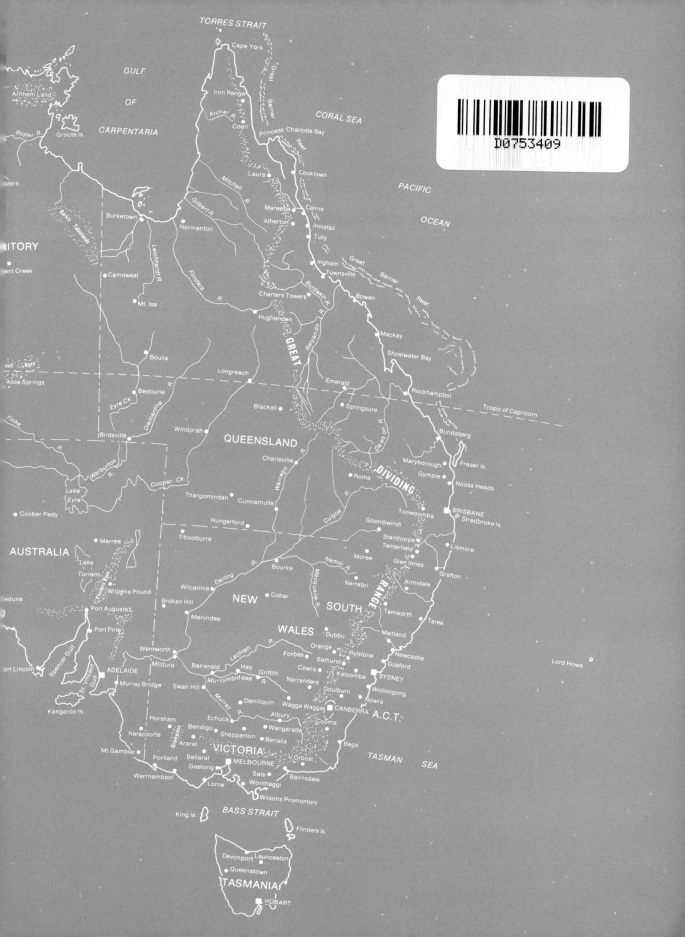

ENCYCLOPAEDIA OF AUSTRALIAN PLANTS

suitable for cultivation

VOLUME ONE

ENCYCLOPAEDIA OF AUSTRALIAN PLANTS

suitable for cultivation

VOLUME ONE

W. Rodger Elliot
David L. Jones

B.Ag.Sc. Dip.Hort.

Line drawings by Trevor L. Blake

LOTHIAN PUBLISHING COMPANY PTY. LTD.

MELBOURNE SYDNEY AUCKLAND

First published 1980
Reprinted with corrections 1981, 1983
Copyright © 1980
W. Rodger Elliot
David L. Jones

Inquiries should be made to the publishers:
Lothian Publishing Company Pty. Ltd.
4 Tattersalls Lane, Melbourne 3000.

NATIONAL LIBRARY OF AUSTRALIA
CATALOGUING-IN-PUBLICATION ENTRY:

Elliot, W. Rodger (Winston Rodger), 1941 —
Encyclopaedia of Australian plants suitable for
cultivation. Volume 1.

Rev. ed.
Previous ed.: Melbourne; Lothian, 1980.
Bibliography.
Includes index.
ISBN 0 85091 142 7.
ISBN 0 85091 148 6 (set).

1. Wild flower gardening — Australia.
I. Jones, D.L. (David Lloyd), 1944 —
II. Title.

635.9'676'0994

Designed by Arthur Stokes

The text has been photo-set in Baskerville
by Acton Graphic Arts, Melbourne

Printed in Hong Kong through Bookbuilders Ltd

Frontispiece — T. L. Blake photo

To Gwen Elliot and Barbara Jones
for their inspiration, tolerance and support,
also to our children Sue and Grant Elliot, and
Sandra and Timothy Jones

Contents

Foreword

Australia is richly endowed with fascinating and colourful native plants that are perfectly adapted to succeed either on coastal sand-plains or in the arid 'red centre', on alpine peaks or in tropical rain-forests; in fact, every conceivable combination of climate and soil supports some of the 15,000 odd species that go to make up our continent's remarkable flora. For too long they had been neglected as candidates for the ornamental garden and, even one generation back, native plants were virtual Cinderellas in their own land. Lack of success attended many early attempts to make them conform to traditional horticulture, so they were branded as intractable, 'difficult' subjects, and passed over in favour of the more amenable rose, iris, hydrangea or other exotic.

The past 20 years or so has witnessed a tremendous upsurge of interest in native flowers. Experimental culture has furnished much valuable information on their requirements, so that today literally thousands of kinds are being grown quite successfully — either blended with introduced species or forming purely native plantations as in grounds of the newer universities, schools and municipal centres, not to mention innumerable private gardens. It is a fine achievement, based on enthusiasm and accompanied by a public demand for more and yet more literature about the indigenous flora. Thus we have recent books of varying depth and approach, with such titles as Growing Australian Plants, Australian Plants for the Garden, West Australian Native Plants in Cultivation and Gardening with Australian Plants.

But there remained a need for some truly encyclopaedic work, to include *all* or most of the species that had ever achieved success under cultivation, and, clearly, this would call for ample experience in the whole field. The authors of this present encyclopaedia, one a horticultural scientist, the other a seasoned nurseryman specialising in native plants, have travelled widely within the continent, studying plants in their natural surroundings. They now join forces to put on record an immense amount of knowledge and personal expertise, in very readable form.

The first of their four-volume work is introductory, covering a wide spectrum; it discusses the general-features of our Australian flora, the

Foreword

history of its cultivation both overseas and at home with a special chapter on eucalypts in cultivation, factors influencing the selection of plants to be grown (climate, soils, aspect, space available etc.), techniques of cultivation such as preparation of ground, maintenance, nutrition and relationship to Australian fauna, pests, diseases and other ailments, methods of propagation, plants for particular purposes, finally a glossary and list of books for further reading. Volumes 2 to 4 are devoted to the encyclopaedia proper, an alphabetical arrangement of genera and species, under each entry of which is given a description of the plant, its distribution, habitat, flowering time, propagation and uses.

One congratulates the authors on this splendid result of their enterprise, feeling confident that the text can aid every grower of Australian trees, flowers and ferns, and also serve to stimulate even wider interest in the potentialities of our native vegetation. It is a most useful reference work for the library.

J. H. Willis,
D.Sc., Dip.For.
Former Assistant Government Botanist
Royal Botanic Gardens and National Herbarium of Victoria

Preface

Australian plants have much to offer the amateur gardener, horticulturist and landscape designer. There is a tremendous variety in form ranging from lowly annuals to lofty trees, and from primitive cycads, ferns and palms, to highly advanced orchids. Flowers vary dramatically in shape from almost standard to the bizarre. Colours range from insignificant, through drab and dowdy, to strikingly flamboyant. Foliage is variable and often interesting, and for some species may be the major feature of interest. In addition many Australian plants are renowned for fragrant leaves and delightful floral perfumes.

Apart from their visual characters, Australian plants have many useful features for cultivation. A large number of species are fast growing, and flower while young. In addition, many species are generally adaptable to a variety of soil types and climates, and hence can be used under a wide range of conditions. One of the main reasons for the increased interest in the cultivation of native plants in Australia is because so many are drought resistant. This interest is renewed regularly following drought years, as was the case in 1968 in southern Australia, when so many introduced plants suffered or died.

The cultivation of Australian plants attracts interest in many parts of the world. They are grown commercially for forestry purposes, as well as for fuel, honey production, cut flowers, foliage, and oil extraction. Others are grown in parks, gardens, conservatories, greenhouses etc., for their ornamental value. Their hardiness under adversity has aroused much interest, and resulted in their use in a wide range of climates, and in difficult conditions such as marshes and bogs, deep sands and rocky soils.

Since the early 1950's, there has been a steady increase in the cultivation of indigenous plants within Australia. This increase took a sudden upsurge in the 1960's and the cultivation of the so-called 'natives' has been maintained at a high level since. This is in keeping with the current trend towards the environment, and many people are now becoming aware of the magnificent Australian plant life. Gardens consisting entirely of native plants are now fairly common, and various species are widely used by municipal bodies in parks, large gardens, streets and highways.

Preface

There has been for many years the need for a comprehensive publication dealing with various aspects of cultivation of the Australian flora. This need was recognised as early as 1892, and is mentioned in 'A Handbook of Australian Horticulture' by H. A. James, F.R.H.S. Although there have been many books dealing with aspects of the native flora since that time, none has presented a detailed cover of all sections of cultivation and propagation of Australian plants.

This volume is intended as the first part of a four volume series. The other volumes will deal with details of Australian plant species and cultivars, and will be arranged in alphabetical order.

In this volume we have tried to cater for the needs of all persons involved with the cultivation of Australian plants in tropical, subtropical and temperate regions. In some cases the information on cultivation in tropical regions is unfortunately limited, due to the authors' lack of wide experience in this field.

In the preparation of this volume, we have drawn on numerous other sources of information, including books, scientific and semi-scientific papers, and articles. A list of the major books is included at the back, for further reading. We have attempted to be as up-to-date as possible, and have included the results of recent and current research where known. In many cases this has resulted from our own studies, but we have also drawn on the results of other workers. The experience and practical knowledge of many other native plant enthusiasts have helped us to provide details that would have otherwise been lacking. We have tried to be as accurate as possible by adopting recent botanical name changes, but, because these changes are not always easy to find, some omissions must be expected.

Common names have not been widely used in the publication, because there is no list, or attempt to standardise such names throughout Australia. We have used them where they are widely adopted or in common usage, or where there has been an attempt at standardization, such as is used for forest and timber trees. The use of a common name is never as accurate as the use of the correct latin name, which is accepted universally. The use of botanical terms has been kept to a minimum, and a glossary is included to facilitate the meanings of those used.

It is important to realise that variations occur in the dimensions, flowering times, and habit of growth of plants, because of habitat factors such as soils and climate. Many Australian plants are also variable because of genetic factors, and it is possible to select out different forms for cultivation. As a general guide, the dimensions of shrubs and trees as considered in this book are —

Tree — Tall over 25 m
           Medium 12-25 m
           Small 6-12 m

Shrub — Tall 4-6 m
         Medium 2-4 m
         Small 1-2 m
         Dwarf up to 1 m

Other terms are used for groups, such as climbers etc. The term ground cover, as used here, applies to any sized shrub that bears dense foliage at or near ground level.

Arrangement of Text

For convenience, the text has been divided into five parts.

1. Introduction to the Australian flora deals briefly with the major families and genera unique to, or well developed in Australia, growth habits and distinctive vegetation types frequently encountered. Of the history of Australian plants in cultivation, it is often thought that many species in cultivation today are of recent introduction, but this section clearly shows that a considerable number (including some very rare species) have been grown for over one hundred years.

2. Factors affecting selection of plants for cultivation — outlines the major points of climate and soil aspects, to be considered when choosing suitable species for an area.

Cultivation deals with various aspects of preparation, planting and maintenance, with special emphasis on problem soils and plant nutrition. A chapter also deals with the cultivation of native plants in containers of various types.

3. The various maladies afflicting plants arc dealt with in Pests, Diseases and other Ailments. A range of problems is described, together with selected methods of control.

4. Propagation is an extensive section, dealing with aspects such as propagation structures, media, and the various techniques of seed and vegetative propagation. Separate sections are included dealing with specialised methods of propagation.

5. Lists of plants suitable for specific conditions and purposes. Where known, these cover both tropical and temperate regions.

Acknowledgements

The initial inspiration, and suggestion for this publication, came from the late Neil Moody, when he was editor of 'Your Garden' magazine. We are indebted to him for the idea, and also to Allan Balhorn, the present Editor, and Arthur Gulliver, Photographer of 'Your Garden'. They have kindly allowed us access to the extensive range of photographs in the 'Your Garden' library, and Arthur has taken many additional shots at our request. These photographs have greatly enriched the publication.

We are particularly grateful to our wives, Gwen and Barbara, for carrying out the onerous task of typing the manuscript. They also provided much help with ideas, constructive criticisms, and in editorial matters.

The volume is enhanced by the line drawings of Trevor Blake. Trevor's contribution has exceeded that of illustrator, and for his knowledgeable assistance, and constructive comments throughout, we say thanks.

Appreciation is expressed to Bruce Gray of Atherton, who selflessly provided much valuable information on tropical plants and their cultivation. Practical knowledge on the use and cultivation of native plants in subtropical areas was passed on by Peter Jones, who has had many years experience in the field.

We thank Jim Willis for writing the foreword, and encouraging the project from the beginning.

Bill Thompson critically read parts of the manuscript, and provided constructive criticism.

We thank David Beardsell for meticulously photographing the pests, diseases and other maladies which affect plants.

The library staff at Melbourne Herbarium were very helpful in locating elusive information.

To Ray Collett, Fred Lang, Betty and George Marshall, Mildred Mathias and Ray Williams of California U.S.A., sincere thanks for their valued assistance and hospitality.

We also thank the C.S.I.R.O. Editorial Publications Service, for permission to reprint the vegetation map, as appeared in 'The Australian Environment'. A special thanks to John Brownlie for preparing the map of Australia used on the endpapers.

Other persons we would like to specifically thank are Beth and John Armstrong, Beryl Blake, Neville Bonney, David Challen, Ron Collins, Kath Deery, John Fanning, Jenny Harmer, Phillip Hicks, Jim Hutchinson, Bill King, Alb. Lindner, A. Ross Lloyd, Ross Macdonald, Grant Mattingley, Bill Molyneux, Ken Newbey, David Nichols, John O'Connor, Pauline Pape, Nigel Quick, Ken Stuckey, Paul Thompson and Glen Wilson.

PHOTOGRAPH CREDITS

Your Garden magazine has been particularly generous in permitting the use of photographs, and all black and white photos, apart from those for which credits are given, have been provided by *Your Garden.*

Abbreviations

aff.	affinity
alt.	altitude
cm	centimetre
cv.	cultivar
diam.	diameter
g	gram
kg	kilogram
l	litre
m	metre
m²	square metre
ml	millilitres
mm	millimetre
ppm	parts per million
sp.	species (singular)
spp.	species (plural)
Qld	Queensland
NSW	New South Wales
Vic	Victoria
Tas	Tasmania
SA	South Australia
WA	Western Australia
NT	Northern Territory

Sandplain Flora W.A.

T. L. Blake photo

Part One

Introduction and History of
Australian Plants in Cultivation

1 The Australian Flora

The Australian flora contains at least 20,000 species of vascular plants, the majority of which are endemic. This figure is by necessity only an estimate since new species are continually being described as little known groups of plants are studied or isolated regions are explored more thoroughly. Changes to existing plant names are also frequent and follow systematic studies by botanists and ecologists.

The Australian flora is remarkable for its diversity of species and growth habit. Vegetation types may change dramatically within a few metres or merge gradually one with the other. In relatively few areas are large stretches of uniform vegetation showing little variation in species to be found. Thus the vegetation contrasts markedly with that of the northern hemisphere where large stands consisting of relatively few species are common, such as in the coniferous forests. Two areas of remarkable diversity are the rainforests of eastern Australia and the sandplains and heathlands of Western Australia. In the latter area approximately 75% of the 3000 or so species are endemic.

The Australian flora is closely linked with the world flora and the endemic species have evolved since the continent was isolated. As it is known today our flora can be roughly divided into 3 main elements. These divisions are based on relationships between species found in Australia and those in various other parts of the world.

The divisions are:

1. Asian: an element that becomes more noticeable from eastern Victoria, through New South Wales reaching a peak in northern Queensland and maintaining a high level in the Northern Territory and to a lesser extent the Kimberley region of north-western Western Australia. Many species have links with the Pacific and Asian region especially those species found in the rainforest.

Despite obvious overseas links a high degree of endemism has developed in some areas and in certain groups of plants. This is especially ob-

vious in highland areas such as the Atherton Tableland where many unique species have originated and proliferated.

2. Antarctic: a southern element which has links with New Zealand, sub-Antarctic Islands and South America. The relationship is obvious in south-eastern Australia, especially Tasmania, but becomes less obvious in northern Australia although some links do extend to New Guinea and New Caledonia.

3. Australian: the unique development of endemic plants that have proliferated since the isolation of Australia and now occupy much of the continent. A remarkable degree of endemism has developed in Western Australia, due to its isolation from the eastern states caused by the dry barriers of Central Australia and the Nullarbor Plain.

COMMON GROWTH HABITS OF THE AUSTRALIAN FLORA

Trees

Trees are a dominant feature of the Australian landscape and there are very few vegetation types from which they are absent. A few hardy species even grow in low-rainfall desert areas, a fact which makes them a valuable source of fuel for similar arid areas in other parts of the world.

Shrubs

Shrubs range in height from prostrate plants to almost small trees. They are a dominant feature of all vegetation types except some grasslands and desert formations.

Climbing Plants

Climbing plants are a familiar feature of some parts of Australia's vegetation but are rare in others. They reach a peak in rainforests of northern Australia where some rainforests have been estimated to be composed of 10% of climbing plants. They are also common in the moist vegetation zones down the east coast but are rare or absent in the dry desert zones.

Herbaceous Perennials

These plants die down to a perennial rootstock to avoid extremes of dryness and temperature (either hot or cold). As a group they are not highly developed in Australia but may be common in some vegetation types such as dry sclerophyll forest, heathlands and riverine plains. Some species may form large stands while others are scattered.

Annuals and Ephemerals

Annuals and ephemerals dominate desert vegetation after periods of good rainfall and carpet huge areas. Their abundance decreases with increasing rainfall and they are virtually absent or very rare in rainforests and other high rainfall situations.

Elements of the Australian Flora
NON-FLOWERING PLANTS

Non-flowering plants are widely distributed throughout Australia but are rarely a dominant feature of any vegetation type.

Mosses

The Australian mosses number about 600 species, only a few of which are endemic. Like ferns they are mainly found in the moist areas of eastern Australia. A unique group however has evolved to survive in the drier areas of the continent and is extremely resistant to desiccation.

Ferns

The Australian ferns number about 110 genera and 350 species. They are mainly found in the moist areas of eastern Australia particularly the fern gullies of the south and the rainforests of the north.

Because ferns are distributed by light spores they are mainly a cosmopolitan group with only one-fifth of the Australian species being endemic. A few species have evolved to cope with dry conditions and are known as resurrection ferns. Similar growth habits are found in some species from South America and Africa.

Fern Allies

The fern allies are closely related to ferns but usually have a very different appearance. They are not a large group in Australia consisting of only 6 genera and about 40 species. They are generally not dominant in any vegetation type although species such as *Phylloglossum drummondii* and *Selaginella uliginosa* may form large colonies in heathland. Some species of tassel ferns such as *Lycopodium phlegmaria* may form prominent epiphytic stands in tropical rainforests. Few species of fern allies are endemic although the genus *Tmesipteris* is well developed in eastern Australia.

Cycads

Cycads are very primitive plants related to both ferns and palms. They occur chiefly in Australia, America and Africa with a few species distributed through Asia. The Australian cycads number 4 genera and about 30 species, the majority of which are endemic. A tropical component is distributed across northern Australia and a well developed subtropical group is found in southern Queensland and northern New South Wales with a solitary species extending to southern New South Wales.

Most are very tough, drought resistant plants found in open forest, gorges or dry situations but a few extend to shady rainforest.

Conifers

Coniferous forests are not a feature of the Australian flora as they are in Europe and America. In fact conifers are quite rare in Australia there being only 9 genera and about 30 species. Although most of the genera are found in other parts of the world all but one of the species (*Araucaria cunninghamii*) are endemic.

The genus *Callitris* forms extensive stands in drier areas and in fact may dominate inland vegetation. Many unusual genera are frequent in parts of Tasmania, most of these having links with species in New Zealand. *Araucaria* species are very prominent in northern areas but rarely form large stands.

FLOWERING PLANTS

Flowering plants dominate the Australian flora in every climatic region and vegetation type. This huge group can be considered in the 2 major subdivisions of monocotyledons and dicotyledons.

Monocotyledons

Rushes and Sedges

Rushes are widespread throughout Australia and extend from open vegetation such as heathland to closed communities like rainforest. They favour wet conditions and are most frequent in marshy or boggy situations or along stream banks. Rushes tend to be cosmopolitan by nature but there is a high degree of endemism in the Australian species.

The term rush is usually used loosely for any member of the 3 families Cyperaceae (36 genera, 560 species), Restionaceae (17 genera, 200 species) and Juncaceae (2 genera, 23 species).

Typical sub-alpine habitat, showing Snow Gums and Herbfields.

W.R. Elliot photo

Shrub Steppe vegetation, showing predominance of Saltbushes and Bluebushes.

T.L. Blake photo

Introduction and History

Strictly, members of the latter family are known as rushes and those of the other 2 families are known as sedges.

Grasses

Grasses are a major feature of the Australian vegetation with about one-sixth of the family being indigenous (about 140 genera, 700 species). Grasses are prominent in many vegetation types, but especially in grasslands, woodlands and open forest. Some interesting species have adapted to closed communities such as wet sclerophyll forest and rainforest. There is a high degree of endemism in the Australian grasses.

Lilies and their kin

The term lily is loosely applied mainly to members of the family Liliaceae and Amaryllidaceae, but also to some members of distant families such as Haemodoraceae, Phylidraceae and Orchidaceae. The lily and amaryllid families are not large in Australia (Liliaceae 9 genera 40 species; Amaryllidaceae 46 genera 180 species) although some species are widespread and common especially in floodplains and heathlands. The Australian species of both families are mainly endemic.

Woody Monocotyledons

Woody monocotyledons are a conspicuous feature of rainforests, open forests and littoral communities of northern Australia, but are virtually absent in southern areas. The genus *Cordyline*, although not large in number, has members which are common in most vegetation types from Cape York to New South Wales. The screw palms (*Pandanus* spp.) are very familiar in eastern and northern Australia along river banks, around the margins of swamps and in forests.

Palms

Palms are not a well developed group of plants in Australia. The Australian palms number only about 19 genera and about 40 species and are mainly peripheral representatives of this great tropical group. A couple of genera and a few species are endemic but the majority are closely related to other species in the Pacific region.

Palms do not form a dominant feature of the Australian vegetation with the possible exception of fan palm colonies in tropical Queensland and stands of bangalow palms in subtropical and temperate areas of the east coast. These however mainly occur in isolated localities and do not form the extensive stands as are found in tropical countries.

Australian palms reach their best develop-

Palms are generally suited to tropical or subtropical regions. The large fan-shaped fronds belong to *Licuala ramsayi*.

W.R. Elliot photo

ment in northern areas particularly in the rainforests of north-eastern Queensland. Most are found in lowland situations but some interesting species are to be found in highland areas up to 1700 m altitude. The number of species and frequency diminishes as one travels south with a solitary species being found in Victoria. Some interesting species are found in isolated gorges in Queensland (such as Carnarvon Gorge), Northern Territory, with a unique species even extending to Central Australia.

Orchids

About 550 species of orchids in 91 genera are indigenous to Australia. They are rarely a dominant feature of the vegetation and are rare or virtually absent from drier regions. Impressive stands of terrestrial orchids are frequently seen in heathlands of southern Australia. Epiphytes are common in forests and rainforests of northern New South Wales and Queensland. Most of the indigenous orchids are endemic especially the terrestrials.

Dicotyledons

The dicotyledons comprise by far the largest group in the Australian flora, and they are found in all areas. Their position in relation to the flora of the rest of the world can be considered on a family basis. Very few families are entirely endemic to Australia and those that are, are mostly small. For example the 2 insectivorous families Byblidaceae with 2 species and Cephalotaceae with a solitary species. Other small endemic families are Akaniaceae (monotypic), Austrobaileyaceae (1 genus, 2

6

species), Blepharocaryaceae (1 genus, 2 species), Brunoniaceae (monotypic), Davidsoniaceae (monotypic) and Idiospermaceae (monotypic). The largest endemic family is Tremandraceae with 3 genera and 43 species all endemic to southern Australia. This paucity of endemism at the family level emphasises the fact that the Australian flora is closely linked with the world flora and that the species unique to the continent have developed to meet the conditions of climate, soils and terrain after isolation by sea. The links have been retained with the floras of other parts of the world and these links are obvious when areas of similar climate are considered.

Certain families have a large Australian component with the majority of species or large unique sections being endemic. Proteaceae is a familiar one with the Australian representatives numbering over 750 species in about 40 genera, the vast majority being endemic. Epacridaceae or the familiar heath family, is also principally indigenous to Australia with over 330 native species in 28 genera. Goodeniaceae has about 300 native species in 13 genera. It is almost exclusively Australian with the exception of a few strand plants scattered through the Pacific islands. Stylidiaceae is also almost exclusive with only 4 species out of 160 (in 6 genera) not being found in Australia. Other families which are predominantly Australian are Centrolepidaceae, Stackhousiaceae and Myoporaceae.

Many other large widespread families have unique groups or genera well developed in Australia. The section Leptospermoideae in the family Myrtaceae provides the most familiar example containing as it does the ubiquitous genus *Eucalyptus*, as well as *Angophora, Baeckea, Callistemon, Leptospermum, Melaleuca* and *Verticordia*. The section Prostantheroideae in Lamiaceae contains the widespread endemic genera *Prostanthera, Westringia* and *Hemigenia*. The section Stenolobeae in the family Euphorbiaceae is well developed in Australia and only extends overseas to New Zealand. It contains such genera as *Amperea, Bertya, Beyeria, Pseudanthus* and *Ricinocarpos*. The section Boroniae in the family Rutaceae also has a solitary representative in New Zealand, this being the only member of the section found outside Australia. It includes such popular and floriferous genera as *Asterolasia, Boronia, Correa, Crowea, Eriostemon* and *Phebalium*.

Some large genera are exclusively Australian (*Daviesia, Dampiera, Dryandra, Hakea, Pultenaea*) however many of the largest have but a few species overseas (*Banksia, Eucalyptus, Grevillea, Prasophyllum, Pterostylis* and *Phebalium*). Many smaller genera are completely endemic.

VEGETATION TYPES

The vegetation can be divided into structures or groups as an aid to understanding the complex variation of plant growth habits. This classification is arbitrary and only the major types and important details are presented here.

Rainforest (Closed Forest)

Rainforests are essentially thought of as being tropical but in fact they extend from north-western Western Australia across the northern coast and down the east coast to Tasmania. They do not form a continuous belt but are scattered in small or large communities. Rainforests are a very dense complex vegetation usually with a multistoried tree layer. They contain a large range of species and reach the greatest diversity in tropical regions where the warm, wet conditions allow luxuriant proliferation of species.

Rainforests develop on deep soils in areas of high rainfall. Trees usually form an upper layer which may be so dense that the floor of the rainforest is dark even during midday. The light is insufficient for the growth of all but very specialised plants such as some ferns and cycads.

Climbing plants are very common in rainforests because they are able to compete very successfully for the all-important sunlight. They have to expend much less energy to reach the outer canopy than do trees and hence are more efficient.

Some unusual growth and flowering habits are common in rainforest plants. Cauliflory or the production of flowers from the trunk, aids considerably in the decorative value of many rainforest trees. Frequently the whole trunk may be covered with large bunches of flowers. This mode of flowering can be seen in *Syzygium cormiflorum, S. moorei* and *Archidendron lucyi*.

Flushes of new foliage of many rainforest species are brightly coloured and very decorative. They are usually of reddish tonings but may be yellowish, pale green or whitish. The reddish colouration is probably an adaptation to the low light conditions, since the reddish leaves are more efficient photosynthetically under low light than are green leaves.

The trunks of many rainforest trees have conspicuous buttresses or flanges at their base. The role of these buttresses is not clear but it is believed that they develop in response to the high humidity which is a common feature of most rainforests.

Epiphytic plants are common on rainforest trees growing on the trunks, larger branches or even on branchlets of the outer canopy. These epiphytes include ferns, orchids, ant plants and members of the family Araceae and Asclepiadaceae.

Rainforests are well developed in Australia but are relatively uncommon. Temperate rainforests are not as complex as tropical rainforests where the warm, wet conditions allow luxuriant proliferation of species.

Rainforests are variable and a few types can be distinguished in Australia.

Tropical Rainforest: dense complex rainforest with a well-developed canopy, numerous vines and epiphytes. Frequently referred to as jungles especially those in coastal areas.

Temperate Rainforest: less complex rainforest with a well developed tree canopy and few vines and epiphytes. There is much less diversity of species with a tendency for some to become dominant.

Monsoonal Rainforest: upper layer is usually smaller and sparser than in the other types. Many of the trees are deciduous, shedding their leaves during the dry season allowing considerable light to reach the rainforest floor. Epiphytes and vines are common.

Sclerophyll Forest

This type of forest is dominated by trees which have flattish crowns and tall, well-developed trunks. The canopy is almost continuous and the ground is well covered by shrubs and herbs. The word sclerophyll means hard leaves and refers to the leathery foliage of most species particularly the dominant species of eucalypts.

Sclerophyll forests are common in southern and eastern Australia in areas of 750 mm rainfall or above. Two main types of sclerophyll vegetation can be distinguished.

Dry Sclerophyll Forest (Open Forest): this forest is basically 2 layered, a dominant upper tree canopy and a ground cover of shrubs and herbs which are usually quite drought-resistant.

Dry Sclerophyll Forest.

Wet Sclerophyll Forest.

Wet Sclerophyll Forest (Tall Open Forest): this forest consists of 3 or more layers, the intermediate zone between the low shrubs and trees being occupied by a discontinuous range of tall shrubs and small trees. Ferns are often present in the ground cover. Some species in wet sclerophyll forests are drought-resistant but the majority are not equipped to survive long, dry periods.

Both types of sclerophyll forest may merge as one moves from the prevailing side of a mountain to the rain shadow side or from a ridge to a gully.

Grassy Forest.

Grassy Forest: this forest is frequent across northern Australia. It is very similar to dry sclerophyll forest but the ground supports very few shrubs and is covered by an almost continuous grass layer.

Woodland

In this type of vegetation, the trees are numerous but do not form a continuous canopy as in sclerophyll forest. The trees have rounded

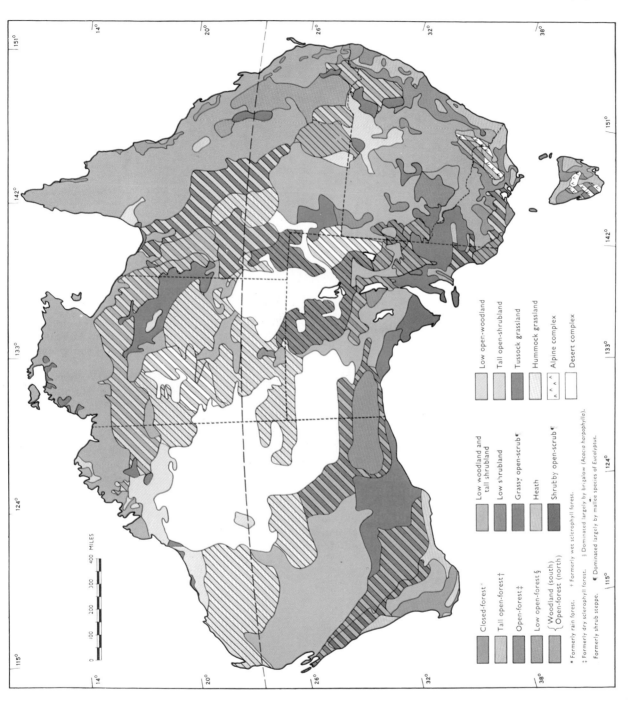

Legend:

Closed-forest *
Tall open-forest †
Open-forest ‡
Low open-forest §
Woodland (south)
Open-forest (north)

Low woodland and tall shrubland
Low shrubland
Grassy open-scrub ⁋
Heath
Shrubby open-scrub ⁋

Low open-woodland
Tall open-shrubland
Tussock grassland
Hummock grassland
Alpine complex
Desert complex

* Formerly rain forest.   † Formerly wet sclerophyll forest.

‡ Formerly dry sclerophyll forest.   § Dominated largely by brigalow (*Acacia harpophylla*).

⁋ Dominated largely by mallee species of *Eucalyptus*.

Formerly shrub steppe.

MILES
0 100 200 300 400

Vegetation Map of Australia
Compiled by R. J. Williams for C.S.I.R.O.

Introduction and History

Woodland.

Mallee habit of growth — branches arise from below ground level.

crowns and short trunks. Tall and low woodland communities are sometimes distinguished on the heights of the trees.

Ground cover varies from continuous shrubs through communities with sparsely scattered shrubs to Savannah Woodland in which shrubs are few or absent and grasses are continuous and well developed. Savannah is a further development where trees occur as isolated individuals or clumps in a continuous grassland.

Heath

This community consists of shrubs varying in height from 0.5-2 m. The growth is frequently thick and tangled but sparse, open heaths also occur. The plants are tough and wiry with numerous drought-resistant features such as reduced, rolled or hairy leaves.

Herbs such as orchids and lilies are frequent in heath communities. Heathlands are floristically rich and produce attractive displays during autumn, winter and spring.

Trees are present in some heathlands and these are known as tree heaths (for single stemmed trees) or mallee heaths (for multi-stemmed trees).

Mallee

A vegetation type dominated by low-growing eucalypts with a characteristic growth habit of many stems arising from an underground lignotuber. The tree crowns tend to be flattened and may form a continuous or more usually discontinuous canopy.

Drought-resistant shrubs are always present and may form a well-developed layer. Annual or perennial herbs are also a feature of the ground layer.

Mallee vegetation is frequently developed on parallel sand dunes with different plant species growing on the ridges compared with the hollows.

Desert Vegetation

Evaporation in desert regions of Australia exceeds precipitation for every month of the year and hence only very drought-resistant plants can survive. Mean annual rainfall is usually less than 200 mm. Annuals dominate such areas and frequently these complete their life cycle within 3 months of rainfall and are in fact ephemerals. A few very tough perennials survive. Desert vegetation can be simple but is frequently quite

Savannah Woodland.

Marlock habit of growth — branches arise together from a point on the trunk.

Mallee Eucalypts showing characteristic growth habit.

complex, with changes resulting from small differences in soil moisture regimes.

Deserts may be sandy with parallel dunes or flat and stony such as the gibber deserts.

Shrub Steppe (Low Shrubland)

Trees are absent in this community that is common in inland and central Australia. The vegetation is dominated by shrubs 1-2.5 m tall. These are usually separated by 1-3 m with grasses and ephemerals growing in the intervening spaces. The shrubs are usually succulent and very drought-resistant. They provide good fodder for stock, particularly the saltbushes (*Atriplex* spp.) and bluebushes (*Maireana* spp.).

Sub-Alpine Vegetation

A complex vegetation made up of numerous communities such as woodland, grassland and herbfield. The last is a low scrub dominated by small perennial herbs which frequently have a mat-like growth habit. The sub-alpine vegetation complex is limited to high mountain peaks of south-eastern Australia and Tasmania.

Tropical Mangroves, Cape York Peninsula, Qld.

Savannah Woodland — predominance of Yellow Box.

Lagoon, Cape York Peninsula, Qld.

D.L. Jones photo

Coastal Heathland.

T.L. Blake photo

2 History of Australian Plants in Cultivation Overseas

18th and 19th Century

The nursery trade in England was well established by 1770 when Captain James Cook arrived in Australia. Many fine, large nurseries flourished and there was considerable interest in botany and the culture of plants. The living collection at Kew Gardens was large and embraced a considerable variety of plant types. As well, there were many extensive private collections, owned by wealthy noblemen and women. Skilled staff were employed exclusively for the maintenance and culture of these collections.

Not only was it fashionable to own a collection of exotic plants, but competition existed between the gentry to have the best. It was considered something of a coup to flower a new exotic species for the first time, and it was not unusual for special meetings to be called so as to display the exhibit. Private expeditions to various parts of the world were financed by the gentry, with the primary purpose of obtaining exciting new plants for their collections.

The English winter climate was too cold for the outside culture of all but the hardiest exotic species, and so expensive glasshouses (or greenhouses) were constructed especially for them. Various types of glasshouses were employed for different types of plants. The hardier types were grown in unheated or cold glasshouses, while the more delicate plants required heated conditions. Those very sensitive species from tropical areas which require year-round minimum temperatures of 15°C and constant high humidity, were grown in a type of glasshouse known as a stove house. The maintenance of the glasshouses and the cultivation of plants in them required considerable skill, and experienced horticulturists were in much demand.

The discovery of Australia slotted into a period when the collection and cultivation of exotic plants was at a very high level, and it is not surprising that the new colony attracted interest from the collectors. First in a trickle, then in a steady stream, species were sent over as seeds, bulbs, roots, or less commonly potted plants. Many did not survive the arduous journey, but a surprisingly large number did, and became established in glasshouses around England.

The cultivation of Australian plants began in England in the late 18th century. Seed was collected on Cook's voyage, presumably by Sir Joseph Banks and Daniel Solander, and again presumably in the vicinity of Botany Bay. These collections were relayed to England, where most went to the Royal Botanic Gardens at Kew, but a few found their way to private nurseries. In 1788 it is known that a private nursery firm had 5 species of Australian plants in cultivation, including *Banksia serrata*. These were presumably from Cook's voyage of 1770, since the second voyage to found the colony was not made until 1788.

It is perhaps staggering for modern Australians to realise that Australian plants were popular in England before the end of the 18th century. Records show that *Melaleuca thymifolia* was growing and flowering as a greenhouse shrub in 1792. *Acacia longifolia* was flowering in 1792, and was propagated from seed and also cuttings. The genus *Crowea* was actually named from specimens of *Crowea saligna* grown from seed, germinated in England in 1790. This record is of particular interest, because at present it is considered to be very difficult to raise *Crowea* species from seed. Many other examples are shown in the accompanying table.

Sir Joseph Banks, who accompanied Cook on his voyage of discovery to Australia, was on his return to England to become the Director of the Royal Botanic Gardens at Kew. He was responsible for the introduction of many Australian species into cultivation in England, through his personal endeavours (*Acacia decurrens*, *Indigofera australis*, *Pittosporum undulatum* and *Pultenaea retusa*), and patronage of collectors. George Cayley was one of the first of these collectors, and he arrived in Australia in 1800. He was appointed superintendent of new botanical gardens which were being established at Parramatta, and collected widely around Sydney, especially in the Blue Mountains. Seed, plants and specimens were sent back to Banks at intervals. It is known that in 1803 Cayley sent Banks the seed of 170 species, including an *Epacris* sp. and *Jacksonia scoparia*. He was also responsible for the introduction to England of the elkhorn *Platycerium bifurcatum* in 1808.

Around about the time that Banks was exerting his influence, other collectors were being sponsored by private individuals. Peter Good, botanical assistant to Robert Brown, and formerly a gardener at Kew, sent a number of seeds to Kew in 1803. These included many species of the family Proteaceae, which aroused considerable interest in enthusiasts. Other species he was responsible for introducing in 1803 included *Acacia alata, Albizia lophantha, Anthocercis littorea, Beaufortia decussata, Bossiaea cinerea Gastrolobium bilobum, Hibiscus heterophyllus, Melaleuca fulgens, Stylidium graminifolium* and *Templetonia retusa*.

The demand at nurseries for Australian plants was becoming considerable, so much so that some of the larger nurseries sent out their own collectors to Australia. David Burton was one such collector who worked in the vicinity of Sydney for 6 months during late 1791 and early 1792, and supplied species to the nursery which employed him.

Allan Cunningham, one of Australia's greatest botanists, also exerted considerable influence on the cultivation of Australian plants in England. He was appointed King's Botanist and in 1817 was sent to Australia with the specific purpose of collecting seeds and plants for His Majesty's Gardens. He collected widely throughout Australia and sent numerous seeds and living plants back to Kew. These included a number of orchids which survived the journey, and were successfully introduced to cultivation in the glasshouses of England.

William Baxter was a gardener, sent out by private enterprise to obtain seeds and roots of Australian plants. He collected in southern Australia in such areas as King George Sound and Cape Arid, WA, and Wilson's Promontory, Vic, between 1823 and 1825 and again in 1829. Specimens from his collections ended up with Sir William Hooker and also Robert Brown. It is recorded that *Correa pulchella* flowered in 1824 in the nursery of Mr. J. Mackie of Clapton, from seed collected by Baxter on Kangaroo Island, SA. One collection of his seeds was purchased in the 1830's for the substantial sum of £1500.

James Anderson was also sponsored by a private nursery, and sent much material back between 1826 and 1830. He later became an independent agent, selling seeds or plants to the highest bidder.

There was considerable interest in the spectacular flora of Western Australia and the plants were in high demand. Soon after the founding of Perth in 1829, James Drummond was appointed curator of the new botanic gardens. He sent large collections of seeds of WA plants to various people in the United Kingdom. By 1837 he was an independent collector who travelled widely and made a living solely from the sale of seeds and plants. Some seeds were collected on spec (especially new species) while others were supplied under contract. Drummond introduced many species into cultivation, including *Boronia megastigma* and *Anigozanthos pulcherrimus*. He was particularly fond of banksias and dryandras, and collected seed of over 60 species.

Many other collectors exploited the flora of WA for its seeds. William Morrison was a gardener and seed collector, who in 1828 sent a large collection of seeds and live plants to Kew. Included were many spectacular members of the family Proteaceae. A Mrs. Molloy living in WA sent seeds during the 1830's to Captain James Mangles, explorer and horticulturist. These seeds were widely distributed, and some such as *Anigozanthos manglesii*, and *Helipterum manglesii* became well established as glasshouse plants.

Many other people were associated with the collection and despatch of seeds and plants to the mother country in the 19th century. These include the explorer Ludwig Leichhardt, who in 1846 collected some 200 kinds of seeds from the interior region of Australia. In 1845 James Kidd collected many live specimens for Kew, including a large specimen of *Xanthorrhoea* which is reported to have 'duly arrived alive'. Frederick Strange introduced the indigenous water lily *Nymphea gigantea* in 1845, and by 1848 seeds of it were being distributed to interested people. Eugene Fitzalan concentrated mainly on tropical species. In 1859 he established a seed and plant shop in Edward Street, Brisbane. In 1887 he moved to Cairns, where for 10 years he exported large numbers of orchids, palms, ferns and others, both as live plants and seeds.

Several large English nurseries carried a good selection of Australian plants for sale in the 1880's and 1890's. The catalogues of William Bull of King's Road, Chelsea, provided an insight into that range, although he carried not only general lines, but also specialised in the introduction of new species and oddities. His 1886 catalogue listed amongst others *Davidsonia*

15

Treed Heathland, Cape York Peninsula, Qld.

D.L. Jones photo

Dry Sclerophyll Forest.

W.R. Elliot photo

pruriens for 10/6d, 15/-, and 1 guinea, and *Hymenosporum flavum* for 7/6d. Further species of interest in that catalogue are *Blandfordia cunninghamii, Brachychiton acerifolium, Castanospermum australe, Crinum flaccidum, Elaeocarpus grandis, E. reticulatus, Erythrina verspertilio* and *Eucalyptus citriodora*. Of particular interest was a unique double-flowered *Epacris*, known as *E. onosmaeflora* 'flora pleno nivalis'. This was considered an 'exceedingly fine plant' and was awarded a First Class Certificate at the Royal Horticultural Society in the 1880's. Although double-flowered *Epacris* is known today, this form, which is probably a cultivar of *E. nivalis*, seems to have been lost to cultivation. Also of special interest in the light of today's protective legislation, is the advertisement for established plants of the tree fern *Dicksonia antarctica*. These specimens ranged in trunk height from 0.3 m to 2.5 m tall, with well-developed crowns, and in price from two to 18 guineas. This surely is an indication of the dedication and zealousness of these early plant pioneers who would have had to collect and transport those large and cumbersome tree fern trunks, before establishing them for sale in the mother country.

Considerable difficulty was experienced in growing some of the species sent back from Australia. Some proved impossible to germinate from seed, because they have inbuilt control mechanisms which even today remain unknown. Even after successful seed germination, others proved difficult to maintain. These were mostly species from heathland areas, particularly of WA. Little trouble was experienced with species from wet forests or from tropical areas, because the gardeners had developed considerable expertise with species of similar requirements from other parts of the world. Fortunately for those difficult species from WA, some English horticulturists had learnt to master some difficult species from sandy areas of South Africa.

These were in many respects similar to the heathland vegetation, and it was known that such plants required well-drained soils of low pH and resented high humidity. A large number were lost when the houses were heated by pumping hot water through pipes. This process maintained a humid atmosphere, and whilst this was ideal for species from wet forests, it was totally unsuitable for plants from areas of relatively low rainfall.

Orchids were a particularly popular group for cultivation, and were widely sought after around the world. Many Australian species were introduced, sometimes with poor results.

In 1823 John Smith, (later the Curator of Kew Gardens) was a foreman at Kew, interested in

Tropical Rainforest, Atherton Tableland, Qld.

W.R. Elliot photo

the growing of orchids. Epiphytic orchids had proved to be difficult to keep alive, due to the dry heat derived from the early heating system used in greenhouses. It was not until many years later that hot water pipes were used, with better results. Orchids were being potted directly into soil, and there were many failures. John Smith received some Australian epiphytic orchids, and for a potting mixture used coarse soil with portions of stems of trees. This mixture was the forerunner of the typical mix used for epiphytic orchids today.

In the 1937 catalogue of Marchants Nursery, Dorset, England, there were 33 species of Australian plants offered for sale. The majority were species that were indigenous to Tasmania. Included in the range were the following. *Bursaria spinosa* 'suited to mild climates', *Eucryphia lucida* — 'the refined beauty of this shrub and the almond scent of the flower combine to place it amongst the most beautiful of plants'. Four species of *Lomatia* were grown, 'they are much hardier than is supposed, and *L. tinctoria* withstands 18°F of frost'. *Prostanthera rotundifolia* — 'suited to a south or west wall', *Telopea speciosissima* and *T. truncata* were also highly prized.

17

Introduction and History

Details of the Introduction of Australian Plants into Cultivation in Britain

Genus	When Introduced	How Propagated	Cultivation	Approx No. of species grown	Examples
Acacia	Late 18th Cent.	Seed or cuttings	Glasshouse, some outside (mainly summer). Equal parts peat, loam and sand.	40	A. alata (1803) A. binervata (1823) A. decurrens (1790), A. leprosa A. longifolia (1792) A. paradoxa (1803), A. pendula A. pulchella
Acalypha	Mid 19th Cent.		Glasshouse	1	A. capillipes
Actinotus	Early 19th Cent.	Seed	Glasshouse	1	A. helianthi (pre 1822)
Albizia	Early 19th Cent.	Seed	Glasshouse	1	A. lophantha (1803)
Ammobium	Early 19th Cent.	Seed	Glasshouse Light, rich soil.	1	A. alatum (Useful for winter bouquets)
Andersonia	Late 18th Cent.		Glasshouse	1	A. sprengelioides
Anigozanthos	Early 19th Cent.	Seed & division	Glasshouse	4	A. flavidus, A. manglesii A. pulcherrimus, A. rufus
Anopterus	Early 19th Cent.		Glasshouse. 2 parts loam, 1 part peat, 1 part sand.	1	A. glandulosus (1823)
Apalochlamys	Early 19th Cent.	Seed	Glasshouse	1	A. spectabilis (pre 1822)
Araucaria	Late 18th Cent.	Seed or cuttings	Glasshouse, plus some in sheltered locations outdoors.	2	A. bidwillii A. cunninghamii
Archontophoenix	Mid 19th Cent.	Seed	Heated Glasshouse. Equal parts loam & leaf mould, ½ part silver sand. Top dress cow manure occasionally.	2	A. alexandrae A. cunninghamii
Anthocercis	Early 19th Cent.	Seed & cuttings	Glasshouse	1	A. littorea (1803)
Atherosperma	Early 19th Cent.	Cuttings	Outside	1	A. moschatum
Athrotaxis	Mid 19th Cent.	Seed	Glasshouse, and outside in mild districts.	3	A. selaginoides, A. laxifolia A. cupressoides
Baeckea	Early 19th Cent.	Seed	Glasshouse		B. virgata (1819)
Banksia	Late 18th Cent.	Seed	Glasshouse, some outside (mainly summer). Equal parts loam and sand.	10	B. serrata (1778) B. dryandroides, B. quercifolia B. speciosa
Beaufortia	Early 19th Cent.	Seed & cuttings	Glasshouse. Equal parts loam, leaf mould & peat, ⅙ sand.	5	B. dampieri, B. decussata (1803) B. purpurea, B. sparsa (1803)
Billardiera	Early 19th Cent.	Seed & cuttings	Outside	1	B. longiflora
Blandfordia	Early 19th Cent.	Division	Glasshouse. Equal parts peat, loam & silver or river sand. Water freely May-Aug, moderately Aug-Oct and Feb-May. None at other times.	1	B. grandiflora (1803) B. nobilis (1810)
Boronia	Late 18th Cent.	Seed & cuttings	Glasshouse, outdoors in summer. 2 parts fibrous peat, 1 part silver sand and pounded charcoal.	10	B. megastigma B. pinnata (1830) B. polygalifolia B. serrulata

Genus	When Introduced	How Propagated	Cultivation	Approx No. of species grown	Examples
Bossiaea	Early 19th Cent.	Seed & cuttings	Glasshouse		B. cinerea (1803)
Brachysema	Early 19th Cent.	Seed, cuttings, layering	Glasshouse, equal parts loam peat, leaf mould and silver sand.	3	B. latifolium (1803) B. lanceolatum (1852) B. undulatum (1822)
Callistemon	Late 18th Cent.	Seed or cuttings	Glasshouse, equal parts peat, loam and silver sand.	6	C. citrinus (1788) C. rigidus (1805) C. speciosus. C. viridiflorus
Callicoma	Early 19th Cent.	Cuttings	Glasshouse	1	C. serratifolia
Calomeria	Start 19th Cent.	Seed	Glasshouse	1	C. amaranthoides (1800)
Calostemma	Early 19th Cent.	Division	Glasshouse. 2 parts loam, 1 part peat, 1 part sand.	3	C. luteum (1818) C. purpureum
Calytrix	Early 19th Cent.	Seed & cuttings	Glasshouse	1	C. tetragona (1818)
Cissus	Early 19th Cent.	Cuttings	Glasshouse	1	C. antarctica
Clianthus	Early 19th Cent.	Seed or grafting	Glasshouse	1	C. formosus
Correa	Late 18th Cent.	Cuttings	Glasshouse. Best grown in mixture of light loam, peat and leafy mould. Needs protection from frost.	5 also forms & hybrids	C. alba C. pulchella C. reflexa (1800)
Crinum	Late 18th Cent.	Seed or division	Glasshouse	2	C. flaccidum (1819) C. pedunculatum (1790)
Crowea	Late 18th Cent.	Seed, cuttings & grafting	Glasshouse. 2 parts peat, 1 part fibrous loam, and a little sand.	2	C. saligna (1790)
Dacrydium	Early 19th Cent.	Seed or cuttings	Glasshouse, and outside in mild districts.	1	D. franklinii
Darwinia	Early 19th Cent.	Cuttings	Glasshouse. Equal parts loam & sand.	10	D. diosmoides D. macrostegia
Daviesia	Early 19th Cent.	Seed & cuttings	Glasshouse. Best grown in sandy, peat soil.	2	D. latifolia (1805)
Dicksonia	Late 18th Cent.	Spore	Glasshouse	1	D. antarctica
Dillwynia	Late 18th Cent.	Seed or cuttings	Glasshouse	3	D. ericifolia, D. hispida D. floribunda
Dracophyllum	Early 19th Cent.	Seed	Glasshouse	1	D. secundum
Dryandra	Mid 19th Cent.	Seed	Glasshouse	1	D. nobilis
Elaeocarpus	Early 19th Cent.		Glasshouse	1	E. reticulatus (1803)
Epacris	Early 19th Cent.	Cuttings & seed sown on ripening, on sandy surface under bell jar.	Glasshouse. 3 parts fibrous peat 1 part silver sand.	7 plus forms & hybrids	E. heteronema (1823) E. impressa E. longiflora E. nivalis (1829)
Eriostemon	Early 19th Cent.	Cuttings & grafting	Glasshouse. Equal parts peat and sand loam.	5	E. buxifolius E. myoporoides
Eucalyptus	Early 19th Cent.	Seed	Glasshouse & outdoors. Silver-leaved species grown for foliage.	4-10	E. coccifera (pre 1850) E. preissiana (pre 1845)

19

Introduction and History

Genus	When Introduced	How Propagated	Cultivation	Approx. No. of species grown	Examples
Gastrolobium	Early 19th Cent.	Seed & cuttings	Glasshouse	1	G. bilobum (1803)
Gompholobium	Early 19th Cent.	Seed & cuttings	Glasshouse. 2 parts rough peat, 1 part each — charcoal, rough loam and sand.	4	G. grandiflorum (1803) G. polymorphum G. venustum (1845)
Grevillea	Early 19th Cent.	Seed, cuttings, layering, grafting.	Glasshouse, and some outside (mainly summer). Fibrous peat, turfy loam and silver sand.	10	G. banksii, G. juniperina G. speciosa (1825) G. robusta
Guichenotia	Mid 19th Cent.	Seed	Glasshouse	1	G. macrantha
Hakea	Late 18th Cent.	Seed	Glasshouse	5	H. myrtoides (1850) H. salicifolia, H. suaveolens
Hardenbergia	Late 18th Cent.	Seed & cuttings	Glasshouse. Equal parts loam & peat, plus a little silver sand.	2 and forms	H. comptoniana (1808) H. violacea
Helichrysum	Early 19th Cent.	Seed or cuttings	Greenhouse or outside. Ordinary soil or rich loam.	3	H. apiculatum (1804) H. bracteatum H. diosmifolium
Helipterum	Mid 19th Cent.	Seed	Outside. Light rich soil.	4	H. manglesii H. roseum
Hibbertia	Early 19th Cent.	Cuttings	Glasshouse. Equal parts loam & peat, with a little sand.	5	H. dentata (1805) H. perfoliata
Hibiscus	Early 19th Cent.	Seed & cuttings	Conservatory Plant	1	H. heterophyllus (1803)
Hovea	Early 19th Cent.	Seed & cuttings	Glasshouse. Outdoors in summer. 3 parts peat, 1 part loam plus a little silver sand.	5	H. elliptica (1810) H. longifolia (1805) H. pungens
Indigofera	Late 18th Cent.	Seed	Glasshouse	1	I. australis (1790)
Isotoma	Early 19th Cent.	Seed & cuttings	Glasshouse	1	I. axillaris
Jasminum	Late 18th Cent.	Cuttings, layering	Glasshouse (commonly)	1	J. simplicifolium (1791)
Kennedia	Late 18th Cent.	Seed or cuttings	Glasshouse. Equal parts loam & peat, with a little silver sand.	6	K. coccinea K. nigricans
Lasiopetalum	Late 18th Cent.	Cuttings	Glasshouse. Best grown in sandy or peaty soil.		L. ferrugineum (1791)
Lepidozamia	Early 19th Cent.	Seed	Glasshouse	2	L. hopei, L. peroffskyana
Leptospermum	Early 19th Cent.	Cuttings	Glasshouse & outside	6	L. grandiflorum (1816) L. prostratum, L. scoparium
Lechenaultia	Early 19th Cent.	Seed & cuttings	Glasshouse, & outside in summer. 2 parts fibrous peat, 1 part silver sand.	4	L. biloba (1840) L. formosa (1824) L. laricina (1846) L. linarioides
Leucopogon	Early 19th Cent.	Cuttings, & seed sown when ripe, on surface of sandy peat beneath bell jar.	Glasshouse. Outdoors in summer.	4	L. lanceolatus L. parviflorus (pre 1822) L. verticillata

Grassy Forest, Cape York Peninsula, Qld.

D.L. Jones photo

Desert Vegetation, Central Australia.

T.L. Blake photo

Genus	When Introduced	How Propagated	Cultivation	Approx No. of species grown	Examples
Livistona	Early 19th Cent.	Seed	Heated glasshouse	2	L. australis, L. humilis
Lomatia	Late 18th Cent.	Cuttings	Glasshouse. Equal parts peat, sand and loam.	4	L. longifolia L. tinctoria
Macrozamia	Early 19th Cent.	Seed & division	Glasshouse. Equal parts loam, sand and peat.	7	M. communis M. riedlei
Melaleuca	Late 18th Cent.	Seed & cuttings	Glasshouse	9	M. armillaris, M. fulgens (1803) M. incana (1818), M. squarrosa M. thymifolia (1792)
Olearia	Mid 19th Cent.	Cuttings	Glasshouse & outside. 2 parts sandy loam, 1 part leaf mould or peat, 1 part sand.	4	O. dentata O. phlogopappa (1850)
Oxylobium	Early 19th Cent.	Seed	Glasshouse	1	O. ellipticum (1805)
Pandorea	Early 19th Cent.	Cuttings	Glasshouse	2 (many colour forms)	P. jasminoides P. pandorana
Parahebe	Early 19th Cent.	Seed	Glasshouse. Outdoors in summer.	1	P. perfoliata (pre 1817)
Patersonia	Early 19th Cent.	Seed & division	Glasshouse. Thrives in peat.	1	P. glabrata (1810)
Pimelea	Late 18th Cent.	Seed & cuttings	Glasshouse. 3 parts fibrous peat, 1 part turfy loam, 1/2 part silver sand.	6	P. ferruginea P. longifolia (1833) P. spectabilis
Pittosporum	Late 18th Cent.	Seed or cuttings	Glasshouse & outside. 2 parts fibrous loam, 1 part fibrous peat, 1/2 part silver sand.	2	P. revolutum (1795) P. undulatum (1789)
Platycerium	Early 19th Cent.	Division	Glasshouse	2	P. bifurcatum (1808) P. superbum
Platylobium	Late 18th Cent.	Seed or cuttings	Glasshouse. 3 parts peat, 1 part loam, plus a a little silver sand.	3	P. obtusangulum (1833)
Podocarpus	Mid 19th Cent.	Cuttings	Outside	1	P. lawrencei
Pomaderris	Early 19th Cent.	Cuttings	Glasshouse	2	P. lanigera (1810)
Prostanthera	Early 19th Cent.	Seed or cuttings	Glasshouse, outdoors in summer. 2 parts sandy loam, 1 part equal proportions of charcoal, broken pots, coarse silver sand.	6	P. lasianthos (1808) P. nivea
Pultenaea	Late 18th Cent.	Seed or cuttings	Glasshouse. Outdoors in summer. 2 parts fibrous peat, 1 part equal proportions of pounded charcoal and silver sand.	17	P. daphnoides P. retusa (1789) P. subalpina P. subumbellata (1833)
Scleranthus	Late 18th Cent.	Cuttings	Outside	1	S. biflorus
Sollya	Early 19th Cent.	Cuttings	Glasshouse. 2 parts peat, 1 part turfy loam, 1/2 part silver sand	2 and colour forms	S. heterophylla S. parviflora
Stenocarpus	Mid 19th Cent.	Seed	Glasshouse	1	S. sinuatus (about 1847)

Genus	When Introduced	How Propagated	Cultivation	Approx No. of species grown	Examples
Stylidium	Early 19th Cent.	Seed	Glasshouse	1	S. graminifolium (1803)
Swainsonia	Start 19th Cent.	Seed or cuttings	Glasshouse. 2 parts fibrous loam, 1 part peat, 1/2 part silver sand.	2 plus colour forms	S. galegifolia (1800) S. greyana (1848)
Tasmannia	Mid 19th Cent.	Seed & cuttings	Outside. Widely grown as a windbreak on the west coast.	1	T. lanceolata (1843)
Telopea	Late 18th Cent.	Seed or cuttings	Glasshouse	1	T. speciosissima
Templetonia	Early 19th Cent.	Seed & cuttings	Glasshouse	1	T. retusa (1803)
Tetratheca	Early 19th Cent.	Cuttings	Glasshouse. 2 parts loam, 1 part leaf mould and a little sand.	4-14	T. ericifolia T. thymifolia
Thysanotus	Early 19th Cent.	Seed	Glasshouse	2	T. junceus (pre 1822)
Tristania	Early 19th Cent.	Seed	Glasshouse	4	T. conferta, T. neriifolia
Wahlenbergia	Early 19th Cent.	Seed, cuttings & division	Glasshouse and outside. Equal parts loam and peat with a little sand.	4	W. gracilis W. saxicola
Waitzia	Early 19th Cent.	Seed	Glasshouse and outside. 1 part sandy peat, 1/3 part leaf mould, 1/3 part loam, 1/3 part decayed cow manure.	3	W. corymbosa (pre 1863)
Westringia	Late 18th Cent.	Cuttings	Outside	3	W. cinerea (1822) W. dampieri (1803) W. fruticosa

The Situation Today

Despite the feverish activity of the late 19th Century, and the large number of species that were successfully cultivated then, very few Australian plants have become firmly established in the English nursery industry. Most, it appears, have died out, but whether this was due to a loss of interest or difficulty in maintaining stock, is impossible to say.

A number of Australian plants flourish in the mild climate of the Scilly Isles. Here the nearness of a warm coastal current moderates the climate. Many eucalypts have been established and now grow as a forest. *Eucalyptus globulus* in particular thrives. Spectacular native shrubs that grow well include *Banksia coccinea*, *B. grandis* and *B. prionotes*.

Some species are still commonly grown, and have become quite popular subjects. A selection of these is listed in the accompanying table, together with comments on how they are used. It is interesting to note that the majority of those grown are easy to propagate and are sufficiently hardy to survive in a sheltered position outdoors.

A few nurseries are showing more than a glib interest in Australian plants for cultivation within the U.K. One such nursery is situated at Wimborne, Dorset, where at the present time there are over 300 species in cultivation. Some plants are in glasshouses, and others planted out, with the objective of trying as many species as possible for hardiness, before presenting them for sale. The nursery lists about 125 species as being currently available. The major genera, and number of species are — *Acacia* (26), *Callistemon* (19), *Casuarina* (4), *Eucalyptus* (24), *Grevillea* (4), *Leptospermum* (12), *Melaleuca* (4), and *Olearia* (3). Other genera represented include *Actinostrobus*, *Agonis*, *Atherosperma*, *Baeckea*, *Banksia*, *Billardiera*, *Bursaria*, *Callitris*, *Conostylis*, *Correa*, *Dodonaea*, *Gompholobium*, *Helichrysum*, *Hovea*, *Ixodia*, *Lomatia*, *Melia*, *Pittosporum*, and *Thysanotus*.

Introduction and History

Details of Some Australian Plants

Grown Outdoors in Britain Today

Species	Position	Remarks
Ammobium alatum	Warm sheltered position	A decorative border plant, grown as an annual. Useful as a cut or dried flower.
Anigozanthos manglesii	Warm sunny position	Grown as a summer annual
Atherosperma moschatum	Sheltered position	Needs plenty of water in summer
Athrotaxis cupressoides	Sheltered position	Slow growing
Athrotaxis laxifolia	Sheltered position	Slow growing
Athrotaxis selaginoides	Warm sunny position	Hardiest of the genus
Billardiera longiflora	South or south-west wall	In mild districts only
Calomeria amaranthoides	Sunny well-drained borders	Plant out in June
Dacrydium franklinii	As a specimen tree in open places	Mild districts only
Grevillea juniperina	Sheltered shrubbery	Grown in the south
Grevillea rosmarinifolia	Warm position	In mild districts
Helichrysum bracteatum	Warm position	Grown as a summer annual, wide range of colours
Helichrysum diosmifolium	Sunny well-drained border	In mild districts only
Helipterum manglesii	Sunny well-drained position	Summer annual, and for winter decoration
Helipterum roseum	Warm sunny position	Also popular as a pot plant
Leptospermum grandiflorum	Sheltered gardens near the seaside, or near a southern wall	In milder districts
Leptospermum myrtifolium	as above	as above
Leptospermum scoparium	as above	as above
Olearia myrsinoides	Sheltered position on southern wall	In milder districts
Olearia phlogopappa	Warm well-drained position	In coastal districts — a range of colours available
Pittosporum undulatum	Warm sheltered position	In coastal districts
Podocarpus lawrencei	Sheltered position	Hardy in milder districts
Prostanthera lasianthos	Sheltered position	In mild districts
Prostanthera rotundifolia	Warm sunny position	Grown in the south
Scleranthus biflorus	In a rockery exposed to full sun	A very hardy plant
Tetratheca ciliata	Warm sheltered position	Half hardy perennial
Tetratheca glandulosa	Warm sunny position	In mild districts
Tasmannia lanceolata	Adaptable to a range of positions	Self seeds in milder districts. Grown as a hedge plant.
Wahlenbergia gracilis	Sunny rockery	Needs plenty of water over summer
Wahlenbergia saxicola	Sunny rockery	as above
Westringia fruticosa	Sheltered shrubbery	In mild districts

FRANCE

France was apparently the first country other than England to collect live specimens of Australian plants for culture in the home country. In 1792 the voyager d'Entrecasteaux visited the very rich flora area of Esperance, WA. The naturalist on board, Labillardière, collected extensively, and many live plants, seeds and herbarium specimens were conveyed back to Paris. Here they were distributed between the Paris Garden (Jardin des Plantes), and the Empress Josephine's garden at Malmaison.

The French explorer Baudin visited WA in 1801, with the purpose of collecting live plants and specimens. The naturalist in the party, Leschenault de la Tour, was to have the honour of having one of the most colourful genera of plants in the world named after him — *Lechenaultia*. Baudin returned to Paris in 1803 with 2 boxes of seeds, and over 60 tubes of living plants. These were again distributed between the Empress Josephine's garden, and the Jardin des Plantes.

Eucalyptus globulus seed was sent to Paris in 1804, and seedlings raised at Malmaison.

Further collecting trips were made in 1818 by Freycinet to the Shark Bay area, north of Carnarvon WA, and by D'Urville in 1826 to King George Sound. Live material was collected on both of these trips, and conveyed back to Paris.

Lechenaultia formosa is known to have been in cultivation in France in 1829, and comments on the beauty of its flowers and ease of propagation were recorded. *L. biloba* followed more than a decade later, and was renowned for its beautiful blue flowers. These colourful Australian species were apparently planted outside during the European summer, and treated virtually as annuals.

There appears to be only limited cultivation of Australian plants in France today. Annuals such as *Brachycome iberidifolia, Helipterum manglesii*, and *Helichrysum bracteatum* are grown in large gardens. In the milder districts of southern France, silver-leaved eucalypts and hardy acacias are grown outside for their decorative foliage, which is harvested and sold in the florist trade.

OTHER EUROPEAN COUNTRIES

Australian plants became widely distributed through Europe during the 19th Century. Most of these were to be found in private collections, such as those of Karl von Hügel in Vienna. This particular collection was very extensive, and included many species of Australian plants, grown mainly in glasshouses. Some annuals and half

The technique of establishing imported rooted cuttings of Australian plants, at University of California, Santa Cruz. (See page 28)

W.R. Elliot photo

hardy species were grown in warm positions outside during summer. Von Hügel's collection aroused considerable interest, and led to Australian plants being more widely grown in European glasshouses.

Other large cities contained gardens which supported collections of Australian plants, of varying size and quality. These included the German cities of Bonn, Essen, Berlin, Frankfurt, Hanover, Dresden and Cologne, Prague in Czechoslovakia, Leningrad in Russia, and Brussels in Belgium. In the 1830's, the collection of plants at Bonn contained many Australian natives, including flowering plants of *Lechenaultia formosa*.

Some plants also found their way into the nursery trade and became firmly entrenched as commercial lines. These included many acacias and eucalypts which were grown as pot plants for their ornamental foliage and flowers. *Lechenaultia formosa* and *L. biloba* were popular subjects in many European nurseries, as were the annuals such as *Brachycome iberidifolia*.

At the present time, in France and other Mediterranean countries, *Acacia dealbata* is commonly grown as a cut flower, known there as 'Mimosa'. *A. farnesiana* is used in the production of perfumes, and has been widely cultivated in the south of France. The perfume is extracted by mixing the sweet scented flowers with melted fat or olive oil, which becomes impregnated with their odour.

In Lokrum, on the island of Dubrovnik which

is part of Yugoslavia in the Adriatic sea, 2 acres of *Eucalyptus*, and shrub species such as *Acacia*, *Callistemon* and *Grevillea* have been planted and are grown as a tourist attraction.

UNITED STATES OF AMERICA

There have been many Australian species introduced to the U.S.A. These are mainly grown in the warmer states such as California and Florida, and to a lesser extent Nevada, Arizona and Texas. Outside of Australia, California is generally regarded as the centre for the growing of Australian plants. Many nurseries list Australian species for sale, but usually only the reliable species are grown. The introduction to cultivation of additional species is mainly left to individual enthusiasts.

It is thought that the first Australian plants reached America early in the 19th Century. What is certain is that most of the early arrivals were sent to America from England, as exchange material to botanic gardens, nurseries and private collectors. The greatest impact was attained by the genus *Eucalyptus*. (See page 32)

Plants in Cultivation Today

As an approximation, there have been over 1000 species of Australian plants cultivated in the U.S.A. The accompanying table gives a list of the main genera, with the number of species cultivated.

Main Genera, and Approximate Number of Species Grown in U.S.A.

Acacia	100	*Ficus*	5
Actinostrobus	3	*Grevillea*	100
Angophora	4	*Hakea*	30
Athrotaxis	3	*Hibbertia*	8
Banksia	15	*Isopogon*	3
Billardiera	4	*Kennedia*	5
Boronia	2	*Kunzea*	8
Brachysema	3	*Lechenaultia*	6
Callistemon	20+	*Leptospermum*	10
Callitris	10+	*Melaleuca*	60+
Calothamnus	10+	*Myoporum*	3
Cassia	8	*Olearia*	6
Casuarina	18	*Pittosporum*	4
Correa	6	*Prostanthera*	10
Darwinia	15	*Stenocarpus*	2
Dianella	4	*Syncarpia*	3
Dodonaea	10	*Verticordia*	5
Eremophila	10	*Xanthorrhoea*	3
Eucalyptus	250+		

Acacias

Records show that over 100 species of *Acacia* have been grown at some time in California.

The accompanying list is of acacias that have proved to be adaptable. Those marked * are especially hardy, under a wide range of conditions. The years, shown in brackets, indicate when the species was introduced into the U.S.A. Those not dated have been introduced comparatively recently.

Acacia Species Grown in the U.S.A.

Acacia alpina

aulacocarpa (1912)	* longifolia (1919)
auriculiformis (1900)	macradenia (1918)
baileyana (1900-1910)	* mearnsii (1871)
biflora (1910)	meissneri (1911)
* boormanii	* melanoxylon (1919)
brachybotrya	microcarpa (1927)
* cardiophylla (1923)	montana
costata (1908)	* pendula
* cultriformis (1919)	podalyriifolia (1909)
* cyclops (1919)	pravissima (1900)
* dealbata	pubescens (early 1900's)
* decurrens (1860-1890)	pycnantha (1919)
diffusa (1918)	* redolens
dodonaeifolia	retinodes
drummondii (1911)	riceana
elongata (1919)	rostellifera (1928)
extensa (1919)	rubida (1937)
falcata (1900)	* salicina (1900)
flexifolia (1927)	saligna
glandulicarpa	simsii (1900)
glaucescens (1909)	* spectabilis (1910)
gnidium	stricta
hakeoides	suaveolens (1912)
holosericea (1905)	trinervata (1900)
jonesii (1926)	triptera
juniperina (1919)	uncinata
linifolia (1900)	* verniciflua (1923)
lineata (1900)	* verticillata (1900)

Other genera

The range of Australian plants in cultivation in the U.S.A. is being increased continually, by the importation of species for trial in institutions such as the Arboretum of the University of California, Santa Cruz, and Saratoga Horticultural Research Foundation, as well as in private nurseries.

There is much interest being shown currently in the genus *Grevillea*, with about 100 species, plus many forms, now in cultivation. Many of these have been introduced to California within the last few years. Trials are very encouraging, and best results have been obtained with plants that have been grown in very well-drained soils.

Some *Grevillea* species and cultivars are already well established in cultivation. These include —

G. juniperina — a form similar to the form from the A.C.T. region. Originally introduced from England as *G.* 'Sulfurea', and still sold by that name. It has pale greenish yellow clusters of flower.

G. 'Aromas' — with light pink flowers. Has affinities with the original type form of *G. rosmarinifolia* from N.S.W.

G. 'Noellii' — very similar to the form of *G. rosmarinifolia* commonly cultivated in Australia. In California this form is the most widely cultivated of all grevilleas, because of its proven reliability, although it is not spectacular in flower.

Species of other genera that are in common cultivation are —

Araucaria bidwillii — large trees are common along the S.W. coastal strip. Popular as street trees. The large cones are removed to prevent injury to pedestrians, or damage to vehicles.

Callistemon citrinus — plants are nearly always in flower, and therefore the species is widely grown. It is used extensively in freeway plantings, where it grows well under harsh conditions of heat, dryness, and pollution. The most commonly grown form is *C. citrinus* 'Splendens'.

Callistemon salignus — some specimens are tree-like and over 12 m tall, with trunks covered in beautiful papery bark.

Callistemon viminalis — is commonly grown in relatively low frost areas. It is appreciated for its weeping growth habit, and long display of flowers.

Castanospermum australe — develop into rounded and spreading trees, and provide a good display of colour in summer.

Cyathea cooperi, and *Dicksonia antarctica* — these are 2 commonly grown tree ferns, and they grow extremely well in suitable moist and sheltered conditions.

Doryanthes excelsa, and *D. palmeri* — grow and flower well under a wide range of conditions.

Ficus rubiginosa — a vigorous species, grown in large gardens, parks, and as a roadside tree where there is room for it to grow to maturity.

Giejera parviflora — a highly sought after tree, because of its pendulous foliage. It was introduced to California by the Saratoga Horticultural Foundation. Widely planted.

Hymenosporum flavum — has adapted very well. Excellent specimens are in cultivation, and they flower prolifically.

Lagunaria patersonii — commonly planted as a coastal tree, where it withstands the harshest of conditions.

Macadamia integrifolia, and *M. tetraphylla* — are commonly grown. They flower and fruit well.

Melaleuca linariifolia — develops into an excellent street tree.

Melaleuca nesophila — has proved very adaptable, and is often grown in gardens, and as a roadside plant.

Pittosporum rhombifolium — is regarded as being one of the showiest small trees planted in California.

Pittosporum undulatum — has adapted extremely well, to the extent that it is becoming a naturalised species in some regions.

Schefflera actinophylla — relishes the conditions, and grows to a large size outdoors. It flowers well.

Syzygium paniculatum — is one of the most commonly grown Australian plants. It is used as a specimen plant, a landscaping shrub, or as a clipped hedge to gain benefit from its reddish new growth.

Tristania laurina — widely grown in gardens, and as a street tree. Selected forms are propagated by cuttings.

Additional Species being grown on the West Coast of U.S.A.

Acmena smithii
Agathis robusta
Agonis flexuosa
  juniperina
Albizia lophantha
Alyogyne huegelii
Angophora costata
  melanoxylon
Anigozanthos flavidus
  manglesii
Araucaria cunninghamii
Asplenium bulbiferum
  nidus
Atriplex semibaccata
Beaufortia sparsa
Boronia heterophylla
  megastigma
Brachychiton acerifolius
  discolor
  populneus
Brachycome iberidifolia
Brachysema lanceolatum
Buckinghamia celsissima
Bursaria spinosa
Callicoma serratifolia
Callistemon macropunctatus
  pinifolius
  sieberi
  speciosus
Calocephalus brownii
Calothamnus quadrifidus
  rupestris
  villosus
Cassia artemisioides
  brewsteri
  sturtii
Casuarina cunninghamiana
  equisetifolia
  stricta

Ceratopetalum gummiferum
Chamelaucium uncinatum
Chorizema cordatum
  ilicifolium
Cordyline stricta
Correa alba
  backhousiana
  'Ivory Bells'
  pulchella
Cupaniopsis anacardioides
Didiscus caerulea
Elaeocarpus reticulatus
Eustrephus latifolius
Ficus macrophylla
  watkinsiana
Flindersia maculosa
Grevillea banksii
  lanigera
  robusta
  rosmarinifolia
  sericea
  speciosa
  thelemanniana
Hakea laurina
  nodosa
  oleifolia
  petiolaris
  salicifolia
  suaveolens
Hardenbergia comptoniana
  violacea
Harpullia pendula
Helichrysum thyrsoideum
Hibbertia cuneiformis
  scandens
Howeia forsteriana
Isopogon anemonifolius
  anethifolius
Kunzea pulchella

Leptospermum flavescens
  laevigatum
  lanigerum
  liversidgei
  petersonii
  scoparium
  scoparium var.
    rotundifolium
Lhotzkya ericoides
Livistona australis
Lomatia fraxinifolia
Macrozamia spiralis
Melaleuca armillaris
  bracteata
  decussata
  elliptica
  ericifolia
  huegelii
  hypericifolia
  incana
  quinquenervia
  styphelioides
  wilsonii
Myoporum debile
  insulare
  parvifolium
  viscosum
Olearia argophylla
  phlogopappa
Omalanthus populifolius

Orthrosanthus multiflorus
Patersonia occidentalis
Pittosporum bicolor
  phillyraeoides
Petrophile biloba
Phymatocarpus
  porphyrocephalus
Platycerium bifurcatum
  superbum
Podocarpus elatus
  lawrencei
Pratia pedunculata
Prostanthera cuneata
  rotundifolia
Rulingia pannosa
Rumohra adiantiformis
Sollya heterophylla
Stenocarpus sinuatus
Tasmannia lanceolata
Templetonia retusa
Tristania conferta
Verticordia drummondii
Viminaria juncea
Viola hederacea
Wahlenbergia gloriosa
  saxicola
Westringia fruticosa
Xanthorrhoea preissii
  quadrangulata

leaving Australia), the rooted cuttings are placed directly into thoroughly prepared ground where the plants are to grow. Care is taken to ensure that the large roots are not damaged, and that all roots are placed pointing down, or slightly spreading outwards, to assist their penetration of the soil as quickly as possible. After planting they are watered, and then each is covered with a specially prepared jar. The base is removed from a 1 gallon glass bottle, and 3/4 of the bottle is covered with aluminium foil. This allows enough light to penetrate, to ensure that foliage will not become chlorotic, and plants will not burn. The open neck of the bottle allows for limited air movement. The bell-jars are positioned so that the sun's rays will not be able to hit the foliage of the plants at any time. Thus warm humid conditions are created, to assist and stimulate new growth.

Plants are watered regularly, but lightly, to maintain moist but not overwet soil. The bell-jars are usually removed after sunset, or if raining, and replaced before the sun has a chance to be on the plants.

As plants become established, the jars are gradually removed for longer periods, to 'harden off' the plants, until the jars are no longer required.

Australian Plants as Noxious Weeds in U.S.A.

A few species of Australian plants have become so well adapted to the environment, that they have become naturalized as weeds, in parts of the U.S.A. The most common species are *Acacia dealbata, A. decurrens, A. melanoxylon* and *A. verticillata. Melaleuca ericifolia* has spread vigorously in many of the wet areas of Florida, and has created a problem which is proving difficult to control. It is known as the punk tree, and its spread has reduced water levels in some swamps, with resultant drastic effects on the wildlife.

Nurserymen and growers are now aware of the likelihood that some Australian species could spread rapidly, threatening their own native species. They are therefore carrying out trials, before releasing plants for general sale.

The Treatment of Imported Rooted Cuttings

At the Arboretum of the University of California, Santa Cruz, an interesting and very successful method of establishing cuttings imported from Australia is being undertaken. It is an adaptation of rooting cuttings with a bell jar.

Prior to despatch from Australia, all soil is washed off the plants for quarantine purposes. On arrival at Santa Cruz (about 2 days after

NEW ZEALAND

There has been interest in New Zealand for many years, regarding the cultivation of Australian plants. Thousands of acres are now planted with eucalypts which were introduced at about 1910, but as happened in California, the timber was found unsuitable for milling and use as a building material. In 1949, the authorities decided that no more eucalypts would be planted, until suitable species had been selected in Australia, and the progeny tested to check stability.

A method commonly used with eucalypts in New Zealand nurseries is that, after germination, they are planted directly into prepared ground, in rows. When grown to about 15-30 cm tall, they are lifted, washed free of soil, and sold as loose rooted seedlings.

Acacias are commonly grown with eucalypts for farm shelter, and other Australian plants that are popular include *Hardenbergia violacea*, and *Kennedia* spp. *Boronia megastigma* is widely grown and readily propagated by layering, and *Telopea speciosissima* is also cultivated for the cut flower trade.

Eucalypts at Santa Monica, California, where testing of various species occurred from 1887-1923.
LHS — *Eucalyptus saligna.* RHS — *E.grandis*

W.R. Elliot photo

Eucalyptus kitsoniana, thriving in a 300mm rainfall in California U.S.A. Its natural habitat is in wet boggy conditions.

W.R. Elliot photo

History of Cultivation Overseas

The very wide range of species grown includes the following:

Acacia baileyana
  dodonaeifolia
  longifolia
  riceana
Acmena smithii
Actinotus cunninghamii
Agonis flexuosa
Astartea heteranthera
Astroloma ciliatum
Banksia baueri
  coccinea
  ericifolia
  integrifolia
  media
  ornata
  prionotes
  prostrata
  repens
  speciosa
  spinulosa
Bauera sessiliflora
Beaufortia purpurea
  schaueri
  sparsa
Boronia crenulata
  denticulata
  heterophylla
  megastigma
Brachysema lanceolatum
Callistemon citrinus
  salignus
  'Violaceus'
Calytrix alpestris
  glutinosa
  sullivanii
  tetragona
Ceratopetalum gummiferum
Chorizema dicksonii
  diversifolium
  ilicifolium
Correa pulchella
  reflexa
Crowea exalata
Diplolaena grandiflora
Dryandra formosa
  nobilis
  polycephala
  praemorsa
Eremaea fimbriata
Epacris longiflora
Eriostemon myoporoides
Eucalyptus ficifolia
  lehmannii
  leucoxylon
  preissiana
Eutaxia obovata

Grevillea banksii
  candelabroides
  dimorpha
  hookerana
  juniperina
  lavandulacea
  longifolia
  longistyla
  petrophiloides
  'Poorinda Beauty'
  robusta
  rosmarinifolia
  speciosa
Hakea laurina
  myrtoides
  purpurea
  sericea
Hymenosporum flavum
Isopogon anethifolius
  cuneatus
  latifolius
Kunzea baxteri
  ericifolia
Leptospermum scoparium
  var rotundifolium
Lechenaultia biloba
Melaleuca diosmifolia
  gibbosa
  huegelii
  lateritia
  megacephala
  nematophylla
  radula
  spathulata
  wilsonii
Olearia phlogopappa
Persoonia pinifolia
Petrophile linearis
Phebalium glandulosum
Pimelea rosea
  spectabilis
Prostanthera incisa
  nivea
  ovalifolia
  rotundifolia
Ptilotus manglesii
Regelia velutina
Scholtzia species
Telopea oreades
  speciosissima
  'Hybrid'
Templetonia retusa
Tetratheca ciliata
Thryptomene calycina
  saxicola
Xanthosia rotundifolia
Westringia glabra

NOTES FROM OTHER COUNTRIES

Australian plants have been introduced to many other countries, although not generally in large numbers. Asian countries such as India have been cultivating some species for a long time. In about 1885, *Acacia melanoxylon* was introduced to Madras, where it was milled for cabinet work. The trees were cut after about 22 years growth. *Acacia dealbata* is highly prized as a fuel timber, and was grown on the hills in India as early as 1840. Other popular species are *Callistemon viminalis*, and *Eucalyptus camaldulensis*.

In neighbouring Nepal, trees such as *Callistemon viminalis*, *Eucalyptus globulus*, *E. grandis* and *Grevillea robusta* have been planted. In some areas of Nepal, Australian trees are being grown to supply fuel, as they are fast growing. They also help to control erosion on the steep hillsides which have been denuded of their natural vegetation by the local people, over the centuries. At the same time, local species are being replanted, to later take over from the introduced Australian species.

In Hong Kong, the following are successfully grown as street and park trees. *Eucalyptus citriodora*, *E. maculata*, *E. sideroxylon* and *Grevillea robusta*.

In recent years, many species of *Callistemon*, *Eucalyptus*, *Grevillea*, *Leptospermum* and *Melaleuca* have been introduced to Japan, both by private organisations, and public authorities. Plantings are in the North, Central and Southern areas of Japan.

The desert she-oak, *Casuarina decaisneana* is commonly grown in Iran for fuel.

Israel has some large areas of Australian plants, with special emphasis on species suitable for cut flowers. (See page 40.)

The Commonwealth War Graves Commission is responsible for planting in war cemeteries around the world, and where possible, those species of plants that are typical of the soldiers' homeland are planted. The Australian War Graves Authority supplies seeds of native plants to overseas cemeteries, so that plants can be grown for this purpose. Many species of Australian plants have been planted, especially in areas with a Mediterranean-type climate. Plants such as *Eucalyptus* spp. have been found ideal to control drifting sands in the cemeteries at Alamein in Africa. In Cairo, initial difficulty was experienced in raising *Eucalyptus* seedlings, as they commonly died when about 20 cm tall. Subsequently, soil from beneath existing eucalypts was gathered, and used in the potting mix, which resulted in healthy, well developed plants. Extreme difficulty in establishing eucalypts at Gallipoli has been encountered, due to the very cold winter temperatures. To date plantings there have not been successful. Recently a selection of Australian species was sent to the United Nations War Cemetery at Pusan in Korea. At this stage it is too early to gauge the success of this planting project.

3 History of Eucalypts in Cultivation

Introduction of Eucalypts to other countries

Eucalypts were easily the most famous plant ambassadors exported from Australia. They became distributed widely around the world, and grew successfully under a very wide range of conditions, from sea level to highland areas, from high rainfall to arid deserts, and in both tropical and temperate regions.

The first known eucalypt seeds to be despatched overseas were a batch of *Eucalyptus globulus*, sent to Paris in 1804. It is also known that they were sent to Chile in the early 1820's (where they were planted in the high Andes mountains) and to South Africa in 1828. The despatches in the first half of the 19th Century were a mere trickle, however, compared with the torrent of seeds which flowed out of Australia between 1850 and 1890. This export was primarily due to the industry and ingenuity of Baron Sir Ferdinand von Mueller, Government Botanist of Victoria. He continually extolled the value of both eucalypts and acacias for afforestation, and personally collected much of the seed that was sent overseas.

Initially, eucalypts were planted for windbreaks, as ornamentals, or for their reputation of having excellent health-giving and medicinal qualities. In some countries, eg. Spain, Portugal, Brazil and the Black Sea coast of U.S.S.R., the leaves were distilled for volatile or essential oil production.

The main use for trees grown today is the production of timber for building purposes, and for fuel.

Eucalyptus occidentalis has been widely planted in arid zones around the world, eg. Israel, where it is common in the northern Negev region. In Zambia, *Eucalyptus camaldulensis*, *E. cloeziana*, *E. grandis*, *E. saligna* and *E. tereticornis* have proved very successful. Local seed was collected for a breeding program to produce hardy hybrids. Hybrids with *E. grandis*, *E. saligna* and *E. tereticornis* as parents have produced better growth than the respective parents. *Eucalyptus camaldulensis* and *E. tereticornis* are widely planted in India,

and resultant hybrids have eventuated, which have proved useful in the climate.

Many other hybrids have developed in overseas countries, eg. *E. cornuta* x *E. occidentalis* in Cyprus, where it is reported as having considerable promise of growing on the island. In U.S.S.R. the development of artificial and natural hybrids has occurred during trials, and some are proving ideally suited to the prevailing conditions.

Other countries in which eucalypts are grown include Congo, Cameroon, Ceylon, Corsica, Cuba, Ecuador, Greece, Indonesia, Iran, Ireland, Japan, Jordan, Libya, Malaysia, Morocco, New Zealand, Nigeria, Papua New Guinea, Paraguay, Peru, Puerto Rico, Rhodesia, South Africa, Tunisia, Turkey, United Kingdom, United States of America, Uruguay.

Eucalypts in the United Kingdom

Eucalypts are not widely grown outside in the United Kingdom, because the climate is generally too harsh for all but the hardiest species. There are however, some well established collections in the milder western counties such as Somerset, Cornwall and Devon. Some of these are quite old, with specimens up to 20 m tall. The plants suffer from periodical severe frosts, which may kill sensitive species, or those at the wrong stage of growth, even in the milder districts. They also may be badly damaged by gales, and hence are often cut back hard, and developed into coppice-growth shrubs. Most species flower in the milder districts, but seed set may be infrequent and irregular. Eucalypts may grow quite quickly in the milder districts, attaining 2-3 m in the one season.

The hardy species of eucalypts which will survive in the colder districts where 20-25 degrees of frost occurs several times in the winter, include *E. de beuzevillei*, *E. glaucescens*, *E. gunnii*, *E. pauciflora*, *E. perriniana*, and *E. vernicosa*.

Those species grown in the milder districts include *E. acaciaeformis*, *E. aggregata*, *E. cinerea*, *E.*

Introduction and History

List of Major Overseas Countries Growing Eucalypts

Country	Approx. area planted (hectares)	Main Uses	Major species used
Argentina	25 000	Timber, fuel, shelter	E. camaldulensis, E. viminalis, E. saligna, E. globulus, E. tereticornis, E. cinerea, E. leucoxylon
Brazil	1 000 000	Timber, fuel, paper pulp, oil	E. camaldulensis, E. alba, E. saligna, E. tereticornis, E. citriodora
Chile	50 000	Fuel, charcoal	E. citriodora, E. cornuta, E. amygdalina, E. maculata, E. polyanthemos
China	40 000	Sleepers, fuel, ornamental	E. robusta, E. citriodora, E. tereticornis, E. camaldulensis, E. exserta
Ethiopia	5 000	Fuel, timber	mainly E. globulus, some E. camaldulensis, E. citriodora
Guatemala		Oil	E. citriodora, E. staigerana, E. smithii
India	1 000	Fuel, oil	mainly E. globulus, some E. pilularis, E. eugenioides, E. punctata, E. resinifera
Italy	40 000	Drainage, shelter, fuel	E. globulus, E. camaldulensis
Kenya	10 000		mainly E. saligna, E. globulus some E. maculata, E. microcorys
Madagascar	140 000	Fuel	E. robusta, E. camaldulensis, E. rudis, E. tereticornis some E. resinifera
New Zealand	10 000	Timber	E. pilularis, E. maculata, E. punctata, E. saligna, E. botryoides, E. tereticornis, E. camaldulensis, E. fastigiata, E. regnans
Portugal	60 000	Paper pulp, fuel	mainly E. globulus, some E. botryoides, E. camaldulensis, E. citriodora, E. sideroxylon.
Spain	400 000	Timber, oil	mainly E. globulus, E. camaldulensis, some E. botryoides, E. citriodora, E. gomphocephala
South Africa	350 000	Timber, paper pulp	mainly E. saligna, some E. viminalis, E. sideroxylon
Hawaii	3 000	Timber	E. robusta, E. citriodora, E. globulus, E. camaldulensis
U.S.S.R.	20 000	Timber, oil, shelter	E. macarthuri, E. rubida, E. macrorhyncha, E. citriodora, E. globulus, E. maidenii, E. smithii

coccifera, E. cordata, E. dalrympleana, E. johnstonii, E. kybeanensis, E. mitchelliana, E. nichollii, E. ovata, E. parvifolia, E. pauciflora, E. rubida, E. stellulata, E. urnigera, E. viminalis.

Eucalypts are also grown as pot plants by the nursery trade throughout England. The glaucous-leaved species are especially popular, and are grown principally as foliage plants. These include E. citriodora, E. coccifera, E. cordata, E. globulus, E. gunnii, E. morrisbyi.

Eucalypts in U.S.A.

Australians visiting the state of California for the first time are usually amazed at the large areas of eucalypts that are grown. Hillsides in some areas are literally covered by Eucalyptus globulus, while roadsides are lined with E. camaldulensis and E. sideroxylon. E. citriodora, E. maculata and E. viminalis are also very popular.

In southern California prior to the gold rush of 1848, there was a dearth of trees, due to harsh climatic and poor soil conditions. In was in San Francisco, immediately after the gold rush, that Dr. H. H. Behr, a native of Germany, suggested the importation of Eucalyptus and Acacia seed from Australia. By 1853 there were 14 species of Eucalyptus growing in San Francisco, and in 1880 seedlings were available for sale from a nurseryman in Oakland.

It seems that the name Eucalyptus was a curiosity to the Californians, as were the trees also, being so different in appearance to the local indigenous plants.

Eucalypts were planted spasmodically in California, until Elwood Cooper started a crusade to convert the barren state into a continuous forest of *Eucalyptus* trees. He contacted the U.S. Consul General at Melbourne, who responded by sending seeds, and reported that the Victorian Government Botanist, Baron von Mueller, had given lectures on the cultivation of eucalypts. These lectures had been printed, but had been sent to London. Baron von Mueller however sent his own original lecture material to Cooper, on the understanding that he would publish it in U.S.A., and give the Baron 50 copies.

In 1875 Elwood Cooper had 50,000 eucalypts growing on his ranch, and gave a lecture entitled 'Forest Culture and Australian Gum Trees', to stimulate people to plant these beautiful trees. He told his audience how some trees grew to 45 feet in 3 years from seed. In 1876 Cooper published his address, with Baron von Mueller's writings. Also included was a listing of 20 species, for which seed was available from Anderson Hall & Co., of Sydney.

Also in 1875 the 'Forest Grove Association' was formed in Los Angeles, 'to convert the barren horizons in both beauty and profit by planting *Eucalyptus* trees'. The State Forestry Bureau undertook experimental plantings at Santa Monica. Today this area has an historical marker, with many species growing. It is an excellent example of grove planting, with low maintenance due to the suppression of weed growth with bush litter.

In 1895 Mr. Abbot Kinney published a monograph on more intelligent utilization of the many diverse species of *Eucalyptus*. He gave locations of sample trees of 51 species, so that they could be inspected and ideas be gained for planting in different areas. Whilst arguing for their value as timber species, he also stressed the host of other uses that could be gained from eucalypts, including medicinal oils, tanning, resin for use as insecticides and astringents, nectar for honey bees, paper pulp, bark for mats, mothballs, nest lining for fowls to control lice, and scouring material for encrusted boilers. One of their major attributes was their ability to drain swampy land and therefore reduce the incidence of malaria.

A further incentive to keep the crusade rolling was provided in 1904 by the Forest Service of the U.S. Department of Agriculture, when it announced that the supply of hardwood from the Eastern states of U.S.A. would be exhausted in about 16 years. As the commonly used woods such as oak, hickory, ash, walnut, maple and mahogany became scarce and their cost rose, substitutes were sought. Australian eucalypts were found to be equal, and in some cases superior.

It was thought that if seedlings were planted immediately, mature trees would be ready for milling as the supplies ran out. At least 50 nurserymen proceeded to propagate these species which were thought best suited to commercial use. The media were behind the venture, and new industries were formed to process the timber and use its by-products. A book entitled 'Eucalyptus, Its History Growth and Utilization,' was published as a guide to commercial growers. It contained much information on the utilization of the timber, for furniture, flooring, agricultural implements, houses, paper, veneer, a superior grade of charcoal, and about a dozen medicinal and cosmetic products made from the distilled oils obtained from foliage and young branchlets.

At this stage eucalypts were planted rigorously. The Santa Fe Railroad Company planted trees along railway tracks, to provide close access for the cutting of railway sleepers. Furniture manufacturers planted large areas. Excellent agricultural land was planted with eucalypts, with the promise of greater profit than from beans or grain. Soon plantings were ready for cutting, but difficulties began to emerge. Trees had to be sawn immediately after felling, otherwise they were too hard for work later. This was so different to the native timbers. Initially the problems were thought to be trivial, but their magnitude increased, as warping, twisting and cracking occurred, no matter how the timber was cured or whenever it was cut. These problems eventually caused the collapse of the Australian Hardwood Timber Industry, and associated ventures.

Many eucalypts were then removed from orchards and farms, cities and towns, and in fact lost favour. Subdividers stipulated in deeds that no blue-gums were to be planted on any part of the development. Some nurserymen propagated smaller ornamental species, but even they lost favour, and other introduced trees such as Magnolia and Jacaranda gained preference.

Eucalypts in California Today

Many of the eucalypts in California have growth habits differing from those common to their natural state. It is often difficult to establish the exact species involved, because of the different appearance, eg. in many cases the trees have pendulous foliage. Nearly every visiting Australian botanist is asked to have a look at gum trees, with a view to identifying them.

Introduction and History

Because of the lack of native pests, most eucalypts grow very quickly and without blemish. This can result in some species having brittle wood, and this combined with the dense foliage causes branches to break. It is only rarely that the foliage of eucalypts is attacked. A local Californian grasshopper eats the leaves of *E. camaldulensis*, but with very limited damage.

Some of the more commonly grown species are —

E. citriodora Widely and successfully grown. Develops into a very graceful tree, even in freeway plantings in Los Angeles.

E. cladocalyx Some street trees are in the vicinity of 100 years old, and have been left to grow without pollarding.

E. cornuta An excellent street tree. Some very old specimens near Los Angeles.

E. deanei Grows well to display its smooth upright trunk. Highly regarded by some Californian horticulturists. Not yet widely grown in Australia.

E. ficifolia Commonly grown on the south west coast, where it usually grows as a round-headed tree. The flowering can be intermittent throughout the year, but occurs mainly during spells of hot weather.

E. globulus Extensively planted. Some forests are cropped for pulp manufacture. Commonly seen in farmlands, as windbreaks and for shade and shelter, with odd plants along the coastline, eg. Big Sur. It has not regenerated to any great extent.

E. globulus var *compacta* This has often been described as an American introduction, but it is not wholly true, as plants of a similar growth habit were observed at the same time in the Canary Islands.

E. grandis Has proved very adaptable. A quick growing tree, reaching about 25 m in 12 years. Widely planted.

E. kitsoniana Has adapted well to very low rainfall.

E. macrandra Grows well. Often has so many flower-heads that branches can crack with their weight.

E. pauciflora Has adapted to varied locations, and proved very hardy.

E. viminalis Widely planted. Some magnificent specimens. Does not usually have the vertical ribbony deciduous bark, as it does in its natural habitat.

Other Eucalypts that have been grown with success in California

Eucalyptus accedens	*Eucalyptus melliodora*
albens	microtheca
angulosa	neglecta
bauerana	nicholii
botryoides	nutans
caesia	orbifolia
caleyi	oreades
calophylla	ovata
camaldulensis	parvifolia
cephalocarpa	perriniana
cinerea	pileata
cloeziana	polyanthemos
coccifera	polybractea
corrugata	preissiana
cosmophylla	pulchella
crucis	pulverulenta
desmondensis	robusta
dundasii	rhodantha
eremophila	rudis
erythronema	saligna
eximia	salmonophloia
forrestiana	scabra
gillii	scoparia
glaucescens	sepulcralis
gracilis	shirleyi
grossa	sideroxylon
lansdowneana	spathulata
leptophylla	tereticornis
leucoxylon var. leucoxylon	tetragona
leucoxylon var. macrocarpa	thozetiana
loxophleba	torquata
macrocarpa	umbra
maculata	vernicosa
mannifera ssp maculosa	woodwardii
magacornuta	yalataensis

34

4 History of Australian Plants in Cultivation in Australia

Australian plants have been grown in overseas countries for longer than they have been cultivated in Australia. It is not certain when the nursery industry became well established in Australia, but it was probably not until after the 1850's. It is known that several nurseries were started in the inner suburbs around Sydney prior to 1848, but how large they were, and what species were grown remains unknown. The nurseries known to be established in Sydney prior to 1848 were Baptist's Nurseries, Guilfoyles' Nursery, Darling's Nursery, Henderson's Camellia Grove Nursery at Double Bay, and Magills of Surry Hills.

It is unlikely that many Australian plants were offered for sale in the early years, because nurseries were probably fully occupied trying to establish and propagate the exotic species imported from the homeland and other countries. For example, during the first half of the 19th Century, the Botanic Gardens of NSW continually exported plants and seeds of Australian species to Europe, and the cases were returned with plants, rare and otherwise, from all parts of the world.

There was however, some interest in the cultivation of Australian plants in Australia during this time. A certain Thomas Shepherd, proprietor of Darling's Nursery in Sydney, encouraged the cultivation of NSW plants, and apparently sold them in his nursery. He also, it seems, lectured on the subject, and these lectures were reported at length in the Sydney Herald in 1834.

Some Australian plants especially the spectacular species such as the Waratah, (*Telopea speciosissima*) became popular subjects for cultivation. Bulbs were popular subjects with horticulturists, and some Australian species attracted interest from an early date. *Crinum flaccidum* was grown in gardens around Sydney before 1810, and in 1844 a William Macarthur had produced a hybrid between *Crinum scabrum* (from Africa) and the native *C. pedunculatum.* This is probably the first man-made hybrid involving an Australian plant, and almost certainly the first in Australia. Macarthur apparently raised a great many *Crinum* hybrids, and this particular one was described as 'a splendid flower'.

Information on the cultivation of Australian plants in Australia, between 1850 and 1890 is not readily obtainable. In 1892 a very comprehensive publication by an enlightened gentleman, actively promoted the virtues of Australian plants to the gardening public. This was 'A Handbook of Australian Horticulture' by H. A. James, F.R.H.S. The following comment was made in a chapter dealing exclusively with Australian plants: 'The plants and flowers indigenous in Australia do not appear to have received from colonial nurserymen and amateur gardeners that consideration which their beauties may fairly claim. True, a few of exceptional merit have found a place in the nurserymen's catalogues, but they are few indeed.' In this chapter, with the help of J. H. Maiden, he listed species suitable for cultivation. There were over 290 shrubs and trees, with special sections dealing with ferns (42 spp.), orchids (24 spp.), cycads and palms (17 spp.) and climbers (16 spp.). Some unusual species were included, such as:

Shrubs and Trees: *Abrophyllum ornans, Abutilon halophilum, Blandfordia marginata, Boronia barkerana, Callitris macleayana, Cassinia aurea, Dracophyllum secundum, Geijera parviflora, Helipterum humboldtianum* (which was described as 'one of the best herbaceous annuals'), *Isopogon baxteri, Oxylobium lanceolatum* (then known as *O. callistachys*), *Sprengelia incarnata* ('amongst the many beautiful flowering shrubs of Australia, there are few which surpass *S. incarnata*'), and *Thysanotus baueri.*

Ferns: *Adiantum formosum, Blechnum patersonii, Cyathea rebeccae, Davallia pyxidata,* and *Marattia salicina.*

Orchids: *Dendrobium bigibbum, Phaius grandifolius* and *Thelymitra ixioides.*

Cycads and Palms: *Cycas media,* and *Pandanus pedunculatus.*

Introduction and History

Climbers: *Diplocylos palmatus, Jasminum simplicifolium* and *Pandorea jasminoides.*

Enlightened comments were also given on factors such as propagation and cultivation:

Elaeocarpus grandis — 'cuttings from ripened shoots and inserted in sandy soil under a bell glass'.

Epacris — 'adapted for pot culture, use light open soils, prune after flowering, propagate from cuttings'.

Hibbertia dentata — 'probably the most useful of the genus'.

Leptomeria acida — 'flowers insignificant but when plant is covered with its green currant-like fruit it presents a distinct and pretty appearance. The fruit is edible and useful for jams etc.'

Macadamia tetraphylla — 'The nut-like kernel is superior to the filbert nut in flavour.'

Pimelea — 'Propagation is effected by cuttings made of young shoots and inserted in sandy soil under a bell glass, or by seed.'

Stenocarpus sinuatus — 'Propagation by cuttings of ripened shoots placed under a bell glass with bottom heat.

Various Australian nurseries offered a range of Australian plants for sale in the late 1890's, but no nursery specialised in their production, and few grew a large range. A good selection was offered by Sewell's Payneham Nurseries in Adelaide. Their 1894 Catalogue listed seeds of at least 125 species, including 23 species of *Eucalyptus.* Over 80 species of native plants were available in pots, including oddities such as a golden-leaved form of *Ficus macrophylla,* and a variegated form of *Lagunaria patersonii.* Other rarities included *Anthocercis viscosa, Boronia spathulata, Desmodium acanthocladum, Elaeodendron australe, Eugenia eucalyptoides, Jasminum didymum, Pithecellobium pruinosum* and *Stenocarpus salignus.*

The 1895 catalogue of Ashfield Nursery in Sydney, listed a range of Australian plants, including the very choice *Barklya syringifolia.*

People who stimulated the cultivation of Australian plants in the early 20th Century included J. H. Maiden, with his book 'The Useful Native Plants of Australia' and many other publications, also W. R. Guilfoyle, whose 'Australian Plants Suitable for Gardens Parks and Timber Reserves' listed a large number of recommended species.

Australian plants were not commonly grown between 1920 and 1950, and they were certainly not actively promoted by general nurseries.

There was only minimal interest in the collection and introduction of species new to cultivation. Those listed in nursery catalogues were mainly established lines, which had been popular for many years. During this period there were only a limited number of specialist Australian plant nurseries, and it was due to their efforts that some headway was made with new introductions.

There was limited, and unco-ordinated interest in the growing of Australian plants, until the formation of The Society for Growing Australian Plants (S.G.A.P.), founded by the writer on Australian plants for 'Your Garden' magazine, A. J. Swaby. The inaugural meeting was held in Melbourne on March 12th 1957, and about 200 people met together. In a very short time, other groups were formed throughout Australia —

Melbourne — 12th March 1957
Queensland Region — 14th June 1957
NSW Region — 31st January 1958
WA (now the WA Wildflower Society) — 18th March 1958
SA Region — 9th April 1958
Federal Council, formed at Canberra — September 1962
Victorian Region/Tasmanian Region — 20th May 1971.

December 1959 saw the publication of Volume 1 Number 1 of 'Australian Plants' a quarterly magazine, and the commonwealth journal of the S.G.A.P. Each issue is now over 15,000 copies, and they are widely distributed around the world.

The theme of 'Preservation by Cultivation' has been to the forefront of the Society's activities. At present the Society has about 8500 members, with many local groups offering information and assistance to anyone who is interested in cultivating Australian plants.

Prior to 1950 there were very few nurseries able to supply more than 15 species of Australian plants, and these were only popular lines such as *Acacia baileyana, Boronia heterophylla, B. megastigma, Callistemon citrinus, Eriostemon myoporoides, Eucalyptus botryoides, E. globulus,* and *Grevillea rosmarinifolia.* There were a few nurseries specialising in the native flora, but these were small, and widely scattered.

From about 1960, and probably due largely to the activities of the S.G.A.P., there began to be an upsurge of interest in the subject. In late 1967 and early 1968, a severe drought ravaged southeastern Australia and badly affected many gardens containing introduced plants. Gardeners realised the value of Australian plants, because they did not suffer to a great extent. This resulted in a dramatic increase in the interest shown in Australian flora. Many nurseries were established, some growing Australian plants exclusively. Also, general nurseries which had hitherto only grown a very small range of

Melaleuca fulgens — Salmon-flowered form. The usual
ɔrm has reddish flowers.

ʿhe attractive flowers of *Isopogon cuneatus* are sold in the
ɔrist trade.

History of Cultivation in Australia

Australian species, increased their range to cope
with the new demand.

The interest has been maintained at a high
level during the 1970's, proving that it is not a
passing phase. Not only are the indigenous
plants now grown by home gardeners, but they
are widely used by municipal and government
authorities, as well as for the planting of commercial and industrial sites.

ROLE OF BOTANIC GARDENS IN AUSTRALIA

The various botanic gardens played a major role
in the early dissemination of Australian plants to
countries all around the world. They have
however played a relatively minor role in the
collecting together, and promoting the
cultivation, of indigenous plants within
Australia. It is only fairly recently that botanic
gardens and annexes have been established to
specifically propagate and cultivate elements of
the Australian flora. Some of these additions
have been prompted by the upsurge in interest in
the environment, Australiana and the cultivation
of Australian plants.

The Sydney Botanic Gardens were established
in 1816, and up to 1850 the export of Australian
plants and seeds from the gardens to Europe was
incessant. The initial collection of plants was
mainly exotic, with a distinct bias towards food
plants and fruit trees. Some natives, such as bulbs
and palms, were introduced into the gardens at a
very early stage, but the main impetus was
provided by the Superintendents Charles Moore
(1848-1896) and J. H. Maiden (1896-1924).

A fair range of natives is included in the
present collection, with many rainforest species.
An annex of the Gardens has been established at
Mount Tomah in the Blue Mountains, for the
purpose of growing species from cool temperate
areas.

Tasmania's Botanic Gardens were established
at Hobart in 1818. They have been mainly
devoted to the cultivation of exotic species.
Recently however, there has been considerable
interest in the cultivation of those species endemic to Tasmania.

Queensland's Botanic Gardens were established at Brisbane in 1828. The main interest
has been in the cultivation of exotic tropical
plants, especially palms. Natives are poorly
represented, however there are some good
specimens of rainforest species. Recently a large
new botanic gardens has been established at
Mount Coot-tha, and there will be more emphasis on native plants in its collection.

Introduction and History

Melbourne's Botanic Gardens began in 1845. They are situated in a very picturesque area close to the city. A considerable number of native plants are grown in the gardens, including many fine specimen plants of species originating in rainforests. The Melbourne climate is conducive to the cultivation of plants from a wide area, and palms and many species from subtropical areas grow quite well. An annex is being established at Cranbourne, south-east of Melbourne, for the sole purpose of cultivating Australian plants, especially those from the spectacular heathland and sandplain flora of WA.

The Adelaide Botanic Garden was established in 1855, and was devoted mainly to the cultivation of timber trees. There has been increasing emphasis on natives, and many more species have been planted recently. Two other botanic gardens are being established, at Mount Lofty (opened 1977) and Wittunga (opened 1975).

The Botanic Garden and Kings Park in Perth, Western Australia has had considerable impact on the cultivation of native plants. Kings Park is a large reserve about 2 km west of the centre of Perth, and the botanic gardens were established within Kings Park. Both specialise in the cultivation of the West Australian flora, and carry out research into various aspects. Over 1400 species are in cultivation, and many are grown in large, impressive stands.

The National Botanic Gardens are the most recent gardens to be established, being opened in 1970. They are devoted exclusively to the cultivation of, and research into, Australian plants. A large collection of plants has already been established, but the range has been somewhat limited by the harsh climate. Research is underway into a wide range of propagation techniques, including grafting, raising terrestrial orchids from seed, and tissue culture of difficult-to-propagate species.

THE HORTICULTURAL DEVELOPMENT OF AUSTRALIAN PLANTS

Australian plants offer considerable scope for horticulture and use in urban areas. Already there has been substantial growth of that section of the nursery industry devoted specially to their production. Most general nurseries now carry a good range of native plants in addition to the usual exotics. As well there are many nurseries specializing in the production of this group of plants. New species, forms, and hybrids are continually becoming available for an expanding group of enthusiasts.

Natives are becoming more common in the urban scene and are widely planted in parks, large public gardens and as street trees. Native plants are also being grown commercially for their cut flowers and a small but expanding industry has been established. These flowers are popular subjects overseas and there would appear to be considerable potential for the development of an international export trade to Europe and Asia.

Native plants will be popular in the Australian horticultural and urban environment for a long period yet. Obviously they are best suited for coping with Australia's particular environmental conditions and offer a large range from which species can be chosen to cope with any situation. Considerable development of native plants has already taken place to meet the needs of horticulture and the urban environment and more will be required to meet future needs. The horticultural development of native plants can be split into stages of collection, selection, hybridization and specialisation.

COLLECTION

This process involves the collection of species from various areas into the particular area in which their performances can be assessed and compared. Often there is some basis for the collection of species, such as those from areas where they are to be tried. Sometimes however the area of origin offers no real clue how the species will perform in a new area because of the species adaptability. Many examples can be given. One example is *Eucalyptus alpina* which in nature can occur as a stunted straggly tree on rocky slopes of the Grampians Mountains in Victoria. In cultivation it is a very hardy species tolerating a wide range of soil and climatic conditions and becoming bushy enough to be a good windbreak shelter. The cootamundra wattle (*Acacia baileyana*) is another example of a species from a restricted habitat which will thrive in a variety of soils and climates over a large area of Australia. *Hymenosporum flavum* from cool sheltered gullies and rainforests of eastern Australia will grow well on poor sandy soils in hot inland and mallee areas.

The programme of collection is well under way mostly initiated by amateur enthusiasts, but also involving nurserymen and government bodies. To date these collections have mainly been at random and haphazard and a more organized approach is needed in the future. So far collectors have tended to concentrate on the more spectacular genera such as *Grevillea*, *Banksia*, *Hakea*, *Anigozanthos*, *Lechenaultia* etc. Less spectacular genera such as *Dodonea*, *Myoporum*, *Baeckea* and *Prostanthera* have much to offer horticulture and in fact may pose less cultural

Double-flowered forms of plants occasionally appear, and these can be perpetuated by vegetative propagation. One example is the double-flowered form of *Eriostemon verrucosus.*

ples are the red or pink flowering forms of *Eucalyptus leucoxylon, E. sideroxylon, E. melliodora* and *E. largiflorens.*

Large flowered forms are also known in eucalypts, the best examples of which are probably the large flowered form of *E. caesia* and *E. leucoxylon* var. *macrocarpa.*

The genus *Grevillea* provides tremendous scope for selection. In *G. glabella* growth habit ranges from low and compact through bushy to tall and lanky; foliage varies from silver to green and flower colours range from cream/green through pink to red, and in various combinations. Each form can be perpetuated by vegetative propagation. The form of *G. hookerana* common in cultivation today is possibly the end result of selection procedures many years ago. It is by no means the most floriferous or spectacular form of the species but is the hardiest and best adapted to cultivation. Forms of this species, such as from sandplain areas of WA have finer foliage and bright orange flowers but are almost impossible to maintain in the eastern states.

Mutations occur with varying frequency among plants and are a useful means of increasing the range of material available. Unusual types should be watched for where large batches of seedlings are being raised. Variegated plants turn up occasionally but are rare. Prostrate forms appear sporadically and can be distinguished by their floppy growth habit even while young. Such prostrate forms can be very valuable because they extend the range of species available for use as ground cover plants. Prostrate forms of *Acacia pravissima, A. baileyana* and *Callistemon phoeniceus* have turned up in this way.

The compact form of *Eucalyptus globulus* is a selection made overseas. It is much more suitable than the normal form for culture in urban environments because the plants are slower growing, remain more compact and retain the attractive juvenile foliage until later in life.

problems than the more spectacular types.

The plants best suited to an area are those indigenous to that area. Local species should be more widely used not only by home gardeners but also by nurserymen and local municipalities. Because they are adapted to the conditions of the area the results obtained from them are likely to be more satisfactory. Local plants when supplied with water and fertilizer can be the equal of most imports.

SELECTION

Selection of forms within species is usually based on factors such as flower colour and flower size. Other less obvious factors however may be of equal importance as criteria for selection. These factors include adaptability to cultivation, resistance to disease and form and habit of growth. Bizarre forms often attract more attention than they deserve. Thus ferns with crested or variously distorted fronds are highly sought after, as are also plants with double flowers e.g. *Bauera rubioides, Eriostemon verrucosus* and *Boronia thujona.*

Eucalypts provide a good example of selection for flower colour and flower size. Red and pink flowering forms occur sporadically in some species which are predominately white flowered, and a high percentage of the progeny from trees with coloured flowers came true to type. Exam-

HYBRIDIZATION

Natural hybridization is common among Australian plants and much of this occurs in gardens when groups of plants are grown together. A number of outstanding hybrids have occurred as the result of accidental crossing when geographically isolated species have been grown together in gardens e.g., the crossing of *Grevillea banksii* and *G. bipinnatifida* to produce *G.* 'Robyn Gordon'. Such hybrids indicate the tremendous potential for a planned breeding programme with Australian natives.

Garden hybrids are quite common especially

in the genus *Grevillea*. The present approach is to propagate any hybrid that is found, however the majority are not worth perpetuating as garden plants. To be of any value the hybrid must possess some character which is superior to its parents, such as better flowers, a longer flowering period or the ability to withstand harsh growing conditions. If it does not possess any superiority it should be discarded.

Deliberate hybridization has played a very minor role in the development of Australian plants for horticulture. Kangaroo paws and a few eucalypts, grevilleas and mint bushes have been hybridized deliberately but the numbers are small and the field is new. Kangaroo paws illustrate the benefits of deliberate hybridization. The spectacular species *Anigozanthos manglesii*, *A. rufus* and *A. pulcherrimus* are difficult to maintain in cultivation in south-eastern Australia for a variety of reasons, whereas the much less showy *A. flavidus* is very hardy. Deliberate crossings have produced showy hybrids with the hardiness and vigour of *A. flavidus*. These will become significant plants not only for gardens but also commercially as cut flowers.

Deliberate hybridization among Australia's epiphytic orchids has produced some spectacular progeny and considerably extends the range available to enthusiasts. Colourful pink or reddish hybrids have been produced by using *Dendrobium kingianum* as one parent and a range of growth forms and flower sizes and shapes has resulted from varying the other parent. Some spectacular hybrids have been produced more recently by using *Dendrobium tetragonum* var. *giganteum* as a parent. This parent gives progeny with spidery flowers and the added bonus of flowering more than once during the year (e.g. *Dendrobium* 'Star of Gold' and *D.* 'Hilda Poxon'). Some attractive hybrids have also been produced by crossing some of the hardcane *Dendrobiums* from tropical Qld. e.g. *D. bigibbum*, *D. canaliculatum*, *D. johannis* and *D. nindii*. Breeding with Australian orchids has now progressed beyond the stage of first generation crosses and the future results promise to be outstanding.

Hybrids are variable and can only be perpetuated by vegetative propagation or if the production of seed from first generation crosses can be maintained. The variation of the progeny of second generation crosses can be large and may defeat the purpose of the original cross. A good example here is the variation obtained from seedlings of *Eucalyptus ficifolia* where hybridization has occurred with *E. calophylla*. Vegetative propagation poses a problem for the perpetuation of some hybrids, especially eucalypts.

The flowers of *Telopea speciosissima* are renowned throughout the world for their long-lasting qualities.

W.R. Elliot photo

SPECIALISATION

Cut Flowers

The cut flower industry in Australia has traditionally grown exotic species for sale. Some indigenous plants have always been popular, but recently there has been more emphasis on natives within the industry. Areas of WA, SA, Vic, and NSW are being planted and farmed with species of *Banksia*, *Dryandra*, *Isopogon*, *Agonis*, *Telopea* etc. The market for these unique cut flowers is increasing in Australia and also more particularly overseas, where the demand is high and prices are good.

Until recently the bulk of the cut flower material of native plants sold in Australia was collected from the bush. Fortunately this practice is no longer widespread, because it not only results in damage to the plants, but it is also wasteful. Not all of the material removed can be sold and the availability of seed for natural regeneration is reduced.

The emphasis now is on the commercial culture of these plants, which allows better control and generally produces better quality cut flowers. It is interesting to note that there was a similar parallel development with the cut flower industry in South Africa. Proteas, leucadendrons and leucospermums were cut from natural stands, however growers responded when urged to grow the plants under commercial conditions.

For many years, in the east and south east outskirts of Melbourne, *Boronia megastigma* has been widely grown as a cut flower. The town of Boronia in the foothills of the Dandenong Ranges received its name because of the plants grown there for cut flowers. The Chandler family were amongst the early settlers in the district and the burgundy coloured form of *B. megastigma*, known as *B. megastigma* 'Chandleri' originated from plantings in this area.

Thryptomene calycina was widely grown in the sand belt to the south of Melbourne, in areas such as Sandringham and Brighton. The NSW Waratah, *Telopea speciosissima*, is very popular in the Dandenongs, where it has been farmed for many years, with large old plants still producing well. *Thryptomene micrantha* has been grown as a cut flower in Tas. for many years.

Australian plants are also grown overseas as cut flowers. Plantations of banksias and dryandras have been established in Hawaii for the production of cut flowers. These same genera are also popular in South Africa and Israel. Israel in particular is carrying out considerable research into Australian plants for cut flowers. Already species of *Dryandra, Banksia, Telopea, Anigozanthos* and *Chamelaucium* are being grown commercially and exported for sale.

Suitable Species

The following species are suitable for cut flowers, with lasting qualities after picking. This is by no means a complete list, and will undoubtedly be increased as more species are tried

A freestyle floral arrangement, by Kath Deery, featuring *Eucalyptus woodwardii* flowers, and dried frond of a Bird's Nest Fern.

'Your Garden' photo

Commercial seed production of NSW Waratah (*Telopea speciosissima*).

D.L. Jones photo

and found to be useful in this regard. Species already grown commercially are indicated with an asterisk.

Acacia
 * dealbata
 decurrens
 terminalis
Actinodium cunninghamii
Actinotus * helianthii
Adenanthos barbigera
 obovata
Agonis floribunda
 * juniperina
 * linearifolia
 marginata
 obtusissima
 * parviceps
Ammobium * alatum
Andersonia caerulea
Anigozanthos * all species
Astartea * fascicularis
 * heteranthera
Banksia ashbyi
 * attenuata
 * baxteri
 * brownii
 * burdettii
 * coccinea
 dryandroides
 elderana

 * ericifolia
 * grandis
 * hookerana
 * ilicifolia
 integrifolia
 laevigata
 * laricina
 lemanniana
 marginata
 meisneri
 * menziesii
 occidentalis
 * ornata
 * prionotes
 pulchella
 * quercifolia
 sceptrum
 serrata
 solandri
 * speciosa
 sphaerocarpa
 * spinulosa
 victoriae
 violacea
Baeckea astarteoides
 camphorosmae
 densifolia

41

linifolia
virgata
Beaufortia elegans
purpurea
sparsa
squarrosa
Billardiera cymosa
longiflora
scandens
Blancoa canescens
Blandfordia *all species
Boronia anemonifolia
(strong foliage odour)
capitata
*clavata
deanei
falcifolia
*floribunda
fraseri
*heterophylla
ledifolia
*megastigma (various forms)
mollis
*molloyae
*muelleri
nematophylla
pinnata (strong foliage odour)
*purdieana
*serrulata
stricta
tetrandra
Brachychiton acerifolium
Burchardia multiflora
Calectasia cyanea
Callistemon — some species with
limited application.
citrinus
pallidus
salignus
viminalis
Calytrix — most species. Some
have colourful calyces after
petals drop.
Ceratopetalum *gummiferum
Chamelaucium *sp. Walpole
*uncinatum
Cheiranthera cyanea
Chorilaena quercifolia
Chorizema cordatum
Clematis aristata (both also attractive glycinoides as hairy seed capsules develop)
Clianthus formosus
Comesperma ericinum
Conospermum *amoenum
bracteosum
*triplinervium
Conostylis aculeata
candicans
Correa backhousiana
*'Mannii'
pulchella
reflexa
Craspedia glauca
*globosa

Crowea exalata
saligna
Cyanostegia *cyanocalyx
*lanceolata
Dampiera stricta
teres
Darwinia citriodora
leiostyla
Dendrobium *discolor
Dianella revoluta
tasmanica
Dichopogon strictus
Didiscus *caerulea
Dillwynia sericea
Dodonaea adenophora
boroniifolia (the coloured seed
capsule, or hops, are decorative)
Dryandra (most species, particularly
those with terminal flowers)
baxteri
carduacea
cuneata
*formosa
fraseri
*patens
*polycephala
*praemorsa
proteoides
*quercifolia
tenuifolia
Epacris impressa
longiflora
microphylla
pulchella
Eremaea beaufortioides
violacea
Eriostemon australasius
buxifolius
hispidula
myoporoides
spicatus
Eucalyptus — many species
including . . .
calophylla
caesia
cornuta
*crucis
desmondensis
erythrocorys
erythronema
ficifolia
*forrestiana
*kruseana
lehmannii
leucoxylon
macrandra
*macrocarpa
megacornuta
*preissiana
pyriformis
torquata
woodwardii
Gahnia radula
sieberana

Geleznowia *verrucosa
Glischrocaryon behrii
Gompholobium grandiflorum
latifolium
Grevillea alpina
banksii
buxifolia
concinna
occidentalis
paradoxa
petrophiloides
sphacelata
Guichenotia angustifolia
macrantha
Hakea bucculenta
francisiana
laurina
multilineata
platysperma
Helichrysum *apiculatum
*baxteri
*bracteatum
cordatum
obcordatum
Helipterum *albicans
floribundum
*manglesii
*roseum
Homoranthus darwinioides
Hypocalymma angustifolium
cordifolium
robustum
strictum
Isopogon anethifolius
baxteri
*cuneatus
dubius
*formosus
*latifolius
petiolaris
trilobus
Ixodia *achilleoides
Jasminum suavissimum
Keraudrenia integrifolia
Kunzea baxteri
Lachnostachys *verbascifolia
Lambertia ericifolia
formosa
inermis
Lasiopetalum behri
Leptospermum myrsinoides
Leucopogon ericoides
Lhotzkya ericoides
Lysinema ciliatum
Macropidia *fuliginosa
Melaleuca fulgens
nesophila
Melastoma denticulata
Micromyrtus *ciliata
Nematolepis phebalioides
Olearia iodochroa
phlogopappa
tomentosa
Oligarrhena micrantha

Passiflora cinnabarina
Persoonia chamaepeuce
   pinifolia
Petrophile biloba
   diversifolia
   linearis
   longifolia
   *serruriae
   sessilis
   *squamata
Pimelea *ferruginea
   *rosea
   *spectabilis
Ptilotus drummondii
   exaltatus
   macrocephalus
   obovatus
   spathulatus
Regelia ciliata
Rulingia hermanniifolia
Scaevola aemula
   crassifolia
Senecio lautus
   linearifolius
Sollya heterophylla
Sowerbaea juncea
   laxiflora
Sphenotoma gracile
Spyridium parvifolium
Stackhousia monogyna
Stirlingia *latifolia
Stypandra glauca

Telopea *mongaensis
   *oreades
   *speciosissima
   *truncata
Templetonia retusa
Tetratheca ciliata
   setigera
   thymifolia
Thomasia grandiflora
   macrocarpa
   petalocalyx
Thryptomene *calcycina
   *micrantha
   saxicola
Verticordia *acerosa
   *brownii
   *chrysantha
   *drummondii
   *grandiflora
   *grandis
   *insignis
   *monodelpha
   *nitens
   *plumosa
Wahlenbergia gloriosa
   saxicola
   stricta
Westringia fruticosa
   glabra
   seniifolia
Xanthosia *rotundifolia
   candida

Annuals are very useful for massed displays, and provide excellent cut flowers. Illustrated — *Helipterum roseum.*

Cut Foliage

There is increasing interest being shown in many Australian plants that have ornamental foliage suitable for cutting, and for use in the decoration of residences and commercial buildings, and also by the florist trade.

Species that are highly prized by florists for their ornamental foliage, and are being grown specifically for this aspect, are *Banksia brownii, B. grandis, Grevillea hookerana* and *G.* 'Ivanhoe'. Many *Eucalyptus* species are used in this manner. In U.S.A. *Eucalyptus gunnii, E. perriniana* and *E. morrisbyii* are popular as cut foliage, and they are sold as 'Silver Dollar Eucalypts'.

Many more Australian plants have foliage suitable for use in this way, and the following list is a selection of such species.

Suitable Species

Acacia baileyana
   brachybotrya
   cardiophylla
   cognata
   cultriformis
   decora
   glaucoptera
   iteaphylla
   pendula
   pravissima
   pyrifolia
   spectabilis
   triptera
   uncinata
   vestita
Adenanthos cuneata
Angophora costata
   hispida

Atriplex nummularia
Backhousia citriodora
Baeckea linifolia
Banksia baxteri
   brownii
   dryandroides
   ericifolia
   grandis
   integrifolia
   occidentalis
   petiolaris
   prostrata
   repens
Beaufortia incana
   orbifolia
Boronia fraseri
Bossiaea linophylla
   (copper foliaged form)
Brachychiton rupestre
Brachysema lanceolatum
Buckinghamia celsissima
Callitris oblonga
   rhomboidea
Calocephalus brownii
Calothamnus quadrifidus
   lehmannii
   longissimus
Cassia artemisioides
   sturtii
Casuarina ramosissima
   torulosa

Darwinia citriodora
Dodonaea adenophora
   boroniifolia
Dryandra calophylla
   formosa
   longifolia
   nivea
   nobilis
   praemorsa
   pteridifolia
   quercifolia
   sessilis
   tenuifolia
Eremaea beaufortioides
Eucalyptus baeurana
   caleyi
   campaspe
   coccifera
   cordata
   crenulata
   crucis
   formanii
   gardneri
   globulus (juvenile)
   gunnii
   kruseana
   macrocarpa
   morrisbyii
   orbifolia
   perriniana
   polyanthemos

43

pulchella
rhodantha
sideroxylon
spathulata
tasmanica
tetragona
urnigera (juvenile)
viridis
Eupomatia laurina
Goodia lotifolia
Grevillea acanthifolia
anethifolia
aquifolium
asplenifolia
baueri
brevicuspis
caleyi
dryophylla
endlicherana
×gaudichaudii
glabrata
hookerana
ilicifolia
'Ivanhoe'
jephcottii
johnsonii
laurifolia
longifolia
longistyla
microstegia
miqueliana
'Poorinda Blondie'
'Poorinda Peter'
ramosissima
repens
robusta
rosmarinifolia
shiressii
sp. 'Glut'
steiglitziana
stenomera
synaphaea
thelemanniana
triloba
willisii
Hakea baxteri
conchifolia
crassifolia
cucullata
elliptica
ferruginea
lasiantha
laurina
pandanicarpa
petiolaris
salicifolia

smilacifolia
trifurcata
undulata
varia
victoriae
Helichrysum obcordatum
thyrsoideum
Hibbertia cuneiformis
Homoranthus flavescens
Hypocalymma cordifolium
Indigofera australis
Isopogon anethifolius
baxteri
Jacksonia furcellata
scoparia
Kunzea pulchella
Lasiopetalum behri
dasyphyllum
Leptospermum lanigerum
nitidum 'Copper Sheen'
petersonii
Lomatia silaifolia
Melaleuca cordata
diosmifolia
elliptica
huegelii
hypericifolia
incana
micromera
rhaphiophylla
seriata
violacea
Nothofagus cunninghamii
Persoonia pinifolia
Phebalium stenophyllum
Pimelea nivea
Polyscias sambucifolius
Pomaderris lanigera
Prostanthera incana
Pultenaea cunninghamii
patellifolia
Regelia inops
megacephala
velutina
Restio tetraphyllus
Spyridium parvifolium
Stenocarpus sinuatus
Stypandra glauca
Swainsonia galegifolia
greyana
Symphionema montana
Thomasia macrocarpa
Veronica formosa
Westringia fruticosa

Commercial Seed Production

Commercial seed collectors have played a very important role in encouraging the cultivation of Australian plants, by presenting a very wide range of seed for sale. The great majority of this is collected from natural stands in the bush, although some comes from roadside plantations.

Seeds of a number of Australian species are now scarce, and highly priced. This includes not only rare species such as *Banksia goodii*, but also species which have suffered from over collecting, such as *Eucalyptus nicholii* and *E. scoparia*. The demand for seeds of these species, from both within Australia and overseas, and their present prices, are such that it is economical to farm some of these species for their seed alone.

Hybridization is a major problem with outcrossing species such as eucalypts, and plantations must be established in isolation from other species which flower at the same time. Genera such as *Banksia*, *Calothamnus*, *Dryandra*, *Hakea*, *Isopogon* and *Petrophile*, are thought to be fairly stable, and not prone to crossing. Therefore they are ideally suited to mixed farming for seed production.

Seed farming can be combined with cut flower production. Even now, many cut flower growers leave sub-standard flowers on the bushes, and harvest the seed later for their own use, or for sale.

Indoor and Glasshouse Plants

The Australian rainforest flora offers some exciting plants, with very decorative leaves and growth, and they appear to have considerable potential for use as indoor plants. Many are adapted to fairly dark situations, as exist on the rainforest floor, and would tolerate the conditions usually imposed on indoor plants. Genera with potential include *Scindapsus*, *Raphidophora*, *Pothos*, *Piper*, *Cissus*, *Cordyline*, *Schefflera* and *Dracaena*. Many ferns and palms also have potential, eg. *Carpentaria acuminata*.

A large range of glasshouse plants is also available from highland and coastal rainforests, including species of *Ceropegia*, *Hoya*, *Remusata*, *Boea*, *Tapeinochilus* and *Curcuma*. Most palms, orchids and ferns are also suited to glasshouse culture, especially in southern Australia.

See Plants for Various Purposes — Indoor Plants page 300.

Hibiscus tiliaceus D.L. Jones photo

Part Two

The Selection and Cultivation of Australian Plants

5 Factors affecting Selection of Plants for Cultivation

FACTORS AFFECTING PLANT GROWTH

Species selection is one of the most important aspects of growing plants in cultivation. The aim is to choose those plants which will grow well in the prevailing conditions of the soils and climate that exist in the area. Numerous factors must be considered about each of these aspects before the plants are chosen, otherwise disappointment may follow. In addition to considering aspects of the soil and climate of the area where they are to be grown, it is wise to consider such factors about the areas of origin of the plants, and other features of the plants themselves. This is discussed more fully in Plant Features, page 56.

CLIMATIC ASPECTS

Climatic Regions

For convenience, Australia can be divided into various climatic regions. The climatic conditions in these regions provide a useful guide to the type and variety of plants which can be grown.

The Tropic of Capricorn divides Australia into tropical and temperate regions. More than one third of Australia lies in the tropical region, north of the Tropic of Capricorn. This includes the majority of Qld and the NT, and less than half of WA. The tropical region can be further divided into the dry tropical and wet tropical zones.

The area south of the Tropic of Capricorn is known as the temperate region. It is the largest area of Australia, and for convenience can be further divided into warm temperate and cool temperate zones. The dry tropical and warm temperate zones merge together in the centre, and for convenience are referred to as the inland zone. As well, a subtropical zone can be distinguished along the eastern coastal part of the warm temperate zone.

Within all of these zones, the climate is modified by proximity to the sea (coastal) and increases in altitude (highland).

Helipterum manglesii.

Wet Tropical Zone

The climate of this zone is characterized by a summer wet season known locally as the Wet, and a winter dry season known as the Dry. This contrast in rainfall is very marked in most wet tropical areas, and floods are common in the Wet, while a drought-type situation exists in the Dry. Localized coastal or highland regions receive scattered showers throughout the year, although the majority of rain still falls in the Wet. Examples of this include the Atherton Tableland and other highland areas such as Mt. Spec, the Windsor and Evelyn Tablelands, Mt. Spurgeon and Mt. Lewis, the coastal strip between Port Douglas and Cardwell, and the

47

Selection and Cultivation

McIlwraith and Iron Range areas of Cape York Peninsula, all in Qld.

Rainfall is highest in the coastal regions, with the Qld coastal towns of Tully and Babinda receiving more than 4000 mm per annum.

Winds are predominantly from the north-west in the Wet and the south-east in the Dry. Cyclones are frequent between December and April, causing considerable physical damage as well as being associated with heavy deluges of rain.

Temperatures are mild in winter and hot in summer, reaching a peak in November-December. Humidity is extremely high for long periods in the Wet, and is much lower in the Dry. Evaporation parallels this, being non-existent in the Wet and extremely high in the Dry. Frosts are absent in coastal regions, but occur sporadically in highland areas such as the tablelands.

Plants: Plants grown in the wet tropical zone are mainly of tropical origin, and local plants are very useful. The main limitation to the cultivation of species from dry tropical, inland and temperate zones, is the high temperature/high humidity conditions experienced for long periods during the Wet. Plants from such areas frequently grow well during the Dry, but quickly succumb in the Wet. Species with hairy stems or foliage, or thickened leaves, are particularly sensitive. Leaf blackening and defoliation followed by plant collapse are the usual symptoms.

Subtropical Zone

The subtropical zone is only of significance in the eastern coastal and adjacent inland strip immediately south of the Tropic of Capricorn and extending into northern NSW. In this zone the rainfall is reliable, and sufficiently high for diversified plant growth.

Rainfall is similar to the tropical regions, having a summer rainfall maximum, and a winter dry. The disparity between the two seasons is not as marked as in the tropics, and scattered rain is common throughout the winter. Rainfall varies from 800-1400 mm per annum, being highest in coastal and highland districts.

Temperatures are mild in winter and hot in summer, reaching a peak in November-December. Humidity is high to extremely high between November and March and much lower in winter. Evaporation is high from April to November, but very low for the rest of the year. Cyclones are rare, but strong winds are frequent. Frosts are rare in coastal districts, but common in highland and adjacent inland regions.

Plants: A wide range of plants can be grown in the subtropical zone including local species and the more adaptable types from both tropical and temperate regions. Plants from areas with a dry climate generally don't grow well because of the high humidity during the summer wet season. Similarly plants originating from hot tropical regions may be very slow growing, because of the cooler winter.

Inland Zone

The inland zone can be thought of as a combination of the dry tropical zone and the inland parts of the temperate zone. Conditions are worst in the centre, which is desert-like or arid, and become better for plant growth towards the margins of the zone.

Rainfall ranges from 100-400 mm per annum. In northern parts of the zone there is some tendency for the rain to coincide with the tropical wet season, but in the central areas which receive 100-200 mm per annum the rainfall is erratic and unpredictable. Mountain areas are generally low, and there is very little modification of climate by altitude.

Temperatures are mild to hot in winter, and extremely hot in summer. Humidity is generally low throughout the year, except after soaking rains, and is extremely low in summer. As a consequence, evaporation is high to very high. Heavy frosts and dews are frequent during winter.

Plants: Very hardy plants are grown in the inland zone, and local species are particularly useful. Annuals are very common and provide impressive displays after rain or if watered. Perennials such as shrubs and trees must have drought-resistant mechanisms to survive. Such mechanisms include reduced leaves, spines, dense covering of hairs, or the ability to shed leaves during stress. As the rainfall increases, so the range of species that can be grown increases.

Plants grown in the dry tropical zone are essentially the same as those grown further south in the warm temperate zone.

Cool Temperate Zone

This zone extends over southern, south-eastern and south-western Australia, including all of Tas. It is not the largest zone, but includes many variable features due to the influence of altitude and proximity to the coast.

Rainfall varies from 300 to over 1600 mm per annum. It is usually well distributed over the year, but with a winter maximum. It is highest in coastal districts and highland areas. Winds are predominantly from the south, with important rain-bearing winds from the south-west. Hot dry northerly winds are common in the summer.

The NSW Waratah, *Telopea speciosissima*, is renowned for its qualities as a cut flower.

Temperatures are generally cold in winter and hot in summer, reaching a peak in January-February. Humidity is fairly high in the winter and fluctuates in the summer from very high to very low, the latter usually occurring on days of hot northerly winds. Evaporation is often very high in summer. Frosts are common throughout the region, and may be particularly severe in inland and highland areas. Snow is not uncommon above 1400 m altitude.

Plants: A very large range of plants can be grown in the cool temperate zone, including local species and those from inland, highland, subtropical and subalpine areas. Climatic limitations are imposed by such factors as snow, heavy frosts and rainfall.

Coastal Influence. The proximity of the sea modifies extremes of climate so that in coastal areas, factors such as humidity and temperature do not fluctuate as much as in inland areas. Frosts are very rare or unknown, but if they do occur they usually cause considerable damage.

There is great variation in coastal areas, from situations exposed to severe wind and salt spray, to lee situations and locations such as sheltered inlets. Thus the range of plants that can be grown in coastal regions is very wide.

Exposed Coastal Areas. Coastal areas are usually very windy, and if the wind has passed over the sea it will be carrying salt. Such salt-laden winds can be very destructive of all but a select group of hardy plants.

To attempt to grow plants that do not naturally exist in such areas can often be an unrewarding experience. It is best to grow a windbreak of plants tolerant of salt spray and wind, to provide protection, and create a micro-climate where more delicate plants can then be grown satisfactorily. The use of hardy, local, coastal species offers a good solution. These can often be slow growing initially, but will give very good long-term results. Species that are tolerant of salt spray and wind are listed on page 281.

Highland Influence. Increases in altitude modify climate. Highland areas of about 100 m altitude have a different climate to those of nearby areas at or close to sea level. The higher the altitude, the greater the modification of climate.

Summer temperatures in areas of high altitude are generally milder, but winters are colder, with severe frosts and snowfalls being common in south-eastern Australia. Rainfall is generally higher than adjacent areas at sea level, and distributed throughout the year with winter or summer peaks depending on latitude. Rain-shadow areas are common in the lee of peaks exposed to prevailing moisture-laden winds, and may be quite large. Fogs are frequent in such highland areas, and may be of several days' duration.

Plant species which are cold resistant, or cold tolerant, are the most suitable for highland areas. Local species, or those from other highland areas perform best. Annual species can be grown over summer, and are useful for rockeries or as fill-ins around other plants.

Climatic Conditions

In the cultivation of any plant, it is imperative that the planner has a knowledge of the local climatic conditions in which plants are to be grown. If unfamiliar with the area, information regarding rainfall and temperatures can be obtained from the meteorological bureau, or it is a very useful alternative to talk to some of the local residents. Observation of local gardens can provide information as to suitable species. These tactics can help to avoid the choice of unsuitable plants that will not survive, or will be severely damaged by the prevailing weather conditions. Plants suitable for a variety of specific climatic conditions are listed in detail in *Part 5*.

If adverse conditions do exist, there may be some steps which can be taken to provide better growing conditions. These are discussed under each of the following specific climatic conditions.

Rainfall

All plants need water, but there are some

aspects of rain that can be damaging to plant growth.

1. Continuous drizzly rain over an extended period does not let the foliage dry out completely. Species with hairy foliage may sweat, which can result in leaf drop. In species with fine, close foliage, development of grey mould and similar fungal attacks can occur.

2. Very heavy rain will cause physical damage, especially during the development of new growth. Judicious pruning may be necessary after such rain, to remove damaged foliage and stems, thus preventing the entry of disease.

3. Heavy rain during hot weather creates ideal conditions for the development of fungal disease, eg. *Phytophthora cinnamomi*. The splashing of rain after hitting infested soil can transfer fungi and nematodes to plant foliage. See Pests and Diseases, pages 161, 168.

4. Cold rain in winter has a chilling effect on plant foliage (ie. sleet-type rain). Species not naturally accustomed to such conditions can be stunted and could suffer tissue damage. Judicious pruning will help to promote new growth. This should be done as the weather warms up, otherwise new growth can be damaged.

5. Many species have adapted to receiving most of the year's rain during one season, but in cultivation they may have to cope with rain distributed throughout the year. Species such as some of the banksias from WA, do not seem to be able to survive such a situation unless very well-drained soils are provided. See Soil Preparation, page 65, for further details.

Temperature

Plants have different temperature tolerance levels, and growth rate can be seriously affected at both low and high temperature levels.

The following can be caused by low temperatures —

1. Injury to plant tissue.

2. A reduction or prevention of growth.

3. The inducing of dormancy.

4. Some species need chilling or freezing, as they may not flower or fruit without such conditions, eg. *Blechnum penna-marina*.

High temperatures can have the following results —

1. A reduction of growth. This is very evident in propagation of cuttings, where cuttings are much slower to produce roots at excessively high temperatures.

2. In association with low humidity desiccation can occur.

3. In association with low soil water content, wilting results.

Windbreaks will help to provide less variation in temperature. See Cultivation, page 75.

Humidity

The level of humidity has a great effect on plant growth.

1. In high humidity, plants can collapse. Results are similar to those experienced with constant drizzly rain. Species with hairy foliage and stems, eg. *Adenanthos sericea*, tend to sweat, and are very susceptible. Many Proteaceae and other species from low rainfall regions do not seem to be able to adapt very well to such conditions. In cultivation, it has been found beneficial to water them only during a cool period of weather, and then to not water the foliage, but thoroughly soak the plant's root zone.

2. In high humidity plus high temperatures, there is a likelihood of a greater abundance of moulds and fungi, affecting plant growth.

3. High humidity and low temperatures. Results are similar to those covered in para 1.

4. Low humidity. Desiccation occurs unless soil is well watered, or plant species are resistant.

Frost

Frost is a potential killer of plants. During frosts plant tissue is frozen and as the tissue in plant cells freezes it contracts and expels water into spaces between the cells. This water freezes to form ice crystals. When thawing begins, the ice melts and the water is absorbed back into the cells by osmosis. If this occurs quickly there is little or no damage to the leaves, but if the ice melts slowly the cells collapse and the leaf tissue 'burns' from desiccation. This can be aggravated by the fact that the atmosphere at or near ground level is dry, due to all moisture being frozen. Frost damage thus occurs when plants are thawing, not when freezing is taking place.

Damage can also result from rapid thawing, as occurs when sun strikes frozen tissue. This damage can possibly be lessened by spraying plants with water, near sunrise, although whether or not this technique is beneficial, seems to be controversial.

Plants are more prone to frost damage during warmer periods. Less damage will occur in the coldest months. Frost hardiness is gained as the growth of plants slows down in autumn, due to colder weather and shorter hours of daylight. Frost damage is more severe on young soft growth than on mature hardened growth.

The main parts of plants in which frost damage occurs is from ground level to 2 m high. The temperature at ground level can be up to 5°C lower than 2 m above. Trees that are frost tender when young, do not become frost tolerant as they mature, but in a large number of species, their increased size enables them to cope without suffering extreme damage, unless grown in areas very susceptible to heavy frosts. They also suffer less because their tops are in the warmer zone.

At this stage there has been little research into the effect of frost on Australian plants. Many species are not susceptible to damage, eg. those from alpine, mountainous and inland regions. Species from high elevations in tropical and subtropical regions have also proved to be frost hardy. Frost damage can vary within the same species. This usually occurs when a species has wide geographical distribution. Seedlings from a coastal form may be prone to frost damage, while those grown from inland forms are more tolerant.

Some courses of action that can help to reduce frost damage are:

1. Before planting, observe which areas are prone to frost, and avoid planting frost sensitive species there. In any area there are usually a number of micro climates.

2. Only grow frost tolerant plants in frost prone locations. Frost tender plants can be grown against buildings, with eaves offering protection, and the walls, especially if brick or some other solid construction, will radiate some warmth.

3. Do not apply nitrogenous fertilizers to young plants later than in mid-summer. This allows for hardening-off of plant tissue. Plants with young growth during autumn and winter will be prone to frost damage.

4. Keep the ground around plants clear of weeds.

5. Keep the ground moist.

6. Do not cultivate the ground around plants. It is best to have a hard, flat surface.

7. Do not mulch with organic material. The best mulch to use in frost prone regions is coarse sand or screenings.

8. Covering of plants with material such as paper or hessian can help to retain the radiated ground heat around plants. Do not cover plants with plastic bags, as they do not always exclude frost, also when the sun reaches the plant, hot air will be trapped within the bag. This will promote rapid thawing of the plant tissue, which can cause severe damage.

9. Protection provided by the canopy of large evergreen trees is most beneficial to smaller shrubs.

10. Solid fences often stop the air flow, and therefore there is a build up of frost, which can cause severe damage.

11. Any pruning should be delayed until further frosts are no longer likely. Premature pruning of frost damaged plants can stimulate

Dryandra quercifolia is an excellent cut flower.

new growth, which will then be readily damaged by future frosts.

Fog

Fog can be beneficial in areas of low rainfall, if it occurs during the late afternoon, night or early morning. In nature, some plants have adapted to absorb moisture as one of their main methods of acquiring water. Fog also helps to cool the foliage, and thus reduce transpiration. This is beneficial in conserving the existing soil moisture.

Plants in regions that are prone to fogs have the following problems.

1. Lack of transpiration and sweating because foliage and stems are continually wet. Leaf drop can occur. This is more common in the species from low rainfall areas that are not adapted to such conditions. Plants can eventually collapse and die.

2. Fog can have a chilling effect during cold weather, with resultant retardation of plant growth.

3. Fog blankets out sunshine, and therefore reduces photosynthesis. This results in a check to the growth rate of plants.

Smog

Photochemical smog may be toxic to some species of Australian plants. It contains several phytotoxic components, eg. ozone, nitrogen dioxide, peroxyacetyl nitrate, sulphur dioxide and other oxidant gases. The effect on plants is mainly on the leaves. In most cases it is the mature leaves that suffer more damage. Growing tips and old leaves usually only show minimal damage. Visible features of smog damage are similar to that which is suffered from leaf parasites or in some cases mineral deficiencies. Banding, silvering, flecking, stippling or bleaching of leaves can occur. It is usual for the upper leaf surface to show damage more so than the undersurface. Generally it is thought that smog affected plants are more susceptible to attacks from insect pests and diseases such as *Phytophthora cinnamomi*.

To date about 250 species have been subjected to tests of sensitivity to sulphur dioxide and ozone. These compounds, when combined, are more damaging to plant tissue than if separate.

Generally, hard-leaved species are less sensitive than softer-leaved species. Three that have proved very sensitive are *Banksia marginata*, *Banksia spinulosa*, and *Eucalyptus nutans*.

For further information, see listing of Smog Resistant Species, page 310.

Wind

Plants can suffer varying degrees of physical damage from wind. This damage can be alleviated in a number of ways, which are discussed further in the section on Cultivation, page 75. Below is a listing of the main damaging factors of wind.

1. Scorching and Drying. Leaf damage occurs in times of low humidity and strong, warm winds. If these persist, plant deaths may occur. Common symptoms are wilting and browning of leaf surface.

2. Strong wind during cold weather can have a chilling effect, and will retard plant growth.

3. Turbulent wind can cause damage to both large and small plants, by breaking branches and snapping or splitting stems or trunks at ground level. Damage to plants can be widespread when strong winds occur from a direction that is not commonly encountered — eg. prevailing winds are westerlies, but strong turbulent winds can come from the east.

4. Damage from strong winds in combination with wet soils. The most common feature is for plants to become loose at ground level. This mainly affects large shrubs and trees. Unless some support is given to the trunks, the plant may suffer irreparable damage. If a large cavity has developed around the trunk, fill it up with soil, and firm it as much as possible. Plants should then be staked, but not too tightly, allowing for some movement of the trunk. In most cases the base of the trunk will swell and be able to support the upper growth. As this happens, release the tie further, and gradually remove it completely. All ties must have a protective covering, eg. rubber or plastic hose, so the outer plant tissue is not damaged.

5. Sandblasting in both coastal and inland situations will severely restrict plant growth. Splitting of the bark and outer stem tissue from sandblasting, will restrict sap flow. Bruising and breaking of the leaves is a common symptom of sandblasting. The erection of temporary screens of hessian or similar material will afford some protection until growth hardens.

6. Salt laden winds severely restrict plant growth. Severe leaf burn occurs due to build up of salt on the tissue. As the salt spray dries, it becomes more concentrated, and leaf damage occurs very quickly. Regular spraying of the foliage with water during cool weather, and the erection of screens similar to those mentioned in para. 5, can reduce the detrimental effect of salt laden winds. It is advisable to grow salt tolerant species in exposed coastal locations. See list of suitable species on page 281.

7. Cyclones can annihilate large areas of vegetation, and large trees can be wrenched from the ground. Studies have shown that some trees are able to withstand cyclonic winds by bending with the wind rather than resisting. (See list, page 286.) Cyclones also include extremes of wind and rain, and salt laden winds can be carried further inland than is customary, resulting in damage to plants that are not used to salt being deposited on the foliage.

Hail

Hail can cause damage that may be readily observed, or in other cases will not show up until some time has elapsed. The latter is the case with young buds, leaves, flowers and fruits. It can often result in malformed growth. Hail storms are usually more severe during summer, because the hailstones are commonly much larger than in cooler weather. They can also be of irregular shape, with sharp edges to damage plant tissue.

Apart from the direct damage upon impact, the hail can have a chilling or even freezing effect if it collects around the stems of young plants.

In areas that are prone to regular hail storms, young plants or valued specimens may be protected by a temporary overhead covering of hessian or shade cloth, or alternatively plants can be grown permanently under a shade house construction which should be able to withstand the weight load of the hail.

Snow

The main effect of snow is to chill or freeze plant tissue. This can seriously damage plants, resulting in the retarding of growth, or death. The careful selection and location of species is very important in areas that receive snow falls.

Damage to plants can also be caused by the weight of snow, when it accumulates over a period on branches and foliage. Even large trees can fall victim to such weight. In cases where pruning or tree surgery is required, make sure this is done in a manner which will ensure healthy future growth of the plant. In areas that receive regular snow falls it can be beneficial to carry out a pruning program prior to winter each year, in order to remove excessive top growth. This can help to eliminate a large amount of snow damage. For procedure on Pruning and Tree Surgery, see Maintenance, page 83.

SOIL ASPECTS

Soils are of utmost significance in the cultivation of any species. It is most important to know and understand the types of soil in which plants will grow, because whilst some plants have a wide adaptability, there are others that will not survive unless they have soil ideally suited to their requirements.

In this section, only soil classes are discussed. Other aspects in regard to soils, eg. soil preparation, are discussed in more detail elsewhere.

Components of Soils

Soils vary tremendously throughout Australia, and frequently complex changes occur over very small areas. This makes soil classification an intricate procedure which can only be carried out accurately by soil scientists. Soils however are made up of physical components in variable combinations, and a knowledge of these components can aid the understanding of soils and soil processes.

The major physical components of soils are classified by their particle size, and are listed below.

Fraction name	Diameter
Gravel	Greater than 2 mm
Coarse sand	2 mm-0.2 mm
Fine sand	0.2 mm-0.02 mm
Silt	0.02 mm-0.002 mm
Clay	Less than 0.002 mm

Soils are known in lay terms by degrees of lightness or heaviness. Light soils are rich in sands or gravels, whereas heavy soils contain high proportions of fine materials such as clay.

SOIL CLASSIFICATION

Soils are classified into classes, depending on the relative amounts of the above components. This is a classification based on texture, and relies on the feel of a moist sample of soil when worked between the fingers and palm of the hand. This technique serves to group soils into the following classes, in increasing order of heaviness:

sand, loamy sand, sandy loam, loam, sandy clay loam, clay loam, sandy clay, clay.

Soils are further classified into types based on such factors as colour, pH, depth, layering into horizons, and the presence of features such as ironstone gravel, lime concretions or gypsum crystals. This classification is complex, and if further information is needed, a publication on soil science should be consulted.

Soil Classes

1. Clay

This is the heaviest of the soil classes. It is composed of many fine particles that have strong cohesive properties. Clay can retain a greater percentage of water than other classes. This does not permit good drainage. When wet it becomes plastic and waterlogging occurs. When dry it is the most difficult soil class for water to penetrate. Shrinkage occurs and it becomes rock hard, often with resultant cracking of the soil. This situation can have a detrimental effect, in breaking the roots of plants, and allowing roots to dry out. It can result in the complete collapse of small shrubs or young plants.

2. Clay Loam

This is basically clay, fortified with fine sand and silt particles. Organic material content is usually higher than in clays. It can be a friable soil, but when wet lacks aeration and retains water. This soil type is usually rich in nutrients, because they are not leached out as easily as in sand. A very wide range of Australian plants can be grown in such a soil, provided that drainage is available for the species requiring this. Many species of *Grevillea* and *Melaleuca* prefer heavier soils rather than light types.

Clay loam is one of the most commonly occurring soil types, and when people talk about having clay soils, it is usually this type that is meant. The depth of clay loam as a topsoil can vary greatly, from a few centimetres to about 50 cm, with a clay subsoil. Clay loams with a percentage of coarse sand are known as sandy clay loams.

3. Loam

Loam is made up of the following components:
silt 10-25%
clay 10-25%
sand 50-65%

Although there is a good proportion of sand, this is not readily felt when the soil is pressed between the fingers. The organic content varies with different types of loam, but is usually fairly high. Some loams that are dark and appear rich in organic matter may in fact be quite low.

This is an ideal soil type, with excellent drainage and moisture retaining qualities. Loams are friable at all times, except when very wet.

4. Sandy Loam

A very well-drained soil type, with a predominance of sand granules. It may also have good moisture retention, provided the organic matter content is high. Many Australian plants occur in sandy soils, and this type of soil has proved to be excellent in gardens, for growing some of the species that have been difficult to establish in heavier soils. Sandy loam varies greatly in depth before it reaches the subsoil. Some sandy loams have an impermeable hard pan layer.

5. Sand

In this soil group the sand grains are visible, and can vary from very fine, to coarse and gravel-like. As a class they are extremely well-drained, but are not high in organic material, and therefore dry out more quickly than other soils. Nutrient content is low because of leaching, and in some cases there is a deficiency of some minerals needed for healthy plant growth.

SOIL TYPES

Features of the major soil types found in Australia are dealt with below. These can only be used as a guide since soils vary considerably and can change character within a very short distance.

Podsols

A widespread and very important group since the 3 major capital cities on the east coast are situated on this type. The topsoil is grey becoming lighter with depth and overlaying a heavy yellowish clay subsoil. The topsoil varies from a sandy loam to a clay loam and ranges in depth from 10-60 cm. Sandy types are common in coastal districts. Ironstone gravel is not uncommon on the surface or as a layer just above the clay subsoil. In very sandy podsols there is a layer of dark-brown rock-like material known as coffee rock. If this layer is hardened enough it may form an impermeable barrier to water and roots. pH is acid throughout, varying from 4.7-5.0 at the surface and in some types becoming more acid with depth (to 4.5) or rising to 5.9. Sandy soils may be very acid throughout (3.5-4.0).

Occurrence: large areas of the east coast from Cape York Peninsula to southern Tas, near Darwin, NT, southern SA and south-western WA.

Problems: podsols are generally excellent for plant growth. The clay layer may be impermeable on some types and create waterlogging in wet periods. Some clay podsols are shallow and inclined to crack when dry. These can be greatly improved by gypsum and mulches. Water retention is a problem in sandy podsols and mulches are desirable to improve the organic matter content. Nutrition is a problem on some very acid types.

Red-brown Earths

Clay-loams with a predominantly reddish-brown colour. The topsoil is relatively shallow (10-20 cm) and there is a sharp transition between the topsoil and a heavy clay subsoil. Lime concretions may be present in the subsoil. The topsoil is inclined to crack when dry. The pH at the surface is 6.5-7.0 rising to 7.5 in the subsoil.

Occurrence: large areas of inland central NSW from the north to the Vic border, north central Qld, southern and central western Vic.

Problems: these soils are often shallow and the heavy clay subsoil hinders the penetration of water and plant roots. Waterlogging is common in wet periods. Some damage associated with cracking occurs when dry. A wide range of hardy plants can be grown.

Black Earths

Dark grey soils which look black when wet. They contain a high proportion of clay and develop a perfect tilth after cultivation. They are usually quite deep ranging in depth from 0.5-1 m, and occur in extensive areas. They are very well structured but the subsoil swells and contracts with wetting and drying. pH is about 8.2 at the surface, rising to 8.7 in the subsoil.

Occurrence: large areas on the inland side of the dividing range from north-central NSW to north-central Qld, the Wimmera region of Vic.

Problems: generally an excellent soil. Some damage associated with cracking when dry. Some nutrient deficiencies such as zinc associated with the high pH. A wide range of plants can be grown.

Red Mountain Soils

Well structured friable loams which are reddish or occasionally chocolate brown in colour. They are also called Krasnozems or red loams. There is usually no sudden change from topsoil

Correa reflexa is recommended for its variety of forms — differing in growth habit, foliage and flowers.
Above — Forest form, with long green bells.

Coastal form, with short red and green bells.

but the soil gradually becomes heavier with depth and often redder. They vary in depth from 0.3-2 m. The pH at the surface is about 5.5 and rises to about 6.5 in the subsoil.

Occurrence: scattered in small to large patches of Tas, Vic, NSW and Qld, usually in hilly or mountainous regions.

Problems: physically these soils are usually excellent but chemically they are often poor and plants grown on them respond well to feeding with complete fertilizers. Despite the fact that they appear rich in organic matter these soils often dry severely in the summer and plants appreciate applied water.

Mallee Soils

Sands to sandy clay loams which vary in colour from yellowish-red to reddish, brown or grey. The lighter sandy soils are typically found near the tops of sandhills whereas the clays are distributed on the lower slopes on flat areas. The subsoil is heavier than the topsoil with concretions of lime scattered throughout. The pH at the surface is 6.5-7.5 rising to 8.5-9.0 in the subsoil.

Occurrence: confined to southern Australia and there widespread in large patches from central western NSW through Vic, SA and WA.

Problems: sandy soils dry very badly and drought resistant plants must be used. Clay soils are poorly drained and may be saline. Soil salt damage is common especially in low-lying areas. Nutrient deficiencies associated with the high lime content are common, especially in sandy soils. Plants tolerant of calcareous or saline soils should be grown.

Laterites

Clay loams to sandy soils which have a dominant mass of ironstone gravel or buckshot over the surface. Soils are frequently shallow or may even be absent and replaced by irregular masses of weathered ironstone. The pH at the surface varies from 4.5-5.5 and is fairly constant with depth.

Occurrence: very large areas of southern WA, large areas of Cape York Peninsula and central Qld, small areas of NSW, southern Vic and SA.

Problems: soils are often very shallow and hard. Sandy types may waterlog in wet periods. Fertility is generally poor and plants may need feeding with organic fertilizers to grow satisfactorily. In WA laterites often support extensive showy stands of plants.

Terra Rossa

These are red brown earths developed on limestone. The soils are typically sandy over a sandy loam and then limestone rubble. They vary in depth from 30-90 cm. The pH is 6.5-7.0 at the surface and rising to 7.5-8.0 in the rubble layer.

Occurrence: south-western WA, south-eastern SA, south of Darwin, NT.

Problems: generally low organic matter content

Selection and Cultivation

and low water holding capacity. Plants need regular watering until established. Nutrient deficiencies associated with the high lime content are common. Plants tolerant of calcareous soils should be grown.

Rendzina

These are black loamy earths developed on limestone. They are very similar to Black Earths except that they are generally shallow with concretions of limestone scattered throughout. The topsoil is well structured clay loam and varies in depth from 10-40 cm. The pH is about 8.0 at the surface rising to 9.0 lower down.

Occurrence: south-eastern SA, south-western WA.

Problems: often shallow and difficult to get plants established. Nutrient deficiencies associated with the high lime content and associated high pH are common. Plants tolerant of calcareous soils should be grown.

Calcareous Sands

Grey to white sands which are usually quite deep without much change in the profile. They occur in dunes in coastal districts and are probably wind blown. Shells and free lime are common. The pH at the surface is 8.0-8.5 rising to 9.5 with depth.

Occurrence: coastal areas of southern Australia.

Problems: these soils dry very severely in summer and may become water repellent. Multi purpose hardy plants resistant to drought, alkaline soils and salt laden winds must be grown. Nutrient deficiencies associated with the high lime content may occur.

Heavy Grey or Brown Soils

Clay loams or clays which are grey or brown and change little with depth. They may be quite uniform over large areas although the subsoils may be mottled. Lime concretions are common. The pH ranges from 7.5 at the surface to 8.5 with depth. Low lying areas may be saline.

Occurrence: extensive areas of inland NSW and Qld with smaller patches in the NT, northern WA, northern SA and western Vic.

Problems: poor drainage in the wet periods, cracking when dry. Overall very good growth of a wide range of plants. Nutrient deficiencies are not common, but may be present in areas of high lime content. Salinity may be a problem in low lying areas.

Brown Sandy Soils

Brown to reddish sandy loams which gradually become heavier with depth. They vary in depth from 30 cm-1.5 m. The pH at the sur-

face is 4.5-5.5 and varies little with depth.

Occurrence: western NSW, north-western Qld, parts of the NT and north-western WA, often in large areas.

Problems: physically these soils are very good but chemically they may be low in nutrients. Rainfall is generally low in the areas where they occur and drought resistant plants should be grown.

Solonets

These are white or grey sands, or sandy loams overlying heavy clays. The depth usually ranges from 10-30 cm. Limestone concretions are common in some types. The pH is 6.0-6.5 at the surface and rises to 8.5-9.5 in the subsoil. These soils are usually found in low lying areas or in large flat expanses.

Occurrence: western Vic, south-eastern and southern SA, south-western WA.

Problems: these soils are generally poorly drained and water-logging is common after wet periods. Those in low lying areas may be saline. The types with lime in the profile may suffer from nutrient deficiencies.

PLANT FEATURES

For best results in the cultivation of any plants, it is necessary to gain a knowledge of the factors that will affect plant growth. The two main factors are soils and climate. Plants may not thrive, or may even die, if they are planted in a wrong position or in a region with conditions different to those it has adapted to in its natural state.

Much can be gained by observing how plants grow in their natural surroundings, and how they are influenced by the soils and climatic aspects. The knowledge gained can be applied to the cultivation of plants in any specific situation.
(a) Do they grow in the open in full sun, or in the protection of other plants, with varying amounts of shade?
(b) Do they need moist, wet, or dry soils?
(c) Can they withstand inundation, or extended dry periods?
(d) Are they frost tender?
(e) What type of soil do they require for optimum growth?
(f) Are they exposed to wind?
(g) Do they grow individually or in groups?
. . . and so on.

Many horticulturally desirable Australian plants occur in very well-drained sandy soils, such as in the sandplain area of WA. Without conditions very similar to those of the natural habitat, it has proved more or less impossible to cultivate some of these species. Others have

A plant of *Blechnum wattsii*, showing sterile fronds (lower and broad), and fertile fronds (narrow and erect).

Billardiera longiflora is a delightful light climber for a cool position.

proved more adaptable, especially when extra soil preparation is undertaken, such as in a sand hill bed. This aspect is discussed more fully in sections on Soil Preparation, page 65.

Adaptability

Plants are to be found in nature, in the situations where their special features enable them to survive. They live in a competitive environment,

and to be successful they rely on special adaptive features. While they are best suited to these particular conditions, it does not mean that this is the only environment in which they can survive. Adaptability is the process by which plants can adjust to new environments such as in gardens. Experience with Australian plants indicates that the majority can adapt, in varying degrees, to different environments.

Variability within a Species

Variability of species is a characteristic of some parts of the Australian flora. This variability may be due to climatic conditions, as for example when plants at high altitudes are procumbent or even prostrate, when compared with plants from low altitudes. Growth under exposed conditions can also cause similar variation. Some of these forms can retain the same characteristics when in cultivation, if they have been vegetatively propagated, eg. forms of *Crowea exalata* and *Grevillea confertifolia*, although this is not always so. If grown from seed, there is the likelihood of variation.

Some species can have 2 or 3 different forms, with similar coloured flowers, growing together within the same region, eg. *Grevillea alpina* — at Mt. Zero in the northern end of the Grampians in western Victoria, there is (a) a prostrate form, (b) a low spreading form to 1 m tall, and (c) a tall upright form to about 3 m high. *Grevillea alpina*, and *Correa reflexa* are excellent examples of variation within a species over a relatively wide area. These two species have numerous forms, with differing plant size, foliage, and flower colour and size.

Heat Loving Plants

The growth of heat loving plants such as *Hakea francisiana*, *Pileanthus peduncularis* and *Verticordia* spp., can pose problems in heavily planted gardens or in cool areas. Such plants need exposure to plenty of sun, and shelter from cold rain and winds. By creating windbreaks, cold winds can be reduced. An ideal site for heat loving plants is where they will be protected by existing buildings. The walls can act as solar panels, absorbing the heat and then releasing it over a long period, often in the evening and night. In some cases heat is reflected by the walls, straight onto plants, thus creating a microclimate which is beneficial to many species.

Cool and Shade Loving Plants

In addition to plants that enjoy sun and warmth, there are others at the opposite end of the scale, and of course very many in between.

Plants that need cool situations are suited to

cultivation in suburban areas, where there are buildings and other structures that give constant protection from the sun's rays. In more open regions, the best method is to plant shade-providing trees and shrubs that can give quick results, but will not become too large as they reach maturity. Large plants can have the un-welcome result of drying out soils, because of their large root systems, and also if only light rain occurs, this often does not penetrate the branches and enter the soil below.

Low growing, shade loving plants often have a small root system, which needs to be kept moist. The moisture content of the soil should therefore be checked regularly. They also do not generally have any drought resisting mechanisms, as found in plants from sunny areas, and hence may suffer severely from stress during hot dry periods.

Leaves

Horticulturists and gardeners are usually con-cerned with the surface of foliage, because it has much to offer in creating an aesthetically pleasing appearance. The foliage of Australian plants is indeed most varied, and some species are even grown for their foliage alone. See listing on page 293.

Leaves are very important to plants, and there are some interesting modifications which have developed so that plants can survive and cope with their environment. As a generalization, species with thin leaves occur mainly in high rainfall regions, and species with thick leaves grow in areas of low rainfall. With species from high rainfall areas, the surfaces of the leaves are mostly smooth and shiny, which means that the water is readily dispersed. Conversely, dry area species often have hairy foliage, giving a grey to whitish appearance. This helps to act as a reflec-tor and reduces the leaf temperature, thus reducing loss of water by transpiration. The hairs also help to collect the minimal rainfall and dew, as many dry area species have adapted to absorb moisture through the foliage. Often in cultivation in cooler climates and higher rainfall, hairy-leaved species are prone to fungal attack, as spores are easily trapped amongst the often moist, fine hairs, which is an ideal environment for fungal development.

A common feature of the majority of *Acacia* species is the production, at the juvenile stage, of true bipinnate leaves (See photo 1) and then to develop phyllodes which are flattened leaf stems that perform the same functions as leaves. For many acacias the change occurs within 2-3 sets of leaves, other species such as *A. rubida* can maintain the true leaves for 1-2 years.

Eucalypts are renowned for the change of foliage from the juvenile to the mature stage. Many species have a dramatic change, eg. *Eucalyptus globulus* and *E. perriniana*, whilst others differ minimally, eg. *Eucalyptus crenulata*, *E. forrestiana* and *E. pauciflora*.

Banksias also have juvenile and adult foliage, although the change is usually subtle. There is also variation in seedlings within the same species, eg. *Banksia ericifolia*, but as plants mature the leaves attain a similarity, even though there was a marked difference in the juvenile stage. (See photo)

Deciduous-leaved Plants

Australia is generally known as having an evergreen flora, but there are some fully or semi deciduous species from northern Australia, eg. *Albizia procera*, *Bombax ceiba*, *Brachychiton acerifolium*, *Cochlospermum* spp., *Erythrina* spp., *Melia azederach*, and *Planchonia careya*.

In the tropical region where there are wet and dry seasons, these plants have adapted to survive by dropping their foliage during the extremely hot, dry season. When rainfall is sufficient to provide soil moisture, new foliage growth begins.

Unique amongst plants from southern Australia is *Nothofagus gunnii*, the deciduous beech from the mountains of Tasmania, which drops its leaves during the winter.

Flowers

People have chosen to cultivate plants, through the ages, for two main reasons, food and or-namentation. Undoubtedly the beauty of the flowers is the main attraction for many people, whether it be the colour, size, fragrance, or the arrangement of the floral parts.

There is a wide variation in the flowers of Australian plants. Some of the features are as follows —

1. Many species have small, even minute, flowers, which are arranged in clusters or spikes, to give the impression of a large flower, eg. *Acacia*, *Callistemon*, *Eucalyptus*, *Melaleuca*, *Pomaderris* and *Ptilotus*.

2. Clusters of flowers, surrounded by decorative bracts. The south west corner of WA is renowned for species of *Darwinia* and *Pimelea* that have developed to produce colourful petal-like bracts. Species such as *Darwinia hypericifolia*, *D. leiostyla*, *D. marcrostegia*, *D. meeboldii* and *D. squarrosa*, occur on or near the peaks of the Stirling Range east of Albany. One theory is that as these species are subject to frequent periods of cloud and fog, they have adapted by producing the bracts to give protection to the reproductive parts of the flower.

Seedling of *Acacia verniciflua*, showing true bipinnate foliage, and phyllodes.

Albizia lophantha is an extremely fast growing small tree, and the bottle brush like flowers are attractive to honey-eating birds.

The majority of *Eucalyptus* spp. have distinct juvenile and adult growth phases, characterised by distinct leaves. *E.goniocalyx.* LHS — juvenile RHS — mature.

The large showy flowers of *Alyogyne huegelii* are produced throughout the year.

Seedling of *Banksia ericifolia*, showing change from larger juvenile foliage (lower) to finer mature leaves (upper).

Seedlings of *Banksia ericifolia*, showing variation in foliage.

3. Tubular Flowers. Australia has a large number of tubular flowered species. There are many variations in the development, and the type of floral tube. Tubular flowers are very attractive to native honey-eating birds, because most species with tubular flowers have a rich supply of nectar. In return for the food supply, it is often the bird which is the pollinating agent. This aspect, of being able to grow plants that will attract birds, not only provides visual enjoyment, but also in many cases helps to maintain a natural balance, as the birds will assist in the control of garden pests. For further information on attracting birds to gardens, see page 117. Some genera with small tubular flowers arranged in dense clusters (eg. *Pimelea*) are readily sought by butterflies for nectar. See list of species attractive to butterflies, page 127.

Variations in the formation of tubular flowers include the following —

(a) Petals joined to form a corolla. Examples of this are *Blandfordia* species, which have colourful orange, red or yellow waxy bells. The Epacridaceae family, of which there are over 300 species in Australia, has many species with tubular flowers, most of which are small in size when compared with the blandfordias, but are prolific in their display.

(b) Tubular flowers arranged in large heads. Some *Banksia* species are outstanding examples, as they can produce heads to over 30 cm long (eg. *B. grandis*), often displayed on long stems above the foliage. Some species have a combination of colour. Initially the buds of *B. burdettii* and *B. prionotes* are greyish, then as the hundreds of flowers open from the base first, the head is transformed to a bright orange. Birds, and small native animals such as pigmy possums, devour the constant supply of nectar from banksias during the flowering period. (See Attracting Native Fauna to Gardens, page 117.) *Telopea* is another genus with many small tubular flowers, arranged to form outstanding terminal floral heads which are very popular as cut flowers.

(c) *Grevillea* and *Hakea* are closely related to *Banksia* and *Telopea*, but have tubular flowers that are usually arranged in clusters or spikes. Some of the variations which occur in these genera are shown in the following examples.

Grevillea speciosa has pink to red flowers, arranged in a horizontal wheel-like formation, and flowers are produced on the new growth, whereas *Hakea orthorrhyncha* has brilliant red clusters of flower, produced along old branches that are usually devoid of foliage. *Hakea francisiana* produces upright spikes of pink to red flowers of about 15 cm in length, in the leaf axils

of the previous year's growth. *Grevillea pteridifolia* has large horizontal toothbrush-like spikes of brilliant yellow, displayed at the ends of branchlets. Many of the brightly coloured species are attractive to birds and insects for food needs, but some of the green or paler coloured flowers of grevilleas, are amongst the most commonly visited by birds, eg. *G. arenaria*, *G. jephcottii*, *G. rivularis* and *G. shiressii*. White and mauve flowered species are seldom visited by nectar eating birds.

(d) *Anigozanthos* is a genus with outstanding ornamental qualities. The tubular flowers are soft and hairy, and resemble the shape of a kangaroo's paw. Brilliant colours such as yellow, red and green are often combined to create eyecatching displays during the flowering period.

4. Pea Flowers. There are about 500 species in the Fabaceae family, with a large degree of endemism, eg. *Bossiaea*, *Chorizema*, *Daviesia*, *Dillwynia* and *Pultenaea*. These genera have small pea flowers, which are usually displayed in profusion, often in leafy spikes. Colours are mainly yellows, oranges, reds and browns, sometimes in combinations, giving colours that are not readily available in other families. The endemic *Hovea* is renowned for its spectacular display of blue to bluish purple flowers. Many of the pea flowers are attractive to butterflies, eg. *Kennedia glabrata*, *Mirbelia oxyloboides*, and *Pultenaea pedunculata*. (See also, listing of Butterfly Attracting Species, page 127.)

5. Cauliflory. Some trees of the tropical rainforest have the unusual feature of the flowers being produced on the trunk, eg. *Archidendron lucyi*, *Castanospermum australe*, *Syzygium cormiflorum*, and *Ficus racemosa*.

6. Honey Flora. Already species that produce copious supplies of nectar have been mentioned. Australia has a rich honey-flora, with *Eucalyptus* being the main genus. Other species such as *Eucryphia lucida* ('Tasmanian Leatherwood') produce a high quality honey of unique flavour. Further information on species is listed on page 300.

7. Perfumed Flowers. Some Australian plants are extremely well-known for their floral perfumes, eg. *Boronia megastigma*, and *B. serrulata*. It is not widely recognised that there are many other species that have pleasant fragrances, some of which are very delicate. Some are sweet, eg. *Jasminum suavissimum*, others are spicy, eg. *Calytrix aurea*. The tropical rainforests are rich in species with perfumed flowers, and as yet little has been done to introduce these into cultivation. There are also some species that have overpowering odours, eg. *Grevillea leucopteris* and some of the white or cream flowered *Hakea* spp. which have

Globular flower-heads and buds of *Acacia saligna*.

The large bracts of *Darwinia macrostegia* are the most showy parts of the flower-heads.

Cylindrical catkins of *Acacia floribunda*.

very strong, sweet odours.

It is common for many of the scented flowers to be pollinated by insects, butterflies and moths which will be attracted to areas in which such species are planted.

Fruits

There are a number of species that have interesting, and in many cases decorative fruits. Some of the large flowered *Eucalyptus* species, such as *E. caesia*, *E. erythrocorys*, *E. forrestiana*, *E. macrocarpa*, *E. preissiana*, *E. pyriformis*, *E. rhodantha* and *E. tetraptera* are suitable examples.

The Proteaceae family has a wide range of attractive fruits. Some *Banksia* and *Hakea* spp. develop large woody fruits that are not only decorative, but require fire or death of the plant for the fruits to open and disperse the winged seeds. *Hakea platysperma* has the largest fruit of the genus. It is hard and globular in shape, developing to about 7 cm diameter. *Grevillea glauca* from Queensland has similar fruits to *Hakea platysperma*. They are not as large, but are produced in clusters.

The fruits of *Billardiera longiflora* are deep blue-purple, and *Hibbertia scandens* produces a cluster of orange berry-like fruits. Colourful fruits are common in the tropical rainforest species. For a listing of plants with decorative fruits, see page 295.

The pods of some *Acacia* species can add a further degree of attraction to the plant. Some are broad and before ripening can be glaucous, eg. *A. obliquinervia*. Others are twisted, with *A. enterocarpa* having unique pods, similar in shape to the jumping jack firework, from which it gains its common name. In their juvenile stage, *Acacia* pods can be translucent, when backlit by sunlight.

Casuarina is another genus with interesting fruits, and they vary in size from species to species. Some are smooth and long, eg. *C. campestris*, whilst others are round to oblong, and covered with triangular valves that open to release the seed, eg. *C. stricta*. *C. leuhmannii* has flattened, broad fruits.

In nature, many fruits provide food for birds and animals. Plants in cultivation will produce fruits that can also attract birds and animals.

Lignotubers

Some species have an adaptive feature of forming a swelling at the base of stem or trunk. This is called a lignotuber. It can be completely below the soil, but in many cases a portion can be seen above. A lignotuber has two functions —
   1. It acts as a food storage.
   2. It bears latent buds, which shoot to form

1. Waxy tubular bells of *Blandfordia* are produced around Christmas time.

2. Banksias are popular because of their large flower-spikes, which are produced in a variety of forms. Illustrated *Banksia integrifolia*.

3. *Banksia prionotes*.

suckers that eventually develop into trunks if the upper part of the plant is damaged or destroyed, such as by fire.

The mallee-type eucalypts, eg. *Eucalyptus behriana*, *E. nutans* and *E. viridis*, and species from alpine and subalpine regions such as *E. pauciflora*, are examples of species with lignotuber development.

There are some Australian plants, the stems of which die back during hot dry periods, to a woody, carrot-like, storage root in the ground. These organs have similar characteristics to lignotubers, and they can be transplanted readily when there is no growth. Examples are *Abelmoschus moschatus*, *Aristolochia pubera*, *Cissus opaca*, *Dioscorea* spp., *Ipomoea* spp. and *Stephania japonica*.

Roots

The root systems of some species of Australian plants are modified in various ways to cope with the environment.

Many species in the families Epacridaceae, Ericaceae, Orchidaceae, Restionaceae and Rutaceae live in a close mycorrhizal association with various soil fungi. The fungi form a fine web over the surface of the roots. In one type of association the fungi penetrate deep into the internal cells of the root (endotrophic mycorrhiza) while in the other type they only enter the epidermis (ectotrophic mycorrhiza).

Mycorrhizal associations are complex and are still not entirely well understood. Some plants cannot grow in the absence of the soil fungi while in other species the association is of less importance. Saprophytic orchids for example lack leaves entirely or have reduced leaves and cannot survive in the absence of the correct mycorrhizal fungus. By contrast the relationship in *Eriostemon myoporoides* is much less complex and the plant can grow well in the absence of the fungus.

As well as fungi many species of plants harbour bacteria within their roots although the reason for their presence is largely unknown. Sometimes these bacteria are contained within special growths on the roots, eg. the nodules on the roots of legumes contain bacteria of the *Rhizobium* genus. The coralloid roots of cycads are another example. These grow upwards, fork repeatedly and resemble coral in shape. They generally proliferate in the humus-rich topsoil around the base of the plant. They are

The flannel flower, *Actinotus helianthi*, can make an outstanding display. The petal-like bracts are the most decorative part of the flowers.

Banksia sphaerocarpa.

inhabited both by bacteria and blue-green algae.

Only specially adapted plants can survive and grow in saline conditions. The mangroves are the most effective group to grow in such conditions and survive because of modified roots. These have an elaborate system of air conducting tissue which becomes active when the roots are exposed during low tides.

The aerial roots of epiphytic plants such as orchids and some members of the family Araceae have a layer of large cells around the root cortex. These roots are important not only for gas exchange but also for absorbing water from the atmosphere.

The roots of members of the family Proteaceae bear dense clusters of rootlets called proteoid roots. These are formed just beneath the soil surface and each cluster lasts only about one month before declining. When in active growth they are white and appear like a mop. Their function is uncertain but is probably related to the nutrition and hormone levels of the plant.

Mangroves

This unique group of plants has adapted to survive in a saline environment, where they play a very important role in erosion control, and provide a breeding ground for sea life and also homes for a large range of wildlife.

Mangroves live in saline water and soil, but will also grow well in non-saline environments. They have adapted to withstand higher concentrations of salt in their sap than most other land plants. The salt is removed by storing it in the oldest leaves, which eventually fall. Plants can also exclude salt from entering the sap system.

Further information will be gained in subsequent volumes under the alphabetical listing of genera, and under Mangroves, Volume 4.

Carnivorous Plants

In Australia there are several types of carnivorous plants, and these are represented by 7 genera, and about 100 species. All have modified leaves, which act as snares to capture small creatures such as insects and spiders, which are then digested and absorbed into the plants' system as a nitrogen supplement.

Leaves of *Drosera* spp. have glistening, sticky hairs, that are capable of moving to entrap the insects. *Byblis* have a simple method of catching insects. Their leaves, with the sticky hairs, act like old fashioned fly paper, and once insects land on the leaves they are caught.

Cephalotus and *Nepenthes* are commonly called pitcher plants, because the modified leaves have a similarity to such vessels. Insects and spiders are attracted inside the pitchers, only to find they cannot escape. *Cephalotus follicularis* is a dweller of swamps in the south-west of WA. Plants usually have conventional leaves, as well as the pitcher leaves. *Nepenthes mirabilis* is renowned for the variation in shape of the pitchers, even on the same plant. It is found on the Cape York Peninsula of Qld.

Utricularia spp. frequent moist situations, and they often grow in water. The bladder-like organs at the base of the stem trap microscopic aquatic animal life, for digestion by the plant.

6 Preparation and Planting

SOIL PREPARATION

Adequate soil preparation, although not always essential, ensures rapid establishment of plants, both above and below ground, without competition. In poor soils, the better the preparation, the better will be the resulting growth. Aeration and good drainage are important for the proper development of a strong root system. Plants die, in many instances, because they are planted without satisfactory soil preparation. Most deaths are in the heavy soil types, where waterlogging can readily occur, although death sometimes occurs in light soils, because there is insufficient moisture retention to keep young roots alive. Some species, eg. many *Callistemon* and *Melaleuca* spp. are adapted to poor drainage, and will tolerate poorly aerated soils.

Below are the steps to adequate soil preparation. Alternatives to planting in existing soils are discussed later in this section.

1. Remove all weeds. If creeping weeds such as couch and bent grasses occur, it is best if these can be completely removed before planting. If left until after planting, they can be particularly hard to control. If they penetrate into the root systems of plants they will be virtually impossible to remove, and will compete with the plants for nutrients, and can smother small plants. Such weeds can be removed painstakingly by hand with a tool such as a fork, which will not chop the underground stems as readily as a spade, or by use of herbicides. Herbicides should be used with utmost caution, to prevent damage occurring to existing shrubs or trees.

2. Dig ground to depth of 25-30 cm, breaking up large clods. If soil is a clay or clay loam and drainage needs to be improved, the addition of gypsum at a rate of 1-1.5 kg per square metre is recommended. Gypsum has a negligible effect on the pH of soils. For best results it should be incorporated evenly throughout the soil. It is not sufficient to let the gypsum lie on the soil surface. The incorporation of well rotted organic matter is also beneficial to clay soils, provided that the soil does not become too loose, and unable to support the base of plant trunks and stems. The addition of well rotted organic material to light soils is beneficial, as it helps to retain moisture, and will provide some nutrients for plant growth.

In large planting schemes such as farms, parks, golf courses etc., it is best to cultivate the area to be planted, preferably in autumn, and leave fallow for 12 months prior to planting. This is especially applicable to low-rainfall areas, as it will build up soil moisture levels after autumn and winter rains. Limited cultivation during the year may be needed to control weed growth, and prevent loss of soil moisture by transpiration.

3. In locations that are badly drained and prone to waterlogging, the drainage must be improved. There are three choices —

(a) To construct underground drains using agricultural pipes, plastic drainage pipe, or coarse screenings of 2-5 cm diameter.

(b) To create surface drains that quickly eliminate excess water. Paths can operate as drainage channels if they are below the level of the surrounding ground.

(c) To raise the level of growing areas, even if only by 10 cm, as this will eliminate the possibility of water lying around the base of plant stems, which is one of the most susceptible points for disease attack.

The raising of the soil level in planting areas can be done in several ways, including the following:

(i) Where paths or pools are planned, remove the topsoil from these areas, and use it to build up growing areas.

(ii) Obtain topsoil from some other source. It is generally better for plant growth if local soil is used, as the plants do not have to cope with a dramatic change of soil texture and sometimes nutrients. If other than local soil is used, it is important that it be thoroughly incorporated with the local soil, to form a

Grevilleas produce flowers which are showy, good for birds, and come in a variety of forms. *Grevillea alpina.*

G. rosmarinifolia.

G. johnsonii

G.asparagoides

homogeneous mixture. When obtaining soil, there is need to be aware that it could result in the introduction of unwanted perennial weeds and fungus diseases such as *Phytophthora cinnamomi* which can attack the root system of many plants (see Cinnamon Fungus).

(iii) For the cultivation of certain species of Australian plants, the creation of a sandhill bed has proved very successful. This is covered in more detail below.

4. Leave the ground fallow if possible for 4-8 weeks. This will allow germination of weed seeds, and growth of any creeping grasses from segments remaining in the soil. These should then be killed or removed by light cultivation. This practice also reduces the number of weeds likely to appear after planting.

5. Lightly Cultivate. After the fallow period, break up any soil lumps, in readiness for planting.

Specific Soil Preparation Techniques

Some species have specific soil requirements, eg. excellent drainage, the preference for light sandy soils, or for soils of high pH. To grow some of these species, especially those intolerant of poor drainage, specific soil conditions must be created. This can be achieved in a number of ways, three of which are considered here. It should be borne in mind that plants from sandy areas are often drought resistant, and if the soil dries out more quickly by being above the natural soil level, this does not usually affect their growth once established. Newly planted species will need regular inspection to make sure soil is moist so the root system can develop and support the growth.

The genus *Hakea* offers a wide range of plant forms. The grass-like leaves and long spikes of *H.francisiana*.

The cupped, broad leaves and clustered flowers of *H.cucullata*.

Preparation and Planting

1. The creation of large mounds of natural soil, with a soil depth of 0.5 m or more.

2. The construction of sand beds or sandhills. Various grades of sand have been used for this purpose with success, although long term results are not yet fully known. Pure sand alone can be used, but it should not be from swampy areas, soakage areas, or beaches, because of salt contamination.

3. Large mounds can be created by using other soil mixtures as follows. There is no set rule, and they can be varied at the discretion of the grower, depending often on the local availability of materials.
   (a) 50% coarse river sand; 50% friable loam
   (b) 75% coarse river sand; 25% friable loam
   (c) 33% coarse river sand; 50% friable loam; 17% gravel or screenings.

IMPROVEMENT OF PROBLEM SOILS

Heavy Clay

At all stages, clay is difficult to cultivate. By the addition of organic matter such as compost, leaf litter, etc., and sand, improvement can be made. The incorporation of gypsum, together with the organic matter and/or sand, is probably the best way to improve clay soil. The gypsum should be applied at the rate of 1-1.5 kg/m², when the soil is slightly moist. It acts by causing the clay particles to aggregate together in little clumps, allowing better moisture penetration and aeration. Gypsum works best in the presence of organic matter, and for best improvement of clays the two materials should be used together. Repeated applications of gypsum every 4-5 years may be necessary, but if possible organic material should be added on a more regular basis.

Clay soils are very prone to surface compaction, and this may lead to reduced plant growth due to the lack of gas exchange at the soil surface. Light cultivation of the topsoil and the application of a mulch, will help to remedy this situation.

The introduction of surface or shallow underground drains will be beneficial if the soils are wet for long periods. (See Waterlogged Soils, below.) This will help to maintain a friable topsoil and remove excess water, allowing root growth to take place.

Waterlogged Soils

Waterlogged soils will suffocate roots of many species of plants, resulting in death. There can also be the possibility of accumulated salts, which inhibit plant growth. (See Saline soils.)

67

Selection and Cultivation

The soft, velvety, tubular flowers of kangaroo paws are unique to WA. Depicted is *Macropidia fuliginosa*.

E. lehmannii

E. preissiana

Many species of WA eucalypts are grown for their decorative buds and fruits, as well as for their flowers. *Eucalyptus platypus.*

E. torquata

E. pyriformis

E. nutans

An insectivorous sundew (*Drosera auriculata*), showing flower, and leaves bearing sticky glandular hairs which trap insects.

The decorative pitchers of *Cephalotus follicularis* — a carnivorous plant, best grown in a pot of peat or sphagnum moss.

Root system of *Banksia* sp., showing proteoid roots. The white clump centre top is in active growth.

Waterlogged soils can be improved in the following ways.

1. The level of the topsoil can be altered to create surface drains. This will help to remove excess water fairly quickly by surface run-off.

2. Construction of underground drains. Trenches are dug 0.5-1 m deep by 0.3-0.5 m wide. The fall of the land must be determined before any trenches are dug. The eye can be deceived by undulations, so always use a string and line level, or other suitable equipment, with the use of temporary pegs for marking the desired fall. The drain must flow to an outlet, and there should be sufficient fall in the drain for it to be self-cleaning. There are different materials and pipes that can be used in the trenches —

(a) Rubble drains can be composed of a lower stratum of broken bricks, large pebbles, or screenings, which are covered by fine screenings or coarse sand. See illustration. This type of drain has a shorter life span than those with pipes, due to a build up of silt.

(b) Agricultural pipe drains. There are now many types of pipes available, including polythene, cement, and glazed or unglazed terracotta clay. Unglazed terracotta clay pipes are the most popular, and probably the best to use in most conditions.

3. Plants that withstand waterlogging can be planted. If it is a large growing area, tall trees can be used. When plants are established, the process of transpiration will remove many litres of water a day. For suitable species, see list on page 274.

69

Selection and Cultivation

Sandy Soils

Sands can be improved by the addition of organic material. This will increase water holding capacity and also reduce the leaching of nutrients. Fertilizers such as blood and bone or slow release fertilizers will be beneficial to growth.

When many of the fine sands are dry, they become water repellent, and it is very hard for water to penetrate the surface. Usually the water will sit near the surface, or often it will run to a low spot where it may penetrate. Close inspection by scratching through the surface is needed, to be sure that penetration has occurred. A light mulch such as pine bark or wood chips can help avert this situation, by preventing the drying out of the sand surface. It will also restrict water run-off, and help to eliminate movement of the sand by strong winds. As the mulch breaks down, it will add further organic material to the soil. When this occurs the mulch should be replenished.

Saline Soils

Saline soils contain an excess of salts which affect plant growth. These salts may be from high concentration of any soluble salt, but the commonest material is sodium chloride.

Coastal soils can become slightly saline, because of excessive deposits of salt spray, which is usually washed through the soil by rain.

Salted soils are frequent in flat areas, where the water table lies close to the surface. Concentrations of dissolved salts build up in the water table, and are carried through the soil in the water by capillary action. On the soil surface, the water evaporates leaving the salt. In severe cases this salt may be visible as a white encrustation on the soil surface.

Isolated pockets of saline soil may occur in hilly country which has porous topsoil over a heavy clay subsoil. They are usually found in country cleared of the natural vegetation. The water flows down the slopes and collects in the depressions. When salt levels build up, the salt can be deposited on the surface following capillary movement of water through the soil.

Ways to improve saline soils are —

1. Create better drainage that will allow for quicker movement of excess water (see Waterlogged soils). Salt is very soluble in water, and can be readily washed down through the soil profile. Usually however, drainage is a major problem in saline areas, and flushing of the soil can only be carried out intermittently.

2. Grow plants, especially trees, on any land vacant at higher elevations than where the

Unglazed terracotta pipes are commonly used for drainage. Joints are covered with bituminous paper to prevent blockage by soil.

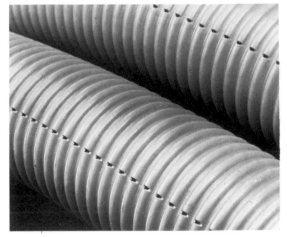

Perforated plastic pipes, suitable for draining wet soils.

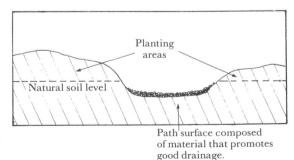

Topsoil from pathways used to raise garden beds, to promote good drainage. The pathway acts as a surface drain.

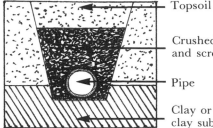

Construction of an underground drain, using agricultural pipes.

- Topsoil
- Crushed rock and screenings
- Pipe
- Clay or clay subsoil

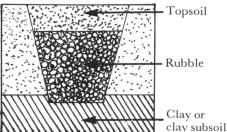

Construction of an underground drain, using rubble.

- Topsoil
- Rubble
- Clay or clay subsoil

salting is occurring. Dense initial planting will be beneficial, even if there is the need for thinning out later.

3. A very useful approach is to plant tolerant species in the saline areas. As wide a variety of species as possible should be established, and they should be encouraged to grow vigorously, by ensuring that they are not short of other nutrients essential for plant growth. Any native plant, with the exception of noxious weeds, should be encouraged, for even the lowliest is better than a bare patch of ground. After some seasons, a dense sward of plants will begin to lower the water table, enabling flushes of fresh water to dissolve and carry away the salt. If this is successful, more desirable species can be introduced and established in the area. With managerial care, such an area can be maintained and improved over the years.

Cracking Soils

Cracking is usually due to two reasons —
(a) the lack of sufficient organic matter to act as a binder with the soil particles,
(b) the soil contains clay particles which have a high shrinkage factor.

Cracking is not only confined to heavy clay soils, as some of the more friable brown earths can also have the same problem.

Improvement of the soil can be gained by the addition of gypsum and organic matter. (See Heavy clay soils.) Mulching is most beneficial, as

it will reduce the loss of soil moisture, and thus limit the degree of cracking.

Alkaline Soils

Soils having an excess of calcium salts have a high pH, and are commonly referred to as limey or calcareous soils. Sometimes such soils also have large quantities of sodium present. This is an element which is not conducive to good growth. Unhealthy growth is common on calcareous soils, often because of low levels of such trace elements as zinc, iron or manganese. Calcareous soils contain lime, in varying quantities, either in a free form or in large nodules.

It is difficult to lower the pH of a soil to any extent, but the topsoil can be improved as follows —

1. The addition of organic matter over a period of years will have some effect on lowering the pH of the soil. The growing of green crops and ploughing them into the soil for 1-2 years before the planting of trees or shrubs, is highly recommended.

2. Elementary sulphur, in powder form, and aluminium sulphate are suitable acidifying agents, however large quantities are necessary for significant acidification. Always use sulphate fertilizers, and do not use carbonate fertilizers as they could raise the pH further.

3. The removal of loose limestone deposits.

4. There are quite a number of Australian plants that grow well in calcareous soils. A selection is listed on page 269. As a general rule, those species from dry or arid areas are tolerant of calcareous soils.

Acid Soils

Acid soils with a pH less than 5.5 benefit from the addition of lime. Lime reduces acidity, supplies calcium which is often deficient in acid soils, and reduces toxic levels of manganese and aluminium.

There are different forms of lime which can be used to raise the pH of soils. Lime is calcium carbonate, and is also known as ground limestone. Slaked lime is also known as calcium hydroxide. Dolomitic limestone is a mixture of calcium and magnesium carbonates. Slaked lime is the most effective in raising the soil pH, and is closely followed by lime. Dolomite is about half as effective as either in raising the pH, but is very valuable, as it also supplies the element magnesium.

The amount of lime to add to a soil depends on many factors, such as soil pH, soil type, and the range of plants to be grown. Soils with a pH of 4.5 will need more lime to reduce the acidity by one unit, than soils at pH 5.5. Clay soils have a capacity to buffer the addition of lime without the corresponding pH change that would occur if lime were added to sandy soils.

Where soils are very acid, it may be a wise procedure to add only small quantities of lime or dolomite to ensure that the elements calcium and magnesium are present for plant growth, and to grow plants suited to acid soils, such as those found naturally in heathland communities.

Acid/Alkaline Soils

Some soils have an acid topsoil and an alkaline subsoil. This has arisen because the original alkaline soil has been leached, leaving the topsoil acid while the subsoil is unchanged. It can be difficult to grow plants in such soils, without careful selection of species. In general, those plants suited to calcareous soils will grow in these soil types. Soils of this type are found in parts of SA and WA.

Variation in growth of container plants of *Acacia myrtifolia.*

CHOICE OF PLANT STOCK

It has generally been found that small, young, healthy Australian plants, establish themselves much better than semi-advanced or advanced specimens. This is especially applicable if plants are to be grown in heavy soils. A good rule of thumb is never to plant specimens that are grown in containers which are deeper than the topsoil in which they are to be planted. The main problem encountered with large plants is that often planting holes need to penetrate the subsoil. If the subsoil is clay, this results in the formation of a sump, with roots being waterlogged, and can lead to the death of the plant.

Most nurseries use artificial fertilizers to stimulate growth. If too much is used, plants can be forced, resulting in very soft top growth whilst the root system has not developed in equal proportions. Avoid leggy, soft plants, and choose stocky, hardened ones. If after purchase, a plant is found to have inadequate root growth, the root system could be watered with a root stimulant. These are available from nurseries and stores. Alternatively the top can be reduced by pruning, to balance with the roots.

Coiling of the roots can take place in containers. This should be corrected at planting time, because the coiling can continue, causing constrictions and restrictions in the main roots. The end result is usually a plant which is not strong, and is prone to being blown out of the ground during strong winds. For the mechanics of handling roots, see Planting Procedures pages 73-75.

Most Australian plants are available in containers such as
(a) rigid plastic pots in various sizes, the most common of which is about 17 cm x 14 cm diameter. Root coiling can occur in such pots.
(b) plastic bags of about 15 cm x 10 cm diameter. These do not readily produce a coiled root system.

With containers of the sizes mentioned, trees grown to about 0.5 m tall are ideal for planting, whilst shrubs to 0.3 m are recommended. Smaller plants are often available in wood veneer or plastic tubes, and these are quite suitable for planting, although extra care may be necessary initially, until the plant is established.

The following points should help in the choice of a well-grown plant.
(a) It should look healthy. Do not buy diseased stock — i.e. with distorted leaves, or having leaves with blackened or yellow edges. A plant which has been eaten by insects or grubs need not be rejected for this reason.
(b) It should not have leggy and soft top growth, with long intervals between leaf nodes. Choose a plant with firm, vigorous growth.
(c) The base of the trunk or stem should be firm in the growing mix.
(d) Do not buy tightly staked plants, as they may not have developed a strong root system. Ties and labels can also penetrate bark; this results in a weakening of the stem or trunk.
(e) The growing mixture should not contain perennial weeds.

Acacia root systems, showing the importance of selecting a healthy plant —
RHS — lacking nodules; LHS — with nodules.

(f) If purchasing leguminous plants, eg. *Acacia, Brachysema, Hovea, Pultenaea* etc., ask if you may inspect the root system for nodules before purchasing. If the plant is in a rigid container and has a well-developed root system, it can be tapped out quite easily. The roots of healthy plants will bear numerous nodules, and should establish easily. If nodules are absent, avoid the plant in preference to another. Occasionally, species imported from interstate do not form nodules, because of the absence of the correct *Rhizobium* bacteria.

The Importance of Legumes

Leguminous plants are common throughout most types of vegetation in Australia. They often grow on poor soils and are of special ecological significance because they increase the fertility of soil by building up nitrogen levels. The root systems of legumes contain nodules which are the site of activity of nitrogen fixing bacteria belonging to the genus *Rhizobium*. These bacteria take nitrogen from the atmosphere and convert it into a form which is available to the legume. This nitrogen then becomes re-cycled and available to other plants, after leaching or death of the legumes.

When establishing gardens, it is a good policy to include some leguminous species, to help build up soil fertility. Legumes belong to the family Fabaceae, Mimosaceae and Caesalpiniaceae. A few non-leguminous plants can also fix nitrogen, eg. *Casuarina* spp.

PLANTING

The planting procedure outlined below will aid the successful establishment of a plant. Correct planting is important, not only in gardens, but also in the planting of large areas such as windbreaks, arboreta or parks.

Planting Sequence

1. Soak plants thoroughly before removing them from containers. It is best carried out about 12 hours before planting, but if this is not possible, soaking an hour before will be beneficial. Pre-soaking is especially important in dry areas. A mixture of water, liquid fertilizer and root stimulant can be used, to promote initial root growth.

Interesting combinations can be created by using ferns and orchids, in association with water and boulders.

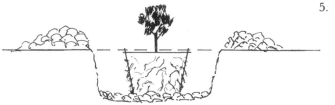

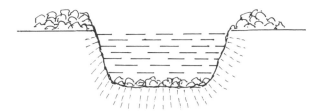

2. The planting hole should be dug at least twice the width of the plant container, and about the same depth, with all soil broken up, especially that at the base of the hole.

3. If soil is dry, fill hole with water at least once, and leave it to drain away before planting. Do not plant in dry soil, because after planting water will not penetrate properly, due to the fine dry soil being water repellent. This effect is particularly noticeable in dry sandy soils.

4. If organic or slow release fertilizers are to be used, they should be incorporated with the loose soil in the bottom of the hole, or mixed thoroughly with the filling soil. Avoid direct contact between fertilizer and the young soft roots. (See Fertilizers, page 97.)

5. Remove plant carefully from the container.

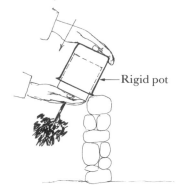

Rigid pot

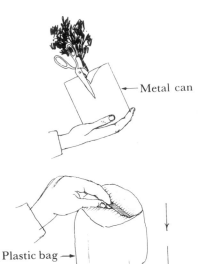

Metal can

Plastic bag

6. Inspect the root systems, and prune where necessary with sharp secateurs. Some disturbance of the root ball is tolerable, but do not break main root ball and expose major roots.

(a) Remove any old, brown, dense, matted roots, to expose young white roots. This allows new roots to penetrate the soil and become established much more quickly.

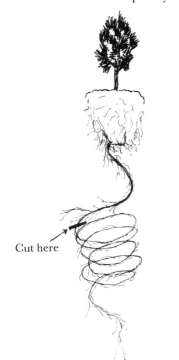

Cut here

(b) If roots are coiled, try to straighten them, or alternatively remove them with sharp secateurs at a point which will not greatly check the plant's growth.

(c) Remove any damaged roots.

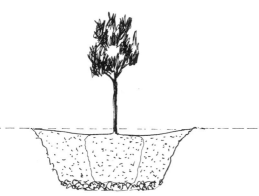

7. Place plant in position, with the plant soil level just minimally below the garden soil level. If a stake is being used, it should be put in place before the back-filling of soil. This eliminates any risk of root damage. It is NOT necessary to stake young plants. They usually grow stronger without stakes. In some circumstances, due to adverse weather conditions, a stake may be needed. (See Staking, page 92.)

8. Place filling in hole.

9. Firm soil around plant, taking care to not damage roots.

10. Water well, with at least 5 litres of water per plant. Repeated waterings of a lesser amount may be necessary to obtain proper penetration and soaking of the soil around roots.

11. Mulch if desired. (See Mulching, page 79.)

Technique of planting in shallow soils

When planting in areas with shallow topsoil and a heavy subsoil, it is most important to not create a situation where waterlogging will occur. To overcome this problem on flat or slightly sloping land, it is recommended that the soil be built up to a height that enables the plant's roots to be just above the subsoil. In most cases, for a plant grown in a 14 cm pot, the extra depth needed would be about 10 cm. The built up soil needs to have a minimum diameter of 1 m, as anything less will dry out too quickly with resultant setbacks to the plant's growth, or even death. Any soil added should be incorporated with the natural topsoil. The subsoil should be broken up, to allow roots to penetrate readily. Sloping areas such as embankments usually present problems in planting. A simple technique, as shown in the illustration overcomes this situation.

WINDBREAKS

Wind can damage or retard plant growth. When the winds are salt laden, severe effect on plants is usually the result, with burnt foliage or even defoliation occurring.

Selection and Cultivation

Windbreak Design

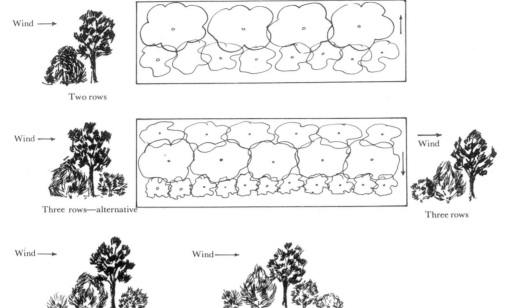

Wind →

Two rows

Wind →

Three rows—alternative

Wind →

Three rows

Wind →

Four rows

Wind →

Five rows

Informal windbreak design.

The poor development of this root system was caused by coiling while in the pot, and insufficient pruning and teasing at planting time.

Techniques of planting in shallow topsoils

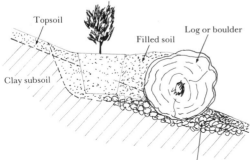

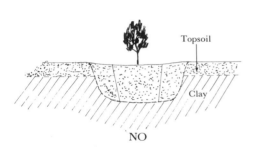

NO

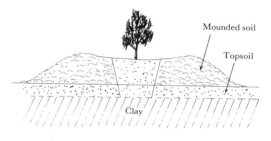

YES

Undoubtedly the best way to cope with excessive wind is to use plants as windbreaks, or to construct some type of wind resistant structure that will protect plants until they are established.

See listing of species that are salt and wind resistant, pages 281, 286.

Vegetative Windbreaks

For vegetative windbreaks to be truly effective, there should be at least 3 strata of plant growth, preferably over a relatively wide area, with the variance of height from low to tall on the windward side. There is the tendency for the winds to be deflected to a higher elevation if there is a gentle upward slope. If the slope is steep, the effect of the windbreak is usually minimised, resulting in a sharp upward deflection, and a responding sharp downward deflection on the leeward side.

For large windbreaks around farms and municipal grounds etc., it is best if there is some airflow through a windbreak, which will result in the diminishing of eddying on the leeward side. In small areas where protection from wind is desired, the principle is still the same, but planting can be more dense.

Experiments have shown that by having a well-grown and developed windbreak, as illustrated, the benefit on the leeward side is effective for about 10-30 times the height of the windbreak, and about 5 times the height on the windward side. Research has also shown that windbreaks, and other planted areas, are directly responsible for reducing the temperature in summer, due to the evaporative processes of the leaves, and there is an increase in temperature during winter because of the reduction of through-flow of cold air, to cool building surfaces. This can result in a reduction of the use of fuels to heat and cool buildings. Windbreaks therefore are very valuable for other reasons, and not only for creating a situation where plants prone to wind damage can be grown.

Selection and Cultivation

Ferns are popular in cultivation, and a wide range can be grown. The Bird's Nest Ferns are best grown as epiphytes.

allow for some penetration of air movement, are tea-tree fences, or brush fences where fine branches and foliage are used.

3. A combination of wire or wooden supports and climbers is very beneficial in reducing the strength of winds. The use of species such as *Kennedia nigricans* and *K. rubicunda*, will enable a quick coverage of the supporting structure.

4. Various long lasting synthetic materials such as shadecloth and interwoven webs, are very useful in restricting winds. In areas prone to very strong wind, the use of fencing wire is beneficial as a framework to act as a support for the cloth. Although the cloth is of open weave, billowing will occur, with resultant strain along the edges of the cloth where it is secured.

Other types of Windbreaks

Many different types of materials are suitable for windbreaks that can be constructed for small specific areas.

1. Fences made from brick or timber will provide effective protection from wind, for plants growing in very close proximity. This type of construction is more suitable for low growing plants, as when taller growing plants reach a height greater than that of the fence, often the trunk cannot cope with the wind then encountered, and breakage of limbs and trunks can occur. On some occasions, trunks are snapped off at ground level.

2. Windbreaks which are fairly dense, but do

7 Maintenance

MAINTENANCE

Maintenance-free gardens are often sought, whether for a suburban home, farmhouse, industrial or commercial planting, public open space, botanical garden, or any other location. Completely maintenance-free gardens are impossible to achieve, although with thoughtful planning many aspects of maintenance can be reduced to a minimum. The following aspects of maintenance are important, and must be considered for any garden:
1. Mulching
2. Watering
3. Fertilizing
4. Pruning and Tree Surgery
5. Weeding
6. Replanting and Renovation
7. Transplanting
8. Staking

Mulching

Mulching can help to provide optimum conditions for plant growth. There are three main reasons for mulching:
(a) To help with retention of soil moisture during periods of hot and dry weather, by reducing evaporation.
(b) To reduce soil temperature fluctuations, and prevent the soil from becoming too hot in the root area.
(c) To help in the reduction of weed growth.

Many different materials can be used as mulches, and some of these are discussed below. Plants themselves can be often used as living mulches (ground covers), and are excellent, especially the ground-covering species of genera such as *Grevillea*, *Kennedia*, *Dampiera* and *Brachysema*, and other mat plants.

Mulching dangers

A major hazard is that often mulches containing decaying organic material are placed too close to a plant's trunk. The trunk near ground level is very susceptible to attack by fungi, and the decaying material can damage the bark and provide conditions for disease entry. When placing organic material such as leaves, sawdust etc., around plants, do not put it close against the trunks. One of the worst materials in this regard is fresh grass clippings. If they are piled up around a trunk, there is usually a generation of heat, and this can kill or damage the bark. Sand, gravel, screenings and crushed rock do not have the same detrimental effect as organic materials because they usually allow for air and moisture movement through the medium.

Mulching in frost prone areas

Some mulches can increase the intensity of frost damage. Research has shown that the best materials to use in such areas are inorganic mulches, of sand, gravels, screenings etc. Organic materials often retain large amounts of moisture, and are readily frozen. This increases the height at which frost damage to plants can occur. (See also Climatic Conditions — Frost, page 50.)

Some suitable mulches

(a) Coarse river sand, or gravel.

This is an excellent mulch, when used about 5-7.5 cm deep. It is highly recommended, despite the fact that it is a relatively expensive material in some areas. It allows very good moisture penetration, helps to maintain a constant soil temperature, and does not break down as is the case with organic mulches. There can be a problem if weeds are left uncontrolled and allowed to seed, as the mulch is excellent for the

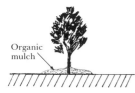

Organic mulch

Do not place organic mulches against the trunks of plants, as it may lead to entry of disease.

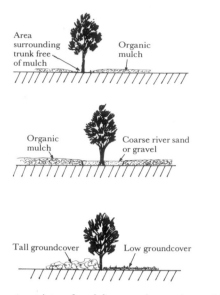

Area surrounding trunk free of mulch

Organic mulch

Organic mulch

Coarse river sand or gravel

Tall groundcover

Low groundcover

A variety of mulches can be used, provided they are correctly applied.

germination of seeds. The mulch can however be used to the gardener's advantage in this regard, as plants such as the flannel flower, *Actinotus helianthii*, can be grown with the purpose of allowing them to self-seed in the garden area.

(b) Screenings and crushed rock.

Similar comments as for the above materials apply here. It is necessary to be aware of whether or not the material has any detrimental factors such as a high pH. Also, some materials can break down, with the resulting formation of strong acids.

(c) Fine Sand.

This material can be good, but problems are often created when the surface dries out and becomes water repellent. Fine sand is also a good medium for the germination of weed seeds.

(d) Wood Chips.

(i) Hardwood: This excellent material allows for air and moisture movement, ages to a pleasant colour, but does not rot quickly. The main disadvantage is that it is not readily obtainable. Mechanical shredders are now in wide use for the purpose of cutting up branches, twigs and leaves.

(ii) Softwood: Excellent for short-term effect, but it rots down more quickly than hardwood.

Wood mulches containing preservative, or other chemicals from treatment plants should not be used, as this can prove deadly to plants. Any diseased plant material should of course not be used for this purpose.

(e) Hardwood Shavings.

These have excellent moisture retention, but can form a crust, and when dry become water repellent. This can be overcome by placing a shallow cover of coarse sand (about 1-2 cm deep) over the material. Shavings do rot down and will need replenishing. Alternatively ground-cover species can be planted, with a view to their becoming effective mulching agents, as the original mulch deteriorates. Care should be exercised in the use of these mulching materials in any area prone to bushfire, or otherwise exposed to burning. Fire can travel within the mulch, and can be very difficult to extinguish, breaking through to the surface of the mulch some time later, and perhaps where not expected.

(f) Bush Litter.

This material, composed of branches, bark, leaves and twigs is also an excellent mulch, but must be used with caution. Fungal diseases such as cinnamon fungus (*Phytophthora cinnamomi*) can be introduced with this medium. Enquire as to whether such diseases do exist in the area from where material is gathered, and do not collect in the vicinity of diseased and dead plants.

(g) Pinebark.

A good mulching material. This is available in many grades and has many applications. A mixture of grades is best for mulching, because if the material is too coarse, weed seeds can germinate, and if too fine it is blown about by wind. Fresh material can be used successfully as a mulch without plant damage, because any toxins are inactivated before they reach plant roots.

(h) Tanbark.

An excellent mulch, but rarely obtainable now, due to the increased use of chemicals for the tanning of leather.

(i) Coffee Bean Husks.

Initially good as a mulch, but the husks break down fairly quickly, often to become soft and mushy. It is best incorporated into the soil as an amendment.

(j) Peanut Shells.

A very good mulch, which must be used fairly thickly. It can be too light and easily blown around by wind, and may also contain weed seeds.

(k) Mushroom Compost.

This fairly good mulch is available from commercial mushroom growers. It should not be placed near plant trunks, and if the surface becomes dry it is difficult for water to penetrate. It is best used for incorporating into heavy soils as an amendment.

(l) Straw or Hay.

This is a good material, and often used for embankments. Water penetration can be poor when the material becomes dry, and another disadvantage is weed growth from seed germination. It has bad fire risk.

(m) Pine Needles.

A good mulch if not used too thickly. It has poor water-penetration properties.

(n) Casuarina Needles.

This is probably one of the best mulches, but it is usually difficult to gather sufficient material.

(o) Grass Clippings.

A fair mulch, but can have disadvantages as previously discussed in this section. It is probably best if used after composting.

(p) Compost.

A good mulch, but needs regular replenishing, and can provide ideal conditions for weed germination. It is best used for incorporating into soils as an amendment.

When applying plastic mulch it must be just below soil level, and not right against the trunk.

(q) Plastic Sheeting.

Black plastic sheeting is commonly used around industrial sites etc. This material is not recommended for flat areas, or heavy soils, but can be beneficial on sloping embankments. It breaks down in time, and weeds may become entrenched beneath the plastic, from where their removal can create many problems. In dry areas, plastic has proved ideal as a temporary mulch when establishing young plants.

For use of plastic around individual plants the plastic should be about 1 m in diameter, with a hole of about 5-10 cm diameter in the centre of the plastic. The plastic should be buried just below soil surface.

(r) Newspaper.

Several layers of newspaper will help to eliminate germination of weed seeds, and can also stifle perennial weeds such as couch grass. It is best used beneath a permanent type of mulch that will hold it in place. This is also important because the newspaper will gradually decompose to become part of the soil. Mulches such as woodshavings, woodchips and pine bark are ideal for this purpose.

Watering

Australia is a dry continent, and many of its plants are drought tolerant once established. It is suggested therefore, that for low rainfall areas

When watering, it is best to thoroughly soak the root system, with a slow application rate.

where water is often in short supply, species which will adapt to such conditions should be selected. Many of these species will grow over a wide range of Australian suburban areas, and their use can help greatly to conserve water, as well as the human effort required in artificial watering. Most Australian plants do not need regular watering, but of course there are exceptions, such as species which grow in constantly moist soil conditions in their natural habitat. It is most important to recognise this need when selecting plants, so a suitable location can be chosen. For watering purposes it is convenient to grow moisture-loving species together.

One of the main reasons that watering is required in gardens is that often more plants are grown in a specified area than would naturally survive. All have roots competing to supply enough moisture for the needs of the plants. In desert areas, plants are more sparsely located, but in moist sandy heathlands or wet forests, plants flourish very well in close proximity, because of the abundant moisture supply. Points to keep in mind when watering Australian plants are —

(a) If the soil about 2 cm down is moist, don't water. There does not have to be a regular watering program (eg. once a week). Inspection of the soil by probing with a finger should indicate if there is a need to water.

(b) It is best to water during a cool period. If possible, it is usually best not to water plants from relatively low rainfall areas during hot weather, even at night or early morning. They have not evolved to cope with such conditions, and it is preferable to wait for a cooler period of a few days or more. With watering during hot weather, there is also a greater possibility of creating conditions for the spread of fungal disease.

(c) Always thoroughly soak the root area. By making sure water seeps to all the roots, conditions will not be conducive to the formation of surface roots which will then require frequent artificial watering. Instead, most plants will form roots which penetrate the subsoil, and find their own moisture supply.

Trickle irrigation is an ideal system for the

watering of Australian plants, and has application in private gardens, public and municipal gardens, roadsides, commercial plantings, and in fact in most areas where plants are grown, either in the ground or in containers. It is very suitable for isolated areas, or if owners are on extended vacations, and is labour saving. This system uses minimum water with maximum efficiency. It is not costly to install, and requires limited maintenance. Further information regarding trickle irrigation can be obtained from your State Department of Agriculture.

Fertilizing

The fertilizing of Australian plants is a topic of much discussion, and the subject of many articles and books, with viewpoints varying from one end of the scale to the other. Most plants need applications of some sort of fertilizer, but at the same time there are species that have been found to be susceptible to overfertilizing (see list below). A general rule is that species from rainforests, mountains or valleys etc., where soils contain more nutrients and are moist for most of the year, are able to withstand higher applications of fertilizer than those species from dry areas, where soils are low in nutrients, particularly phosphorus (see also Phosphorus Excess, page 179).

To be effective, fertilizers must be applied to moist soil. If the soil is dry, it is of considerable benefit to water it thoroughly, and allow excess water to drain away, before applying the fertilizers. It is also beneficial to water in fertilizers after application.

Fertilizers should not be used in excessive quantities, and it is best to make two or three small applications, rather than one heavy dose. Fertilizers should be applied in a balanced mixture. Excess nitrogen for example can lead to excess top growth at the expense of root growth, resulting in top-heavy plants that are not stable in the ground.

Type of Fertilizer to Use

The type of fertilizer to use will depend on the species, season, soil type, and age of the plant. (For details on Fertilizer Types, see page 97.) Organic and slow-release fertilizers are the safest to use, since they release their nutrients slowly, and the nutrients can be used by the plants as they become available. If using soluble inorganic fertilizers, it is best to apply them in a complete balanced mixture, unless correcting a deficiency. Liquid fertilizers are very good for tub, pot, hanging basket or indoor plants, but can also be very useful in the garden where a rapid response is required.

Placement of Fertilizers

Fertilizers are best scattered over the surface of the ground within the drip line or canopy of the tree. They should not be concentrated around the trunk, or else they may burn the bark and allow disease to enter.

When to use Fertilizers

(a) At Planting

Fertilizers are most commonly applied at planting, but this is not always necessary. If the soil is rich in organic material and has not supported plants previously, there will be enough available food for most plants. If plants purchased from a nursery have recently received an application of a slow-release fertilizer, a further application at planting could result in overdosage. If possible, discuss this aspect with your nurseryman, or look for signs of recent fertilizing in the plant, eg. granules in the soil, or abundant new leaf growth. When applying fertilizers at planting time, never exceed the dosage rates recommended by the manufacturer. Often half the dosage rate recommended is ample for most species. Make sure that the fertilizer is thoroughly dispersed throughout the soil and not allowed to come in contact with the plant roots.

(b) On Established Plants

Fertilizers broadcast on the surface and watered or lightly cultivated in, are a very good means of replenishing nutrients and stimulating growth in established plants. Most species respond well to such treatment, but heavy applications should be avoided. For most species a once yearly application is sufficient, but many members of the family Myrtaceae, such as callistemons, syzygiums and melaleucas, respond well to applications of fertilizers in the autumn and spring. Weeds are a common by-product of fertilizing, and should be removed when noticed as they compete with other plants. Blood and bone, and other fertilizers with odours can attract animals such as dogs and cats, unless incorporated in the soil.

Sensitive Plants

Some plants have been found to be sensitive to the over use of fertilizers, and must be treated carefully. (See also Nutritional Disorders, page 177.)

Sensitive species belong to genera *Adenanthos, Banksia, Boronia, Brachysema, Conospermum, Dryandra, Grevillea, Hakea, Isopogon, Kennedia, Lambertia, Petrophile* and *Pultenaea.*

Pruning and Tree Surgery

There are three major rules for pruning and tree surgery that should be adhered to at all times.

(a) All cutting tools must be kept sharp. This enables smooth cuts to be made, thereby restricting the possibility of disease organisms entering the plant through damaged tissue.

(b) All tools must be kept clean, by regular washing, or soaking for short periods in a germicide or disinfectant (commonly available through supermarkets etc.).

(c) In situations where branches have been removed from plants, or damage has occurred to the bark and cambium layer, it is important that a heavy dressing of a wood sealant be applied. There are specific wood sealants available, which help to promote new cambium growth, and also act as a temporary bark and prevent the entry of organisms detrimental to plant growth.

Pruning

Why prune Australian plants?

(a) To promote healthy growth.

(b) To be able to direct the growth of a plant in a particular manner.

(c) Pruning can extend the life of plants, especially rapid growing, short-lived species such as some acacias, prostantheras and westringias.

(d) Pruning can result in a greater display of flowers.

Some plants, such as *Telopea speciosissima*, respond well to hard pruning. This plant has been cut back to the base of the trunk.

Tip pruning, by pinching out growing shoots, is an effective way of keeping plants bushy.

(e) For the removal of diseased, dead or injured material, thus restricting the spread of unwanted diseases.

As with the fertilizing of Australian plants, there are many theories on whether plants should, or should not be pruned. In nature plants are regularly pruned by animals. The soft new growth of low species such as *Hibbertia empetrifolia* is enjoyed by kangaroos, wallabies, introduced rabbits etc., thus producing a dense ground-cover, whereas in a garden this *Hibbertia* is bushy, and can act as a climber if in contact with other shrubs. Many eucalypts are pruned by members of the parrot family as they gather seed from branchlets. As a general rule, most Australian species will tolerate pruning, with some responding extremely well.

When pruning, the cut should be just above a bud, a side branch, or a main branch that is pointing outwards from the centre of the plant. This rule may need to be varied if it is necessary to prune a plant to a particular shape.

The best and most reliable pruning method is to tip-prune. It is also the simplest method. This can be done regularly, when the plant is small, by simply pinching out the tips or terminal buds, between thumb and forefinger. The result is a bushy plant that may not need pruning later in its life. This method is highly recommended for shrubs of all sizes.

Time of Pruning

Apart from tip-pruning, which can be done at any time, the recommended time for pruning is after flowering has finished, because there is less likelihood of removing the developing flower buds. This is usually a period when plants are very active, with new growth being produced. If desired, plants may also be cut whilst in flower, to provide flowers for indoor decoration. This

Selection and Cultivation

practice is regularly used with popular cut flowers such as *Boronia megastigma*, and *Thryptomene calycina*.

Pruning to a natural or desired shape.

The natural shape of a plant may be destroyed by indiscriminant pruning. A mark of good pruning is if the plant has retained its basic shape, and there are no readily visible signs of pruning. It is very easy to cut all the growth in a horizontal plane, but it also leaves a jarring sight. With a little more time and care, a much more pleasing plant can result.

On some occasions it is necessary to prune to shape, to improve the visual quality of the plant. The lower branches of small trees can be gradually removed, to produce a canopied plant that can be easily walked under. Attractive trunks can be accentuated by the removal of side branches whilst plants are young. An attractive feature of many of our Australian plants is their tendency to produce multiple trunks, eg. eucalypts and angophoras. By selective pruning the strongest trunks only need be retained.

There is often the need for thinning out of growth to allow light to reach lower growing species. The pruning of lateral growth on some tall shrubs, or trees, will allow more sun to penetrate gardens or buildings in winter, but because of the canopy, there will be shade in summer. Pathways, narrow garden beds, and building features are some of the other aspects which can lead to plants being pruned to a particular shape. Careful initial selection of plant species will minimise the need for such pruning, and conversely, large-growing species poorly positioned into areas of limited size will need regular attention.

Similar care in regard to the shape of plants should be exercised when collecting material for propagation by cuttings. Basic principles of good pruning should be adhered to, in order that the plant might benefit, rather than being impaired by indiscriminative cutting.

To enhance and strengthen trunks of young trees, it is advisable to progressively shorten side branches.

Lower branches can be removed from trees, to highlight a trunk or allow access.

Cut here

Before

After

Strengthening of Plants

Sometimes plants can grow very vigorously, producing top growth that is too heavy for the trunk to support. They can be damaged by wind or the weight of water on leaves and flowers. In this situation, branches can be shortened, and this pruning will help to produce stronger trunk and branches. In the pruning of specific forms such as weeping plants, care must be exercised in order not to spoil the natural growth habit. Most eucalypt species can withstand very hard pruning, because of dormant buds maintained beneath the cambium layer.

Tree Surgery

This section is merely an introduction to tree surgery, and the following topics are discussed:
(a) Branch removal (for safety or aesthetic reasons, or due to insect or fungal attack).
(b) The treatment of physical injury to trunks, or branches.
(c) The treatment of cavities.

(a) Branch removal

Three simple steps will save irreparable damage from occurring to the plant:
(i) A light cut just into the outer wood should be made on the underside, about 30 cm

84

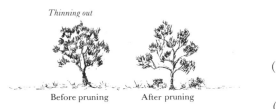

Thinning out

Before pruning   After pruning

Dense plants can be opened up by strategic pruning to allow light to reach the ground.

from the trunk, to prevent the bark stripping when the severing cut is made.

(ii) The severing cut should be made on the upper part, about 5-10 cm beyond the undercut. If the work is in a limited area, where falling branches could cause damage to buildings, plants or people, the piece to be cut must be secured tightly with a rope, to the trunk or a strong branch. It can then be lowered safely after cutting.

With large branches, the above two points are carried out in succession, from the outer growth first.

(iii) The flush cut should be made as near to the trunk or bark as possible, following the contour. A wood sealant is then applied. At all times, cuts must be made to allow for water run off, otherwise decay can start, and cavities will be formed.

(b) Treatment of Physical Injury to Trunks or Branches

Trees can suffer damage from climatic conditions, or receive injuries caused by animals, a wide range of mechanical equipment from lawn mowers to motor vehicles, or numerous other means. Treatment is best done immediately, to enable quick healing of the wound to commence.

(i) All damaged material should be removed until healthy bark and wood is reached. The sides and top of the wound should be cut at right angles to the trunk or branch. The lower cut should be sloped slightly to allow for run-off of moisture. Moisture should not be allowed to lie in a cavity, as it will stimulate decay of the wood.

(ii) Remove excess woodchips or sawdust, by

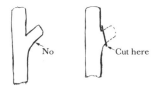

No   Cut here

When pruning, do not leave stubs, always trim flush to a branch or trunk.

hosing with a strong stream of water. This will also moisten the bark and exposed wood, and allow for better coverage and adhesion of the wood sealant.

(iii) Apply a heavy coating of wood sealant, paying special attention to the bark-wood junctions.

(iv) Healthy, vigorous trees should quickly produce good callus growth, whereas unhealthy trees might respond to application of a complete fertilizer, to promote better growth.

(v) If the original injury was large, and/or callusing is slow, a slight cutting of the callus, and repetition of steps (ii) to (iv) will usually promote quicker growth.

In addition to being responsible often for broken branches or trunks, strong winds can cause young trees to become loose in the ground. For the procedure in relation to injury of this nature, see Climatic Conditions — Wind page 52.

(c) The Treatment of Cavities

Cavities form in plants due to the entry of wood rotting organisms. Often cavities eventuate from ill-treatment of a previous cutting or branch-removal program. On other occasions it can be from build up of organic material in the trunk and branch forks. The effect of cavities is to reduce the strength of trunks and branches, and they should be treated immediately they are noticed. If cavities extend a long way it could mean that treatment would render the branch or trunk unsafe, in which case they should be removed. If the cavity can be readily treated, the following steps should be followed:

(i) Remove all debris and decayed or dead material, until healthy wood is revealed. In a deep cavity the introduction of a drainage hole, using plastic pipe, is beneficial, to remove any moisture which may enter the cavity. Woodchips and sawdust can be flushed out with water from a hose.

(ii) Leave to dry.

(iii) The application of a fungicide or wood preservative will help to prevent spread of disease organisms.

(iv) Allow to dry.

(v) Apply wood sealant liberally, to inner surface, making sure all parts are covered.

If the cavity is large, the following action may be necessary:

(vi) Fill cavity with suitable material (see below for list of materials), allowing for free run-off of water.

(vii) Apply wood sealant to filler and bark,

Reducing excessive top growth helps strengthen slender trunk.

After pruning.

Example of correct pruning.
Branch has been removed, flush with trunk, to allow quick healing. Wound should be sealed with a protective compound.

making sure that the filler-bark junction is properly covered.

(viii) Periodic inspection is recommended, to check callus growth and/or deterioration of filling materials.

Suitable filling materials:

(i) A mixture of wood sealant and sterilized sand is recommended. This has the property of being able to expand and shrink if needed. It is also easy to remove in the event of further treatment to the cavity becoming necessary.

(ii) Mortar or concrete. This is relatively cheap, but its main disadvantage is the difficulty of removing the filling for inspection of the cavity.

(iii) Rigid foam fillers, such as polyurethane and urethane types. This technique is not widely used at present. The material is supplied as two liquids, and when they are mixed, a chemical reaction takes place to form a rigid foam. It has been found with polyurethane that moisture can penetrate between the foam and the bark as it retracts.

Examples of incorrect pruning.
The stubs should have been cut flush, where marked, to allow quick healing, and prevent disease entry.

Incorrect pruning. This trunk should have been removed where indicated.

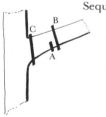

Sequence of branch removal
A — Undercut to prevent bark tearing.
B — Cut through branch to remove weight.
C — Final cut, flush with trunk to allow wound to heal quickly.

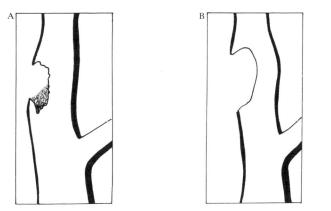 

Sequence of cavity treatment.   A. Cavity before treatment, filled with debris.
B. After removal of debris and trimmed of dead wood to allow drainage of water.
C. With large cavity it may be necessary to use a filling material.

Weeding

It is advisable to remove all weeds when they are small, and before they have had the opportunity to set seed or spread by underground rhizomes. The main reason for weeding is to reduce competition, particularly for water, between the weeds (which are generally more efficient) and the plants being grown. The absence of weeds allows stronger and quicker growth of the plants being established.

There are annual and also perennial weeds. The greatest competition comes from perennials such as the creeping types, and large vigorous annuals which smother weak or small plants. It is highly desirable that these be eliminated or controlled before any planting occurs.

To reduce time spent on weeding, it is often wise for the home gardener to develop small areas at a time. This will enable most weeds to be controlled until ground covering shrubs are large enough to help prevent germination of weed seeds. Any areas not being planted should be mown or otherwise maintained, to avoid weeds or grasses maturing, to spread seeds into nearby garden areas.

There are several methods of weed control, including

    (a) manual,
    (b) mechanical,
    (c) chemical,
    (d) mulching.

(a) Manual

This involves hand-weeding, or light cultivation with a hand-hoe or fork. With this method there is less likelihood of damage occurring to plants, but there is a need for care if using digging tools. Spades are not recommended. Make sure roots of plants are not damaged, as disease can enter the wound. If main roots are completely severed, this can affect the stability of the plant during heavy winds, and it may blow over. Particular care should be exercised when cultivating under plants of the family Proteaceae, because their root systems are developed right to the soil surface.

(b) Mechanical

Machines such as rotary hoes can be useful in large areas such as public gardens, roadsides, farms etc. If the weed problem involves species which are spread by underground rhizomes or bulbs, the rotary hoe can be detrimental, by helping to spread the weed. Rotary hoes should not be used close to established plants, as they destroy any surface roots, and generally reduce the plants' feeding area.

(c) Chemical

There are numerous chemical sprays (herbicides) available for weed control, and some of these are very selective as to the species they will kill. Caution should be exercised, as some will sterilise the soil for extended periods, and can be very harmful to existing plants. Always make sure before using any herbicide, what effect it will have on soil or plants. There are some compounds available that will break down on contact with the soil, and only kill foliage that they contact. These are very suitable for the control of weed species in areas already planted. There must be no contact with the foliage, young branches, or green trunks of plants other than the weeds.

Herbicides can be toxic to the handler, and should be used carefully. (See Spraying Rules, page 137.)

Selection and Cultivation

(d) Mulching

Mulching can play a very important role in the control of weeds within a garden area. There are a number of different mulching materials which may be used, and the subject is discussed in detail at the beginning of this section. (See page 79.)

Renovating and Replanting

In any type of garden, there is always the need for renovation and replanting. This may be caused by changes in attitudes or needs, but also plants become old, unthrifty or diseased, and may even die. It is often difficult to grow new plants amongst older established plants. This is especially so if the existing plants are old and include some tall trees which produce a high degree of shade, and the extensive root systems maintain a level of dryness in the soil.

Some points worth consideration are as follows —

(a) Undertake a pruning program to increase the light available in areas to be renovated.

(b) Thoroughly prepare soils as described under Soil Preparation, page 65. In particular, remove all roots and root pieces belonging to plants that were removed. Slow release fertilizers such as blood and bone are very beneficial, as the soils may be exhausted of nutrients. Lime may be of benefit in correcting pH, and killing off some pests. The introduction of rotted organic matter such as compost will also improve the soil texture.

(c) A very careful selection of plant species is recommended. Not all species will be suitable, and if in doubt, choose the hardy types, especially if the area is relatively shady and dry.

(d) After planting, a constant vigil will be needed to make sure that the new plants do not dry out, because they must grow in an area with competition from many other roots. Regular watering could be needed for 6-12 months, until the new plants are established.

(e) Side dressings of blood and bone at 6 monthly intervals will ensure that new plants survive the competition, and become established.

The Changing of Soil Level around Existing Plants

To alter the soil level around plants can often retard the growth and eventually lead to the plant's death. Unless it is absolutely necessary, this practice is not recommended.

Building up Soil Level

The most common occurrence is to build up soil levels. If this is done completely around a plant, the added soil will cut off the air supply to

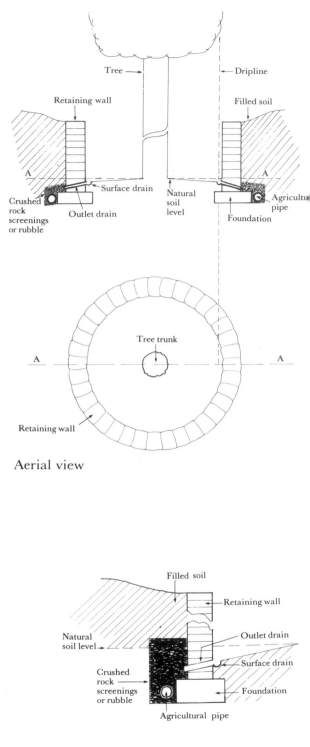

Aerial view

Technique of raising soil level around existing trees.

A pleasing combination of small trees, tussock plants, and water.

the plant's roots. Building up of soil on one side will give the plant more chance of survival.

The following course of action can be helpful, if the siting allows for its use.

(a) Construct a retaining wall, at a distance from the trunk, of about one-third of the tree's foliage diameter.

(b) Provide adequate drainage behind the wall.

Lowering Soil Level

The majority of nutrients are taken up by the

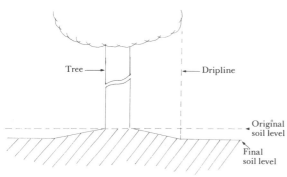

Lowering soil level around a tree.

feeder roots, which are situated in the top metre of soil. To remove this soil and the roots will drastically affect the plant's growth. If removal is necessary the following steps may help to maintain healthy growth.

(a) It is best to grade the soil on a gentle slope away from the trunk to outside the drip line. This will limit the amount of damage to the main root system. A light top dressing of soil to cover any exposed roots will help to re-establish feeder roots.

(b) It is beneficial if the original soil level can be maintained for at least half, but preferably the full diameter of the tree's foliage, by constructing retaining walls that are slightly higher than the new soil level. This helps to act as a water catchment too, as the soil around the trunk will now dry out more quickly because of its elevation from the surrounding soil level.

Any large roots that are broken or damaged during construction must be treated. Ensure that the cuts are clean, and then coated with a wood sealant. Applications of a slow release fertilizer, and/or injection of a root stimulant and slow release fertilizer, would be beneficial. The reduction of the canopy growth will also help to balance the loss of any roots.

Transplanting

Established specimens of Australian plants are not commonly transplanted, but there has been

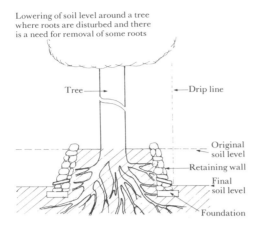

Lowering of soil level around a tree
where roots are disturbed and there
is a need for removal of some roots

Tree

Drip line

Original
soil level

Retaining wall

Final
soil level

Foundation

A retaining wall with adequate drainage should be constructed when lowering soil level around an existing tree.

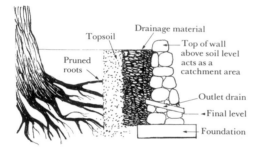

Drainage material

Topsoil

Top of wall
above soil level
acts as a
catchment area

Pruned
roots

Outlet drain

Final level

Foundation

Detail of wall construction.

some success with species in genera such as *Acmena*, *Agonis*, *Bauera*, *Boronia*, *Brachychiton*, *Callistemon*, *Calytrix*, *Casuarina*, *Eriostemon*, *Erythrina*, *Ficus*, *Kunzea*, *Melaleuca*, *Schefflera*, *Syzygium*, *Tristania*, *Verticordia* and *Xanthorrhoea*.

Some nurseries have traditionally grown Australian species in the open ground, to obtain uniform growth and faster development. The plants are generally grown in the ground for 6-24 months before being lifted and potted or balled for sale. This practice is not so common nowadays, but was popular from about 1900 to 1950, with species such as *Bauera rubioides*, *B. sessiliflora*, *Boronia denticulata*, *B. heterophylla*, *B. megastigma*, *Eriostemon myoporoides*, and *Thryptomene calycina*.

Some species of eucalypts are grown in the U.S.A. and sold as advanced plants 5-8 m high. These are grown in the open ground for 2-3 years, and the root system is trenched at regular intervals (about every 3 months) to encourage a compact, fibrous root system. Trenching consists of digging a circular trench a certain distance from the trunk, to cut all roots and encourage them to branch. The trench is refilled with soil after the roots are cut. When large enough the plants are lifted and balled, or sold in large containers. This technique is successfully used on *Eucalyptus sideroxylon*, *E. citriodora* and *E. globulus*.

There is sophisticated machinery available now, capable of transplanting large trees, and there is no reason to believe that more Australian plant species could not be successfully transplanted. The transplanting of *Ceratopetalum gummiferum* trees, over 6 m tall, has been successful, and in a recent test of large machinery on the Gold Coast in southern Qld, 47 out of 50 *Melaleuca leucadendron*, between 3 and 6 m tall, were successfully transplanted.

It is not advisable to carry out transplanting operations during hot weather. Select a cool time of year, when plants are not growing vigorously, or are dormant but are about to break into growth.

Transplanting method

In any transplanting there must be adequate preparation of the specimen to be removed. Below are recommended steps, the first of which can be started as early as 3-6 months before the projected transplanting.

(a) Sever the roots by cutting vertically with a sharp spade in a circle around the trunk. The diameter of the circle will depend largely on the type of plant, whether it is a tree or shrub, and its size. The diameter can also be reduced if there are no large roots to be cut. With shrubs, it is good to initially cut the roots near the drip line of the foliage. If no large roots are encountered, cutting closer to the trunk can be executed. This will make the final removal much easier, because of the reduced soil weight. By cutting the roots 3-6 months in advance, or as early as possible from the projected transplanting time, this will promote a dense system of fibrous roots that will be able to support the plant after removal. The removal of some branches and foliage at this time is recommended, to reduce strain upon the reduced root system. After cutting, plants can also be watered with a root stimulant. This can be repeated at intervals prior to removal.

(b) 4-7 days before removal, soak the plant thoroughly with water containing a root stimulant.

(c) 3 days before removal, dig a trench, with the original cutting operation of 3-6 months ago being the outside wall of the root ball. Make the trench wide enough for easy digging.

Sequence of transplanting large shrubs or trees.

(i) If the plant is small and easily handled, it can be lifted out carefully.

(d) If the roots on exposed ball are not large, more soil and roots can be removed, making sure to not remove large roots which are important to the plant, and will be necessary to enable it to survive the process of transplanting.

(e) The removal of soft tip growth and some branches at this stage will help to reduce the strain on the root system after transplanting. Large trees may have to be pollarded back heavily.

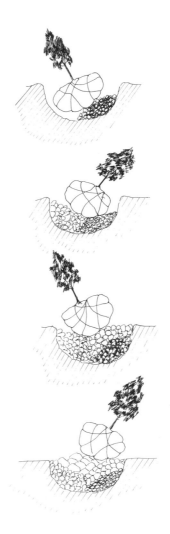

(f) Cut under plant to halfway, at a depth to avoid the cutting of large roots. Make room to fit hessian or similar material under plant.

(g) Put rolled hessian under the cut side, so that when the other side is cut, the plant can be placed onto the hessian and the excess roll can be pulled underneath the recently cut side.

(j) With large plants, machines can be used if available, otherwise a method such as the following can be employed. Gradually place a small amount of soil underneath one side of the balled plant, roll it carefully onto the soil. Place soil underneath the other side, and continue the process until at ground level, when the plant can be placed on a low wheeled trailer or trolley, for easy removal. Take care to not damage the soil ball at any stage.

(h) Hessian should then be tied tightly around the soil ball, to prevent the breaking away of soil.

Selection and Cultivation

(k) The soil into which the plant will be placed should be well prepared. (See page 74.) Place the plant in the hole then remove the hessian and string from soil ball, by rolling the ball carefully first to one side then the other. For further details on this aspect of transplanting, see Planting Instructions, page 74.

(l) If the plant is in a windy situation, a stake should be placed on the windward side, making sure to not damage any roots. If trees are large, they must be supported by guys from 3-4 points. It is most important to make sure that allowance is made for movement of the upper trunk and stems, as this will eliminate the need for permanent stakes or guys.

(m) Water thoroughly. The inclusion of a root stimulant can help when watering.

Aftercare

(a) If any subsidence of soil occurs, refill, and water further.

(b) Carefully maintain moisture content of soil, so it is not waterlogged, but just moist. Waterlogging can result in the plant's death, as it reduces the air availability, which the roots need in order to grow.

When transplanting *Cyathea australis*, a good portion of the root system must be retained. The stump on the right hand side has little chance of survival. (The Soft Tree-fern — *Dicksonia antarctica*, can be transplanted in similar manner to the trunk on the right-hand-side.)

(c) Regular watering of foliage is also beneficial, as it keeps the leaves cool, and thus reduces transpiration.

Transplanting Plants with Lignotubers

Limited success has been gained in transplanting young plants, and in some cases well-developed plants that have developed lignotubers. (See Plant Features, page 61.) Species include *Banksia dentata*, *B. spinulosa*, *Eucalyptus ptychocarpa*, *Stephania japonica* and *Verticordia grandis*. The top growth is removed to just above the lignotuber, and the roots are cut below it. Probably the best procedure is to re-establish the plants in containers, where growing conditions can be more readily controlled than if they were replanted into the ground immediately.

Staking

Staking is usually not necessary if healthy young plants are being planted, and it is rarely needed for established trees and shrubs. Some movement of a plant's trunk is necessary for strengthening, and staking should never completely immobilize a plant. There are however, circumstances in which staking can add support to trunks, and be beneficial to the growth of plants.

1. When planting is undertaken in extremely windy areas.

Example of poor staking and tying.
Stake should not be placed on leeward side of prevailing wind.

Example of poor staking and tying — tying too close to trunk, and tie too tight.

Example of correct staking and tying.

Use of these wire twitches to support the trunks has caused considerable damage, and provides entry points for pests and diseases.

2. When large container-grown trees or shrubs are being planted, or if established plants are being transplanted.
3. If established plants become top-heavy. This can result from unbalanced use of fertilizers, or because roots have continued to coil, due to lack of attention to this aspect at the time of planting.
4. When a hole has been created at the base of a trunk due to constant movement of the upper growth, caused by excessive wind. This situation occurs mainly in wet soils.
5. If protection from prevailing winds is suddenly removed, (eg. building, fence, or other screening plants).

Suitable Staking Materials
   Stakes: These should be strong, and able to withstand lengthy periods in the ground without rotting, eg. good quality hardwood, or metal star pickets. If the stakes have been used previously, soaking in a disinfectant to remove any disease is recommended.
   Ties: Broad, long-lasting material that will not damage the bark should be used. Never use wire or thin string, unless these have been threaded through plastic water hose or a similar material. (See Illustration — Guying of a recently transplanted tree, page 92.)

Staking Procedures
1. Always place the stake on the windward side of a plant. There is less chance of abrasion to the plant's trunk.
2. Do not place the stake too close to the trunk, as main roots may be damaged (See also Planting, page 75).

The informality of garden settings using Australian plants.

3. When tying, allow for some trunk movement, in order that the plant does not become reliant on the stake. Rigidly tied plants often collapse after removal of ties.
4. Check ties regularly. Make sure they do not penetrate the bark, (see photograph) which can lead to ring-barking or weakening of the trunk. In strong winds, trunks can snap off at the weakened area.
5. Removal of ties. A gradual loosening of ties before complete removal is recommended, so that the plant is able to adjust to its lack of support.

Multiple Staking

With large shrubs or trees, 2 to 4 stakes may be needed to offer adequate support. Care must be taken when tying, to not allow the trunk to come in contact with the stakes. Wire guys fastened to short stakes are also very useful for large trees. The provision of a protective covering for the wire is imperative. (See Transplanting, page 90.)

Small Stakes

Short, small stakes, are very useful, and several can be placed in the ground amongst the foliage, to provide support for small and brittle shrubs, eg. *Hibbertia stellaris*, *Lechenaultia biloba*, and *L. formosa*. Suitable materials are bamboo or light twigs.

The Use of Boulders as an alternative to staking

Large boulders can be used as anchors, to help stabilize fast growing plants. This method is gaining rapidly in popularity. Plants such as *Eucalyptus caesia* and *Hakea laurina*, have been successfully treated in this manner.

It is best to incorporate the boulders below, or just above ground level, at the planting stage. Established plants can be treated, if care is exercised when placing the boulders near the roots. Interesting rock outcrops can be created in addition to providing support for the plant.

8 Plant Nutrition

PLANT NUTRITION

Plants extract different elements from the soil in order that they can grow, flower and produce fruit. Most of these elements are essential for normal plant growth. Some elements are required in large quantities and are known as the major elements, while others are required in small quantities and are known as the minor or trace elements. Both types of elements are listed in the accompanying table.

Major Elements	*Minor Elements*
Nitrogen	Iron
Phosphorus	Manganese
Potassium	Boron
Magnesium	Zinc
Calcium	Copper
Sulphur	Molybdenum
	Chlorine
	Cobalt

Most elements are generally available from soils in sufficient quantities for normal plant growth. Soil reserves, however, may be depleted by cropping or leaching following heavy rains and it is often necessary to build up the reserves again by the addition of organic materials and fertilizers. The absence of an element from soil or its tie-up by soil factors affects the growth of plants and causes symptoms of deficiency (for the various symptoms see page 177).

Plants take up nutrients as they are available to them from soils. The nutrients interact within the plant and an imbalance can upset the plants' growth. Plants grow better if a balance of nutrients is available to them in the soil rather than if there is an excess of one particular element.

Soil pH

The pH unit is a logarithmic function of the concentration of hydrogen ions in the soil. Put more simply it is a measure of the acidity or alkalinity of a soil. The pH scale ranges from 0-14 with 7 being neutral, 14 very alkaline and 1 very acid. Soils commonly range from pH 4 to 9. The accompanying figure illustrates the pH scale.

The measure of pH in a soil is of critical importance to plant growers for 3 reasons:

(1) Plants have pH preferences, some being suited to grow in acid soils, whereas others prefer alkaline soils. Some plants have a very narrow pH tolerance whilst others grow in a wider range.

(2) Extremes of pH can indicate a deficiency or excess of some of the major elements. In very acid soils phosphorus and molybdenum can become deficient whereas in alkaline soils sodium or calcium is probably in excess.

(3) Interactions occur among the major elements and the trace elements and soil pH. Thus, under very acid conditions aluminium and manganese may reach levels which are poisonous to plants. Similarly under very alkaline conditions trace elements such as iron and zinc may be immobilized to the extent that plants cannot obtain sufficient supplies for normal healthy growth.

THE SOIL pH SCALE

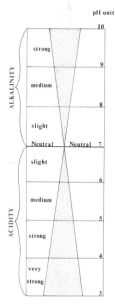

pH unit

ALKALINITY
strong — 10 — 9
medium — 8
slight
Neutral   Neutral 7
slight
ACIDITY
medium — 6 — 5
strong — 4
very strong — 3

Selection and Cultivation

The optimum soil pH at which most plants like to grow is in the range 6-6.5.

Details of each Element

The various elements used by plants are important for the structure and day-to-day chemical reactions. Some elements have a variety of roles to fill while others are very specific.

Nitrogen

This element is important in the formation of chlorophyll which is the green pigment in leaves, etc., essential for photosynthesis. It is also used in the formation of amino acids which are the building blocks of proteins. Nitrogen encourages vegetative growth and produces a lush greenness in foliage. If used in excess it can have some detrimental side effects such as delaying flowering and maturity, weakening the strength of stems and increasing the plants' susceptibility to some diseases.

Fertilizers: a large range of nitrogen fertilizers can be used and the selection of one depends on price and the speed at which the nitrogen is made available to the plants. Commonly used fertilizers are listed in the accompanying table. (See also Legumes, page 73.)

Informal paths incorporated into a natural bush setting.

Fertilizer	% nitrogen	Avail- ability	Application rate kg/10 square metres	Comments
Blood and Bone	7	slow	1-1.5	slow release
Hoof and Horn	12-14	slow	1-1.5	slow release
Dried Blood	12-13	slow	1-1.5	slow release
Ammonium nitrate	35	rapid	0.25	rapidly available
Calcium nitrate	15	rapid	0.5	rapidly available
Ammonium sulphate	20	rapid	0.5	acidifies soil
Potassium nitrate	13	rapid	0.5	also supplies potassium
Sodium nitrate	15	rapid	0.5	useful in winter
Urea	46	rapid	0.15	use carefully

Phosphorus

This element plays an important role in the storage and use of energy in chemical reactions such as are involved in respiration and photosynthesis. It is also particularly important for the development of flowers, fruits and seeds and in root development and the strengthening of stems.

Fertilizers: superphosphate is the most commonly applied form of phosphorus fertilizer. It contains 9% phosphorus. Triple superphosphate is a concentrated form which contains 19-20% phosphorus. Monocalcium phosphate is expensive but is very soluble and useful where rapid applications are needed. Phosphate fertilizers work best if finely ground. Blood and bone, and hoof and horn manures are also rich in phosphorus.

Application Rates: superphosphate can be applied at 0.3-1 kg/10 square metres. Triple superphosphate should be applied at about one third the rate. Some native plants are sensitive to excess quantities of phosphorus (see page 179).

Potassium

This is essential for the production and transport of carbohydrates in plants especially starch. It strengthens plants and builds up their resistance to disease. It is also important in chlorophyll formation, respiration, flowering and root development.

Fertilizers: the commonest fertilizers used are potassium chloride which is also called muriate of potash, potassium sulphate and potassium nitrate which also supplies nitrogen. Potassium is also found in seaweed (25%) and ashes (3-10%).

Application Rates: potassium sulphate and potassium chloride can be safely applied to soil at the rate of 50-100 g per 10 square metres.

Calcium

This element is important for the structure of cell walls and proteins, and in the formation of flowers and in a number of chemical reactions. It is also very important for healthy root growth.

Fertilizers: calcium can be applied to the soil as lime (also known as ground limestone or calcium carbonate), slaked lime (or calcium hydroxide), gypsum (or calcium sulphate) and dolomite (a mixture of calcium and magnesium carbonate). All except gypsum raise the pH of soils (see page 95).

Application Rates: the rates will vary depending on the pH and the soil type. Responses should be obtained after applications of 1-3 kg per 10 square metres.

Magnesium

Magnesium is an important constituent of chlorophyll and photosynthesis. It is also related to the use of phosphorus in the plant.

Fertilizers: magnesium can be supplied as magnesium sulphate (Epsom Salts), magnesium carbonate or dolomite (a mixture of calcium and magnesium carbonate). The last 2 compounds raise the soil pH while magnesium sulphate has a negligible effect.

Application Rates: magnesium sulphate is commonly applied at 50 g per 10 square metres.

Sulphur

Sulphur is a constituent of many important chemicals such as amino acids. It is also important for chlorophyll synthesis and in the formation of roots.

Fertilizers: sulphur is present as a constituent of many fertilizers and is usually not applied intentionally, eg. the sulphate forms of magnesium, potassium and calcium.

Application Rates: gypsum at 1-3 kg per 10 square metres should supply most sulphur requirements.

Iron

Iron is necessary for the proteins used in chlorophyll synthesis and in enzymes. It is needed in continuous small quantities.

Fertilizers: the fertilizer used depends on the soil pH. Ferric sulphate is used if the soil pH is between 5 and 6, ferrous sulphate if between 6 and 7 and iron chelates if the pH is above 7.

Application Rates: the sulphates are commonly applied at the rate of 0.5 kg per 10 square metres. The chelates are applied to the soil around the plant at rates of 50-200 g per plant depending on its size.

Manganese

This element is required for the function of important enzyme systems concerned with oxidation and the formation of sugars and chlorophyll. It is concentrated in green tissue and also has an important interaction on the solubility of iron.

Fertilizers: manganese sulphate is commonly used. The best soil pH for manganese availability is about 6.5.

Application Rates: commonly applied at the rate of 50-150 g per 10 square metres.

Boron

This element is important in actively growing areas such as stem and root tips. It is important in protein synthesis in plants and is related to the use of calcium and potassium.

Fertilizers: borax or boric acid.

Application Rates: 2-4 g per 10 square metres.

Copper

This element is required in small quantities for the function of important enzyme systems. It is concentrated in green leaves.

Fertilizers: copper sulphate is mainly used.

Application Rates: 12 g per 10 square metres.

Molybdenum

Molybdenum is needed for the formation of nodules in legumes and in enzymes used in nitrogen nutrition.

Fertilizers: sodium molybdate.

Application Rates: 1 g per 10 square metres.

Types of Fertilizers

Organic Fertilizers

These are composed of organic waste materials such as blood, blood and bone, bone meal, hoof and horn, etc. They were once very commonly available but are now becoming less readily available and more expensive. They release their nutrients slowly for plant growth

Fertilizers: 1 Superphosphate; 2 Lime;
3 Blood and Bone; 4 Potassium sulphate;
5 Ammonium nitrate; 6 Urea.

growth or low nitrogen, high phosphorus and potassium for flowering and fruiting.

Complete fertilizers are very useful as maintenance dressings for established plants. They are usually readily soluble and supply nutrients quickly to plants.

Slow Release Fertilizers

These are manufactured chemicals which only release their nutrients for plant growth slowly. They are prepared either by using only very slowly soluble chemicals or by coating mixtures of soluble compounds with slowly soluble materials such as polymers or sulphur compounds. Most are granular pellets but some are large lumps and others have been compressed into pills and tablets. They are an excellent means of supplying nutrients but must not be applied too heavily and are best scattered rather than applied in concentrations. Some slow release fertilizers only supply nitrogen while others supply nitrogen, phosphorus and potassium.

and in general are ideal for application at planting or as a maintenance dressing. Details of the nutrients supplied by some commonly used organic fertilizers are shown in the accompanying table.

Constituents of Commonly Used Organic Fertilizers:

	% Nitrogen	% Phosphorus	% Calcium
Dried Blood	12-13		
Blood and Bone	4-7	4-7.5	5
Bone Meal	2-4	2-5	3-5
Hoof and Horn	12-14	1-2	3-5

Inorganic Fertilizers

These are manufactured chemicals which supply one or more nutrients for plant growth. They are widely used in agriculture and horticulture and are a cheap means of supplying nutrients for plant growth. They are usually readily soluble and supply nutrients quickly to plants.

Complete Fertilizers

These are inorganic fertilizers which have been mixed together to supply different combinations of the nutrients needed for plant growth. Some complete fertilizers only supply nitrogen, phosphorus and potassium whereas others may supply all major and minor elements (see also page 96). It is possible to obtain complete fertilizers with different ratios of nutrients to be used for different purposes eg. high nitrogen, low phosphorus and potassium for

Four types of Slow Release Fertilizers.
1 Granular; 2 Polymer coated; 3 Urea-formaldehyde chip; 4 Coarse granular.

Liquid Fertilizers

Inorganic compounds that are very soluble in water can be applied in a liquid form. These can be specific chemicals applied to correct a deficiency (eg. calcium nitrate to supply nitrogen, potassium sulphate to supply potassium) or prepared mixtures which supply all major and minor elements for plant growth. Various commercial preparations are available all of which are fairly comparable. Liquid fertilizers are very useful for plants in containers or where a rapid response is needed for a plant in the ground, because the fertilizers are soluble and can be rapidly taken up by plant roots. Most fertilizers are made from inorganic materials but some organic preparations are also available.

Animal Manures

Animal manures are a good source of plant nutrients and are also rich in organic materials. Their use on problem soils before planting is very beneficial and greatly improves growth. On sandy soils they increase the water-holding capacity and on clay soils they help to aggregate the particles and improve drainage. Manures can also be used to make compost or as a top-dressing on established plants.

Manures must be used very carefully on native plants particularly when the manure is fresh since it can burn roots. Old or aged manure is much safer to use, especially as a top-dressing or if plants are to be planted soon after its application. If in doubt the manure should be stored in a heap for at least 6 months or used to make compost. Fresh manure should never be applied around the bases of trunks, as it can burn the bark and lead to the entry of disease organisms. Some manures (such as sheep manure) contain many grass and weed seeds and should be used with care or preferably composted first.

Manures vary in their chemical composition according to the animals from which they were obtained. They contain a minimum of 0.5% nitrogen, 0.25% phosphorus and 0.5% potassium. The composition of commonly encountered manures is shown in the accompanying table.

Manure	% nitrogen	% phosphorus	% potassium
Chicken	0.8-1.0	0.7-0.85	0.2-0.4
Sheep	0.8-0.9	0.3-0.4	0.8-1.0
Cow	0.5-0.6	0.1-0.2	0.4-0.5
Horse	0.6-0.8	0.1-0.3	0.4-0.6
Pig	0.5-0.6	0.3-0.4	0.3-0.4

This specimen of *Eucalyptus ficifolia* has been ruined by thoughtless pruning.

W.R. Elliot photo

Mechanical transplanting of an established plant of *Melaleuca quinquenervia.*

P.D. Jones photo

9 Cultivation of Container Grown Plants

CULTIVATION OF CONTAINER GROWN PLANTS

The scope for growing Australian plants in containers is very wide. There are many different types of containers, including pots, tubs, hanging baskets and planter boxes. A wide range of materials is used in their construction. Ceramics are amongst the most common, and are the longest lasting of all containers if treated with care. Many clay types are used, and containers can be glazed or unglazed. Concrete is useful in the construction of large containers. Long lasting woods such as river red gum, jarrah and cedar are ideal materials. Wood that has been chemically treated or preserved should not be used where the roots can come in contact with such materials. Hollowed logs are very suitable as containers. In this age where plastics are in common use, there are many types of plastic container to choose from. They can be rigid, flexible, or of the foam type.

Much of the knowledge regarding the cultivation of Australian plants in containers has been gained from nurseries, as nearly all Australian plants grown for sale are cultivated in containers.

A wide range of plant sizes, including large trees can be grown successfully in containers. An example is in a landscape construction, where there may not be enough soil to support large tree growth, so large containers are constructed in situ, filled with soil and then planted. Opposite to this example, there are bonsai specimens which are cultivated in very small containers.

Two or more plants can be grown in one container at the same time if desired. The combination of height, foliage and flower can be used most aesthetically.

Regardless of the type of container chosen, there will be a need for continued maintenance, for successful cultivation of the plants. Container grown plants involve a greater time spent on maintenance than do plants grown in the

Excellent examples of Bonsai, using Australian Plants by A. Ross Lloyd

Above *Leptospermum laevigatum*

W.R. Elliot photo

Below *Casuarina littoralis*

W.R. Elliot photo

101

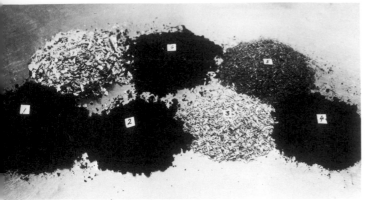

Organic Potting Materials
1 Peat Moss; 2 Sedge Peat; 3 Rice Hulls; 4 Brown Coal; 5 Sawdust; 6 Pine Bark; 7 Peanut Shells.

ground, but the reward is certainly worth while.

The range of species that can be cultivated is enormous, because with containers, great variation in growing conditions can be achieved. Excellent drainage can be provided, and growing conditions are easily regulated by watering and fertilizing. Climatic conditions can be varied if necessary, because the containers are readily moved to a suitable location.

Species that grow in sandy soils in low rainfall regions, require very well-drained conditions, and easily adapt to container cultivation, eg. *Darwinia*, *Hypocalymma*, *Lechenaultia*, and *Verticordia* spp. In areas of heavy clay-type soil, container-growing opens new horizons for Australian plant cultivation. There are also many orchids, ferns and palms that thrive when grown in containers. Suitable species for container growing are listed on page 291.

Potting Mixes

A growing medium that will produce healthy plants is of utmost importance whether the plants are for later planting out or for display purposes. Many materials have been tried for the growth of plants in containers and new materials are constantly being tested. Whatever materials are used, the potting mixture must supply a suitable anchorage for a plant and also encourage root and top growth by ensuring:

(1) adequate aeration (oxygen is important for root growth).

(2) that it holds sufficient water available to plants.

(3) that it holds adequate nutrients for plant growth.

(4) that it is free of any organisms that may be detrimental to the plant.

Potting mixtures are usually a combination of more than one material because it is difficult to find a single material which has all of the above features. Mixes are usually composed of soil, coarse sand and an organic material.

A useful and safe mixture which combines all of the above features is:

5 parts coarse washed sand
4 parts organic material
3 parts friable loam.

Potting Materials

Soils

Soil provides the capacity to hold moisture and nutrients available for plant growth. Only good quality topsoils rich in organic matter are suitable for use in potting mixes. Soils vary considerably in their drainage properties and some soils behave poorly when placed in a pot losing their structure and tending to set hard.

Soil Substitutes

A number of materials have properties similar to those of soil and can be used in potting mixes.

Brown Coal: this material has properties intermediate between soil and organic matter. The pH is about 6.0. Chunky samples of brown coal with a low percentage of dust are best to use. Brown coal should not be used in high proportions in mixtures as it is very easily overwatered.

Scoria: scoria is crushed basalt pumice which has properties very similar to soil. The most useful grade has particles less than 0.5 cm across. The pH varies from 7-10 and iron deficiency may result from this high pH. Scoria has proved to be a useful addition to potting mixes.

Sand: sand is added to potting mixes to provide drainage and aeration. Only coarse sands or gravels should be used as fine sands tend to pack and add little to a mix. Sands with angular particles are better than those with rounded particles. If the sand is dirty or contains weed seeds it should be washed before use.

Sand Substitutes

Inert coarse materials such as perlite or polystyrene balls or chips can be used as sand substitutes. They lighten the weight of a mixture but contribute little else except providing drainage and aeration.

Organic Materials

Organic materials are necessary in potting mixtures for their capacity to increase water retention and nutrient availability. A range of materials can be used successfully.

Peat Moss: this is the organic material most commonly used in potting mixes however it is becoming scarce and expensive. Good quality peat moss is derived from sphagnum moss bogs. These are scarce in Australia and high quality peat moss is all imported from Europe, Canada and New Zealand. Peat moss has a high water holding capacity and an acid pH (4.5-5.0). It is low in nutrients but has the ability to hold added nutrients in a form available for plant growth.

Sedge Peats: this is organic material derived from the accumulation of litter in swamps and bogs where rushes and sedges grow. There are extensive deposits in NSW and WA with smaller deposits in most states. Some samples may contain high quantities of salt and must be used with care. The pH is about 6.0 and the material contains about 1% nitrogen which is useful for plant growth.

Pine Bark: bark from pines grown for the softwood industry can be used successfully in potting mixtures after treatment. The bark is mainly available from 2 species of pine (*Pinus radiata* and *P. elliotii*) both of which have similar properties. Pine bark contains toxic materials when fresh and these toxins can stunt or kill roots. The toxins are easily removed by thoroughly wetting the bark and keeping it moist in a heap for about 6 weeks. The best size bark for potting mixes has particle sizes of 0.5 cm or less and the bark should be milled and sieved before it is wetted and aged in the heap. The pH of pine bark is initially about 5 but rises in time to about 6.5.

Sawdust: sawdust has excellent physical properties with good aeration and water holding capacity. It does however have many chemical problems and should be used with care. Fresh sawdust contains toxins which stunt or even kill roots. These are easily removed by thoroughly wetting the sawdust and keeping it moist in a heap for about 8 weeks. The quantity and type of toxins vary with the species from which the sawdust was cut.

Sawdust is extremely low in nitrogen and even ties up added nitrogen so that it is unavailable for plant growth. This can be somewhat offset by adding some nitrogenous fertilizer to the moist heap when the sawdust is being aged. Slow release fertilizers are useful in combination with potting mixtures containing sawdust. The pH of sawdust is about 4.5 and needs the addition of lime.

Rice Hulls: these are a waste product from the rice industry and are often used in potting mixes. They contribute very little having no water holding properties although they are useful for increasing aeration and lightening a mix.

Fertilizers in Potting Mixes

There is a popular belief that native plants as a group do not need or indeed may be killed by fertilizers. All plants in fact need nutrients for growth and if the plants are growing in artificial potting mixtures then the addition of fertilizers will be of considerable importance. The amount of fertilizer used is the critical factor and varies considerably with the species being grown. If in doubt it is a good policy to under-fertilize rather than over-fertilize a plant.

As a guide Australian plants can be roughly divided into two groups:

(1) those which respond to high levels of fertilizer. Plants in this group are generally found in high rainfall areas in such vegetation types as wet sclerophyll forest and rainforest. They have high nutrient requirements and respond well to the addition of fertilizers at normal levels.

A suitable fertilizer balance which could be added to a potting mixture for this type of plant would be as follows:

Fertilizers	per 12 shovels	per cubic metre
Ammonium nitrate	8 g	1.5 kg
Superphosphate	5-10 g	1-2 kg
Potassium sulphate	3 g	0.5 kg
Dolomite	5-10 g	1-2 kg
Iron sulphate	3 g	0.5 kg

(Note that 12 shovels can be made up easily on the 5:4:3 mix outlined under Potting Mixtures.)

Lime may be needed to adjust the pH of the potting mixture to 6. Trace elements can be added as a prepared mixture.

(2) those which resent high levels of fertilizers, especially high levels of phosphorus. Plants of this type are usually found in low rainfall areas on infertile soils of heathland or sandplain communities. Such plants generally require lower fertilizer levels than other commonly grown plants and species in the family Proteaceae are especially sensitive to high levels of phosphorus (see Phosphorus Excess page 179).

The sensitivity to phosphorus varies greatly with the species but a number of species in the following genera are affected: *Banksia, Grevillea, Hakea, Isopogon, Petrophile, Conospermum.* It is interesting to note that the less sensitive species in these genera are found in the higher rainfall areas.

A suitable fertilizer balance which could be added to a potting mixture for this type of plant would be as follows:

Fertilizers	per 12 shovels	per cubic metre
Ammonium nitrate	5 g	1 kg
Superphosphate	nil-3 g	nil-0.5 kg
Potassium sulphate	3 g	0.5 kg
Dolomite	5 g	1 kg
Iron sulphate	3 g	0.5 kg

(Note that 12 shovels can be made up easily on the 5:4:3 mix outlined under Potting Mixtures.)

Lime may be needed to adjust the pH of the potting mixture to 6.0. Trace elements can be added as a prepared mixture.

Slow Release Fertilizers

As the name suggests these fertilizers release their nutrients slowly and are extremely useful for maintaining plant growth. They can be substituted for some of the fertilizers mentioned in the previous paragraphs. They should not be used too heavily on potted plants or else they will promote excessive top growth at the expense of roots. Common rates for native plants are between 0.5-3 kg per cubic metre or 3-15 g per 12 shovels.

Some commonly-used organic fertilizers such as bone meal, hoof and horn, or blood and bone, act by releasing nutrients slowly, and are very useful in potting mixtures. Commonly used rates are 1-3 kg per cubic metre or 5-15 g per 12 shovels. It should be noted that the commonly-used blood and bone is high in phosphorus (7%) and can be responsible for phosphorus toxicity to sensitive species when used at excessive levels (for phosphorus-sensitive plants it should not be used at rates higher than 1.5 kg/cubic metre, 9 g/12 shovels).

Many slow release fertilizers are manufactured inorganically and act by being combined with insoluble chemicals or by being coated with slowly soluble chemicals such as plastic polymers or sulphur compounds. It is important to realize that some of these slow release fertilizers supply nitrogen only, while others supply nitrogen, phosphorus and potassium. Those containing phosphorus must be used carefully on species sensitive to phosphorus toxicity (at rates no higher than 1 kg/cubic metre; 5 g/12 shovels).

Liquid Fertilizers

Liquid fertilizers are very useful for maintaining growth in containers. They are also useful for stimulating growth because their nutrients are soluble and are rapidly taken up by plant roots. Various commercial preparations are available, all of which are fairly comparable. They should be used at regular intervals and diluted according to the recommendations on the label. For any plants that are sensitive to high levels of fertilizers it is advisable to apply liquid fertilizers at half or three quarters of normal strength.

Choice of Containers

Containers must be able to meet specific

Water containers gently, so as not to disperse growing medium.

Growing medium has shrunk due to drying. Water applied carelessly may run down side of container, without wetting the area of root system. The best policy is to soak container by immersion in a larger container of water, for a couple of hours.

requirements that will help to produce healthy, well-grown plants. These are listed below:

1. To have long lasting physical qualities.

2. To have adequate drainage holes, or be constructed of porous material.

3. To have suitable room for root development of the plant chosen. Repotting can be required, if plants become too large, so it is wise to use containers that enable the plant to be removed easily. Some containers available commercially have a neck which is smaller than the width elsewhere, thus making removal of the plant difficult. Careful selection of plant species will be necessary if such a container is to be used.

4. The container material should not have toxic properties. (See Treatment of Containers Before Potting.)

Trickle irrigation systems are an effective way of watering plants in containers.

Size of Containers

Container size depends very much on the species of plant chosen. Recommended minimum size would be 10 cm diameter, which would accommodate a small plant, e.g. *Brachycome multifida*, or *Stylidium graminifolium* for a season, but plants may then need repotting to a larger size.

Treatment of Containers before Potting

The following steps should prove beneficial for good plant growth.

1. Concrete containers can have a high pH, due to the lime content of the cement used in construction. This could adversely affect plant growth if not corrected before potting. The best method is to wash the container with a mixture of 1 part hydrochloric acid (spirits of salts) and 5 parts water. Then rinse the container thoroughly to remove the acid mixture.

2. If the container has been used previously, wash thoroughly with germicide or disinfectant. Rinse several times with water.

3. Leave to dry and air for 2-3 days.

4. If there is no detectable smell of germicide, it is ready for planting.

Planting

Planting procedures in regard to container-grown plants is the same as for potting on of cuttings or divisions. See page 233.

Watering

Container-grown plants have a need for constant moisture. The ideal is to not over-water, (especially if combined with regular fertilizing), as this promotes lush growth. A barely moist growing medium should be maintained. This allows for the hardening up of the foliage, and it will not wilt if the growing medium becomes slightly dry. Plants are therefore more likely to survive for a longer period if watering is not possible, or is neglected.

The potting mixture should be flushed with a good soaking about once a fortnight, to remove accumulated salts from fertilizers.

The introduction of a trickle irrigation system is fairly simple, and most suitable for watering containers, although it undoubtedly interferes with the aesthetics and can add inconvenience if the containers must be shifted. Such a system can be operated by hand or electrically, and details are available from state agricultural departments.

Fertilizing

If a repotting program is carried out regularly, there should not be a need for extensive fertilizing of containers. Application of a slow release fertilizer once or twice a year is usually suitable. Liquid fertilizers can be used in moderation, to give quick results if foliage becomes yellow. (See Fertilizers, page 97.)

Repotting

To gain maximum growth, and maintain healthy container-grown plants, repotting is necessary. This practice could be needed every 1-3 years, depending on the size of the container. In most cases it is advantageous to use a larger size container when repotting, although this is

Established plants in need of repotting.
LHS — *Boronia deanei* RHS — *Banksia aspleniifolia*.
Note clumps of proteoid roots on *Banksia*.

not absolutely necessary. Repotting is best done after a dormant growth period, when new roots are just being formed.

Repotting procedure:

1. Water plant thoroughly 12-24 hours before removal, a root stimulant can be included.

2. Remove plant carefully from container, without damaging main ball of roots.

3. Tease edges of ball to remove old or dead roots, and up to 1/3 of the existing soil. Thick roots must be cut with clean sharp secateurs.

4. Place fresh potting mix into the base of selected container.

5. Place the plant in container, and fill with fresh potting mix to desired level.

6. Water thoroughly. The addition of a root stimulant and fungicide is usually beneficial.

7. Place container and plant in a sheltered location for 3-10 days, to allow for re-establishment.

8. If new potting mix subsides, refill to level and water again.

3 Re-potting *Banksia aspleniifolia*.
Fill new container with soil mixture to a slightly higher level than finally desired, to allow for settling.

1 Lightly teasing root system when repotting *Banksia aspleniifolia*, to expose fresh young root growth.

2 Plant of *Banksia aspleniifolia*, ready for potting in new container. Note teased roots.

4 Firming growing medium around roots of re-potted *Banksia aspleniifolia*.

5 Knocking out a plant of *Dendrobium kingianum* to be re-potted.

6 Cutting a clump of *Dendrobium kingianum* in half.

9 Division of *Dendrobium kingianum*, potted up.

7 Trimming dead roots off a clump of *Dendrobium kingianum.*

8 Potting division of *Dendrobium kingianum.*

10 Plant of *Cymbidium madidum*, in need of repotting.

11 Plant of *Cymbidium madidum*, showing root system, broken down potting mixture, and weeds.

Selection and Cultivation

1 Removing old potting mixture from the roots of *Cymbidium madidum*.

2 Splitting a clump of *Cymbidium madidum* by dividing the rhizome.

3 Thinning out roots on division of *Cymbidium madidum*.

4 Trimming dead roots on division of *Cymbidium madidum*.

5 Placing the division of *Cymbidium madidum* in pot — note new shoot.
Suitable potting mix for epiphytes (ferns, tassell ferns, orchids etc.) — equal quantities of pine bark, charcoal, gravel.

6 Division of *Cymbidium madidum* potted up.

Permanent water is a very important aspect of attracting birds to gardens. *W.R. Elliot photo*

Anigozanthos flavidus is the hardiest of the Kangaroo Paws, and is freely visited by honey-eaters.

D.L. Jones photo

Banksia spinulosa is excellent for attracting honey-eating birds. *W.R. Elliot photo*

The flowers of the cultivar, *Grevillea* 'Robyn Gordon', provide nectar throughout the year. *D. L. Jones photo*

109

Grevillea hookerana makes a decorative container plant.

A healthy plant of *Dendrobium* × *delicatum*.

Cycads are ideal for containers — *Lepidozamia peroffskyana*.

Hanging Baskets

Some Australian plants are eminently suited to culture in hanging baskets, and can be a decorative addition to a home or glasshouse. Many different types of baskets can be used, but the two most common types are of galvanised wire lattice, or moulded plastic. The latter type has the advantage that it is ready to use immediately, as the wire baskets must be lined with moss, elkhorn peat, paperbark or some similar material to prevent the soil mixture from falling through. Baskets are also occasionally cut from tree fern trunk sections. These make excellent baskets as the roots of the plants can penetrate between the fibres. Hanging baskets made from ceramic material are also readily available, but sometimes drainage holes are inadequate. Some ceramic baskets, hand-made by potters are ideally suited for cultivation of Australian plants.

Baskets dry out rapidly, especially if hung in windy or sunny areas. Ideally baskets should only be used in protected areas, but if they must be exposed, then only hardy plants should be chosen. Baskets must be watered regularly, and if a well-drained potting mixture is used, they are almost impossible to overwater. If drying is a major problem the plant may have to be repotted into a mixture rich in well rotted organic material. A layer of moss or hessian on the soil surface will reduce evaporation and drying out. When planting baskets, the soil mixture should be pressed down to leave an adequate catchment of about 3 cm for watering. Basket plants respond to the occasional use of slow release or liquid fertilizers.

Native plants suitable for baskets include:

Aneilema acuminatum	Hardenbergia comptoniana
Arthropteris beckleri	Hibbertia dentata
tenella	Hoya australis
Billardiera cymosa	keysii
longiflora	rubida
scandens	macgillivrayii
Cissus antarctica	nicholsoniae
repens	Kennedia eximia
Dampiera diversifolia	prostrata
linearis	Lechenaultia formosa
rosmarinifolia	Lycopodium squarrosum
Davallia pyxidata	Microsorium diversifolium
solida	scandens
Dendrobium kingianum	Piper caninum
striolatum	mestonii
teretifolium	novae-hollandiae
Dischidia nummularia	rothianum
ovata	
Fieldia australis	
Goniophlebium subauriculatum	

Cyathea cooperi is a hardy fern for a container.

Hollowed sections of dead tree-fern trunk make ideal containers for some plants. A fine specimen of *Asplenium simplicifrons*.

Dendrobium kingianum

Rhododendron lochae

Agapetes meiniana

Pyrrosia adnascens, growing well.

Selection and Cultivation

Asplenium bulbiferum — well suited to a hanging basket.

Arthropteris beckleri in a tree-fern basket.

Pyrrosia rupestris is a hardy fern for a wire basket.

An unusual method of growing in the elkhorn (*Platycerium bifurcatum*) on a terracotta pot. The clump will eventually envelop the pot.

A handsome specimen of *Lycopodium squarrosum* in a wire hanging basket.

Lycopodium phlegmaroides, Layered Tassell fern, in a wire basket filled with staghorn peat.

Fieldia australis is an epiphyte found in shady moist gullies, and is suited to culture in a terrarium.

Terraria

The use of terraria for indoor decorations in homes and offices has become very popular. Once established they are self contained and if set up properly require little maintenance. Some species of native plants are suitable for terraria although because of the high humidity the number of species that can be used is limited.

Any good potting mixture can be used for plants in a terrarium although if it contains soil it is best sterilized before use (e.g. in an oven at 93°C for 30 minutes). The mixture should then be thoroughly moistened before planting and the plants watered after planting.

Suitable plants for terraria include:

Adiantum aethiopicum	Gratiola peruviana
diaphanum	Libertia pulchella
Aneilema acuminatum	Mentha diemenica
Asplenium flabellifolium	Mimulus repens
Athyrium japonicum	Nertera depressa
Australina pusilla	Peperomia enervis
Blechnum chambersii	leptostachya
penna-marina	Ranunculus collinus
Boea hygroscopica	Selaginella australiensis
Claytonia australasica	brisbanensis
Doodia caudata	longipinna
Fieldia australis	uliginosa
Goodenia elongata	umbrosa
hederacea	Viola hederacea
humilis	
lanata	

Bonsai

Australian plants are successfully grown as bonsai specimens, although they are not com-

monly used for this purpose. Excellent results have been gained using *Casuarina littoralis*, *Eucalyptus citriodora*, *Leptospermum laevigatum*, *Melaleuca styphelioides*, and *Nothofagus cunninghamii*.

There has been doubt about the use of Australian plants for bonsai, because it is often thought that many species are short lived, but there are many that have extremely long life-spans, e.g. native conifers such as species of *Athrotaxus*, *Callitris* and *Diselma*. These should be extremely suitable, as would be many of the eucalypts.

It is recommended that Australian plants be started as bonsai specimens when they are still in the seedling stage. Natural methods of pruning or weighting are recommended, as the unnatural method of wiring often causes the death of branches.

Further species grown successfully are:

Acmena smithii	Ficus macrophylla
Agonis flexuosa	obliqua
Araucaria bidwillii	platypoda
cunninghamii	rubiginosa 'Variegata'
Banksia dentata	
marginata	Grevillea longifolia
serrata	'Poorinda Constance'
Brachychiton acerifolium	'Poorinda Elegance'
discolor	'Poorinda Queen'
populneum	rosmarinifolia
rupestre	Kunzea baxteri
Callitris columellaris	Leptospermum flavescens
Cassia brewsteri	juniperinum
Eucalyptus erythronema	Melaleuca ericifolia
ficifolia	hypericifolia
torquata	incana
woodwardii	Sterculia quadrifida

Liparis nugentae is a hardy epiphytic orchid for bush house culture in southern Australia.

Drynaria rigidula, growing on a tree-fern slab —
note two different types of fronds.

Platycerium veitchii, established on a tree-fern slab.

Dendrobium lichenastrum, growing on a piece of
weathered hardwood.

Pyrrosia, growing on fern slab.

Slab Culture

Many epiphytic plants prefer to grow on a
slab, where their roots are exposed to the atmosphere, rather than in a container where their
roots are enclosed in potting mix. Such plants
are generally very sensitive to waterlogging and
prefer to develop their roots where they can dry
out after watering.

Suitable materials for slabs include weathered
hardwood, trunks of dead tree ferns, compressed
cork and bark of the cork oak. Tree fern slabs
are most commonly used and are suitable for a
wide range of plants, especially epiphytic ferns.
Weathered hardwood and cork are excellent for
epiphytic orchids.

Slabs should be hung in a protected position
where they do not receive too much direct sun
and wind. Some air movement is necessary but
this should not be excessive. Watering plants on
slabs is variable with the weather conditions
however it is generally difficult to overwater a
plant grown in this way. Watering should be
thorough so that the plants' roots are soaked.

Plants to be grown on slabs are tied on
securely with nylon fishing line, thin wire or
strips of panty hose. A pad of sphagnum moss
beneath the plant helps difficult species to get
started. Once established the plants benefit from
applications of liquid fertilizers two or three
times a year.

Dendrobium aemulum, growing on a piece of aged hardwood.

Dendrobium aemulum, growing on a piece of aged hardwood — showing roots.

Saccolabium rhopalorrhachis, growing on tree-fern slab.

Dendrobium teretifolium, growing on cork bark — showing roots.

Dendrobium teretifolium, growing on cork bark.

115

With careful selection and planting it is possible to encourage native birds to breed in a garden —
Clockwise from top left
White-naped Honeyeaters.

W.H. King photo

Blue wrens actively feed on small insects.

W.H. King photo

Eastern Rosellas feed on fruits and seeds of a wide variety of native plants.

W.H. King photo

Bottom left: Red Wattle-birds are common visitors to nectar producing plants.

W.H. King photo

10 Attracting Fauna to a Garden

ATTRACTING FAUNA TO A GARDEN

Gardens should be thought of as a living, viable system which can support not only the plants but also a variety of creatures. The activities of these creatures add an extra dimension to a garden and as well as being educational can greatly increase the enjoyment obtained. Some creatures will migrate naturally to the garden as it develops while others must be introduced and specially catered for by growing food plants or creating the right conditions. Some of these creatures may be destructive of plants but are tolerated because of the interest they create. Others aid in the control of pests (see also Biological Control).

BIRDS

Usually after a native garden has been established for 2-3 years, there is a gradual influx of native birds that pay short visits to the plants. These birds are colourful and active, and add an extra dimension of enjoyment to the growing of Australian trees and shrubs. With proper planning in selection of plant species and planting locations, birds such as honeyeaters and some of the insect eaters, may become permanent residents, and even breed if the right conditions are created. Other species will be spasmodic visitors, arriving when conditions for food supply are good, or during their migration.

Birds can play a very important part in pest control, even to the extent that there will be no need to use dangerous pesticides. See Pests and Diseases, page 137.

There is one aspect of domestic life that will scare birds, or reduce any bird population, and that is the domestic cat. The cat is undoubtedly a menace to wildlife, especially to birds in suburban gardens. It is not the cat's fault, as it only acts according to its natural instinct, and it is a very efficient hunter. Owners may think their cat does not catch birds because it is too well fed, but this is usually not so, unless cats are confined

to quarters or kept on a leash when outside. If a small neck bell is placed on a cat's collar, this will in some cases at least give warning to the birds, but it is really not a satisfactory way of protecting the birds.

Attracting native birds to gardens, where they can be studied and enjoyed, has become a popular pastime in capital cities and country areas alike. Birds have 3 main needs and these should be catered for if they are to be attracted to a garden. They are:
1 — Food
2 — Water
3 — Shelter.

1. Food

Birds usually visit gardens to obtain food. Often the first visitors to native gardens are honeyeaters, because grevilleas, correas and other commonly grown nectar-producing plants are in flower. To encourage the birds to stay, or visit throughout the year, it is important to consider plant flowering times. There should be at least some food plants in flower at any given period of the year, to maintain a constant supply of nectar and insects.

To increase the range of birds in a garden, it is necessary to incorporate a range of plant types. Insect eating birds (which also include honeyeaters, as they supplement their nectar diet with insects, and often pollen too) need a good supply of insects. Plants that attract insects often have perfumed flowers. This does not necessarily mean a pleasant perfume, because such plants can have very strong odours, making it unwise to plant them too near buildings e.g. *Hakea sericea*, *Kunzea ambigua*, and *Leptospermum flavescens*. Some other plants will be host to insects such as scale, that become food for some small birds such as silver-eyes, thornbills, or pardalotes. This raises the point that there must always be some insects on plants, as they are an important part of the food chain for birds. There is therefore a need for discipline in the use of toxic sprays. As the birds eat insects in sprayed areas, they can also

117

Selection and Cultivation

be accumulating poisons which can be the cause of infertile eggs, or lead to the birds' death. It is much safer to try to create a balance of nature, by planting suitable shrubs, and by tolerating a level of insects, unless they are in plague proportions. (See Pests and Diseases, p. 134.)

Seed-eating birds, such as rosellas, bronze-wing pigeons, etc., are not common visitors to gardens, unless there is some large natural bush area close by. Food can be provided for these birds by planting acacias and eucalypts. Ideal eucalypt species are those that have a bounteous supply of small flowers, and set seed readily, e.g. *Eucalyptus polybractea*, *E. radiata*, and *E. viridis*.

Artificial feed can be provided for birds, and there are now various types of feeders available, to handle both liquid and solid food. An important disadvantage of this type of food provision, is that birds will become reliant upon regular supplies, and if these cease, due to any number of reasons, especially during holiday periods, it could have disastrous results. It is recommended that natural food be supplied, via a range of suitable plants, and this will keep the birds at a viable level, rather than build up a larger population than the plants are capable of supplying with food. If feeding is necessary, it is not recommended that commercial honey be used as a food, because honey bees will collect it, and there is a danger of introducing disease to the hives if the honey is impure.

2. Water

A necessity for maintaining a regular population of birds in a garden, is to ensure that there is a permanent supply of water available for their use. This can be achieved in a number of ways —

(a) The simplest is to have a bowl of water that is filled regularly. Make sure that it is not likely to be within reach of a cat, as any cat will soon realise that permanent water is a regular visiting place of birds.

(b) A constantly, dripping tap, set off the ground, with a container to prevent unnecessary wastage of water.

(c) The construction of pools. Any size from small to large will be suitable, provided there is permanent water. It is ideal to have a shallow edge, so birds can use this area to bath if they wish. If large enough, some type of landing such as a dead branch, log or boulder, will help to give the birds confidence, knowing that there is water between themselves and land, and will also provide protection from animals. It is recommended that pools be planted with some suitable native water plants (see Aquatic Plants, Vol. 2). Rushes and similar types of plants will

Lambertias bear heads of tubular flowers that are rich in nectar. Illustrated *Lambertia formosa*.

Correa 'Mannii'. The tubular flowers are excellent for attracting small honey-eating birds.

Lambertia inermis.

provide a breeding ground for frogs and other aquatic animals, which will provide a further source of food for birds such as kookaburras. It is also possible that kingfishers, waders such as white faced herons, or grebes may visit for food. (See also, Plants for Waterlogged Areas, page 274.)

3. Shelter

Shelter is also a very important aspect, if birds are to remain within a garden for any period. There is a need for dense bushy areas that have a number of prickly plants. Such areas can create a refuge for the birds. If the plants have prickly foliage or thorns, it will restrict the entry of animals and predators. *Grevillea tripartita* and *Hakea sericea* are excellent for this purpose. Further species are listed on page 306. It is in these situations that nesting and breeding may also occur. Ideal locations in suburban gardens are in a back corner of the block, or at the side of a house, where there is little or no foot traffic. If birds accept these areas as being safe, they will visit other parts of the garden for food.

The planting of clump forming plants, such as grasses, sedges, and lilies is recommended, as these are often used for nesting materials, as is the bark of stringy-barked eucalypts, e.g. *Eucalyptus baxteri*, *E. cephalocarpa*, and *E. macrorhyncha*. *Melaleuca* species with papery bark are also useful in this regard, e.g. *M. linariifolia*, and *M. styphelioides*.

Small pools are useful for attracting birds.

BIRD ATTRACTING PLANTS

Highly Recommended Species

The following species are excellent for bird attraction, and at least one plant should be present in every garden. Their use by municipal authorities is to be encouraged.

Rock pool.

FOR TEMPERATE REGIONS

Anigozanthos flavidus
Banksia ericifolia
  spinulosa
Correa reflexa
Epacris longiflora
Eucalyptus lehmannii
  leucoxylon
Grevillea arenaria
  'Poorinda Constance'
  shiressii

FOR TROPICAL AND SUBTROPICAL REGIONS

Antidesma dallachyanum
Banksia integrifolia
  dentata
Callistemon viminalis
Eucalyptus ptychocarpa
Grevillea banksii
  pteridifolia
  sp. 'Coochin Hills'
Syzygium cormiflorum
Xanthostemon chrysanthus

Selection and Cultivation

BIRD ATTRACTING PLANTS

Nectar Producers
For Temperate Regions

Acacia pycnantha
Albizia lophantha
Angophora costata
  floribunda
  melanoxylon
Anigozanthos bicolor
  flavidus
  manglesii
  pulcherrimus
  rufus
  viridis
Banksia aspleniifolia
  caleyi
  canei
  ericifolia
  integrifolia
  marginata
  occidentalis
  prionotes
  robur
  serrata
  serratifolia
  speciosa
  sphaerocarpa
  spinulosa
Beaufortia orbifolia
  sparsa
  squarrosa
Billardiera longiflora
  scandens
Blandfordia grandiflora
  nobilis
Brachysema lanceolatum
  latifolium
  praemorsum
  sericeum
Callistemon citrinus
  comboynensis
  'Harkness'
  macropunctatus
  phoeniceus
  speciosus
  viminalis
  viridiflorus
Calothamnus gilesii
  homalophyllus
  quadrifidus
  rupestris
  sanguineus
  validus
  villosus
Castanospermum australe
Conostylis bealiana
Correa aemula
  backhousiana
  baeuerlenii
  calycina
  decumbens
  lawrenciana
  'Mannii'

  pulchella
  reflexa
  schlechtendalii
Darwinia citriodora
  fascicularis
  leiostyla
Doryanthes excelsa
  palmeri
Dryandra formosa
  praemorsa
  quercifolia
  sessilis
  tenuifolia
Epacris impressa
  longiflora
Eremophila denticulata
  glabra
  maculata
Eremaea beaufortioides
  violacea
Eucalyptus annulata
  burdettiana
  caesia
  calophylla
  calycogona
  cornuta
  crucis
  diversifolia
  eremophila
  erythronema
  erythrocorys
  ficifolia
  forrestiana
  gardneri
  goniocalyx
  grossa
  gummifera
  kitsoniana
  kruseana
  lehmannii
  leucoxylon
  macranda
  macrocarpa
  megacornuta
  nutans
  orbifolia
  platypus
  polybractea
  pyriformis
  rhodantha
  sideroxylon
  spathulata
  steedmanii
  stellulata
  stoatei
  stricklandii
  tetraptera
  torquata
  'Torwood'
  woodwardii

Banksia marginata, one of the best flowers for bird attraction.

The flowers of *Eucalyptus lehmannii* are recognised as being excellent for attracting birds. The buds and fruits add a further decorative aspect.

Callistemon 'Harkness' is one of the most adaptable plants for a variety of situations. The flowers also produce nectar for honey-eating birds.

Animals such as lizards add interest to a garden, and are useful in pest control.

W.R. Elliot photo

Ring-tail Possums are widespread and common throughout south-eastern Australia.

W.H. King photo

Selection and Cultivation

Grevillea alpina
  aquifolium
  arenaria
  asparagoides
  'Audrey'
  banksii
  barklyana
  baueri
  bipinnatifida
  chrysophaea
  'Clearview David'
  'Crosbie Morrison'
  'Dargan Hill'
  dielsiana
  diminuta
  dimorpha
  dryophylla
  floribunda
  ×*gaudichaudii*
  glabella
  hookerana
  ilicifolia
  jephcottii
  johnsonii
  juniperina
  lanigera
  laurifolia
  lavandulacea
  longifolia
  longistyla
  macrostylis
  miqueliana
  mucronulata
  pinaster
  polybractea
  'Poorinda Beauty'
  'Poorinda Constance'
  'Poorinda Queen'
  rosmarinifolia
  shiressii
  singuliflora
  speciosa
  steiglitziana
  stenomera
  thelemanniana

  tripartita
  victoriae
Hakea bucculenta
  cinerea
  francisiana
  laurina
  multilineata
  obtusa
  orthorrhyncha
  petiolaris
  purpurea
Hymenosporum flavum
Kennedia beckxiana
  macrophylla
  nigricans
  rubicunda
Kunzea baxteri
  pulchella
Lambertia ericifolia
  formosa
  inermis
Melaleuca armillaris
  calothamnoides
  coccinea
  diosmifolia
  elliptica
  fulgens
  hypericifolia
  lateritia
  leucadendron
  steedmanii
  wilsonii
Prostanthera calycina
  chlorantha
  microphylla
  walteri
Regelia megacephala
  velutina
Schefflera actinophylla
Stenocarpus sinuatus
Telopea oreades
  speciosissima
  truncata
Templetonia retusa

For Tropical and Subtropical Regions

Abarema grandiflora
  hendersonii
  muellerana
  sapindoides
Adansonia gregorii
Agapetes meiniana
Albizia basaltica
  canescens
  procera
  toona
Backhousia hughesii
Banksia aspleniifolia
  dentata
  ericifolia
  integrifolia
  marginata
  robur

  serrata
  serratifolia
  spinulosa
Barklya syringifolia
Barringtonia acutangula
  asiatica
  calyptra
  racemosa
Blandfordia grandiflora
  nobilis
Bombax ceiba
Brachychiton acerifolium
  bidwillii
  discolor
  diversifolium
  paradoxum
  populneum

The flower-heads of *Melaleuca elliptica* are borne on the old wood. It is also an excellent bird attracting plant.

Callicoma serratifolia is an efficient screening plant, and the flowers attract insects.

The creamy flowers of *Hakea varia* are strongly scented, and attract insects.

Open-petalled flowers, such as *Leptospermum nitidum*, are excellent for attracting insects.

refracta
robusta
'Robyn Gordon'
striata
venusta
wickhamii
 sp. Coochin Hills
Hakea bakerana
 chordophylla
 lorea
 purpurea
 suberea
Hibiscus tiliaceus
Hymenosporum flavum
Kennedia rubicunda
Macaranga tanarius
Melaleuca argentea
 cajuputi
 dealbata

hypericifolia
lasiandra
leucadendron
magnifica
nervosa
symphiocarpa
 sp. aff. symphiocarpa
 viridiflora
Mucuna gigantea
Nauclea coadunata
Schefflera actinophylla
 versteegii
Stenocarpus sinuatus
Strongylodon ruber
Xanthostemon chrysanthus
 paradoxus
 whitei
 youngii

BIRD ATTRACTING PLANTS

Insect Attracting

For Temperate Regions

Buckinghamia celsissima
Callistemon citrinus
 comboynensis
 formosus
 montanus
 pachyphyllus
 polandii
 rigidus
 salignus
 viminalis
Calophyllum inophyllum
Cassia brewsteri
 queenslandica
 tomentella
 marksiana
Capparis arborea
Castanospermum australe
Cordia myxa
Crateva religiosa
Deplanchea tetraphylla
Doryanthes excelsa
 palmeri
Eremophila maculata
Erythrina indica
 phlebocarpa
 verspertilio
Eucalyptus acmenioides
 alba
 cloeziana
 corymbosa
 crebra
 dichromophloia
 eugenioides
 foelscheana
 grandis
 haemastoma
 intermedia
 jensenii
 leucoxylon
 maculata
 melliodora
 microtheca

miniata
paniculata
papuana
pellita
peltata
phoenicea
polyanthemos
polycarpa
populifolia
porrecta
pruinosa
ptychocarpa
resinifera
setosa
tereticornis
terminalis
tessellaris
tetradonta
torelliana
Eugenia
 kuranda
 wilsonii
Euodia bonwickii
 elleryana
Gmelina leichhardtii
Grevillea banksii
 cyranostigma
 decora
 decurrens
 dryandri
 floribunda
 glossadenia
 goodii
 heliosperma
 hookerana
 johnsonii
 juncifolia
 juniperina
 longistyla
 parallela
 pteridifolia
 pungens

Acacia dealbata
 decora
 elata
 fimbriata
 glandulicarpa
 howittii
 mearnsii
 podalyriifolia
 verniciflua
Acmena smithii
Actinotus helianthii
Agonis flexuosa
 juniperina
 parviceps
Albizia lophantha
Anthocercis frondosa
Baeckea astarteoides
 linifolia
 virgata
Banksia ericifolia
 media
 meisneri
 pilostylis
Boronia denticulata
 muelleri
Brachycome multifida
Bursaria spinosa
Callicoma serratifolia
Callistemon paludosus
 salignus
 shiressii
 sieberi
Calocephalus brownii
Calytrix alpestris
 sullivani
 tetragona

Cassia artemisioides
 sturtii
Cassinia aculeata
 arcuata
Ceratopetalum gummiferum
Celmisia asteliifolia
Chamelaucium sp. Walpole
 uncinatum
Chorizema cordatum
Cordyline stricta
Craspedia glauca
 globoidea
Dichopogon strictus
Didiscus caerulea
Diplarrena moraea
Doryanthes excelsa
 palmeri
Eriostemon myoporoides
Eucalyptus cephalocarpa
 cinerea
 cosmophylla
 crenulata
 diversifolia
 ficifolia
 globulus
 gomphocephala
 gracilis
 leucoxylon
 melliodora
 pauciflora
 sideroxylon
 spathulata
 viminalis
 viridis
Eupomatia laurina

123

Selection and Cultivation

Frankenia pauciflora
Gahnia sieberana
Goodia lotifolia
Grevillea acanthifolia
  anethifolia
  australis
  brevicuspis
  crithmifolia
  leucopteris
  phanerophlebia
  vestita
Hakea corymbosa
  costata
  cristata
  leucoptera
  lissocarpha
  nitida
  nodosa
  prostrata
  salicifolia
  sericea
  suaveolens
  teretifolia
  undulata
  varia
Helichrysum apiculatum
  baxteri
  bracteatum
  dendroideum
  obcordatum
Helipterum roseum
Hibbertia dentata
  scandens
Isopogon anethifolius
Ixodia achilleoides
Jacksonia scoparia
Kennedia glabrata
Kunzea ambigua
  ericifolia
Leptospermum flavescens
  laevigatum
  lanigerum
  nitidum
  phylicoides
  scoparium
Melaleuca armillaris
  decora
  decussata
  ericifolia
  halmaturorum

  linariifolia
  nodosa
  polygaloides
  squarrosa
  styphelioides
Mentha australis
  diemenica
Mirbelia oxyloboides
Myoporum floribundum
  insulare
  parvifolium
  viscosum
Olearia argophylla
  dentata
  phlogopappa
Orthrosanthus multiflorus
Passiflora cinnabarina
Patersonia occidentalis
Phebalium lamprophyllum
Pimelea ferruginea
  rosea
  spectabilis
Pittosporum phillyreoides
  undulatum
Pomaderris lanigera
  pilifera
Pratia pedunculata
Pultenaea daphnoides
  pedunculata
  polifolia
Scaevola hookeri
Sowerbaea juncea
Spyridium parvifolium
Stylidium graminifolium
Stypandra caespitosa
  glauca
Thryptomene calycina
  saxicola
Thysanotus multiflorus
Tristania conferta
  laurina
Verticordia chrysantha
  mitchellii
  plumosa
Viminaria juncea
Xanthorrhoea australis
  minor
Xanthosia rotundifolia

The wiry, prickly growth of *Dryandra polycephala* provides a refuge for birds.

BIRD ATTRACTING PLANTS

Insect Attracting

For Tropical and Subtropical Regions

Acacia aulacocarpa
  auriculiformis
  bancroftii
  calyculata
  decora
  falcata
  fimbriata

  flavescens
  holosericea
  leptostachya
  podalyriifolia
Acmena australis
  graveolens
  smithii

Alphitonia excelsa
  petriei
  whitei
Alstonia muelleri
  scholaris
Backhousia anisata
  bancroftii
  citriodora
Backhousia myrtifolia
Baeckea camphorata
  virgata
Barringtonia racemosa
Bauerella simplicifolia
Beilschmiedia bancroftii
  obtusifolia
Bosistoa euodiiformis
  pentacocca
Brombya platynema
Bouchardatia neurococca
Buckinghamia celsissima
Bursaria incana
  spinosa
Callicoma serratifolia
Cardwellia sublima
Cerbera inflata
Commersonia bartramia
Darlingia darlingiana
  ferruginea
Decaspermum fruticosum
Eucalyptus alba
  crebra
  dichromophloia
  intermedia
  paniculata
  pellita
  torelliana
Flindersia acuminata
  australis
  brayleyana
  ifflaiana
  pubescens
  schottiana

Grevillea glauca
  hilliana
  leiophylla
  mimosoides
  pinnatifida
  sessilis
Hakea eriantha
  florulenta
  pedunculata
  persiehana
  plurinervia
  salicifolia
Helcia diversifolia
  ferruginea
Hollandea sayerana
Jacksonia scoparia
Kunzea ambigua
Leptospermum fabricia
  flavescens
  lanigerum
  longifolium
  scoparium
  wooroonooran
Mallotus discolor
Medicosma cunninghamii
Melaleuca armillaris
  bracteata
  decora
  linariifolia
  minutifolia
  nodosa
  styphelioides
Melia azederach
Neolitsea dealbata
Pithecellobium grandiflorum
  pruinosum
Pittosporum rhombifolium
  undulatum
Pomaderris tropica
Stenocarpus salignus
Tristania conferta
  laurina
  neriifolia

The stiff, pungent leaves of *Hakea corymbosa* provide protection for small birds.

BIRD ATTRACTING PLANTS

Seed and Fruits

For Temperate Regions

Acacia baileyana	*goniocalyx*
boormanii	*leucoxylon*
cultriformis	*macrandra*
myrtifolia	*macrorhyncha*
paradoxa	*melliodora*
pravissima	*obliqua*
prominens	*polyanthemos*
pycnantha	*polybractea*
retinodes	*radiata*
verticillata	*sideroxylon*
Acmena smithii	*spathulata*
Alectryon subcinereus	*stellulata*
tomentosus	*viridis*
Alyxia buxifolia	*Gahnia radula*
Angophora costata	*sieberana*
floribunda	*Goodia lotifolia*
Banksia integrifolia	*Grevillea banksii*
marginata	*robusta*
Callitris columellaris	*Juncus australis*
rhomboidea	*polyanthemos*
Carex inversa	*Lepidosperma elatius*
Casuarina stricta	*Lomandra longifolia*
Coprosma hirtella	*Omalanthus populifolius*
quadrifida	*Pittosporum phillyreoides*
Cordyline stricta	*undulatum*
Cyathodes acerosa	*Poa caespitosa*
Danthonia brownii	*Podocarpus elatus*
Dianella revoluta	*Polyscias sambucifolius*
tasmanica	*Pultenaea gunnii*
Elaeocarpus reticulatus	*scabra*
Eucalyptus calycogona	*Solanum aviculare*
cephalocarpa	*laciniatum*
cinerea	*Stipa elegantissima*
crenulata	*Syzygium coolminianum*
dives	*paniculatum*
globulus	*Themeda australis*

Attracting Fauna to a Garden

BIRD ATTRACTING PLANTS

Seed and Fruits

For Tropical and Subtropical Regions

Acmena australis	*Calamus australis*
graveolens	*caryotoides*
hemilampra	*motii*
smithii	*muelleri*
Acronychia acidula	*Callicarpa pedunculata*
haplophylla	*Canthium coprosmoides*
laevis	*lucidum*
melicopoides	*Celtis paniculata*
vestita	*Cinnamomum laubatii*
Alectryon subcinereus	*oliveri*
tomentosus	*Corida subcordata*
Alphitonia excelsa	*Cordyline stricta*
petriei	*Cryptocarya angulata*
whitei	*cinnamomifolia*
Alyxia ruscifolia	*corrugata*
Antidesma bunius	*hypospodia*
dallachyanum	*mackinnoniana*
erostre	*murrayi*
ghaesembilla	*rigida*
parvifolium	*triplinervis*
Arytera lautererana	*Delarbrea michieana*
Austromyrtus acmenioides	*Dillenia indica*
bidwillii	*Elaeocarpus bancroftii*
dulcis	*ferruginiflorus*
tenuifolia	*grandis*
Backhousia bancroftii	*reticulatus*
Beilschmiedia obtusifolia	*Elaeodendron australe*
Brackenridgea australiana	*Endiandra cowleyana*
Breynia oblongifolia	*hypotephra*
stipitata	*longipedicellata*
Buchanania arborescens	*microneura*
muelleri	*muelleri*
obovata	*sieberi*

Pimeleas are excellent for attracting butterflies. This species is *Pimelea spectabilis*.

subtriplinervis
virens
Ervatamia angustisepala
Eugenia kuranda
Euodia elleryana
Euroschinus falcata
Ficus albipila
  australis
  benjamina
  coronata
  crassipes
  destruens
  fraseri
  gracilipes
  henneana
  hispida
  leptoclada
  macrophylla
  microcarpa
  obliqua
  opposita
  platypoda
  racemosa
  septica
  triradiata
  variegata
Galbulimima belgraveana
Halfordia drupifera
Heterodendron oleifolium
Litsea bindoniana
  glutinosa

leefeana
Melia azederach
Myristica muelleri
Neolitsea dealbata
Omolanthus populifolius
  stillingiifolius
Pleiogynium timorense
Podocarpus amarus
  dispermus
  elatus
  neriifolius
Polyscias elegans
  mollis
  murrayi
Premna lignum-vitae
Rhodamnia spongiosa
  trinervia
Schefflera actinophylla
  versteegii
Symplocos cyanocarpa
  paucistaminea
Syzygium coolminianum
  cormiflorum
  corynanthum
  fibrosum
  floribundum
  longipes
  moorei
  paniculatum
Tetrasynandra laxiflora

nicrocorys
obliqua
ovata
paniculata
pilularis
polyanthemos
* punctata

radiata
regnans
* resinifera
* rubida
saligna
* tereticornis
* viminalis

KOALAS

Koalas are not common in built up areas but some well treed suburbs are favoured by their visits. The peaceful dozing daytime appearance of a koala, which is so appealing, is deceptive however because at night they are often noisy, quarrelsome creatures. Despite these drawbacks they are still a very popular and appealing animal.

The present colonies of koalas living in partially built up areas feed on existing trees left after clearing. There is usually very little regeneration of their natural food trees and the gardens are planted with unsuitable species. If the koalas are to stay in the area young trees must be planted from time to time to supplement the established trees.

The following species of eucalypts are known food trees of the koala in various eastern states of Australia. Not all of these are eaten by koalas throughout the year as some species are only eaten on occasions when their main food trees* are unacceptable.

Eucalyptus botryoides
* camaldulensis
  globulus
  goniocalyx

haemastoma
maculata
melliodora
microcarpa

POSSUMS

Possums are charming creatures but they can also be a nuisance in suburbs living in the roofs of houses and damaging favoured garden plants. The larger possums such as the brushy tail can be particularly bad in this respect. The smaller species such as the ring tails and sugar gliders are less troublesome and are quite captivating creatures. They have a very sweet tooth and are readily attracted to such luxuries as bread spread with jam. They are also fond of fruit especially apples. Ring tailed possums can be encouraged to reside and nest in a garden by planting dense bushy trees such as Acmena smithii and Syzygium coolminianum.

BANDICOOTS

Bandicoots are frequently common close to large cities and are still known from the outer suburbs of a couple of capital cities. Their activities are revealed by small conical holes which they make in soil with their noses while searching for food. They are engaging little animals which cause minimal damage and should be encouraged and protected where they occur. They are fond of tussock grass communities and these should not be cleared or mown if it is known that bandicoots are in the vicinity. Their enemies are cats and dogs.

LIZARDS

Lizards are a very active attraction in any garden and aid considerably in insect control. The easiest kinds to establish are the various species of small skinks which are very efficient at catching a variety of insects. They thrive where there is abundant litter on the ground and rocks with crevices to shelter in. They lay their eggs in loose friable clay soil and a couple of small heaps will encourage them to breed.

The larger lizards such as blue-tongues and bearded dragons can be successfully introduced into gardens but require protection from cats and dogs. They need to find a permanent place in which to shelter, such as among rocks, or else they tend to wander.

126

The papery daisies of *Helichrysum baxteri* are excellent for attracting butterflies.

FROGS

Frogs are interesting creatures that add a dimension of sound to a garden especially on moist nights. Some species will appear naturally as a garden develops especially if water is present but other varieties can be readily introduced. Their successful establishment requires the presence of permanent water and logs, vegetation etc. for food and shelter.

FISH

Fish are rarely native to a garden but some species are readily introduced into suitable ponds or dams. There are many species of small native fish which can be successfully established if the conditions are right.

Most fish require water with a minimum depth of about 20 cm. The pond should be large enough so that it does not dry out rapidly nor reach too high a temperature in the summer. There should be plenty of shelter gained from plants such as rushes around the edge and also water plants growing in pots or in the mud. It is best to set up and plant a pond 3-6 months before the introduction of fish so that sufficient shelter and food for their needs can develop. Pesticides should never be sprayed near a pond as they are lethal to water life.

BUTTERFLIES

Butterflies are attracted to a native garden, and their presence adds beauty and interest. In the

northern areas of Australia, butterflies are continuously present throughout the year. In the southern areas, butterflies are in flight mainly from August to April, with a peak in the summer. Therefore plants suitable for them should be blooming during this period.

Butterflies visit gardens for 2 main reasons, seeking food for themselves, or plants on which to lay their eggs and which will provide food for their caterpillars. The butterflies seek nectar from a wide variety of flowers, including everlastings, pea-flowers, tubular flowers, and open-petalled flowers such as jasmines. They are also attracted to plants which produce masses of small flowers, such as *Bursaria* spp., or flowers in heads, e.g. *Pimelea* spp.

Food plants for butterfly larvae are wide and varied, and it is possible to attract particular species of butterflies to a garden by planting the food plants. Good examples in tropical areas are *Euodia elleryana* for the magnificent mountain blue butterflies, and various *Aristolochia* spp. for the birdwing and greasywing groups. In temperate areas the decorative painted lady is attracted to the everlastings *Helichrysum bracteatum* and *H. apiculatum*. Other nectar producing and food plants attractive to butterflies are to be found in the accompanying list.

Butterfly Attracting Plants

Abarema hendersonii	*Brachycome multifida*
muellerana	*Buckinghamia celsissima*
sapindoides	*Burchardia multiflora*
Actinodium cunninghamii	*umbellata*
Actinotus helianthii	*Bursaria spinosa*
Adenanthera abrosperma	*Calocephalus brownii*
pavonina	*Calytrix alpestris*
Agonis juniperina	*aurea*
parviceps	*depressa*
Albizia basaltica	*glutinosa*
canescens	*sullivanii*
lophantha	*tetragona*
procera	*Capparis arborea*
retusa	*canescens*
thozetiana	*lasiantha*
toona	*mitchellii*
xanthoxylon	*Cassia artemisioides*
Alphitonia excelsa	*brewsteri*
Ammobium alatum	*nemophila*
Archidendron lucyi	*Celmisia asteliifolia*
vaillantii	*Chamelaucium axillare*
Aristolochia deltantha	*·uncinatum*
pubera	*Chorizema cordatum*
Astartea heteranthera	*Claytonia australasica*
Asterolasia asteriscophora	*Clematis aristata*
Baeckea linifolia	*microphylla*
virgata	*Clerodendrum inerme*
Bossiaea linophylla	*tomentosum*
Brachychiton acerifolium	*Conospermum mitchellii*
discolor	*Craspedia glauca*
diversifolium	*globoidea*
populneum	*Dichopogon strictus*

Clockwise from top left

Spider webs can be decorative in a garden.
W.R. Elliot photo

Butterflies are attracted to perfumed flowers.

Imperial White Butterfly on *Xanthorrhoea minor*.
T.L. Blake photo

Common Imperial Blue Butterfly on *Bursaria spinosa*.
W.N.B. Quick

Emperor Gum Moth caterpillars are destructive, but are
also very decorative, and add educational interest.
D.V. Beardsell ph

Diplarrena moraea
Doryanthes excelsa
  palmeri
Euodia elleryana
Eupomatia laurina
Eutaxia microphylla
Frankenia pauciflora
Gompholobium huegelii
  latifolium
Goodenia ovata
Goodia lotifolia
Helichrysum apiculatum
  baxteri
  bracteatum
  elatum
  leucopsidium
  scorpioides
  semipapposum
Helipterum albicans
  roseum
Hoya australis
  keysii
Hypocalymma angustifolium
  cordifolium
  robustum
Ipomoea digitata
  gracilis
Ischnostemma carnosum
Jasminum aemulum
  didymum
  lineare
  suavissimum
Kennedia glabrata
Leptospermum epacridoideum
  flavescens
  'Horizontalis'
  lanigerum
  nitidum
  scoparium

Libertia pulchella
Loudonia behri
Mazus pumilio
Mirbelia oxyloboides
Olearia ciliata
  dentata
  floribunda
  iodochroa
  myrsinoides
  phlogopappa
  ramulosa
  teretifolia
Pimelea ferruginea
  linifolia
  nivea
  rosea
  spectabilis
  sylvestris
Pithecellobium grandiflorum
Pomaderris lanigera
  pilifera
Pongamia pinnata
Ptilotus obovatus
Pultenaea daphnoides
  gunnii
  humilis
  pedunculata
Sowerbaea juncea
Spyridium parvifolium
  vexilliferum
Stylidium bulbiferum
  corymbosum
  spathulatum
Stypandra caespitosa
Trichosanthes pentaphylla
Verticordia acerosa
  chrysantha
  densiflora
  plumosa

The Emperor Gum Moth is an attractive addition to the garden.

MOTHS

Moths are mainly night flying creatures but some active species fly by day and are attracted to colourful flowers on which they feed. Of particular interest are the various hawk moths or sphinx moths which fly extremely rapidly. Some species beat their wings so fast while in flight that they produce a distinctive burring noise. They feed on flowers while hovering and are particularly attracted to colourful tubular flowers such as species of *Ipomoea*.

Some large night flying moths are familiar subjects because they often shelter in houses or under eaves during daylight hours. Many also have large conspicuous caterpillars which are popular with children. One of the best known species is the emperor gum moth, the adults of which measure 10-12 cm across and are pinkish-buff coloured with a blue eyespot on each forewing. The large fleshy caterpillars are bluish-green with rosettes of non-stinging red and blue spines scatterd over the body. They are excellent subjects for nature study being easy to keep needing only fresh leaves daily. They feed on *Tristania conferta* and a variety of eucalypts including *E. leucoxylon*, *E. nicholii*, *E. doratoxylon* and *E. polybractea*. The emperor gum moth is restricted to eastern Australia but a very similar species feeds on eucalypts in SA and WA. The large, handsome atlas moth is found in northern Qld.

BEETLES

Australia possesses many colourful beetles both large and small. Many are destructive on occasions but the presence of a small population in a garden is tolerable. The christmas beetles are amongst the most familiar beetles and are a favourite group with children. They come in a variety of colours from bright purple through green to pinkish-buff. They are generally very shiny and conspicuous. In some years they gather in large colonies, and may strip the leaves

Selection and Cultivation

from the eucalypts on which they feed. Their numbers however are easily reduced by collection methods and the eucalypts usually recover quickly from their attacks.

The golden or greenish stag beetles are also conspicuous and decorative. They feed on the young shoots of a variety of eucalypts but seem to be especially fond of *E. leucoxylon* and *E. chapmaniana*. They rarely cause any major damage.

Many large colourful beetles such as the jewel beetles feed on flowers and are attracted particularly to plants which produce masses of fluffy flowers such as species of *Austromyrtus, Backhousia, Bursaria, Eucalyptus, Kunzea, Leptospermum, Melaleuca* and *Xanthorrhoea.*

SPIDERS

Spiders render a valuable service in gardens by preying on many pests. However, they are often treated with suspicion by people. A number of species are decorative and are a source of interest and education. Some species will appear naturally as a garden develops but others can be readily introduced from natural populations.

Among the web spinners the most distinctive are the orb weavers that produce circular webs from strong strands. The web of the St Andrew's Cross spider has a distinctive cross of white webbing in the centre, while the golden orb weaver spins webs of golden threads. Other spiders of interest include the various jumping spiders, the delicately coloured flower spiders and the unusual bird-dropping spider.

Boronia pulchella W.R. Elliot photo

Part Three

Pests, Diseases
and other Ailments

11　Pests and their Control

PESTS

Australian plants in their natural environment suffer from attacks by a large range of creatures, and it is unusual to see a plant which has not been damaged in some way or other. Most of these attacks are of a minor nature causing superficial damage and slight setbacks to the plants. Sporadic attacks, however, also occur which are of major significance and can result in stunting or even death of the plant.

By contrast, when they are grown away from their natural environment, such as overseas or even interstate, the plants are in a situation free of their indigenous pests and do not suffer the constant depredations experienced in their native environment. Consequently they often grow faster and with an entire unblemished appearance. This is a feature of eucalypts which are grown overseas. Macadamia nuts in their natural situation grow in rainforests of NSW and Qld. When grown commercially in these areas they suffer from constant attacks by pests. By contrast if they are grown in inland or semi-desert areas and regularly watered they suffer few attacks and the foliage is dark green, lustrous and unblemished.

Severe attacks which cause major setbacks or even kill plants occur in one of two ways:

1. When an insect is introduced into a new environment which is free from its natural enemies. Such pests are mainly those which have been introduced from overseas as have most of the aphids in Australia. Pests from interstate may also come under this category.

2. When the natural balance between a pest and its predators is upset. This natural balance is delicate and subject to small fluctuations, but can be upset by outside influences such as bushfires, clearing of vegetation, or spraying with insecticides. If the balance is tilted in favour of the pest, then its numbers build up very rapidly until it reaches plague proportions. At very high population levels the pest causes severe damage and only a corresponding increase in the num-

bers of its natural enemies will bring it under control. If this happens quickly then the plants will usually recover but with a minor setback (even after complete defoliation). If the attacks persist at serious levels over several seasons then stunting or even death of the plants can follow. Sometimes natural catastrophes upset the balance as in outbreaks of wattle blight, cup moths, saw flies and phasmids. More frequently, however it is man who upsets the balance.

For reasons which are not understood some insects undergo population explosions at irregular intervals. Their numbers increase enormously, sometimes suddenly, or more often over a period of time. The insects may reach plague levels and devastate large areas or be confined to individual trees. These sporadic increases in the populations of insects cannot be predicted and considerable damage may be caused. Sometimes the outbreaks decline as rapidly as they occurred.

Pests in gardens are subject to control from natural enemies and have similar fluctuations in population as they have in the bush. Outbreaks of pests are frequently a problem in new gardens, but their incidence lessens as the gardens become established. When new suburbs are created much of the natural bush is cleared for houses, roads etc. and only a skeleton of the original vegetation remains. Often some plants of the original species will become weakened or die out under the new conditions of increased light and transpiration imposed by the clearing and only those adaptable species will survive. All of these changes affect the balance between insect pests and their predators, and new gardens planted in such estates are often ravaged as a result of this imbalance. As an example, borers are commonly a problem attacking a variety of plants grown in such areas. These pests are usually well entrenched in the weak or dying eucalypts and wattles which have been left, and are almost impossible to adequately control.

As a new suburb settles down and gardens become established a balance is again achieved

A weakened eucalypt, severely attacked by pests.

causing problems, e.g. the scale-like covering in lerps is conspicuous but may not be noticed until after the insects have been controlled by natural enemies. Spraying at this stage would only kill harmless and even beneficial insects.

4. If natural control systems are becoming established do not interfere — see Biological Control.

5. If the pest is a potentially serious one such as aphids, leaf skeletonizers or borers, act as soon as the symptoms are noticed. Such pests can build up in numbers rapidly, or cause considerable damage in a short time and if action is delayed then control may be much more difficult to achieve.

6. Do not try to eliminate all pests but attempt to reduce them to safe levels.

7. Use the safest control systems first and only use toxic sprays as the last resort.

Biological Control

The majority of insects are not harmful to man or his animals or plants and many are indeed beneficial. Some are deadly enemies of the worst plant pests and their activities are to be encouraged in gardens. If sufficient numbers of such beneficial insects can be established, then outbreaks of damaging pests are greatly reduced.

This system of control is known as biological control and offers the best hope of controlling the worst pests. In the U.S.A. quantities of such beneficial insects as ladybirds and lacewings are bred and offered for sale. These can be purchased and released into gardens where they materially contribute to the control of such pests as aphids and mealy bugs. This sophisticated degree of pest control is not yet available in Australia but it is hoped that it will reach here soon.

Biological control is based on the balance achieved by nature. Fluctuations occur between a pest and its natural enemies but overall these are balanced out. Thus when a particular insect builds up to plague proportions so its natural enemies also build up and eventually reduce it back to a tolerable level. Such a balance is possible to achieve in a garden or any natural system and can be aided if certain rules are followed.

Random or indiscriminate spraying with all but very safe pesticides should be abandoned because of the danger of upsetting the balance between pests and their natural enemies. Often a spray applied to control one pest will result in the upsurge of another because the spray has destroyed or reduced its natural enemies.

A garden bed planted with mixed species is better able to cope with pests than expanses of

between the pests and their natural predators and parasites, although this will probably be different to the balance in the original bush. This new balance is subject to similar fluctuations as was the original balance and outbreaks of pests will occur when the balance is upset.

Pest Control

Control of pests and diseases is a continual process in crop production where losses are of economic significance. In most parks and gardens, however, outbreaks are sporadic and pest control occupies only a small proportion of the time spent in maintenance.

Principles of Pest Control

There are 7 basic rules which should be adhered to if adequate control is to be achieved.

1. Vigorous healthy plants are able to resist attack better than weakened plants. If plants are continually attacked by pests then perhaps this is an indication of some other ailment, e.g. waterlogged soil weakening the tree. The answer in this case is to improve the drainage of the soil. The use of fertilizers often dramatically increases a plant's resistance to pests, especially if the plants have been previously starved.

2. Identify accurately the culprit causing the damage. This is of paramount importance because the particular control system chosen will vary with the species of the pest.

3. Ensure that the pest is still active and

Webbing Caterpillars form large shelters. They are very destructive of a wide range of plants.   *D.L. Jones photo*

Larvae of the Steel-blue Sawfly congregate during the day and disperse at night to feed.   *D.L. Jones photo*

The larvae of the Gum Tree Moth severely skeletonise glaucous-leaved Eucalypts.
   D.V. Beardsell photo

Larvae of the Citrus Butterfly feed on citrus or related plants.   *D.V. Beardsell photo*

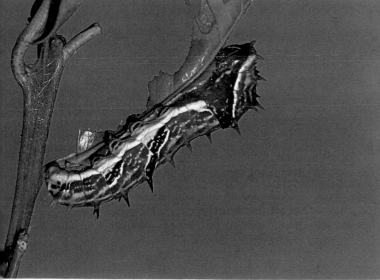

one kind of plant. Mixed plantings are better able to support beneficial insects than are stands of a single species which invite attack by pests which thrive on it.

Remove weeds which are often a harbour for pests and diseases e.g. marshmallows are a haven for harlequin bugs, while thistles and capeweed provide excellent shelter and food for aphids.

Beneficial Insects

A number of insects found on plants cause no damage and are in fact beneficial because they destroy insect pests. Their activities should be encouraged and it is of benefit to be able to distinguish them from injurious insects. Beneficial insects include such well known creatures as ladybirds, lacewings, praying mantids, and also a range of lesser known species such as ground beetles, assassin bugs, ant lions, wasps and hover flies.

Ant Lions: the adults are gauzy winged insects similar to lacewings. They are clumsy fliers and are sometimes called helicopters. The brown, oval larvae (about 1 cm long) lives at the bottom of a small cone shaped pit excavated in sandy soil. It has large sickle shaped jaws which it uses to catch and feed on ants and other insects which blunder into the pit.

Assassin Bugs: these are ugly, dull brown or blackish bugs which feed by sucking the body juices from ants and immature forms of other insects. They move fairly slowly. Some Australian species have their hind legs intricately clothed with large brushes of hairs.

Ground Beetles: these are active dull brown or black beetles which hide during the day and roam abroad at night to feed. They have relatively long legs and can run rapidly when disturbed. Their food consists of other insects especially caterpillars and grubs.

Hover Flies: the adults of these insects hover, almost motionless, over plants and flowers with the wings vibrating so fast that they appear as an indistinct blur. Eggs are laid among colonies of aphids. The small, green or brownish maggot-like larvae, feed actively on the aphids by sucking their body juices.

Lacewings: the adults are attractive insects with gauzy wings. They are usually yellowish or green with large eyes. Eggs are laid in rows, on long, slender stalks. The larvae grow to about 0.8 cm long and are narrow with large prominent hooked jaws. They attack a range of small insects including thrips, scales, aphids, mealy bugs and also mites.

Ladybirds: These popular insects are very beneficial in home gardens and glasshouses. Both the larvae and the familiar adult beetles actively feed on aphids, mites, scales and mealy bugs. The adults can be moved onto colonies of aphids where they will remain feeding until all of the aphids have been destroyed. The small ladybird (*Rhizobius ruficollis*) is an active predator of mealy bugs and has been successfully introduced into glasshouses to control this pest.

Praying Mantids: large familiar insects which adopt a praying attitude on plants or flowers while awaiting prey. The commonest species found in gardens is green but there are many species with greyish or brown tonings, including some quite small species which can run actively. The adults feed on a wide range of insects, including many pests, while the young feed on small insects including aphids and thrips.

Wasps: large wasps and hornets attack spiders and a range of insects including cicadas, caterpillars and grubs. Numerous species of small ichneumon wasp parasitise other insects by laying their eggs inside the bodies. These eggs hatch into larvae which consume the body of the host eventually killing it. They are very important in the control of a range of pests.

Other Beneficial Animals

Spiders are generally frowned upon but provide a very active service by reducing insect populations. The nomadic hunting types such as the huntsman and wolf spider can be very beneficial as are the many species of web spinners. The tiny jumping spiders attack a range of small insects including many pests. Spiders are present in most gardens but additional species can be readily introduced.

Frogs add extra interest to a garden as well as being beneficial by consuming ground dwelling pests such as earwigs, slaters, slugs and cut worms. Numerous varieties can be introduced into a garden, but their successful establishment requires the presence of permanent water and logs, etc. for daytime shelter.

Lizards, especially the various species of small skinks, are also useful animals for reducing the levels of pests in gardens.

Birds are the major enemies of most pests and their activities in gardens should be encouraged (see Lists of Bird Attracting Plants, page 119).

The tiny two spotted mite is a major pest of many plants. It is attacked voraciously by a larger predator mite (*Typhlodromus occidentalis*) which quickly reduces the numbers of the pest to a safe level.

Integrated Pest Control

This system of pest control combines the best

features of both biological control and spraying. Every effort is made to achieve biological control but where necessary, sprays are applied strategically to achieve control. Selection and application of sprays is made after due consideration of the natural balance that exists between pests and their natural enemies.

Other Controls

Banding

A strip of hessian or cloth tied around the trunk of a tree offers a haven for some pests. The material can be inspected and removed at intervals and the pests destroyed. This technique was commonly employed in the early years of fruit culture in Australia. The strip of material should be tied to the tree in such a way that a flap hangs downwards and encourages the entry of travelling pests.

This technique has proved very successful for trapping the adult weevils of root borers when they migrate to the above ground parts of the plant. It is also extremely effective against the hairy white cedar caterpillars, so much so that it need be the only control system adopted for this pest.

A modification is to smother the band with a sticky non-drying adhesive material, which effectively traps travelling insects. This system is particularly effective for preventing the passage of ants up a tree.

Hand Picking

Individual large pests such as solitary caterpillars or case moths can be removed by hand and squashed. Pests which cluster together such as aphids, sawflies and processional caterpillars can be removed by snipping off the shoot where they are living or feeding, and squashing or burning it. Pests such as leaf skeletonizers or leaf beetle larvae are often gregarious while young but disperse as they get older. If caught early enough whole colonies can be squashed before they have done much damage. Colonies of eggs can be destroyed before they hatch, e.g. *Paropsis* beetle on eucalypts.

Water Jet

A reducing nozzle attached to the end of the garden hose narrows the stream and increases the pressure of the water. Such a jet will not damage shrubs or trees but is very effective at dispersing colonies of pests such as aphids, sawflies, scales, beetles and bugs. Aphids readily drown in water and a powerful jet may stun larger pests such as bugs and sawflies rendering them susceptible to attack by predators.

Spraying

Sprays should only be used as a last resort when all other methods have failed and the pests are doing intolerable damage to the plants. Unfortunately there is a general tendency to use sprays as the first control measure but in the garden this approach usually creates more problems than it solves.

Most pesticides are harmful to the environment and they affect birds and other wildlife, fish, spiders and beneficial insects such as bees. Pesticides frequently upset the natural balance between predators, parasites and the pests they control. Thus it is not uncommon for a pesticide to cause an outbreak of a pest different from the one which it has been used to control, e.g. pesticides killing ladybirds and allowing aphids to build up.

Pesticides frequently achieve spectacular results when they are first applied against a specific pest which they are designed to control. After a while however the results are not so spectacular and higher concentrations may be needed to achieve the same control as that of earlier sprays. After continual spraying it is common for pests to become resistant to the effects of the spray either by a change in their habits or genetic changes which induce immunity. If there is a genetic change then continued spraying effectively selects those which are resistant, and soon this control measure is ineffective. Thus a new pesticide must be found to replace the ineffective one and the system becomes a vicious circle with the pests adapting and the environment suffering from pesticide pollution.

Unfortunately in some cases it is only possible to achieve pest control by using a chemical spray. If spraying is unavoidable then spray properly and observe all of the correct procedures.

Spraying Rules

1. Choose the safest and most effective pesticide for the job.

2. Carefully read the label and use only at the recommended strength and for the purpose stated.

3. Mix up sufficient spray to cover the affected plants only.

4. Spray thoroughly to wet the pests but not so that a great deal of excess spray drips to the ground.

5. Spray on a still, calm day (avoid spraying on windy days at all costs).

6. Preferably spray towards evening to lessen the chance of birds contacting the fresh spray.

7. Spray only the affected plants and if there is excess spray do not apply it to other plants at

random. Such random spraying could easily result in the destruction of beneficial insects and an upsurge in the levels of hitherto insignificant pests.

8. Never spray near fish ponds or pools as fish, frogs and other waterlife are easily killed by chemicals.

9. If there is excess pesticide dispose of it by digging a deep hole and pouring it in. Flatten and bury pesticide containers.

Chemical Sprays

Most chemicals are handled under a common name but where they are widely used they may be sold under a variety of labels known as trade names. If a chemical is not widely manufactured then often a common name will be the same as the trade name. In this book we have only listed chemicals under their common names.

Labelling

It is required by law under the Pesticides Act that all pesticides sold, must be labelled with the chemical name and the name and amount of the active ingredient contained in the spray. Where there is an approved common name this is used instead of the chemical name of the active constituent. The label also contains other information such as recommended strengths to use, and compatibilities with other sprays. The labels should always be read carefully before a spray is used.

Safety Directions When Handling Pesticides

All pesticides should be treated as if toxic and handled accordingly. If pesticides are used carefully they will create little hazard.

1. Check spraying equipment for leaks or blockages before adding the pesticide.

2. Wear protective clothing which includes gloves, a boilersuit or waterproof cape, woollen socks, a hat and if necessary spray goggles.

3. Wear an efficient face mask respirator when handling concentrates or very toxic chemicals. These masks should have a replaceable cartridge.

4. Do not eat or smoke while spraying or handling spray materials.

5. Shower after spraying.

6. Wash protective clothing after each use and wipe goggles or mask.

7. Be especially careful when handling concentrates before dilution.

Pest Types

Pests primarily feed on plants by either chewing the parts or sucking the sap. It is important to determine the method of feeding since this influences the choice of control measures to be used. The major pests can be split into 2 groups depending on how they feed.

SUCKING	CHEWING
Aphids	Borers
Bugs	Caterpillars and
(Crusader, Harlequin)	Grubs
Cuckoo Spit	Earwigs
Galls	Leaf-eating Beetles
Hoppers	Locusts and Grasshoppers
Jassids	Millipedes
Lerps	Sawflies
Mealy Bugs	Slugs and Snails
Mites	Stick Insects
Nematodes	Termites
Scales	Thrips

Spray Types

Sprays basically kill pests in one of 3 ways and an understanding of the mode of action is an important facet of effective control and also ensures that the correct spray is chosen for the job.

Contact Sprays: as the name suggests these kill on contact. They will kill virtually any insect contacted either good or bad. They are most effective when moist and fresh but some sprays are persistent and retain some contact properties for a few weeks after spraying.

Stomach Poisons: These kill after they have been ingested by the insect. They are only effective against chewing insects such as caterpillars, locusts and sawflies.

Systemic Sprays: these are absorbed into the sap stream and distributed throughout the plant. They are effective against sucking insects such as aphids and mealy bugs which feed on the sap. Once absorbed by the sap of the plant they only kill sucking insects (not chewing insects) and hence are safe for wildlife. Unfortunately many of the systemic sprays are toxic to handle and their widespread use is not encouraged.

Other Sprays

Wetting Agents: these are important materials which increase the effectiveness of sprays. They are usually soapy or detergent type solutions which overcome the waxy nature of leaf surfaces and help the spray to spread evenly over the whole surface. They must be used at no higher than recommended strength as they can cause damage to foliage at higher rates.

Attractants: these are chemicals, which resemble an insect's food source or its sex hormones. They are used to lure insects to an area where they can be destroyed by pesticides. Food attractants, such as fermenting sugars, lure a wide range of insect species, whereas sex attractants

This colourful Cutworm is extremely destructive of plants in tropical regions. *D.V. Beardsell photo*

Pittosporum leaves are often disfigured by the activities of the Pittosporum Leaf-miner. *D.V. Beardsell photo*

Leaf damage on a *Callistemon*, caused by the larvae of the Leaf-blister Sawfly. *D.V. Beardsell photo*

The Painted Apple Moth caterpillar is readily identified by the 4 tufts of bristles on its back. It feeds on a wide variety of plants. *D.V. Beardsell photo*

are specific to a species. Sex attractants have been used with some success against fruit fly infestations.

Safer Sprays

Some sprays are relatively safe to use and do not have a drastic effect on the environment. If used correctly they can give as effective a control as the more toxic sprays. The details of these are given below.

Bacterial Spore Suspensions: the bacterium *Bacillus thuringiensis* is a very effective antagonist of caterpillars, but does not affect any other form of life. Its spores are available in various preparations and sold under commercial trade names. They are sprayed onto the foliage where caterpillars are active and when ingested, germinate in the caterpillar's gut and kill it.

The bacterial spores themselves are readily killed by ultra violet light from the sun and to be effective should be applied in the evenings or during cloudy weather. For continuous protection sprays must be applied every 10-14 days.

Clensel: is a soapy type solution of very low toxicity. It has some properties as a contact material and also kills by coating the insect and blocking its air supply. It has some effect on caterpillars but is best for controlling aphids and scales. Two or three sprays at intervals of 1-2 days may be necessary to clean up persistent attacks.

Derris Dust (Rotenone): this material is a natural compound obtained by crushing and drying the roots of various *Derris* species. It acts as a stomach poison and is effective when sprayed or dusted on foliage where caterpillars are active. It is broken down by sunlight and is best applied towards evening or during cloudy weather.

Garlic Spray: a natural spray made from cloves of garlic. It is effective against a wide range of pests including aphids and caterpillars. It acts as both contact spray and a deterrent and is safe for the handler. It is a very effective deterrent for cats.

To make garlic spray crush 85 g of garlic cloves and mix with 10 ml of paraffin oil. Leave for about 48 hours and then add 562 ml of water and 7 g of an oil based soap. Mix thoroughly, filter out the lumps and store the concentrate in a plastic drum. This will keep for ever and can be used as needed. Dilutions range from 1 in 50 to 1 in 100 parts with water.

Nicotine sulphate: this is a naturally occurring material extracted from tobacco. It acts as a contact poison and fumigant and is effective against a wide range of pests. It must be handled with care as it is toxic to humans but breaks down quickly after spraying and is therefore safe to wildlife (unless contacted while fresh). It is commonly used at the rate of 1½ teaspoons of nicotine sulphate and 28 g of soap to 4.5 litres of water.

Pyrethrum: is a naturally occurring compound extracted from the daisy flowers of the genera *Pyrethrum* and *Chrysanthemum*. It acts as a contact spray and is effective against a range of pests including aphids, caterpillars and bugs.

Sulphur: wettable sulphur which can be dissolved in water has some insecticide properties although it is mainly used as a fungicide.

White Oil: a viscous material which is effective against scale insects. It kills by coating the insect with a layer of oil which cuts off its air supply and the insect suffocates. A thorough coverage is essential for effective control. Two or three sprays at close intervals can also increase its effectiveness as can the inclusion of a contact insecticide such as pyrethrum or maldison. White oil may stunt growth of species such as ferns and orchids and for these plants it is best used at about three quarter strength. Damage is accentuated by high temperatures and white oil should not be sprayed on hot days (above 25°C).

Less Safe Sprays

Carbaryl: a manufactured chemical which acts as a stomach poison and is thus effective only against chewing insects such as caterpillars. It is quite effective and may persist on the foliage for several weeks. Although fairly safe to use it should only be resorted to if safer sprays such as derris dust, lead arsenate or bacillus spores have proved ineffective.

Dimethoate: a manufactured chemical which acts as a systemic poison and when sprayed is only effective against sucking pests. It is also effective against both leaf-eating and sucking pests when applied by trunk injections. It is toxic and must be handled with care. It is highly toxic to bees and should not be used when plants are in flower.

Lead Arsenate: a fairly safe material which is not readily soluble and is applied to foliage as a suspension. It coats the foliage and acts as a stomach poison against chewing insects such as caterpillars. It may persist on the foliage for several weeks but as it only acts if ingested, it is safe for other forms of life. It is used at the rate of 9½ level teaspoons to 4.5 litres of water. If used too frequently arsenic may build up to toxic levels in the soil.

Maldison: this is a manufactured chemical which acts by killing insects on contact. It is effective against most insects including caterpillars, aphids and bugs. It is most effective while fresh but has some persistence on the foliage. Its effectiveness is increased if used in combination with white oil. It is one of the more toxic sprays and should be used with due care and only if safer sprays such as pyrethrum have proved ineffective.

Combination Sprays

Some sprays are more effective when used in combination than when used separately. The effectiveness of white oil is increased by adding a contact insecticide such as maldison or pyrethrum. This combination also increases the effectiveness of the insecticide because the white oil aids its spreading and sticking powers.

A useful control against lerps can be achieved by using a combination spray of white oil and nicotine sulphate (28 ml nicotine sulphate, 224 ml white oil, 18 litres water).

It should be emphasized that not all sprays are compatible and some cannot be mixed together. Information on compatibility can be obtained from the Department of Agriculture or spray firms.

Trunk Injections

Control of pests on large trees is generally impractical however some success has been achieved against both sucking and chewing insects by using trunk injections of systemic materials. The injected insecticide is taken up in the sapstream and transported to the leaves where it is ingested by the pests.

Holes are drilled through the bark to penetrate the wood near the base of the trunk. These holes are about 1 cm in diameter and are drilled at a slight downwards angle. They are spaced evenly around the trunk about 15 cm apart. The systemic material is placed into the holes in a concentrated form from an eye dropper. The holes can be reused if later treatments are necessary although it is probably a better

policy to seal them completely and drill new holes. If old holes are used, they should be slightly enlarged to expose fresh tissue. After use or between uses the holes should be plugged with a mastic material to prevent entry of diseases and aid healing.

The best insecticide readily available for trunk injection is dimethoate. The dosage rate varies with the leaf cover because the material is concentrated in the leaves. Thus sparse leaved trees would end up with a higher concentration of insecticide in the leaves than would trees with a dense canopy if the same dosage was applied. Common dosage rates of dimethoate range from 1-1.5 ml per 1 cm of trunk diameter. The holes are filled until the insecticide reaches just below the bark level. They are then topped up as the insecticide is taken in to the sap until the required dosage has been applied to the tree.

Other Useful Materials

Baits

Baits containing stomach poisons are effective against pests such as cutworms, armyworms, slugs, snails, earwigs and millipedes. The baits are generally scattered in the vicinity of the plants to be protected and may be effective for several weeks, although this depends on the weather conditions. Baits can be used strategically if something is known about the habits of the pest to be controlled. Examples are baiting dark, humid areas for millipedes, baiting on humid or rainy nights for slugs and snails and baiting weedy areas for cutworms.

Commercially prepared baits are available that are effective against the pests mentioned above. Alternatively an effective bait can be prepared by mixing 5 g of Paris Green or

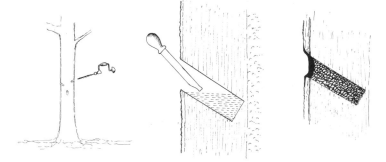

Technique of injecting insecticide into tree trunks.
A — Boring injection holes   B — Placing insecticide   C — Sealing injection hole.

metaldehyde with 120 g of bran. Immediately before use, sufficient water is added to form a crumbly mash and the bait can then be placed in small heaps. This bait is best applied in late afternoon or early evening as it becomes less attractive to caterpillars when it dries. Another useful bait can be made by mixing one part by volume pyrethrum powder or derris dust to 2 parts flour. Baits are poisonous and should not be placed where they can be eaten by pets or children.

Deterrents

Some materials are useful because they act as a deterrent to pests and will protect plants if used in their vicinity. Naphthalene flakes are an excellent deterrent for a wide range of pests and can be used to good effect in glasshouses, cutting frames or around seedlings. Garlic sprays are similarly effective against pests and have the added bonus of deterring cats. Bands of creosote can be used as a deterrent to prevent ground pupating pests such as root borers and weevils from climbing tree trunks. Lime is a good deterrent to many ground dwelling pests. The fungicide thiram is an effective deterrent of rabbits and hares.

Borers can be prevented from egg laying by painting the trunks and limbs of trees with deterrent pastes. The most commonly used paste is bluestone paint made up of copper sulphate 750 g, quicklime 500 g, water 5 litres. The copper sulphate is dissolved in approximately half the amount of water and the lime in the remainder. The two are then mixed in a wooden, earthenware or copper container (never iron) to form the paint which can be brushed over the trunk. A small amount of linseed oil will help the material spread and stick.

Dusts

Insecticides contained in powder can be applied to foliage or soil as dusts. Arsenic compounds can be applied in this way but should be handled carefully. A very useful combination against chewing insects is 1 part lead arsenate to 10 parts talc, hydrated lime or flour. Derris dust is probably the best dust and is widely used for the control of caterpillars in vegetables. Nicotine sulphate can also be used as an effective dust, commonly at a 3% formulation (28 g nicotine sulphate to 6 kg hydrated lime). It is best mixed at frequent intervals and used fresh. Fine sulphur can also be applied as a dust against aphids. A dust composed of equal parts by weight of fine sulphur and hydrated lime has been used with some success against mites. A combined dust made from 1 part fine sulphur to 9 parts lead ar-

senate powder is effective both as an insecticide and a fungicide. Leaf eating beetles can be controlled by dusting with a mixture of one part by weight of pyrethrum powder to 2 parts by weight of talc. Foliage damage may result from dusts if used at temperatures above 30°C.

12   Chewing Insects

BORERS

As the common name suggests, these insects bore holes and tunnels through the heartwood and sapwood of plants. A range of insects is involved, mostly beetles and their larvae, and they attack the wood of the trunk or branches. Many species of plants are subject to borer attack including *Callitris* spp., *Prostanthera* spp., *Melaleuca* spp., *Banksia* spp., *Callistemon* spp. and *Grevillea* spp. but perhaps the most susceptible are *Eucalyptus* and particularly *Acacia* spp. Borers can severely reduce the life of a tree and in bad cases cause its death. Often plants will linger for many years, frequently producing new growth which is vigorous until attacked by the borers.

It has been claimed that borers only attack trees which are weakened or have lost vigour. While this is probably true in the majority of cases the authors know of many instances of healthy vigorous garden plants being attacked. This is a frequent occurrence in gardens that are established in areas where there are numerous weakened or dying eucalypts and wattles. These trees support a large population of borers and the excess spread out to attack some of the native plants in the nearby gardens.

Healthy plants are normally able to tolerate borer attack and usually produce vigorous new growth that outgrows the weakened branches which often break off. Borer attack in healthy eucalypts is often confined to the outer parts of the branches and causes little damage. Attacks on large branches or the trunk are generally sealed off by the exudation of gum or kino. This exudate greatly restricts the borers' activities and will eventually cause their death.

Stem Borers

These attack the above ground parts of plants, principally the trunks and larger branches.

Root Borers

These pests are less obvious because they attack the below ground parts of the plants. Their

Borer on stem of *Callistemon* — note chewed wood and webbing covering hole.

Borer in stem of *Callistemon* — hole uncovered to show extensive damage to bark.

Borer in stem of *Callistemon* — probing with wire to kill larvae.

effects however are similar to stem borers and frequently the die back or death of a single branch can be traced to the destruction by borers of the roots below it. In severe cases trees can be killed. Plants which are frequently attacked include *Acacia* spp., *Eucalyptus* spp. and *Casuarina* spp.

Symptoms of Borer Attack

In small trees the grubs feed around the stem under the bark, cutting the sapwood and causing the branch to snap off where it has been weakened. Similar effects occur on the young parts of older trees. On older branches and the trunk, damage shows up as patches of gum, piles of chewed sawdust and peeling bark which lifts easily. When the bark, gum or piles of sawdust are removed the tunnels of the borers can be seen.

In the early stages borer attack shows up as yellowing of the tips of affected branches. The yellowing extends into older leaves and the tips die. Eventually the whole branch may die back. Severely attacked trees look very unthrifty, usually with a number of dead branches and much of the trunk damaged. Because the trees are weakened they frequently shed branches during winds and may become a hazard.

Borers often use damaged tissue as points of entry although this does not seem essential. Storm damaged trees or those that have been heavily pruned or lopped are often severely attacked.

Many species of insects are borers, attacking a variety of trees. Sometimes they bore in distinctive modes. Most damage is done by the larvae which are usually flattish, fleshy grubs.

Control: some measures should begin as soon

as borer activity is noticed. The holes can be probed with soft pliable wire or filled with solutions of a mild contact insecticide. Kerosene or soap solutions will cause the grub to emerge and it can then be destroyed. Severely affected limbs should be removed and burnt and all cuts painted with a good wound sealing compound. Dying or dead trees should be removed to prevent infection of healthy specimens. Bluestone paste will deter females from egg laying if applied in spring (see Deterrents). Persistent borer attacks should be used as an indicator that the tree has been weakened by some factor in its environment and this cause should be corrected.

Examples

Auger Beetle (Bostrychopsis jesuita) — A common borer, both the adults and larvae of which tunnel into a wide variety of species including wattles, eucalypts, kurrajong (*Brachychiton populneus*), white cedar (*Melia azederach*) and silky oak (*Grevillea robusta*). The larva is a thickset, white grub which fills its tunnels with droppings and undigested wood particles. The adult is 1-2 cm long, glossy black, with a roughened surface and a long downturned head.

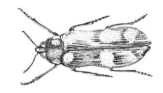

The grubs of Jewel Beetles are destructive borers, which attack a wide variety of plants.

Jewel Beetles (Buprestidae) — a common group of handsome beetles. They are widespread throughout Australia, especially in the drier regions. The larvae attack the stems, trunks and/or roots of a variety of trees including *Acacia* spp., *Banksia* spp., *Casuarina* spp., and *Leptospermum* spp. The murray pine borers (*Diadoxus erythrurus* and *D. scalaris*) are at times very destructive on *Callitris* spp.

Longicorn Beetles (Cerambycidae) — a large group of beetles all of which have long feelers. Some species are slender and others are large and stout. They are frequently common and cause much damage. The larvae usually do not bore deep into the timber but excavate in the sapwood and just below the bark. Some species ringbark twigs. Common examples are the yellow box borer, fig tree borer (*Dihammus vastator*) and various wattle borers.

Web Covering Borers (Cryptophasa spp.) — These are common borers with the characteristic of

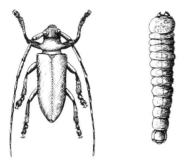

Longicorn Beetles are borers, attacking a variety of plants.

covering their tunnels by an accumulation of sawdust-like material enclosed in a fine web. If this is scraped aside the tunnel is revealed. This is a slanting hole about 0.5 cm across, frequently with the green bark under the covering completely eaten away. The tunnel extends through the centre of branches, considerably weakening them. These are very destructive insects which should be controlled when first noticed. Affected limbs become yellowish and sickly, and usually snap off in a strong wind. The fruit tree borer (*Cryptophasa unipunctata*) attacks a variety of plant genera including *Eucalyptus*, *Acacia*, *Melaleuca*, *Leptospermum*, *Cassinia* and *Prostanthera*. *C. rubescens* tunnels in the stems of wattles and *C. melanostigma* feeds on the bark of many species often ringbarking branches.

Weevils (Curculionidae) — an abundant group in Australia, many species of which are destructive. They can be recognized by the front part of the head being drawn into a snout. Boring types attack such trees as silky oak (*Grevillea robusta*) and kauri (*Agathis* spp.). After felling they may riddle the logs with numerous small holes. The kurrajong weevil (*Axionicus insignis*) is sometimes very destructive of kurrajongs (*Brachychiton populneus*) in western areas. The elephant beetle

Longicorn Beetle.

D.V. Beardsell photo

(*Orthorrhinus cylindrirostris*) attacks brush box (*Tristania conferta*), black bean (*Castanospermum australe*) as well as many species of eucalypt. Many large weevils are root borers attacking a range of plants particularly wattles.

Wood Moths (Cossidae, Hepialidae, Zeuzeridae) — large brownish moths, the larvae of which tunnel in species of *Acacia*, *Leptospermum*, *Eucalyptus* and *Banksia*. The grubs are very large and bore broad tunnels through the heartwood of the tree. The wattle goat-moths (*Zeuzera* spp.) are very large (wingspan to 12 cm across) and with grubs up to 12 cm long. They bore tunnels about 2 cm across in various species of *Acacia* and may be very destructive.

CATERPILLARS AND GRUBS

Caterpillars of moths, butterflies and beetles, attack the leaves of new shoots of a wide range of native plants. Some are of minor importance but others are extremely destructive. Their incidence varies from season to season and in bad years some species may ravage large areas. They are usually controlled by a range of natural predators and parasites but occasionally the balance is upset and the pests increase in numbers to plague proportions.

Control: caterpillars are usually readily controlled with sprays or dusts. Pyrethrum based sprays kill on contact and are safe for the environment because they break down upon exposure to sunlight. Dusts containing pyrethrum or derris are also effective and safe but must be used while fresh. Preparations containing spores of the bacteria *Bacillus thuringiensis* (see Sprays) can be very effective but must be sprayed in the evenings or during cloudy weather. Severe and persistent infestations can be controlled with moderately safe sprays such as carbaryl or lead arsenate but these should only be used with due consideration for the environment.

Examples

Banksia Moth (*Danima banksiae*): The caterpillars of this species are very destructive of *Banksia* spp. and other Proteaceae including cultivated grevilleas. The handsome caterpillars grow to about 5 cm long and are brown, with circular black bands, the end parts being mauve. When disturbed they react by jerking the head backwards and extrude a red forked process from the underside near the head. The moths are up to 8 cm across, and are grey with black and white markings and an orange body.

Case Moths; Bag Moths: These insects get their names because the larvae shelter inside a silken case which is frequently reinforced with sticks or

Pests and Diseases

The Stick Case Moth (*Clania ignobilis*) is common on fine-leaved plants.

The Ribbed Case Moth (*Thyridopteryx herrichii*) constructs a spindle shaped case, without any protective covering.

Saunders Case Moth (*Matura elongata*) is a large species, constructing a case about 15cm long.

leaves. The larvae do not leave the case but the upper parts of the body emerge for feeding or when crawling about. If disturbed the head and legs are quickly withdrawn and the opening of the bag held closed. The males are small slender-winged moths and the female case moths are wingless and never leave their case.

Case moths feed on a variety of plants particularly eucalypts, but seldom cause much damage and in fact add interest to a garden. If severe infestations occur individuals can be picked off by hand and squashed until the numbers are sufficiently reduced. Natural parasites and predators also kill large numbers.

The leaf case moth (*Hyalarcta huebneri*) is sometimes destructive on eucalypts and *Leptospermum* spp. especially in coastal districts. It is easily recognised by the case adorned with leaves and pieces of bark.

The stick case moth (*Clania ignobilis*) usually attacks fine leaved species such as pines and conifers. Its case is protected by stout sticks with a single stick extending much longer than the others. The ribbed case moth (*Thyridopteryx herrichii*) builds an unprotected bag-like case.

Saunders case moth (*Matura elongata*) is the largest species, constructing a case about 15 cm long. The stout caterpillar is dark with yellow markings and eats a wide variety of plants.

Casuarina Caterpillar (*Perna exposita*): A very destructive species which feeds on the stems and leaf scales of *Casuarina* spp., leaving white patches where it has fed. The caterpillars may ringbark branches and severe infestation during dry periods or on weakened trees may result in death of the tree. The larvae are hairy and slender, with a relatively large head. They grow to about 2.5 cm long and spin a small, white parchment-like cocoon on the branches. The adult moths are stout bodied with the females being larger and sluggish compared with the small fast males. When disturbed, the caterpillars drop to the ground and this can be used as an aid in their control. If plastic sheets are spread on the ground and the branches beaten with sticks the caterpillars can be easily collected and destroyed.

Citrus Butterfly (*Papilio anactus*): The handsome butterflies of this species are very decorative but the caterpillars are destructive of citrus trees and the native *Microcitrus* spp. The caterpillars have a greasy appearance and are greenish with dark spots and a forked reddish protuberance near the head. They are voracious feeders and quickly strip foliage from the stems where they are active. The caterpillars are attacked by a variety of predators including the birds known as silver eyes which consume them in large numbers.

Cup Moths (also called Chinese Junk): The caterpillars of these insects are very distinctive being flattish, fleshy, bluish-green and with groups of yellow or brownish retractable hairs near the head and tail. These hairs can sting painfully if contacted, and the larvae are often called stingers. They grow to about 2.5 cm long and appear in large numbers in some seasons

Cup Moth caterpillar.

D.V. Beardsell photo

146

Cup Moth caterpillars attack a variety of eucalypts. The cocoon is cup-shaped.

and may cause considerable damage to a variety of eucalypts. Initially they skeletonize the leaf surfaces but as they grow they eat the whole leaf down to the midrib and may strip large trees.

Several different species of moth produce almost identical caterpillars. The caterpillars build a cup or egg-shaped cocoon in which they pupate. This is a very neat structure which opens by a circular lid. The moths are about 4 cm across, greyish with marbled markings.

Cutworms (Noctuidae): Cutworms are so called because of the habit of the grubs of living in the soil and chewing off seedlings at ground level so that the whole plant topples over. They are fleshy hairless grubs in a variety of colours. When disturbed they have the habit of coiling and remaining motionless for some time. They usually feed at night and hide during the day but they are often seen about during cloudy weather. The adults are brownish moths.

There is quite a variety of cutworms widely distributed throughout Australia. They are very destructive of seedlings of a wide range of species and will also attack and damage older plants. They congregate in weedy areas and seedbeds should be cleared of all weeds and well prepared before sowing. Seedlings should be baited or seedlings sprayed or dusted for continuous protection, if these destructive pests are around. The common cutworm of south eastern Australia (*Agrotis infusa*) produces a dull brown grub while

The Common Cutworm of south-eastern Australia feeds on a variety of plants.

D.V. Beardsell photo

those of tropical areas are more brightly coloured (e.g. *Aedia acronyctoides*).

Emperor Gum Moth (*Antherea eucalypti*): A large insect familiar to most people both as the adult moth and handsome caterpillar. The caterpillars grow to about 10 cm long, are fleshy, bluish green with numerous tufts of non-stinging orange hairs along the body. They are black for about the first week after hatching. They mainly feed on eucalypts but have also been recorded on *Tristania conferta* and a few other species. They chew the leaves right to the midrib and can be very damaging when present in large numbers.

Despite their destructiveness they are very decorative and add interest to a garden. Their numbers can be easily checked by handpicking and squashing or transferring to other host plants. They are avidly eaten by large birds such as cuckoo shrikes and currawongs. Two favourite host plants are *Eucalyptus leucoxylon rosea* and *E. doratoxylon*. The moths have a wing span up to 15 cm and are brown with 4 conspicuous eye blotches on the wings.

Kurrajong Bag Moth (*Sylepta clytusalis*): *Brachychiton* trees are frequently attacked by this pest which forms shelters (bags) by rolling leaves and joining them together with silken threads until a large mass is formed. Numerous caterpillars form colonies within these bags. Each caterpillar grows to about 2.5 cm long and is pale green and hairless. The bags eventually become brown as the leaves die. The adult is a bright yellow moth about 2.5 cm across. The bags can be removed easily with secateurs and burnt. Weak contact insecticides should be jetted into the bags if spraying is necessary for control.

Leaf Skeletonizers

As the name suggests these pests strip off the outer layer of eucalypt leaves leaving a network of veins as a skeleton. The veins quickly brown off and the affected parts become very conspicuous. Damage is caused by caterpillars of several moths. The caterpillars are extremely ravenous and quickly devastate whole branches. In severe infestations, whole plantations of gums may be affected giving the appearance of devastation by fire. The caterpillars are especially fond of eucalyptus with glaucous leaves. Details of two common examples follow.

Blue Gum Caterpillar (*Mnesampela privata*): The caterpillars of this species are hairless, bluish green and grow to about 2 cm in length. They are fleshy and are a severe leaf skeletonizer attacking a variety of eucalypts. Occasionally they also feed by eating the whole leaf, leaving the midribs intact. The caterpillars are gregarious

Pests and Diseases

The Blue gum caterpillar feeds by either skeletonizing the leaf surface, or eating the entire leaf.

D.V. Beardsell photo

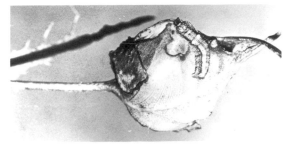

The Blue gum caterpillar shelters between joined leaves during the day.

D.V. Beardsell photo

and during the day cluster together in shelters made by joining leaves together with silken thread. When clustered together they are easily killed by squashing or dropping the cluster into boiling water.

Gum Tree Moth (*Roeselia lugens*): Easily recognized by the small caterpillars covered with white hairs. They are frequently bad on young eucalypts, attacking a variety of species. The caterpillars grow to about 1.5 cm long and have the unusual habit of piling cast-off skins on their head.

Light Brown Apple Moth (*Tortrix postvittana*): One of the commonest and most destructive insects attacking a wide variety of plant species. The grubs usually attack the young growing tips, joining the leaves together with silken threads and feeding within this shelter. They grow to about 1 cm long and are fleshy and light green. When disturbed they wriggle very actively and frequently drop to the ground. The moth is brownish and about 1 cm across.

Loopers: The larvae of various species of moths produce caterpillars that are known as loopers from their characteristic means of locomotion. The front legs are extended forward and the rear ones are brought up to form a characteristic loop in the body of the caterpillar. They may be in shades of grey, brown or green. Some species are camouflaged and hold themselves stiffly amidst the foliage. They feed on a wide variety of native plants and usually appear in numbers without warning. Outbreaks are sporadic and usually occur in spring.

Painted Apple Moth (*Teia anartoides*): A destructive species which attacks a wide variety of plants including *Acacia* spp., *Melaleuca* spp. *Callistemon* spp. and *Grevillea* spp. The caterpillars are hairy with 3-4 conspicuous bundles of reddish hairs on the back. They grow to about 4 cm long and are voracious feeders. They may eat the whole leaf (as in fine-leaved plants) or skeletonize it by eating the upper surface layer (as in broad-leaved plants such as *Acacia pycnantha*). They may be found throughout the year but seem to be particularly active during the cool winter months. The adult males are brightly coloured moths about 2.5 cm across, and the females are wingless.

Procession Caterpillars; Itchy Caterpillar (*Ochrogaster contraria*): A severe pest which attacks a variety of plants but which is particularly fond of wattles such as *Acacia pendula* and *A. salicina*. The caterpillars grow to about 5 cm long and are covered with long, reddish-brown hairs. These hairs are sharp and stiff and cause intense skin irritation if contacted.

The larvae shelter by day in large brown silken bags and come out at night to feed on the foliage. The bags are very conspicuous especially in trees which have been denuded of foliage. The bags should not be handled as they contain numerous irritating hairs and old skins cast off by the caterpillars.

The caterpillars move from tree to tree in long processions each with its head in contact with the caterpillar preceding it. The adult moths are brownish with a wing span of about 5 cm.

Procession caterpillars should be controlled when first noticed as they are rather unpleasant and very destructive. The community bags

A Looper-caterpillar.

D.V. Beardsell photo

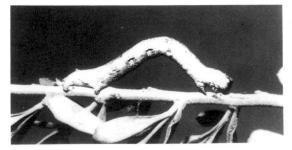

should be clipped off and burnt during the day and/or the trees sprayed with a stomach poison such as carbaryl. The caterpillars are particularly easy to destroy while on the move over the ground.

Webbing Caterpillars: These caterpillars spin a protective webbing over the stems and leaves of the plants on which they feed. This webbing becomes filled with their droppings, chewed leaves and other plant debris and becomes unsightly. The webbings vary from small clusters to large bundles. The caterpillars grow to about 2.5 cm long and bear many black hairs. They feed on a variety of plants but are particularly fond of fine leafed *Melaleuca* and *Leptospermum* spp.

White Cedar Moth (*Leptocneria reducta*): The larvae of this moth are hairy and travel in a procession in a similar way to the procession caterpillars. They grow to about 4 cm long and the hairs cause irritation. They attack only white cedar (*Melia azedarach*) and may completely strip even large trees of foliage. They usually feed at night and during the day migrate to the lower parts of the tree where they hide in crevices in the bark. They may also move from tree to tree in long processions.

Banding is a simple and very effective means of controlling this pest. If a bag is tied around the trunk the larvae will seek shelter in it and can be picked out and squashed during the day. Spraying the foliage towards the evening with carbaryl also gives effective control.

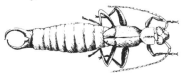

European Earwig (*Forficula auricularia*) is an introduced pest, attacking seedlings and flowers.

EARWIGS

Earwigs are familiar insects which have a pair of forceps at the rear end of the abdomen. They hide under logs, stones, rocks etc. and are common in weedy areas where there is an abundance of decaying organic matter. The native species are not troublesome but the introduced european earwig (*Forficula auricularia*) is a serious pest attacking seedlings and eating the leaves and flowers of a wide variety of plants, including many natives. It is a nuisance in glasshouses where it attacks and destroys the root tips of orchids.

Control: Numbers can be reduced by trapping the insects in balls of crumpled newspaper to which they are attracted for shelter. These can be collected at intervals and burnt. Breeding sites should be dusted with lime or naphthalene flakes. Baiting is a useful technique for protecting valuable plants.

Christmas Beetles (*Anoplagnathus* spp.) feed on eucalypts during the summer months.

Larvae of *Anoplagnathus* spp. are curl grubs, feeding on the roots of plants.

LEAF-EATING BEETLES

Christmas Beetles (*Anoplognathus* spp.): These handsome and familiar beetles which appear during the warm months feed on young eucalypt foliage. They occasionally swarm in large numbers and may completely defoliate the trees. They have a shiny metallic appearance and are coloured green, blue, brown or orange. The grubs, commonly known as curl grubs, feed on the roots of grasses etc.

Control: These beetles are rarely troublesome in gardens and in fact are interesting and decorative additions. If they reach plague proportions the colonies can be disrupted by beating with sticks or jets of water and individuals squashed. Defoliated eucalypts recover quickly.

Paropsis Beetles: Both the adults and larvae of these beetles feed on eucalypt leaves and at times cause considerable damage to the trees. The leaves are eaten in an irregular manner and may be stripped right to the midrib. The grubs are about 1 cm long, pale green or yellowish, hairless and fairly active. The beetles are rounded (pie-dish type) about 1 cm long and yellowish-brown, grey, green or black. When disturbed they usually drop to the ground.

Wattle Blight (*Paropsis orphana*): A number of the larger true-leaved wattles such as *Acacia dealbata*, *A. mearnsii* and *A. decurrens* are attacked by this small pest which causes the leaves to go a reddish-brown as if they had been scorched. Whole trees or whole colonies may be attacked, as under ideal conditions the insects increase in numbers very rapidly. The adults are small beetles about 0.6 cm long, light green with white stripes. The grubs are stout, greenish and taper to a point at the tail. They attack the leaves eating off the surface layer and the damaged parts turn brown. In some seasons they are very severe and may kill even vigorous trees. They were off particular importance in the early 1900's when plantations of wattles were established to provide bark for the tanning industry.

Weevils (Curculionidae): The adults of a number of species of weevils are destructive of plants by chewing leaves, young bark and buds (the larvae are also borers). When in sufficient numbers their depredations can cause serious damage to young trees. The elephant weevil (*Orthorrhinus cylindrirostris*) has been found to be destructive of brush box (*Tristania conferta*), black bean (*Castanospermum australe*) and various eucalypts.

Leaf miners construct tunnels, and excavate areas just below leaf surfaces.

LEAF MINERS

The larvae of a range of insects, including beetles, moths and flies, feed on the internal tissues of leaves. Their activities can be seen from the surface after the area they have fed upon dies off. This shows as narrow lines which are in fact tunnels or broad sometimes blistered areas. The tunnels are rarely straight and usually twist and convolute around in a most irregular manner. The larvae are generally flattened so that they can feed in the confined areas of the inner leaf tissue.

Control: leaf miners are very difficult to effectively control without resorting to highly toxic chemicals, because the larvae are shielded by the leaf surfaces. Fortunately serious outbreaks are sporadic and most attacks are of a minor nature. Affected leaves should be removed and destroyed so as to reduce the population of future generations.

Examples

The jarrah leaf miner is an undescribed species of moth, the larvae of which sometimes tunnel extensively ·in the leaves of jarrah (*Eucalyptus marginata*). Patches of the leaves die off and severe infestations give the trees a scorched appearance. Many eucalypts are attacked by· leaf miners as well as a wide range of other

The larvae of the Leaf Blister Sawfly (*Phylacteophaga eucalypti*) excavate blisters below the leaf surface.

plants. The larvae of the moth *Nepticula anazona* attack the leaves of *Tristania suaveolens* and those of *Lithocolletis aglaozona* feed on *Kennedia* and *Glycine* species. The larvae of the leaf blister sawfly (*Phylacteophaga eucalypti*) feed on various eucalypts, callistemons, and brush box (*Tristania conferta*) causing blotching and large papery blisters. The wattle leaf miner (*Acrocercops plebeia*) attacks wattles with silver phyllodes such as Qld silver wattle (*Acacia podalyriifolia*). The phyllodes become blotched, discoloured and eventually covered by a large blister. The pittosporum leaf miner (*Phytobia pittosporophyllii*) damages the leaves of *Pittosporum* spp. but rarely causes severe effects.

Grasshoppers are common pests of gardens. Some species can swarm in plague proportions.

LOCUSTS AND GRASSHOPPERS

Locusts and grasshoppers are familiar insects. Grasshoppers are generally regarded as solitary insects while locusts are gregarious. There is a range of species of both types all of which feed on plants. Some gregarious species reach plague proportions in years with a particular set of climatic conditions, e.g. the Australian plague locust (*Chortoicetes terminifera*). All species feed by chewing large lumps out of leaves usually leaving only the midrib. Locust plagues strip foliage from any plants in their path, and may even chew the green stems if they are ravenous enough.

The solitary-type grasshoppers are not usually as great a problem as the swarming types although if present in sufficient numbers they can cause considerable damage. The katydid (*Caedicia olivacea*) and green gum tree hopper (*Torbia perficta*) are common green species with flattened wing covers resembling a gum leaf. Both species have long slender antennae and camouflage well in the foliage. They are usually an interesting addition to a garden but occasionally assume pest proportions.

One species to be actively discouraged is the large ridge-backed locust (*Goniaea australasiae*). The adults grow up to 8 cm long, are brownish, and are very strong with sharply pointed teeth on the hind legs. They are extremely voracious feeders eating a variety of plants but are particularly fond of palms and the cottonwood (*Hibiscus tiliaceus*) which they may strip of foliage. This insect is widespread but is most damaging in tropical and subtropical areas.

Control: control of locust swarms is extremely difficult and is usually carried out on an area wide basis. Continual spraying is necessary but even this may not protect plants because the damage is done before the insects die. Valuable plants should be completely covered to deny access to the foliage.

Solitary grasshoppers are best controlled by squashing (if they can be caught) or beating with sticks. Spraying with a stomach poison such as arsenate of lead is effective but a continual spray cover must be maintained as the creatures are nomadic. Research is under way to determine if the micro-organism *Nosema locustae* offers a method of biological control. Experience in the U.S.A. indicates that this organism can suppress grasshopper populations for several seasons.

SAWFLIES

Sawflies, also sometimes called spitfires, are common insects the larvae of which congregate in groups during daylight hours. When disturbed they jerk up their heads and tails, at the same time emitting a sticky yellow fluid which usually smells strongly of eucalyptus oil. At night they move in procession to the young shoots which they systematically strip of all leaves. They mainly attack eucalypts but *Callitris*, *Ficus*, and *Leptospermum* spp. may also be eaten.

The grubs of the large steel-blue sawfly (*Perga affinis*) are very common in eastern Australia during winter and spring. They grow to about 5 cm long, are black with white hairs and their lower abdomen curls like an elephant's trunk. They form large, dense clusters on a variety of eucalypts with swamp gum (*E. ovata*) being one of their favourites. Small greenish roughened grubs with a long pointed tail are often found attacking tea-trees (*Leptospermum* spp.) sometimes

causing severe damage. They belong to the genus *Pterygophorus*. *Callitris* branches are sometimes defoliated by the slender green grubs of the pine sawfly (*Zenarge turneri*). The leaf blister sawfly feeds on the tissues beneath the leaf surface (see Leaf Miners).

Control: sawflies frequently cause consternation when found on garden eucalypts. Although destructive, their occurrence is sporadic and they are readily controlled by picking off the clusters and squashing them or dropping them in boiling water. They can also be knocked to the ground with sticks or jets of water. Once on the ground they are not very mobile and are subject to attack by predators. Large birds such as currawongs and cuckoo shrikes feed on them while on the tree, in the process knocking many to the ground.

STICK INSECTS

These are unusual insects, the numbers of which occasionally blossom to plague proportions and they can be very destructive to forests. They seldom cause much damage in home gardens and are an added feature of interest. The large stick insect *Didymuria violescens* may completely defoliate large areas of forest however it is rarely encountered in gardens. The leaf insects (*Extatosoma* spp.) are found in gardens and feed on a wide variety of plants.

TERMITES

Termites are very destructive communal insects widely distributed throughout Australia and especially abundant in tropical regions. Some species build the familiar termite mounds, but others are less conspicuous, living in trees or underground tunnels. They eat wood and wood products and can be very destructive of trees, both living and dead. Their attacks are often insidious, entering the trees below ground level and working up into the trunk and branches. The trees usually become sickly and affected parts are brittle and break off easily. On some eucalypts, particularly of the bloodwood group, the termite tracks show up as dark strands in the bark. Affected trees eventually collapse and die.

Control: Termites are very difficult to control and preventive measures seem better than cures. All dead or dying trees should be removed completely (roots and all) and burnt, and any nests destroyed. Unfortunately feeding lines range a long way from a termite colony and large areas may have to be treated. Resistant trees such as *Callitris* spp. may be used in areas of severe infestation. Garden trees should be examined regularly and if infested the termite tunnel should be excavated and poisoned before the tree is killed. If infested trees are apparently healthy and worth saving, a hole 0.5 cm across can be drilled into the centre of the tree near the base and a dust, such as paris green or maldison, blown in and the hole sealed with grafting wax or wood putty.

THRIPS

Thrips are tiny insects very difficult to see but their effects are usually obvious. Some species attack delicate tissues such as flowers or young growth causing distortion of the affected parts frequently accompanied by papery patches. Older leaves take on a silvery mottled appearance and fall prematurely. Young shoots of *Callistemon* species are a favourite target with the leaves becoming twisted, reduced in size and often reddish. Flowers with delicate petals and stamens such as *Hibbertia*, *Eucalyptus*, *Leptospermum* and *Baeckea* spp. are attacked and seed formation may be prevented. The flowers of NSW christmas bush (*Ceratopetalum gummiferum*) are subject to attack and usually brown off and fall without developing into the attractive red bracts for which the species is renowned.

Thrips are generally not a major problem to native plant growers, although in years with a warm winter they may build up rapidly to plague proportions and swarm in immense numbers.

Another type of thrip, called gall-making thrips, produce bladder-like galls on the leaves of *Syzygium*, *Acmena* and a few other Myrtaceae, *Geijera*, *Casuarina*, and also some wattles such as *Acacia pendula* and *A. aneura*.

The glasshouse thrip (*Heliothrips haemorrhoidalis*) attacks the foliage of tender species such as ferns, *Cissus* spp., and *Passiflora* spp. They favour cool moist conditions and are sometimes severe on glasshouse plants. Their numbers are drastically reduced by hot, dry weather.

Control: spraying with a contact material such as a pyrethrum based spray. A nicotine sulphate and soap spray is also effective but must be used with care (see Combination Sprays).

13 Sucking Insects

APHIDS

Aphids are small soft-bodied insects which congregate in colonies on young shoots. There are no species native to Australia but a number have been introduced which are troublesome pests of glasshouses and some native plants growing in the open. They can be very damaging to new fronds of ferns, and new shoots and flower spikes of orchids. *Callitris* stands are sometimes attacked very heavily by the pine aphid (*Cinara thujafolia*). This is a fairly large, dark brown, hairy aphid which casts the trees with a sticky honey-dew followed by sooty mould. *Hymenosporum flavum* is subject to attack by the green peach aphid (*Myzus persicae*).

Aphids feed by sucking sap from the young succulent parts of the plant. They excrete considerable amounts of honey-dew which is fed upon by ants. Honey-dew also provides an excellent substrate for the development of sooty mould. Some aphids live underground feeding on the roots of plants, generally herbaceous species such as lilies, grasses, etc. Root feeding aphids congregate in colonies and are generally globular in shape and are covered with white or grey waxy secretions.

Control: Aphids build up in numbers very

A typical plant-feeding bug.

D.V. Beardsell photo

quickly and should be controlled as soon as noticed. Small infestations can be squashed between the fingers but large infestations may need spraying with a contact insecticide such as maldison or a nicotine sulphate-soap solution (see Combination Sprays). Soap solutions applied under pressure can also be effective. Hosing with jets of water disrupts the colonies and kills some of them by drowning. Excellent control in glasshouses has been achieved by using pest strips which release insecticidal vapours into the atmosphere. Ladybirds and lacewings are very fond of aphids and their activities should be encouraged. There is no ready means of controlling root feeding aphids.

BUGS

Bugs are sucking insects some species of which attack plants. They usually congregate in mixed colonies of adult and immature stages and attack soft new growth. When handled they emit a nauseous odour.

Control: Small infestations cause minor damage but large swarms should be controlled before they cause significant damage. Complete control is difficult but levels can be reduced by shaking the colonies into a collecting device such as an upturned umbrella or sheet of plastic. The collected insects can then be killed by burning, immersion in hot water or water topped with kerosene. The insects are sluggish in the early morning or during cool weather and are then easier to catch. If spraying is necessary it is best to use a pyrethrum-based contact spray.

Examples

Crusader Bugs (Coreidae): These are occasional pests which attack eucalypts, wattles, hibiscus and cassias by sucking the tender young shoots and causing them to wilt and die back. They are large, distinctive bugs which give off an unpleasant smell if handled. The holy cross bug (*Mictis profana*) is a common, very destructive species found in eastern Australia, especially in

153

subtropical regions. The adults can be easily recognized by the distinctive white or yellow cross on the back. The immature stages are brown with 2 small orange spots on the abdomen. These pests become particularly active during hot weather.

The Holy Cross Bug (*Mictis profana*) is a common destructive pest, of eastern Australia.

Harlequin Bug (*Dindymus versicolor*): A strikingly marked bug which is a familiar sight in waste areas often on the weed marshmallow. The adults are about 1 cm long and are red and black with a green or yellowish abdomen. Immature forms are wingless and brighter coloured than the adults. The bugs cluster in colonies which are a mixture of adults and immature forms in various stages of development. If handled they emit a noxious odour. They are not usually a troublesome pest but occasional outbreaks damage such plants as *Alyogyne*, *Hibiscus*, *Abutilon* and *Thomasia macrocarpa*.

Metallic Shield Bug (*Scutiphora rubromaculata*): This brightly coloured bug is a decorative addition to the garden, although sometimes it reaches nuisance levels and must be controlled. The adults are about 1 cm long, shield-shaped, and are deep metallic blue mottled with black and with 2 bright red blotches on the thorax. They feed on a variety of plants including figs (*Ficus* spp.), cottonwood (*Hibiscus tiliaceus*) and *Melaleuca* spp. They are particularly fond of *Ficus* fruits and may swarm over the trees. Their feeding may be followed by sap exudation.

Other Bugs: Various native plants are attacked by other bugs such as the stainer bug (*Dysdercus sidae*) and the leptocoris bug (*Leptocoris lurida*). The former species grows to about 1 cm long, and is reddish brown with a black spot on each wing cover, and yellowish beneath. The leptocoris bug grows also to about 1 cm long but is much more slender. It also is reddish brown and is dull red beneath.

CUCKOO SPIT

Cuckoo Spit or Frog Hoppers are small cicada-like insects the young of which cover themselves with a frothy sticky secretion as a protective device. They attack a variety of succulent plants including salt bushes and also the young growth of woody plants such as wattles and grevilleas.

They are rarely a problem and in fact add interest to a garden. If troublesome infested branches can easily be snipped off and the insects squashed or burnt.

GALLS

Galls are mis-shapen swollen objects found on various plant parts but particularly on stems, leaves or blossoms. They are growth malformations of the plant and are induced by the stimulus of insect or fungal attack. This stimulus results in an increased level of hormones flowing to the site of irritation and the promotion of abnormal growth around this point.

Galls vary tremendously in shape and size. The particular shape depends on the interaction of a range of factors between the species producing the galls, the site of attack and the host plant. Some galls have a shape so characteristic and repeatable that it can be used in their classification. Sometimes the galls caused by male and female insects of the same species are of different shapes.

Control: control of galls is generally not a practical proposition as regular spraying is necessary throughout the spring, summer and autumn months. Infestations on young trees or small, localized infestations should be removed and destroyed so as to reduce attacks by future generations. Spraying may be of some use in severe infestations which threaten to weaken or kill a tree, however this is rare. Because the insects are protected inside the gall they must be killed by using systemic insecticides (see Sprays). These are generally toxic to animal life and their widespread use is not encouraged.

Galls are caused by a wide variety of creatures. Insect galls may be caused by the larvae of wasps, flies, scales, lerps and thrips. Galls may also be caused by fungi, eg. *Uromycladium Gall.*

Flower-galls on *Eucalyptus polyanthemos.*

D.V. Beardsell photo

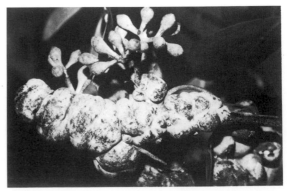

Damage caused by incorrect tie, has allowed the entry of Borers into the trunk of this tree.

D.V. Beardsell photo

A section of stem, showing Borer tunnel, and larva of Fruit Tree Borer.

D.V. Beardsell photo

Dying branches often indicate the presence of Borers.

D.L. Jones photo

Three stages in the life cycle of a common leaf-eating beetle (*Paropsis*).

D.V. Beardsell photo

Flower-galls on *Acacia longifolia*.   *J. Fanning photo*

Pimple-galls on leaves of *Eucalyptus nicholii*.

D.V. Beardsell photo

Examples

Blossom Galls on eucalypts are produced by the maggots of small flies. If attacks are severe they may prevent seed production. Galls are also commonly formed on the flower heads of various wattles.

Casuarina Gall (Cylindrococcus spp.): these coccid insects produce galls on various species of *Casuarina*. The galls are remarkable in that they closely mimic the fruiting capsules of the tree even down to the overlapping scales. The insect feeds inside the gall. The galls of *Cylindrococcus spiniferus* are common on *Casuarina littoralis*.

Coccid Galls: these are usually found on eucalypt branches and may be of weird shapes. They are frequently elongated with projecting horns near the apex. Galls produced by male and female insects are of different shapes, the females being very large, and the males small and horn-shaped. Both sexes frequently make galls in clusters often with the males growing upon the side of the female gall.

Gall making Thrips cause small bladder-like galls on the leaves of *Syzygium* and *Acmena* spp.

Pimple Galls: numerous small pimple-like swellings on the surfaces of gum leaves. These

are usually caused by wasp larvae. The red-flowering gum (*Eucalyptus ficifolia*) is sometimes especially prone to attack by these wasps.

Psyllid Galls cause large ball-like swellings on eucalypt leaves. These swellings are often solitary on a leaf and may be reddish in colour.

Uromycladium Gall — see Diseases page 174.

JASSIDS

Jassids or Leaf Hoppers are small insects which are usually deep metallic blue or black variegated with white, red or yellow bands. They resemble miniature cicadas, and when disturbed jump and fly or move around the tree keeping on the far side of the branch or trunk. They feed in clusters on young eucalypt growth which may wither and die if the infestation is severe enough. They secrete copious quantities of honeydew upon which ants feed, and which forms a site for the growth of sooty mould.

Control: jassids are usually a minor pest and only a problem in some years. Large clusters are readily dispersed by jets of water or hitting with sticks. Many can be killed by these procedures.

LERPS

Lerps (Psyllids) are small sucking insects which attack the leaves of a variety of native plants, but particularly eucalypts. The majority of species feed on the leaf surface and are protected by a small waxy scale-like covering which may be of intricate design. They usually congregate in colonies and cause discoloured dry patches in the leaves which shed prematurely. Severe infestations may partially defoliate trees and if attacks persist for a couple of years, dieback of the branches may occur. Honeydew is secreted by the feeding insects and becomes a site for the development of sooty mould.

The mahogany gums *Eucalyptus botryoides* and *E. robusta* are very prone to attack by lerps which

Casuarina-gall on stem of *Casuarina littoralis* — the gall mimics the fruits of the plant.

D.V. Beardsell photo

render the trees very unsightly. Moreton Bay Figs (*Ficus macrophylla*) are also attacked by lerps which cause blobs of sticky sap to exude from the damaged areas. The leaves shed prematurely and these are sticky to the touch and become a nuisance to pedestrians. Severe attacks may cause dieback of mature figs and cases of death are known.

A distinct group of lerps causes galls on eucalypt leaves (see Galls). A couple of species including the unusual star psyllid (*Tyora sterculiae*) feed on *Brachychiton* spp.

Control: lerp infestations vary considerably each season and are not usually a major problem. Control of bad infestations is not practical and the populations of lerps are soon reduced usually by natural predators and parasites. If attacks persist the levels can be reduced by spraying with a nicotine sulphate — white oil mixture (see Combination Sprays). Trunk injections of systemic sprays can also be used to good effect (see page 141).

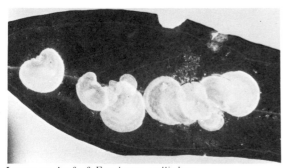

Lerps on leaf of *Eucalyptus melliodora*.

D.V. Beardsell photo

MEALY BUGS

These are plump soft insects closely related to scales. They exude a dense covering of waxy filaments which act as a protective device and are water repellant. The insects congregate in colonies and suck the sap from soft young shoots. They attack a variety of plants but are particularly fond of ferns, orchids, palms and large leafed liliaceous species such as cordylines. On occasions they may also attack other plants such as grevilleas and wattles. Attacks on palms centre around the central developing crown and may be very persistent and severe. Developing fronds become misshapen and stunted, and prolonged attacks may weaken and even kill plants.

Control: small infestations can be cleared up by squashing or dabbing the insects with methylated spirit. The insects are difficult to

Passion Vine Hopper *(Scolypopa australis)*, is a common, widespread pest, attacking a variety of plants. The adults (left) have clear wings borderd with brown. The immature stage (right) has white hairs, and jumps when disturbed.

wet because of their waxy coating, but severe infestations can be controlled by spraying with a mixture of white oil and maldison, or white oil and nicotine sulphate (see Combination Sprays).

PASSION VINE HOPPER

Passion Vine Hopper (*Scolypopa australis*) is a common widespread species which is a severe pest of *Passiflora* species. The adults are about 1 cm across, triangular, with clear wings bordered by brown and black bands. They jump and fly when disturbed. The immature stage are small, white hairy insects which spring actively when disturbed and are popularly known as hairy rockets.

These pests feed by sucking sap from young plant parts and in bad years congregate in large colonies. They frequently attack uncoiled fern fronds causing distortion and dry papery patches in the tissues. As well as *Passiflora* species and ferns they attack a variety of plants such as *Grevillea* spp., *Acmena* spp. and *Hymenosporum flavum*. Honeydew is exuded by the insects and attacks are accompanied by growth of sooty mould.

Control: small infestations can be controlled by squashing or disturbing with jets of water. Severe infestations must be controlled by contact sprays such as pyrethrum, nicotine sulphate or maldison.

SCALES

Scales are sucking insects which conceal themselves beneath waxy, leathery or cottony shells or secretions. They often cluster in colonies and may cause serious damage to plants. Sooty mould usually grows on the sugary exudates secreted by the insects and they are frequently attended by ants.

Control: small or localized infestations can be removed from the branch and squashed or burnt.

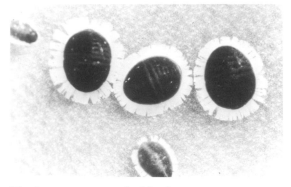

The immature stage of white fly.

D.V. Beardsell photo

Larger infestations should be sprayed with applications of white oil until the insects have all been killed. White oil may damage young soft growth, or stunt soft species such as ferns. In such cases it should be sprayed at about three quarters recommended strength. Soap solutions applied under pressure can also be useful. Combination sprays of white oil and pyrethrum or maldison may prove more effective (see Combination Sprays).

Examples

Brown Olive Scale (Saissetia oleae): a very common scale which attacks a wide variety of plants especially members of the family Rutaceae. Copious quantities of honeydew are excreted, resulting in ant activity and strong growth of sooty mould. The adults are dark brown, oval, domed and with a raised "H" marking on the back. They usually cluster along the twigs and on the undersides of leaves.

Casuarina Scale (Frenchia casuarinae): an unusual shaped scale which produces a tall helmet-like hard black covering over the insect which is pink and jelly-like. The insects become attached to the young branches causing swellings around where they are situated. These swellings increase in size as the branches age, and become woody and gall-like. In severe attacks the trees become weak and frequently die from the depredations of the pest.

Cottony Cushion Scale (Icerya purchasi): a readily recognisable scale because the females frequently have a conspicuous white egg sac attached which is covered with cottony threads. Adults are usually about 0.5 cm long, are reddish black, hairy and with black legs. The males are winged. They usually cluster along the midribs and veins on the undersides of leaves but may also be found on the bark of the branches and trunks. They attack a variety of trees and shrubs

Thrip damage, on young shoots of *Callistemon salignus*.

D.V. Beardsell photo

in subtropical and temperate areas, and are particularly fond of fern-leaved wattles such as *Acacia dealbata*. Outbreaks occur sporadically but are usually cleaned up within a few months by parasites and predators such as ladybirds.

Globular Wattle Scale (Cryptes baccatus): very similar in appearance to the eriococcid scale of eucalypts but attacking a wide variety of wattles. Both phyllodinous species (such as *Acacia longifolia*, *A. linearis* and *A. floribunda*) and ferny leaved types (such as *A. decurrens* and *A. mollissima*) are attacked. At times this pest causes serious damage to stands of *A. pendula* and *A. aneura* in inland areas. The adult scales are globular, up to 0.8 cm long and vary in colour from white to brown or slaty blue. They congregate together in clusters and can weaken or kill a healthy tree. Control steps should be taken when the scales are first noticed as they increase in numbers very rapidly.

Gum Scale (Eriococcid Scale — Eriococcus coriaceus): a widespread scale which attacks a range of eucalypt species (and some other Myrtaceae). The adults are yellowish or cream,

Green Peach Aphids, on young leaf of *Hymenosporum flavum*.

D.V. Beardsell photo

Eriococcid Scale, smothering young branches of *Eucalyptus caesia*.

D.L. Jones photo

Eriococcid Scale attended by Ants, on a branch of *Eucalyptus caesia*.

D.V. Beardsell photo

Root aphids.

D.V. Beardsell photo

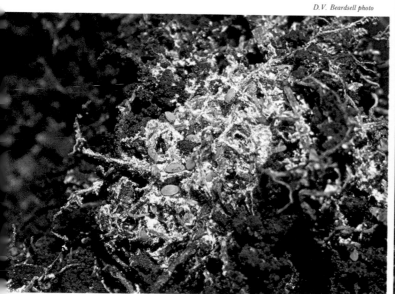

domed and leathery in texture. They cluster in dense masses along the stems and branches and exude a reddish sticky gum on which sooty mould grows. They are a very strong pest and, if unchecked, can kill a healthy vigorous young tree. Once established they can be very difficult to eradicate and steps should be taken when first noticed. They are controlled by a range of predators including ladybirds, but these frequently seem to be absent, allowing the scales to rapidly build up numbers and become established. Small infestations can be cleaned up by squashing between the fingers or removing and burning the infested branches. Weak trees are more susceptible to attack as are also some species of *Eucalyptus* such as *E. perriniana*, *E. morrisbyi*, *E. pulverulenta*, *E. crenulata* and *E. caesia*.

Saltbush Scale (Pulvinaria maskellii): a scale which may cause severe damage to various species of saltbush in particular *Atriplex nummularia*. In severe infestations the plants appear as if they have burst into masses of white flowers. Adult females are about 0.5 cm long and exude a cottony secretion to protect the eggs. Outbreaks are sporadic probably associated with fluctuations in predator levels.

Soft Brown Scale (Coccus hesperidium): the adults of this scale are about 0.4 cm across, oval in shape, very flat and pale yellow-brown. They characteristically cluster in small dense colonies on isolated branches and twigs and don't usually spread over the whole plant. They attack a variety of trees and shrubs in tropical and subtropical areas and are also found on ferns and orchids in glasshouses. Because of their habit of clustering in isolated colonies, control can frequently be obtained by cutting off the affected branch and burning.

Tea Tree Scale (Eriococcus orariensis): this scale is very similar to both the gum scale and globular wattle scale but is found principally on *Leptospermum* spp. Severe attacks weaken plants considerably and are invariably accompanied by sooty mould which blackens leaves and stems and gives the whole plant a blasted appearance.

Wattle Scale (Pseudococcus albizziae): a leathery scale generally similar in appearance to the eriococcid scales, but the adults secrete cottony threads. It mainly attacks *Acacia* and *Albizia* spp. It is particularly fond of ferny leaved wattles and severe infestation may kill healthy trees. Sooty mould grows on the honeydew secreted by the insects giving the tree a blackish appearance. Ants also feed on the honeydew. The adults are 0.2-0.3 cm long, deep reddish brown and surrounded by a white cottony margin. They are gregarious and congregate in dense colonies along the branches.

White Louse Scale (Unaspis citri): infestations of this scale resemble shredded coconut sprinkled over the leaves and stems of the plants upon which it feeds. These are in fact the coverings of the male scales, the females being duller and less conspicuous. Attacks of this scale may be very persistent and last for several seasons, causing twig dieback, bark splitting and general weakening of the afflicted plant. Heavy attacks give the branches an appearance of being covered by snow. This scale attacks a wide variety of species including many members of the family Rutaceae. It is usually controlled by predatory caterpillars of a small moth.

WHITE FLY

White fly (*Trialeurodes vaporariorum*) are small insects 0.2-0.3 cm long. The adults are winged and are covered with fine white powder giving rise to the common name. They rise in clouds when disturbed while feeding. The young are wingless and congregate on the undersides of developing leaves, sucking the sap. White flies are mainly a pest of vegetables but also attack a variety of glasshouse plants including many species of ferns.

Control: white fly is very difficult to control and a sequence of sprays may be necessary. Small infestations can be cleared up by dabbing with methylated spirit. Severe infestations can be controlled by spraying with a mixture of white oil and nicotine sulphate (see Combination Sprays, page 141).

14   Other Animal Pests

ANTS

Ants are not often a problem in a garden and in fact most kinds are usually beneficial. Small black ants, however, are attracted to the honeydew excreted by sucking insects such as lerps, scales, mealy bugs and jassids, and frequently encourage the activity of such pests by guarding them against predator attack and moving the young onto fresh growth. The introduced Argentine ant (*Iridomyrmex humilis*) is one of the worst culprits.

Control: sticky solutions containing weak insecticide will reduce the incidence of ants, when applied to the bark near the base of the plant.

MILLIPEDES

Millipedes are hard-shelled, many jointed, worm-like creatures which have numerous legs and a characteristic habit of coiling when disturbed. They mainly feed on rotting vegetation but will also eat tubers, bulbs and fleshy roots of plants such as orchids, lilies and palms. They build up in damp situations where there is an abundance of decaying organic material.

Control: numbers can be reduced by collecting and squashing. This technique can be effective at night aided by a torch. Organic material should not be allowed to accumulate in dark, moist places. Potential breeding sites should be raked free of organic material and dusted with lime or naphthalene flakes.

MITES

Mites are tiny animals some species of which are serious pests of plants. They are not insects but are closely related to spiders since they have 8 legs. Adult mites are so small that they are difficult to detect even with the aid of a magnifying glass. They are found on the undersides of leaves and feed by sucking the sap. They spin fine, delicate webs and reproduce very rapidly during warm, dry weather.

Mites attack a large variety of plants and are often a serious pest of plants in glasshouses. Afflicted leaves take on a yellowish mottled colour with a dry or sometimes silvery appearance. In severe infestations, the leaves turn yellow and fall prematurely.

Control: control measures should be initiated as soon as the pests are noticed because they build up in numbers very quickly. Jetting the undersides of the leaves with water helps reduce the population but spraying with a suitable miticide is the control measure most commonly used. A dust consisting of a mixture of equal parts by weight fine sulphur and hydrated lime has been used with some success. A predator mite (*Typhlodromus occidentalis*) has been released onto some commercial crops with considerable success in reducing the pest mite populations. Another predator mite (*Amblyseius womersleyi*) has been found to control two-spotted mite in subtropical areas. Small black ladybirds of the genus *Stethorus* also feed actively on mites.

Examples

The two spotted mite (*Tetramychus urticae*) is also called the red spider. Both it and the bryobia mite (*Bryobia arborea*) are the major pest species in Australia attacking a wide range of plants.

NEMATODES

Nematodes (Eelworms) are tiny (microscopic) round worms that are ubiquitous in soils. The vast majority of species are harmless to plants but a few are parasitic and can be of considerable importance. They feed by sucking the contents of plant cells. Most attack the root systems, bulbs and rhizomes but some species are found on the aboveground parts of stems, leaves and flowers. Most species feed from the outside but some root feeding nematodes enter the cells and cause lesions.

Soil nematodes occur in a wide variety of soil types but require good aeration and the presence of moisture. They are tolerant of acidity, alkalinity and salinity. They prefer infertile soils rather than highly fertile soils.

Symptoms of nematode attack vary with the species. Root feeding nematodes disrupt water and nutrient uptake, resulting in stunted plants which exhibit leaf yellowing and various deficiency symptoms. Stem nematodes cause stems to become swollen and distorted and affected plants are stunted. Leaf nematodes cause small black patches on the leaves of susceptible species.

Control: control of root nematodes is only practical under nursery conditions by pretreating all soil with steam-air mixtures. Field populations can be reduced by using fumigants such as methyl bromide but this is impractical and dangerous for home gardens. Population levels can be reduced by growing resistant plants such as grasses, and antagonistic plants such as african marigold or species of *Crotalaria.*

Control of stem and leaf nematodes has been achieved by spraying with fenaminiphos.

Examples

Root Nematodes: root knot nematodes (*Meloidogyne* spp.) have been found on a wide range of species including *Grevillea* spp. and *Myoporum parvifolium.* This nematode produces swellings and galls on main and lateral roots, disrupting normal root function. Root lesion nematodes (*Pratylenchus* spp.) are extremely widespread and have been found on many species of the family Myrtaceae including the Tasmanian blue gum (*Eucalyptus globulus*) and other plants such as *Grevillea alpina* and *Hardenbergia violacea.* This nematode can kill the plant in extreme cases. It causes a stunted much-branched root system and infected roots show small black patches. The burrowing nematode (*Radopholus similis*) has been found on such species as *Lagunaria patersonii, Syncarpia glomulifera* and *Tristania conferta.* It forms burrows in the soft outer tissues of roots. These burrows can form entry points for pathogenic root fungi such as the honey fungus (*Armillaria mellea*).

Above Ground Nematodes: the stem nematode (*Ditylenchus dipsaci*) has been found on the stems of wattles and species of *Cassia.* It can be transported on seeds but these are killed if the seeds are treated by the boiling water technique. The same nematode also attacks bulbs causing them to become soft and spongy with brown rings.

The leaf attacking nematodes (*Aphelenchoides* spp.) have been found on a wide range of native plants of the family Asteraceae as well as kangaroo paws (*Anigozanthos* spp.) and many ferns (e.g. *Asplenium bulbiferum* and *Pteris tremula*).

They reduce the vigour of infected plants and in extreme cases cause death. Their attacks are worse during the cooler months of the year.

POSSUMS

Possums feed on a variety of vegetation and may be destructive in gardens. They are especially fond of developing shoots and buds and can ruin a year's flowering in a couple of nights' feeding. The large brushy tailed possums are the most destructive and may travel long distances each night in search of food.

The use of metal bands around the trunks of isolated trees prevents access by possums. These bands should be loosened at intervals and checked to see that insect pests are not building up in numbers beneath them. In shrubberies spraying with the fungicide thiram has some benefit as a repellent. If attacks persist the animals should be trapped and released in a forest where they can find shelter and food. Garlic spray would also be worth a try as a repellent.

RABBITS AND HARES

These animals often damage young trees by gnawing the green bark on the trunk. This damage sets back the growth and development of the trees, as well as providing entry points for pests and diseases. If trees are ringbarked they can easily die.

In areas where these animals are pests the trees should be protected until established. The following techniques can be useful.

1. Wrap bituminous paper around the trunk to about 60 cm high. Special bands can be purchased for the purpose.

2. Circle the trunk with a wire netting guard. This should be about 30 cm from the trunk at any point and supported by stakes.

3. When establishing plantations they should be surrounded by a secure fence of rabbit proof netting.

4. The fungicide thiram and also garlic spray act as a repellent to rabbits and hares and can be sprayed on the trunks and surrounding areas.

SLATERS

Slaters (Wood Lice) are greyish, jointed, creatures which have numerous legs. They congregate in damp, shady places where there is an abundance of organic matter and are frequently in decaying wood. They mainly feed on decaying plant material but also eat soft shoots and root tips. They are especially fond of the root tips of

Scale, on leaves of *Eucalyptus alpina*.

D.V. Beardsell photo

The slug-like larvae of a Syrphid Fly, feeding on Cottony Cushion Scale.

D.V. Beardsell photo

Globular Wattle Scale, on branches of *Acacia viscidula*.

D.L. Jones photo

Lady Bird and larvae, feeding on Cottony Cushion Scale.

D.V. Beardsell photo

163

orchids and can cause considerable damage in glasshouses.

Control: numbers can be reduced by clearing up accumulations of organic matter, and spreading lime or naphthalene flakes. Baiting provides the best method for keeping this pest under control.

SLUGS AND SNAILS

These familiar and common pests attack a variety of plants but are very destructive of seedlings and succulent species such as lilies, bulbs, kangaroo paws, ferns and orchids. In severe infestations the green bark at the base of sappy species such as mint bushes, grevilleas and salt bushes may be eaten and the plants ringbarked. The white cedar (*Melia azedarach*) is particularly prone to attack. Severe ringbarking can result in death of the plants.

The leaves of succulent species such as kangaroo paws, and many bulbs are continually browsed and the surface layers stripped off exposing the sappy cells. These damaged areas become slimy from the exudation of sap and are a point of entry for other diseases. Such plants may be eaten right back to the bulbs and even the surfaces of the bulbs are eaten.

Control: regular baiting with commercial preparations is the best means of controlling these pests. Succulent species should be protected continually and young plants should be baited until established. Baits should be applied before rain to coincide with the maximum activity of these pests.

15   Diseases and their Control

DISEASES

Australian plants are afflicted by a range of diseases with the severity of the attack depending on many factors but chiefly the health of the plant. Some diseases are extremely virulent and can cause death of large well established plants and may spread to ravage whole areas. Most diseases however, only cause limited damage and occur sporadically when a particular set of conditions favours an outbreak. A few diseases are insidious and cause stunted growth or reduced flowering over many years without ever really becoming obvious.

Causative Agents

Diseases are primarily caused by 3 groups of pathogens — fungi, bacteria and viruses.

Fungi: these are the commonest pathogens attacking native plants. All parts of the plants may be attacked but the leaves, roots and timber are particularly susceptible. Fungi spread by spores and some types are very troublesome during warm, humid, still weather. They can spread rapidly under ideal conditions and control steps should be taken immediately damage is noticed.

Bacteria: in fruit crops, pathogenic bacteria cause wounds associated with cankers, gumming and blight of blossoms and young leaves. The only bacterial pathogen known to significantly damage native plants is the crown gall organism but there are probably others of importance.

Viruses: viruses are minute particles which live within plant cells. If present in sufficient numbers or in combinations of different virus species plant damage can occur. Typical virus symptoms include irregular mosaic patterns on leaves, distortion of young shoots and leaves, colour breaks in flowers and reduced size and rosetting of leaves. Virus attacks stunt plant growth and severe attacks can kill. Viruses are transmitted by sucking insects such as aphids, hoppers, jassids, etc. Plants raised from seed are generally free of viruses although a couple of viruses are known to be seed transmitted.

Viruses are known in a few native plants and are suspected in many others because of symptoms such as mosaic patterns which appear in the leaves of species such as *Solanum aviculare, S. lacinatum, Pterostylis curta, P. baptistii* and *P. nutans.* Research is needed to clarify these suspicions. The orchid *Cymbidium madidum* is known to suffer from Cymbidium mosaic virus. This causes yellowish and black streaks in the leaves and weakens infected plants. Passionfruit suffer from woodiness virus which causes distorted leaves and fruit. Similar symptoms have been observed in the native *Passiflora cinnabarina* but it is not certain if the virus is the cause.

The effects of virus are promulgated by vegetative propagation. Cuttings, divisions or scions for grafting should only be taken from healthy vigorous plants and never from unthrifty plants with distorted or mosaic-patterned leaves. Plants suspected of being virus infected should be destroyed. Aphids and other possible vectors of virus transmission should be controlled when noticed. Secateurs or knives should be sterilized if they have been used to cut plants suspected of being virus infected.

DISEASE CONTROL

Methods of disease control vary with such factors as plant health, stage of advancement of the disease and the type of disease involved. The best disease control relies on prevention rather than cure.

Practices to Reduce Disease Incidence

1. Vigorous healthy plants are better able to resist disease than are weak or unthrifty plants. Only select those plants which are healthy and vigorous. Attend to all of the plants' needs such as drainage, fertilizers, and watering and remember that any setback can contribute to the entry of disease.

2. Avoid sowing seed or planting gardens too thickly. Air movement is an excellent control of some fungus diseases such as moulds. Thick

planting encourages rapid spread of disease. Thick planting can be useful to give a rapid effect in a garden but thinning may be necessary after a couple of years.

3. Avoid large areas of a single species, as this encourages rapid spread of any disease which attacks that species.

4. Trim ragged edges of large wounds with a sharp instrument, and dress with a suitable sealing mastic to prevent entry of disease. Large pruning cuts should be treated in a similar manner.

5. Remove weak or dying trees and check plants at regular intervals.

6. Initiate control measures as soon as diseases are first noticed. Use fungicidal treatments as a last resort and then in strict accordance with safety procedures and the manufacturer's directions.

7. Choose the correct fungicide for the job and wet the affected area thoroughly.

Symptoms of Disease

Necrosis: death or decay of tissue common, following attacks on young tissues.

Lesions and Cankers: growths on the leaves, branches or trunks which are usually black and hardened by the exudation of gum. They are often irregular in shape.

Wilting followed by Dieback: the young shoots wilt followed by dieback which extends down the branches. This symptom indicates interruption to the water supply system of the plant such as a vascular blockage or damage to the roots.

Stunting: reduced growth and stunting is characteristic of many diseases.

Fungicidal Sprays

Fungicidal sprays, pastes or dusts can be extremely useful for controlling diseases but they should be handled carefully and with all due respect to the environment and health, as outlined in the Chapter on Pest Control. Not all fungicides are compatible with each other, or with pesticides, and may cause problems if mixed together. Information on compatibility can be obtained from the Department of Agriculture or spray firms.

Benomyl: a systemic fungicide which is very useful for controlling botrytis and other moulds. It is not very soluble in water and must be kept agitated while spraying. It is toxic to humans and must be used with care. A good combination fungicide or drench can be made by mixing benomyl with wettable sulphur (7.5 g sulphur, 1 g benomyl, 2 ml wetting agent, 2.25 l water).

Bordeaux Mixture: this mixture is one of the oldest fungicides known but is still very effective. It is not very soluble in water and must be kept agitated while spraying. It can damage foliage and should only be applied while fresh, and during cool weather. It is effective against a variety of diseases and is relatively safe to use. It can be made up by dissolving 40 g of copper sulphate in 5 l of water in one plastic bucket and 40 g of hydrated lime in 5 l of water in another plastic bucket. The two can then be mixed together with constant agitation. Bordeaux paste is a useful protectant to cover wounds (see page 83).

Captan: this material is used as a protectant fungicide or drench. It is very useful against botrytis (grey mould) and damping-off of seedlings. It can also be used as a dust to prevent fungus damaging stored seed. It is relatively safe to use but the concentrate must be handled with care.

Copper Oxychloride: this material is a useful substitute for bordeaux mixture because it requires less preparation and is more soluble in water. It is however generally less effective than that material. It has proved very useful for controlling the various leaf spots that infect a variety of plants. It is relatively safe to use.

Dinocap: a useful material for the control of powdery mildew. It must be sprayed with a wetting agent and must be handled carefully especially as a concentrate.

Fenaminosulf: a useful soil drench for the control of damping-off in seedlings. It also inhibits *Phytophthora* to some extent. It should be handled carefully.

Sulphur: this element is available as a wettable powder which is effective as both a fungicide and an insecticide. It is safe to use and gives control of diseases such as powdery mildew and blights.

Thiram: a useful fungicide for the control of leaf spots. It is a very good repellent for hares and rabbits.

COMMON DISEASES OF NATIVE PLANTS

Armillaria Root Rot

Armillaria mellea is a vigorous fungus which attacks the root systems of established plants causing dieback or death. A wide range of species is susceptible including both natives and exotics. It is commonly known as the honey fungus and is also sometimes called shoe-string fungus.

The fungus becomes established in old stumps or pieces of large roots or other dead wood. It is spread through the soil by means of thick, flat, black fungal strands which resemble shoe laces

Adult Long-tailed Mealy Bug and young.

J. Fanning photo

The leaves of Mahogany Gums are
frequently disfigured by Lerps.

D.V. Beardsell photo

Cuckoo Spit.

D.L. Jones photo

Flower Galls on *Acacia baileyana.*

D.V. Beardsell photo

167

and are known as rhizomorphs. These can enter roots and are the means of infection of the fungus. After entering the root, the fungus spreads through the root system and base of the trunk beneath the bark. In infected roots the fungus can be seen as a creamy layer beneath the bark.

Infected trees lose vigour and become unthrifty. Branches die back from the tips and eventually the whole plant dies when the fungus encircles the bark of the trunk. Clusters of honey coloured toadstools are produced from the base of the dead tree and also from the source of infection such as the decaying stump.

Control: plants infected by *Armillaria* may linger for many years, dying slowly. Control of infected plants is impractical and they are best removed and burnt. If noticed early, plants may benefit from having a trench of soil dug around to locate and destroy the rhizomorphs. Prevention is much better than cure and an important control measure is the complete removal and destruction of all stumps, large roots and pieces of decaying wood. Infected soil areas must be fumigated before replanting.

Cinnamon Fungus (*Phytophthora cinnamomi*)

Cinnamon fungus is a vigorous pathogen which kills a wide range of plants by attacking the root system. It is very widespread and is spreading through much of the forests of southern Australia where it is causing great destruction. About half a million acres of the magnificent jarrah forests of WA have been destroyed since about 1927, and it is estimated that much more is doomed. In Vic the important coastal strip of east Gippsland is severely infected as well as the Brisbane Ranges and parts of the Grampians to the west of Melbourne. The fungus is present in Qld and northern NSW, but does not appear to cause severe damage there except in coastal areas or on cultivated crops. There are indications that the fungus has been present in northern Australia for a considerable period but has only recently been introduced into southern Australia.

Fungal threads and resistant spores of the cinnamon fungus survive in infected soil and decaying plant roots. Soil containing these is the usual source of infection when it is used for gardens or in nursery containers. The fungus invades the fine feeding roots of plants causing them to die and reducing the feeding surface available. The fungus also produces swimming spores which travel in water and hence spread with the natural drainage of water. These spores are produced during warm, wet weather and are chemically attracted to live roots which they in-

fect. It has been estimated that in warm wet conditions, (such as occur during heavy rainfalls during summer) the fungus can complete its life cycle within 24 hours.

Cinnamon fungus is common in home gardens, orchards, parks and nurseries and causes horticulturists much anguish. It has devastated some gardens including the Botanic Gardens in Canberra where large areas were devastated within 2 years of its introduction.

Cinnamon fungus causes a variety of symptoms in plants, depending on the species attacked and the soil conditions where it is growing. The most startling appearance of the disease is the sudden and dramatic collapse within a couple of days of a plant which was apparently healthy. This type of collapse is common in susceptible species such as those originating in areas with a dry climate (e.g. many *Banksia* spp., *Dryandra* spp., *Isopogon* spp., *Adenanthos* spp. and some *Hakea* spp., *Grevillea* spp. and *Eucalyptus* spp. from WA). Such sudden collapses may occur in either well drained or waterlogged soils if the species is very sensitive to cinnamon fungus. The collapse usually occurs during hot weather and is a direct result of the decay of the plant's root system. Often plants which collapse in this way have been infected for several months but have been able to survive because the remaining roots have gathered sufficient water for the plants' needs. This is not possible in severe stress conditions and the plants collapse rapidly.

Cinnamon fungus becomes much more virulent in heavy or waterlogged soils and virtually only resistant plants can survive such a combination. In well drained soils, cinnamon fungus may not kill the plants but will cause stunting, slow growth and die-back of the growing tips. The small feeding roots are attacked and the leaves of affected plants are often yellow with brown margins and apices. Plants in such situations may survive for quite a long time but often succumb after warm wet periods of 24 hours or longer, when conditions favour the fungus.

Control: improvement of soil drainage by installing drains, raising garden beds and/or using sunken paths greatly increases the chances of plants surviving attack. In areas known to be infected with cinnamon fungus only tolerant species should be grown (see list).

Infected soil should be fumigated before replanting unless resistant species are being used. Such soils can also be sown down to grass for at least 3 years to eliminate any resistant spores of the fungus. Some chemicals offer some hope of control but most are still in the experimental stage of development. Fenaminosulf prevents the fungus developing in the soil while the chemical is present, but does not cure infected plants.

Uromycladium gall on *Acacia mearnsii.*

Plants believed to be tolerant of Phytophthora cinnamomi

*—highly tolerant

Acacia acinacea
baileyana
*dealbata**
decurrens
fimbriata
floribunda
howittii
longifolia
mearnsii
pravissima
prominens
retinodes
*riceana**
salicina
saligna
verniciflua
*Acmena smithii**
*Agonis flexuosa**
*juniperina**
parviceps
Albizia lophantha
Angophora costata
floribunda
hispida
melanoxylon
*Anigozanthos flavidus**
Astartea heteranthera

Baeckea imbricata
linifolia
virgata
Banksia integrifolia
robur
spinulosa
Brachychiton acerifolium
populneum
Callistemon acuminatus
*citrinus**
comboynensis
linearis
linearifolius
*macropunctatus**
paludosus
*salignus**
*sieberi**
*viminalis**
Calytrix alpestris
Castanospermum australe
Casuarina cunninghamiana
glauca
pusilla
Ceratopetalum gummiferum
Darwinia camptostylis
citriodora
Elaeocarpus grandis

reticulatus
Epacris longiflora
microphylla
Eucalyptus alba
alpina
astringens
bancroftii
bosistoana
*botryoides**
*camaldulensis**
*camphora**
cephalocarpa
cinerea
citriodora
cladocalyx
cloeziana
*coccifera**
cordata
cornuta
crenulata
*deanei**
dwyeri
eximia
ficifolia
gardneri
*globulus**
*gomphocephala**
goniocalyx
gummifera
*gunnii**
haemostoma
incrassata
intermedia
*kitsoniana**
lansdowneana
lehmannii
leucoxylon
maculata
maidenii
mannifera ssp. *maculosa*
melliodora
nicholii
*ovata**
pauciflora
*perriniana**
polybractea
pulverulenta
risdonii
*robusta**
rubida
saligna
scoparia
*sideroxylon**
smithii
spathulata
stellulata
tasmanica
tereticornis
tessellaris
torelliana
vernicosa
viminalis
Eupomatia laurina
Goodia lotifolia

Grevillea acanthifolia
asplenifolia
arenaria
banksii
buxifolia
'Clearview David'
glabella
hookerana
lanigera
mucronulata
juniperina
longifolia
robusta
rosmarinifolia
shiressii
Hakea dactyloides
*nodosa**
petiolaris
*salicifolia**
scoparia
suaveolens
Howittia trilocularis
Hymenosporum flavum
Indigofera australis
Kunzea ambigua
Leptospermum ellipticum
epacridoideum
*flavescens**
grandiflorum
'Horizontalis'
*lanigerum**
*squarrosum**
Lomatia longifolia
polymorpha
*Melaleuca armillaris**
*bracteata**
*decussata**
*diosmifolia**
gibbosa
*halmaturorum**
*hypericifolia**
lanceolata
leucadendron
linariifolia
macronycha
nesophila
pulchella
spathulata
squamea
*styphelioides**
thymifolia
viminea
violacea
wilsonii
Melia azederach
Myoporum insulare
*Pittosporum phillyreoides**
*revolutum**
*rhombifolium**
*undulatum**
Pultenaea daphnoides
Swainsonia galegifolia
*Syzygium coolminianum**
paniculatum

Pests and Diseases

Plants believed to be sensitive to Phytophthora cinnamomi

*— very sensitive

Acacia aculeatissima*
　alata*
　aspera
　botrycephala
　brownii*
　continua
　drummondii
　glandulicarpa
　gracilifolia
　lanigera
　pulchella
　rigens
　spinescens
　triptera
　varia*
Anigozanthos bicolor
　humilis*
　manglesii
　pulcherrimus*
　rufus*
　viridis
Asterolasia asteriscophora
Astroloma ciliatum*
　conostephioides*
　pinifolium
Baeckea astarteoides
　behrii
　crassifolia*
　ramosissima
Banksia ashbyi*
　attenuata
　audax
　baueri*
　baxteri*
　benthamiana*
　brownii
　burdettii
　caleyi
　canei
　candolleana*
　coccinea*
　dryandroides
　elderana*
　grandis*
　hookerana*
　laevigata
　laricina
　lindleyana
　media*
　meisneri
　nutans
　occidentalis
　ornata
　petiolaris
　pilostylis
　praemorsa
　prionotes*
　prostrata
　quercifolia
　repens

　sceptrum
　solandri*
　speciosa*
　sphaerocarpa
　verticillata
　victoriae*
Beaufortia decussata
　heterophylla
　purpurea
　squarrosa*
Boronia anemonifolia
　denticulata
　heterophylla
　megastigma
Calothamnus gilesii
　quadrifidus
Chamelaucium sp. 'Walpole'
Conospermum mitchellii*
　triplinervium*
Crowea saligna
Darwinia lejostyla
　micropetala
Dryandra baxteri*
　calophylla*
　conferta*
　formosa*
　fraseri*
　polycephala*
　serra*
Eucalyptus caesia
　calycogona
　campaspe
　consideniana
　cosmophylla
　crucis*
　delegatensis
　desmondensis
　diversifolia*
　dives
　dumosa
　eremophila
　erythrocorys*
　forrestiana
　gracilis
　grossa
　kingsmillii*
　kruseana*
　macrandra
　macrocarpa*
　muellerana
　nitens
　nutans
　obliqua
　occidentalis
　oleosa
　orbifolia*
　platypus
　preissiana
　pyriformis
　radiata

　regnans
　rhodantha*
　salmonophloia
　salubris
　scabra
　sepulcralis*
　sieberi
　stricklandii
　tetragona
　tetraptera
　torquata
　viridis
　websterana*
　woodwardii
Grevillea acerosa
　alpina
　aquifolium
　asparagoides*
　baueri
　bipinnatifida*
　brevicuspis
　capitellata
　chrysophaea*
　dielsiana*
　dimorpha
　dryophylla
　endlicherana
　evansii
　floribunda
　ilicifolia
　insignis*
　jephcottii
　lavandulacea
　leucopteris
　miqueliana

　pilulifera*
　steiglitziana
　stenomera
　triloba
　victoriae
Hakea bucculenta*
　cucullata
　francisiana*
　lehmanniana
　subvaginata
　multilineata*
Hypocalymma angustifolium
　robustum
Isopogon buxifolius
　dubius*
　formosus*
　latifolius*
Lechenaultia biloba
　formosa
Melaleuca coccinea
　nematophylla
Petrophile biloba*
Pultenaea humilis
　pedunculata
　subternata
Telopea speciosissima
Thryptomene baeckeacea
Verticordia densiflora*
　insignis*
　mitchelliana*
　plumosa*
Xanthorrhoea australis
　minor
　resinosa

Collar Rot

As the name implies the part of the plant to be damaged by this disease is the lower part of the trunk at soil level. Collar rot is caused by species of *Phytophthora* other than *P. cinnamomi* (e.g. *P. cactorum*). The trunk is usually infected within 15 cm of soil level and the rot may completely encircle the trunk. The plants appear unthrifty and the leaves yellow. The bark above the rot may crack and exude gum. If the infected bark is removed the tissue below is brown and often has a sour smell. Usually there is a distinct margin between the healthy and diseased tissue.

Control: collar rot is favoured by saturated soil and practices such as hilling soil or mulches around the trunk. Drainage must be improved and every effort should be made to reduce humidity in the area of the trunk. A heavy dressing of lime on the soil surface around the trunk is claimed to reduce the incidence of collar rot. Budded or grafted plants should be planted with the union well above soil level. The bark of afflicted plants can be cut away to expose healthy tissue and the area painted with bordeaux paste or a mastic containing a fungicide. If

Flower Gall on *Acacia pycnantha.* *D.V. Beardsell photo*

Stem Galls on *Eucalyptus robusta.*

D.V. Beardsell photo

Eriococcid Galls assume bizarre shapes.

D.V. Beardsell photo

Leaf Galls often severely disfigure *Eucalyptus ficifolia.*

D.V. Beardsell photo

the fungus is killed and the wound is not too extensive the plant will survive and recover from such treatment.

Crown Gall

Crown gall is a widespread bacterial disease that is known to attack over 600 species of plants around the world. It is caused by the bacterium *Agrobacterium tumefaciens* and attacks the root system and underground stems of plants, causing swollen lesions, galls and cankers. These are usually roughened and misshapen and constrict the flow of sap through the area attacked. Plants are stunted and severe attacks can kill even healthy plants. The galls also weaken the attacked area and badly affected plants may blow over.

Crown gall is mainly a pest of cultivated soils and appears to be unknown on undisturbed areas. Native plants known to be sensitive or resistant to the disease are listed in the accompanying table.

SUSCEPTIBLE TO CROWN GALL

Abutilon theophrastii	*Cordyline stricta*
Araucaria bidwillii	*Eucalyptus tereticornis*
Brachychiton acerifolium	*Ficus benjamina*
Brachychiton populneum	*Lythrum salicaria*

RESISTANT TO CROWN GALL

Acacia longifolia	*Grevillea robusta*
Callitris endlicheri	**Melia azedarach**
Crinum asiaticum	*Tristania conferta*
Eucalyptus melliodora	

Control: crown gall is extremely difficult to control once established in a plant. Vigorous healthy plants will withstand infections better than weak plants and may not even show symptoms. Soils known to be infected with crown gall should be fumigated before planting. A sterile strain of the crown gall bacterium which does not cause the disease is available commercially. This competes actively with the disease producing type and prevents infection. It is known as Isolate 84 and the usual method of application is to dip the plants in solutions of it before planting.

Damping-off of Seedlings

Damping-off is a disease which attacks young seedlings, particularly during warm, moist weather. The first obvious symptoms of attack by a damping-off fungus are when seedlings begin toppling over. This usually occurs suddenly and without warning. Close examination of afflicted seedlings will show a constriction of the stem at the soil surface associated with a watery-brown discolouration of the tissues. Seedling damping-off is commonly caused by fungi belonging to the genera *Pythium* and *Rhizoctonia*, but occasionally species of *Phytophthora* are involved.

Damping-off spreads very rapidly and should be controlled when first noticed. It is worst when seedlings are sown too thickly, and in warm conditions the affected area can be seen spreading through the batch. Occasionally some seedlings will survive the attack but usually have a withered constricted stem at soil level.

Control: control can be achieved by drenching the soil with a mixture of benomyl and sulphur, captan or fenaminosulf at the rate of 10 level teaspoons in 22 litres of water over 2 square metres. Seed can be treated with captan or some fungicidal dust before sowing. It is always best to sow into sterilized or pasteurized soil (some control can be achieved by heating the soil in an oven at 98°C for 30 minutes). Care must be taken to prevent recontamination of pasteurized soil as the disease is much more severe under these conditions.

Ink Disease of Kangaroo Paws

Kangaroo Paws are subject to attack by a fungus commonly known as Ink Disease. This disease is readily identified because it causes blackening of leaves and flower stems. The blackening usually shows first at the leaf tips then spreads down the leaves into the rhizomes. If uncontrolled, Ink Disease can kill weaker species such as *Anigozanthos manglesii* and *A. viridis*, although vigorous species such as *A. flavidus* are generally resistant. Vigorous plants are more resistant to the infection than weak ones.

Control: control of Ink Disease is fairly difficult as a range of factors influences the results. Plants growing in cool moist climates are much more susceptible than plants growing in hot dry climates and there is some indication that nutrient deficiencies in soils (particularly potassium and calcium) may increase the plant's susceptibility. The best means of control is to keep the plants vigorous and healthy. If they are still attacked, then spraying with a fungicide such as copper oxychloride at recommended strength may be beneficial. Applications of potash and calcium are also worth a try. On badly infested plants it is best to remove and burn affected leaves. In cool moist climates, species which are susceptible, such as *A. manglesii*, are difficult to grow for more than 12-18 months. In such areas it may be best to treat this species as an annual, raising a fresh batch from seed each year.

Leaf Spots

The leaves of a variety of species of native plants are disfigured or distorted by various fungi. Most attacks are sporadic and do little more than render the leaves unsightly. Severe infestations occasionally occur and these can cause defoliation of part or all of the plant. Mature plants recover from such attacks with little more than a setback but young trees may be stunted and seedlings killed. Leaf spots are generally more prevalent in tropical and subtropical regions than in temperate zones.

Eucalypt leaves are disfigured by blotches caused by the fungus *Phaeoseptoria eucalypti*. Severely affected leaves are shed and the fungus causes little damage to mature trees. It can however have disastrous effects on eucalypt seedlings and should be controlled as soon as noted. The juvenile leaves of blue gum (*E. globulus*) may become badly marked by species of *Mycosphaerella* and *Hainesia lythri*. Black velvety blotches on *Hakea* leaves and fruits are caused by the fungus *Cladosporium*. Damage to mature plants is minor although weakened plants, such as those growing in poorly drained areas, may become severely disfigured. Leaves of *Ficus* spp. may be blotched and damaged by various fungi such as *Fusarium hypocreoideum* and *Phyllachora rhytismoides*.

Control: most leaf spots can be controlled by copper sprays such as bordeaux or copper oxychloride or thiram.

Moulds

Under still, very humid or drizzly conditions mould may grow on seedlings or bushy plants which have fine foliage. Attacks are mostly short lived and cause little damage but in long periods of still, humid or drizzly weather persistent attacks can cause leaf damage and rotting of seedlings. Grey mould (*Botrytis cinerea*) is one of the commonest types covering affected foliage with a mass of fine grey threads. It can kill seedlings and damage fine leaved species such as *Astroloma ciliatum*, *Acrotriche serrulata*, *Grevillea pilulifera* and *Thryptomene baeckacea*. Damage is more severe if the species is planted in an unfavourable situation, such as frequently occurs with *Eremophila* spp. grown in shaded situations in southern Australia. Plants grown in sunny, well ventilated situations do not suffer to the same extent if at all.

Control: moulds are readily controlled by spraying with benomyl or captan.

Powdery Mildew

Leaves, young shoots, flowers and fruits of a variety of species are attacked by these diseases which cover the afflicted part with a white or greyish fungal growth and masses of white powdery spores. The disease is most prevalent in spring and spreads very rapidly in warm, humid, still conditions. Leaves become distorted and are often folded or cupped. New growth is infected as it is produced and older leaves become hard and brittle before being shed prematurely.

Powdery mildews are a common disease of nurseries and glasshouses, but can also occur in gardens during periods of still humid weather or where plants are planted too thickly. It spreads extremely rapidly and should be controlled when first noticed. Seedlings can be killed by the disease.

Control: powdery mildew can be controlled by improving ventilation of glasshouses or nurseries, or moving afflicted seedlings to a position where there is more air movement. Sprays of a mixture of benomyl and sulphur, wettable sulphur, dinocarp or sulphur dust should be applied at regular intervals until control is achieved.

Shoot Blight

This disease, which affects a variety of *Eucalyptus* species and a few closely related plants, is caused by species of the fungus genus *Ramularia*. Young shoots and leaves are attacked and develop masses of white globules. These become brown and eventually develop into necrotic lesions. The stems become distorted and in severe cases the shoots defoliate and die back.

This disease attacks young trees in warm humid areas and is sometimes severe in coastal districts of NSW and Qld. It is particularly severe on *Eucalyptus maculata* and *E. citriodora*.

Control: spraying with copper oxychloride.

Sooty Mould

A common fungus disease which covers plants with a black, sooty material, rendering them very unsightly. It grows on honeydew secreted by sucking insects such as scales, aphids, mealy bugs, jassids and lerps. Occasionally it is found on secretions exuded by young fast growing tissues.

Control: control of sooty mould involves removing the source of honeydew on which it grows, i.e. the sucking insect. If the infestations of these pests are controlled, the sooty mould usually disappears within a couple of weeks.

Stem Canker of Red Flowering Gum

The spectacular flowering gum *Eucalyptus ficifolia*, is severely attacked in its native state by a fungus

Two-spotted Mite, feeding on *Pandorea*.
D.V. Beardsell photo

Powdery Mildew on eucalypt seedling.
D.V. Beardsell photo

Leaf Galls on *Acacia dealbata*.
D.V. Beardsell photo

disease *Sporotrichum destructor*. This disease enters through bark injuries and causes large cankers on stems and trunks. These swell and split to reveal the wood beneath and eventually become coated with a powdery mass of white spores. The leaves and small branches wither off, followed by larger branches and finally the death of the tree.

Stem canker also attacks *E. calophylla* and *E. haemotoxylin* in WA, although with less vigour than on *E. ficifolia*. Strangely enough stem canker is only found on *E. ficifolia* that have been planted and not on those growing naturally.

Control: control of stem canker is extremely difficult and to date no fungicides have been found to be effective. Wounds should be trimmed and dressed to prevent the entry of the fungus and affected branches should be removed when noticed. Trees should be inspected regularly to minimize the chance of infection. Some trees are known to be resistant to stem canker and these provide hope for future control however, to date, attempts at vegetative propagation have proved extremely difficult.

Uromycladium Gall

Large galls on wattle stems and developing seed pods are usually caused by the fungus genus *Uromycladium*. The galls are generally brown, misshapen and with a powdery or granular texture. Galls of this type on stems of *Acacia mearnsii*

174

The distinctive fruiting bodies of Honey Fungus, are produced on dying and dead trees.

W.R. Elliot photo

Cladosporium Leaf-spot, on *Hakea elliptica*.

D.V. Beardsell photo

Cinnamon Fungus has killed one plant in a group of this prostrate *Banksia*.

D.L. Jones photo

Leaf-spot on *Eucalyptus lehmannii* seedling, caused by *Hainesia lythri*.

D.V. Beardsell photo

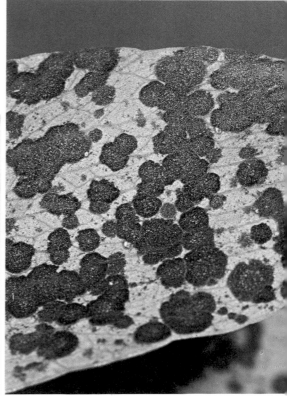

may be up to 15 cm across. Bad infestations are injurious and weaken or may even kill a tree. Severe attacks on developing pods may completely inhibit seed production.

Control: weakened trees are attacked more severely than vigorous, healthy trees. Control of badly infected trees is impractical and they are best removed to prevent infection of others. Trees should be maintained in a healthy condition and galls removed when noticed.

Wood Rotting Fungi

Many types of wood rotting fungi attack the trunks and branches of established trees. Most enter through damaged tissue, such as where a branch has been torn from the trunk in a storm, or from borer holes, termite holes or other injuries and then spread through the wood around the entry point. The genus *Fomes* can enter through the roots in a manner similar to that of *Armillaria* and like that fungus also becomes well entrenched in dead trunks. *Polystictus* spp. may spread through the larger branches, killing them off one at a time. The appearance of plate-like or bracket fruiting bodies is a sure indication of infection and usually indicates an advanced stage of decay.

Control: control of wood rotting fungi is generally impractical except if noticed in the very early stages and badly affected trees are best removed before they infect others. Prevention is better than cure and all wounds should be trimmed and dressed with bordeaux paste or a protective mastic to prevent infection. Sick or dying trees and dead stumps should be removed from the area as a hygienic measure.

16 Nutritional Disorders and other Ailments

NUTRITIONAL DISORDERS

Nutrient Deficiencies

Nutritional disorders occur regularly in soils. Each plant species produces a characteristic set of growth symptoms when growing in soils low or deficient in an element. These symptoms are related to the use of the element within the plant's structure and chemistry. Such deficiencies have been studied for many years and the basic symptomatology related to deficiencies (or excess) of each element is known although this varies with each species.

Correction of Deficiencies: most deficiencies are readily corrected by adding the deficient element to the soil in the correct quantity. Speed of response by the plant will be variable depending on such factors as the element involved, the temperature and time of the year and how deficient and stunted the plant became before the missing element was added.

Occasionally adding the element to the soil may not give the desired response. This is common in alkaline soils where some elements such as zinc are tied up by the high calcium levels and are unavailable for plant growth. Zinc added to the soil is similarly tied up and is best applied as liquid solution to the foliage. Similar results may happen with phosphorus and molybdenum in very acid soils (see Soil pH page 95).

A single deficient element can stop, stunt or cause distorted plant growth. The only way to restore normal growth is to add that missing element. Increasing the levels of the other elements will bring no response until the deficit of the missing element is corrected.

Nutrient Toxicities

Some elements are toxic to plants when present in the soil in excess quantities. Usually this excess is due to an imbalance such as an extremely low or high soil pH or a low level of some other element. Nutrient toxicities produce characteristic growth symptoms and these are outlined where known under each of the elements in the following pages.

Correction of Toxicities: Toxicities are more difficult to correct than are deficiencies. Often it is necessary to change the pH of the soil or else increase the level of some other element with which the toxic element interacts. Toxicities are fortunately rare in soils and are usually caused by overuse of fertilizers or lime.

The nutrition of native plants is a relatively new subject and little is known about the responses of the vast majority of species. As a general rule plants have basic similarities in their behaviour to nutrient disorders and thus symptoms for crop plants can be used as a guide for other plants. The following deficiency symptoms are based on those for food crops but have been modified where the authors have had experience with a deficiency in native plants. For convenience the elements are dealt with in alphabetical order. For more details on fertilizers see also the chapter on Plant Nutrition.

Boron

Deficiency Symptoms: wilting and defoliation of the upper parts of shoots followed by death of the terminal bud and dieback of the shoots. Leaves may become thickened and lateral buds often develop.

Correction: boron compounds such as borax or boric acid applied at low concentrations to the soil or as a foliar spray (boric acid at 1 g per litre).

Remarks: deficiency symptoms of boron are extremely variable depending on the species. Wattles (*Acacia* spp.) may be badly affected by boron deficiency particularly *A. adunca* and *A. spectabilis*. Only small amounts are required by plants and excessive quantities are very toxic. Boron is immobile in plants.

Calcium

Deficiency symptoms: partial or complete failure of terminal buds. Young leaves, if they develop, are distorted with necrotic areas. Die back of twigs and stunting of plants occur. The root system is greatly reduced.

Correction: by the addition of lime or gypsum to the soil. Lime is best used on very acid soils since it raises the pH (see page 97).

Remarks: calcium deficiency is usually common only on very acid soils. Calcium interacts with many other elements in the plant.

Copper

Deficiency symptoms: terminal parts of the shoots wilt and eventually die-back. Leaves of legumes show a greyish or bluish colouration. Gum may be exuded from the bark.

Correction: copper sulphate ($CuSO_4$) applied to the soil or as a foliar spray (0.5 g per litre).

Remarks: copper can be very toxic if available to the plant in appreciable quantities. Care must be taken not to over-correct its deficiency.

Iron

Deficiency symptoms: earliest symptoms are pale green new growth. This is followed by chlorosis of the leaf areas between the veins which remain green, giving the leaves a mottled appearance. In severe cases all of the green may disappear from the leaves which die and are followed by dieback of the stems. In some species such as *Hypocalymma cordifolium* the deficient new growth may be pinkish instead of pale green.

Correction: by applying salts to soils or by foliar applications. Ferric sulphate is used only for soil applications. It is only useful in the pH range 5-7 and acidifies the soil. Iron chelates are effective in the pH range 6.5-8.5 and are useful for correcting iron deficiency in calcareous soils. Applications are usually between 50-200 g per plant. Foliar sprays of ferrous sulphate at 30 g per litre have been found to be effective. Up to 3 sprays may be necessary to completely correct the deficiency.

Remarks: iron is rarely at deficient levels in soils but is frequently held in a form unavailable to plants, such as in calcareous soils. Iron is very mobile in plant tissues.

Magnesium

Deficiency symptoms: usually show up first on older leaves. Chlorosis of parts of the leaves with the veins especially the midrib remaining green. A green band or vee is often conspicuous along the midrib. In severe cases the whole leaf becomes pale yellow and eventually necrotic. Old leaves may become reddish and are shed. Root growth is poor and flowering is frequently affected adversely.

Correction: magnesium sulphate ($MgSO_4$) (Epsom Salts) applied to the soil or as a foliar spray (20 g per litre). Foliar sprays work rapidly but are not long lasting and both soil and foliage treatments may be necessary.

Remarks: magnesium is most commonly deficient in very acid sandy soils and in the presence of high levels of potassium. The element is highly mobile within plants.

Manganese

Deficiency symptoms: appear on young leaves first. Chlorotic patches on the leaves with the veins remaining green. Very similar to iron deficiency but often associated with cupping of the leaves and with brown flecks or patches on the chlorotic areas. In severe cases the leaves become entirely yellow with necrotic patches.

Correction: manganese sulphate ($MnSO_4$) applied to the soil or as a foliar spray (5 g per litre).

Remarks: deficiency is common in calcareous soils rich in organic matter. Liming of an acid soil to an alkaline soil is a common cause of deficiency. Manganese is immobile in the plant.

Manganese excess: manganese becomes available in large quantities in very acid soils and can be toxic to plant growth.

Correction: liming of the soil to reduce the acidity. A pH of 6-6.5 is optimum.

Molybdenum

Deficiency symptoms: lack of nodules on the roots of legumes. A slight mottling of the leaves associated with curling of the leaf margins.

Correction: sodium molybdate (Na_2MoO_4) applied lightly to the soil or as a foliar spray (0.05 g per litre).

Remarks: deficiency is most common in very acid soils and liming of such soils will be necessary to prevent added molybdenum becoming unavailable to plants. It is only required in minute amounts.

Nitrogen

Deficiency symptoms: usually appear on the older leaves first. Leaves become a uniform pale yellow and the plants are stunted. Younger leaves may be green. In severe cases the leaves become bleached and develop necrotic patches which spread until the whole leaf dies.

Correction: soil applications of various nitrogen fertilizers such as ammonium nitrate, ammonium sulphate, urea, potassium nitrate, calcium nitrate and sodium nitrate. Organic fertilizers such as blood and bone and animal manures are also rich in nitrogen. Foliar sprays of calcium nitrate (2 g per litre) or urea (1.5 g per litre) are also effective as are liquid fertilizers such as ammonium nitrate (10 g per litre) or calcium nitrate (12 g per litre) applied to the roots.

Remarks: nitrogen is extremely important for

plant growth and adequate supplies are characterized by deep green leaves and vigorous healthy growth. Nitrogen is not commonly deficient in native plants.

Nitrogen excess: nitrogen is readily supplied in excess, the symptoms being lush soft growth and a retardation or inhibition of flowering. Excess nitrogen increases a plant's susceptibility to disease and frost damage. The stems may become thin, sappy and weak.

Correction: nitrogen is readily leached from the soil by heavy watering. An application of phosphorus should help counteract the effects of excess nitrogen.

Phosphorus

Deficiency symptoms: stunting of the plant and the development of deep green leaves sometimes associated with purplish or bronze tinges in the leaves and stems. The root system is greatly reduced.

Correction: soil applications of superphosphate or soluble orthophosphate compounds. Organic manures such as hoof and horn, bone meal or blood and bone are rich in phosphorus.

Remarks: phosphorus deficiency is very rare in Australian native plants except perhaps in rainforest situations. Heathland communities have developed on phosphorus deficient soils and have evolved a very tight phosphorus cycle so that the element is not wasted. The element is usually withdrawn from all old leaves before they are shed and specialized root systems (such as proteoid roots) probably play a part in the uptake of phosphorus. Phosphorus is very mobile within the plant.

Phosphorus excess: excess quantities of phosphorus can be toxic to some plants. Toxicity symptoms are marginal leaf burn and necrosis of the older leaves. The dieback starts at the tip of each leaf and spreads towards the base and is followed by premature defoliation giving the plants a sparse appearance. The toxic effects of high levels of phosphorus are largely offset if balanced by high levels of nitrogen. Plants sensitive to high levels of phosphorus are mainly found in the family Proteaceae and include species of *Grevillea*, *Hakea* and *Banksia*. Phosphorus toxicity arises from the use of high levels of fertilizers containing phosphorus. Superphosphate and especially the newer concentrated phosphates must be used with care. Blood and bone is high in phosphorus and can cause damage from phosphorus toxicity if used in excess. Phosphorus toxicity is mainly a problem of plants grown in containers and is not common in garden grown plants because the phosphorus is fixed and rendered immobile by soil.

Correction: phosphorus toxicity is difficult to correct and often results in the death of plants. It can be offset to some extent by increasing the levels of nitrogen and potassium available to plants. Do not increase calcium as this element makes the toxicity worse.

Potassium

Deficiency symptoms: usually appear first on older leaves. Leaves develop a marginal necrosis or burn which spreads towards the tip. Eventually the whole leaf may become necrotic.

Correction: soil applications of potassium sulphate (K_2SO_4) or potassium chloride (KCl). Potassium sulphate is preferable for soils with high chloride levels.

Remarks: potassium is required in large quantities by plants. It is usually present in soils in sufficient quantities but may not be readily available to plants. It may be deficient in sandy soils. It is mobile within the plant.

Sulphur

Deficiency symptoms: retardation and stunting of growth. Uniform pale green chlorosis of all leaves except those which are very young. Sometimes the veins show up pale in an otherwise green leaf.

Correction: soil applications of elemental sulphur or gypsum. Elemental sulphur increases soil acidity which may be useful in calcareous soils whereas gypsum does not affect pH.

Remarks: symptoms are very similar to nitrogen deficiency. Sulphur is not commonly deficient. It is mobile within plants.

Zinc

Deficiency symptoms: appear on young leaves first. Irregular yellowish or chlorotic areas between the veins, stunting of growth and shortened internodes giving a rosetted appearance. Leaves become pale and the older leaves brown and drop off. Stems die back from the tips.

Correction: zinc sulphate ($ZnSO_4$) applied to the soil or as a foliar spray (3-5 g per litre).

Remarks: zinc is a complex element and deficiency can occur under a wide variety of conditions. It is required in minute quantities and high levels are toxic to plants. Deficiency is common in calcareous soils. Zinc is immobile in the plant.

OTHER DISORDERS

Certain factors in the plant's environment, other than those dealt with in the previous chapters, may adversely affect the growth of plants. These factors vary from pure physical injury and ad-

Pests and Diseases

verse climatic conditions to chemical poisoning, and the symptoms vary correspondingly.

Cold Damage

Many plants show a reaction to cold which is not necessarily associated with frost damage. These plants are usually from subtropical or mild coastal districts where they are not usually exposed to much cold weather. Examples are *Grevillea* × *gaudichaudii. Buckinghamia celsissima* and *Omolanthus populifolius*. Typical symptoms are a darkening of the leaves frequently with black patches appearing on the margins. New growth during the warm weather is quite normal. On some species the leaves redden following periods of cold.

Dryness

Wilting is the most common symptom of dryness and is an indication that the roots cannot supply water fast enough to the top of the plant to keep up with losses from transpiration from the leaves. Wilting is most common in dry ground where the soil is so dry that it cannot meet the requirements of the roots. Temporary wilting however can also occur in moist or wet soil and this is usually caused by sudden increases in transpiration which the plant cannot cope with in the short term. It is most often seen on vigorously growing plants on days of intermittent cloud and hot sun. It is also common on potted plants that have just been moved from a shady or protected position into the sun.

Wilting is only apparent on plants with soft, young growth, and ·dryness on non-growing plants exhibits different symptoms. The leaves of hard-leafed species of *Hakea, Grevillea* and *Banksia* lose their lustre, take on a dryish appearance and often curl inwards towards the stem. The older leaves yellow and fall off prematurely. In shallow rooted species such as *Lechenaultia, Goodenia* and *Scaevola*, the leaves take on a dry appearance and fall prematurely making the plants appear sparse. Such plants frequently die from dryness. In large leafed species such as *Tristania conferta* the leaves droop downward against the stems and numerous older leaves yellow and fall prematurely.

Fasciation

Fasciation is a disfiguration whereby the upper part of a stem becomes flattened and bears multiple leaves and ridges as if many stems had been joined together. It is usually found on young shoots which are growing rapidly. It is believed to be purely a physiological disorder developing with the very rapid growth, although similar symptoms occur occasionally following insect

Iron deficiency in *Banksia integrifolia.*

D.V. Beardsell photo

and mite attack or with some viruses. There is no method of control and if unsightly the fasciated stems should be pruned off. Fasciation does not seem to weaken a plant or stunt its growth.

Fog Damage

Continuous fogs cause sweating of plants because foliage and stems are continually moist. The sweating is worst in plants with a compact growth habit rather than open sparse types. It is also aggravated in species with hairy leaves. Fine leafed hairy species may suffer badly when the fogs last 2-4 days or more. Leaf drop is common after the leaves turn brown or black.

Hail Damage

Hail causes physical damage such as laceration of leaves and bark. It can also bruise flowers and fruits but the damage may not show up until later when the fruits ripen abnormally or the flowers are malformed. Large concentrations of hail can also have a sudden chilling effect checking growth and causing the fall of leaves that are still green.

Magnesium deficiency in *Garcinia* sp.
D.V. Beardsell photo

Nitrogen deficiency in *Lagunaria patersonii*.
D.V. Beardsell photo

Boron deficiency in *Acacia spectabilis*.
D.V. Beardsell photo

Manganese deficiency in *Hymenosporum flavum*.
D.V. Beardsell photo

Humidity

Long periods of high humidity can cause collapse of susceptible plants. These are usually species from dry inland areas where humidity is usually low over most of the year. They are often also hairy plants such as *Banksia ornata* and *Adenanthos sericea*. Long periods of misty or drizzly weather also cause similar problems.

Long periods of hot weather and very low humidity cause extreme drying and desiccation of plants.

Lack of Myccorrhiza

Some plants have associations with symbiotic fungi in their roots. These are known as myccorrhizal fungi and they aid in the plants' nutrition. In the absence of these fungi some plants grow weakly and appear unthrifty. They lack vigour and also may have yellowish leaves. Such plants do not generally respond to the application of fertilizers. The addition of some leaf mould from under established bushes of the same species will generally produce a marked improvement in the plant, although not always. Myccorrhizae are common in plants growing on poor sandy soils such as heathlands. Their root system contains short knobby or distorted roots that are the site of myccorrhizal activity. Myccorrhizae are found in such groups as orchids (*Caladenia, Calochilus, Dipodium, Gastrodia, Prasophyllum*), rushes and sedges and also a number of shrubs (e.g. *Ricinocarpos pinifolius*). The proteoid roots found in members of the family Proteaceae do not contain myccorrhiza.

Lack of Root Nodules

Legumes which have no nodules on the roots or a poor development of nodules are stunted and grow weakly. The plants generally have a yellowish appearance and the older leaves go bright yellow and are shed prematurely. Such plants grow slowly and linger for a time before dying. The addition of some bush litter or leaf mould from under other legumes may induce nodule formation. It is a wise procedure to check the root systems of legumes for nodules before purchase from nurseries.

Salt Damage

Salt damage can occur in a few different ways but the two most widely encountered are windborne or cyclic salt and salting in soils.

Windborne Salt

Salt is picked up from the sea and transported inland by onshore winds. Plants growing in coastal areas are frequently buffeted by these winds and damage can result from salt deposition on exposed foliage. Damage is more severe following strong winds in storms because more salt is transported and deposited.

Symptoms are usually a burning of the leaves which may blacken, or may develop brown papery patches. New growth withers and dies back and leaves may be shed. Symptoms vary greatly with the species, some being quite tolerant (see list of Coastal Plants tolerant of salt wind, page 281).

Soil Salt

Soils in low lying zones, where drainage water collects, are frequently subject to salting because the water is continually evaporating during warm weather and the dissolved salts become concentrated. The water need not ever appear on the soil surface for salting to occur, but if the water table rises near enough to the soil surface for evaporation to occur by capillary action then salt will build up and vegetation will be affected. Such salting is common in hilly country which has been extensively cleared of vegetation. In severe cases salt may appear as a white encrustation on the surface.

Symptoms of soil salt include reduced growth, reduced leaf size and an inward cupping of the leaves with associated brown or papery patches (see Treatment of Saline Soils page 70).

Smog

Damage from air pollution is relatively common close to the larger capital cities of Australia. The damage is mainly caused by ozone although there are some effects from sulphur. The symptoms vary from water soaked areas to dark necrotic spots or bleached areas in the leaves. Affected leaves are shed prematurely. The upper surface of the leaf is affected more than the lower surface. Young leaves and very mature leaves appear to be most resistant to smog damage. There is a considerable range of sensitivity of species to smog damage (see list of resistant plants page 310).

Snow

Snow causes physical damage from its weight when it accumulates on plants. It can also cause chilling injury and sweating if it lies on plants for long periods.

Sun Scorch

Some species are sensitive to too much exposure to hot sun and scorch if planted in an exposed situation. Shade loving plants often have large thin textured leaves which damage easily. Young shoots often wilt and leaves show large scorched patches which turn papery and white. Sensitive species include *Cuttsia viburnea*, *Hollandea sayeri*, *Alpinia coerulea* and many ferns.

Scorching can also occur when protection is suddenly removed such as occurs to sheltered plants in a summer storm. The plants suddenly exposed to hot conditions may scorch badly especially on tender leaves. The drying effects of sun are exaggerated by hot winds. Scorching is also common when plants are removed from glasshouses or plastic houses during hot weather and are not placed in a sheltered position to harden off for a few days.

Scorching can also occur on the bark in areas suddenly exposed to sun such as after defoliation by insects or following storm damage. Bark scorch shows up as brown, orange or reddish patches. Bark may be killed on species with thin bark. Protection can be given by applications of whitewash (lime and water) until the natural cover is returned.

Waterlogging

Waterlogging of soil occurs when water replaces air in the soil pores for long periods. This replacement is a normal phase of drainage following watering or heavy rains but in this case is only temporary. Waterlogging may occur for long periods in low lying areas or in heavy soils and in such situations plant roots of many species cannot extract sufficient oxygen for normal growth, and the plants suffer.

Symptoms vary but are usually associated with cupping of the leaves and the appearance of irregular dead patches on them. If new growth is present, wilting is common on sunny or windy days. Branches die back and leaves are shed from the upper parts giving an unthrifty appearance. Some plants die rapidly when waterlogged, while others linger on, dying slowly, and others exhibit little or no symptoms although generally making little growth (see list of plants tolerant of waterlogging, and also Treatment of Waterlogged Soils page 67).

Waterlogging can be complicated by other factors such as soil sulphur levels and the presence of disease organisms. Under waterlogged conditions sulphur becomes reduced to compounds such as rotten egg gas and these are toxic to roots. Very few plants can survive waterlogged soil when vigorous root pathogens such as *Phytophthora cinnamomi* are present (see Cinnamon Fungus page 168).

Wind Damage

Apart from the obvious physical damage caused by wind it can also be responsible for scorching and withering of soft new growth and chilling of plants preventing growth. Hot summer winds may desiccate new growth leaving it withered and blackened or cause white papery patches in leaves which unfold or develop later. Cold winds may chill plants stunting growth and causing a sudden and premature shed of leaves which are usually still green (see Windbreaks page 75).

Lechenaultia tubiflora W.R. Elliot photo

Part Four

Propagation

17 Propagation Structures and Materials

INTRODUCTION TO PROPAGATION

Amongst the first plants to be propagated by man were the cereals. It was during the Neolithic Period, around 5000 BC that man began to cultivate wheat, raised from seed. During this period the Egyptians organised plant collecting expeditions to many areas of the then known world.

The Chinese carried out specialised plant selection and propagation, before the advent of western civilisation. Spaniards were propagating grape vines from cuttings and by grafting during the 14th Century, yet even today there are many problems encountered with the propagation of this crop.

Man has been interested in propagating plants for this long period for two major reasons —

   (a) the provision of food, and
   (b) to beautify the environment.

There was an upsurge in horticulture from about the middle of the 18th Century. From about 1920 there have been many advances made in propagating methods, and the development of specific tools and equipment has helped achieve great things in plant propagation. There is still however the need for basic knowledge on the propagation of plants. With this knowledge, and simple equipment, many species can be easily multiplied.

Plants can be propagated by two basic methods.
1. Sexual Propagation. Plants are reproduced from seeds and spores.
2. Asexual or Vegetative Propagation. Plants are propagated from sections of living plants, e.g. cuttings, grafting and budding, layering, division, and tissue culture.

PROPAGATION STRUCTURES

There is a wide range of equipment and structures suitable for the propagation of Australian plants. Excellent results can be obtained by using the simplest of equipment, and there are

Left Simple propagating structure using plastic bag with supports in pot.

Right Simple propagating structure, using an upturned glass jar, placed over cutting. Useful for a small number of cuttings.

many alternatives suitable for enthusiasts. Some of these are discussed below.

1. A pot and plastic bag. This is probably the simplest, and involves a pot filled with a propagation medium, and covered with a polythene bag. The bag should be supported on a framework of wire or wood, and secured at the open end to prevent it from blowing around. This system is very efficient for the rooting of cuttings of a range of species. It is most important that the pot should not be placed in direct sunlight, as overheating occurs very easily. An alternative to the plastic bag is to use an upturned glass or plastic jar.

2. Box and plastic. An adaptation of 1 is to have a box instead of a pot. The box can be half filled with sand or sawdust, and pots containing the cuttings are embedded in this medium. This is ideal for general use. Shade-cloth or hessian can be placed over the plastic cover during hot weather, to reduce temperature. Polystyrene fruit boxes make ideal containers for this type of propagation.

There are commercial products obtainable, based on 1 and 2. These are made of rigid

Propagation

Commercially available propagating unit.

Small bottom heat propagation unit, suitable for enthusiasts.

plastic, and have been used with success.

3. Cold frames. These are unheated frames, with solid sides, and a hinged or otherwise movable roof. They are commonly used, and have proved to be very efficient. Frames can be of any length, and are commonly up to 1.5 m wide. The minimum depth should be about 30 cm at the front, and about 45 cm at the back. They may be constructed of wood, cement sheeting or bricks. A wide range of materials is available for covering the top, including glass, rigid PVC or plastic sheeting, and fibreglass. Old window frames have been used effectively.

Inside the cold frame, the base can be covered with sand or sawdust, which helps to maintain a humid atmosphere. Fresh animal manure was used for many years in the base of these frames to supply warmth over winter.

4. Heated propagating frames and hot beds. The main advantage with this type of equipment

Small cold frame, suitable for propagating a wide variety of species.

is that ideal propagating conditions can be maintained throughout the year. This usually results in a quicker and greater output of rooted cuttings or seedlings. Basically heat is provided below the propagating medium, and keeps the bases of the cuttings at an ideal temperature for root formation. High resistance wire cables, hot water or steam pipes are the most commonly used forms of heating. There are many electrically heated models available commercially, or alternatively beds of any size can be constructed, according to the needs of the propagator. Construction details are available from offices of the electricity authorities in each state.

Automatic misting equipment is often used in conjunction with bottom heat, to reduce the danger of the cuttings drying out. Heated beds or frames can also be incorporated in existing glasshouses or greenhouses. In California U.S.A. success has been gained in rooting many species of Australian plants, by using heated beds with intermittent mist in a lath house.

5. Glasshouses. This type of construction has been used successfully for many years, and there are now many designs and sizes available. Some can be purchased in kit form. Glass screens out ultra violet rays from the sun, and allows infra red rays to pass, thus heating the house. Glass is still one of the best materials available for covering propagating structures, or growing-on areas, but it is difficult to handle, heavy, and relatively expensive. Glass must be covered with whitewash or glasshouse paint in summer, to prevent overheating and burning of the plants by the sun.

6. Fibreglass. This material has been used as an alternative to glass in recent years. It is lighter, and hence requires less support than similar structures in glass. It also comes in long

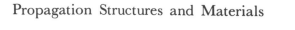

Phosphorus toxicity in *Macadamia integrifolia*.

D.V. Beardsell photo

Fasciated stem of *Templetonia retusa*.

D.L. Jones photo

Waterlogging damage on leaves of *Eucalyptus lehmannii*.

D.V. Beardsell photo

Frost damage to fronds of *Cyathea cooperi*.

D. L. Jones photo

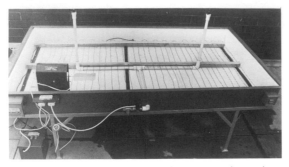

A combined bottom heat and mist propagation unit, suitable for hobbyists and small nurseries.

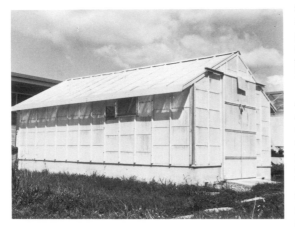

Typical small glasshouse.

Bottom heat unit, showing cuttings and wires.

sheets, and can be erected more quickly than glass. Only good quality fibreglass which contains a protective layer of ultra violet inhibiting material should be used. Cheap fibreglass lacks this protection, and breaks down rapidly with the resulting loss in light transmission. Fibreglass is available in various colours, but only light colours should be used for propagation or growth structures. Clear fibreglass is probably the safest choice. Fibreglass builds up heat around it, and hence plants should not be placed close to it, or they will burn. This heat build up can be reduced by whitewashing or spraying with glasshouse paint.

7. Rigid PVC or Plastic. These materials are similar to fibreglass and the remarks under that material apply here also. Some materials in this group are short lasting, and darken after a couple of years. Most become brittle after a few years, although some are reputed to last for 10-15 years before deterioration.

8. Polythene or Polyethylene Greenhouses. Although relatively new to horticulture in Australia, these structures have been readily accepted. They are not expensive, and have proved very useful for the propagation of Australian plants. Kits are available in varying sizes, and can be assembled in a short period of time. Their main disadvantage is the breakdown of the plastic cover, due to the constant exposure to the ultra violet rays of the sun. The polythene covers usually need replacing about every 18-36 months. The life span can be extended by careful maintenance, including the following steps —

(a) Cover the iron or aluminium structure with lagging, or other insulating material, to prevent the metal becoming too hot.

(b) Do not stretch the polythene cover too tightly when initially placing over structure. The polythene shrinks with age, and if too tight splitting will occur, particularly at the end frames.

(c) Spray with white glasshouse paint during the warm weather. This protects the polythene from the radiation, as well as prevents burning of the cuttings or plants inside. Alternatively a cover of shade-cloth can be used. It is best if this is set at 15-30 cm above the polythene cover.

PROPAGATION MEDIA

Until recently, the main components of propagating mixes have been sand and sphagnum peat moss. Because of increasing costs of these materials in some areas, research is being undertaken to find substitutes.

For best results, a propagating medium needs to have the following characteristics:

Polyethylene greenhouses, for propagation or other horticultural purposes, are available in various sizes.

Interior of polyethylene greenhouse used for propagation of Australian plants — note misting system, and also use of individual plastic pots for propagation.

(i) To be able to hold cuttings or seeds firmly in place.

(ii) It must not expand or shrink excessively when wet or dry.

(iii) To be able to retain moisture for lengthy periods, but be porous, to allow free flow of excess moisture, and adequate penetration of air.

(iv) It should be of correct pH for root initiation (4.5-5.5).

(v) It should be free from weeds, wccd sccds, pests and disease organisms.

(vi) It must be able to be readily sterilized by steam or other compounds, without any damaging side effects or changes in character.

(vii) It should contain some nutrients, especially for seed germination.

(viii) It must not be saline.

Some of the materials at present used regularly are:

(a) Peats (b) Perlite (c) Pine bark (d) Sand (e) Sawdust (f) Scoria gravel (g) Topsoil (h) Vermiculite

(a) Peat. Peats consist of rotted organic material, sometimes of great age. There are two types commonly available, formed from either sphagnum moss or sedges. Sphagnum peat is available as a shredded material. It has a low pH of about 4.5, is sterile, and light in weight. It has a high water holding capacity, but at the same time has excellent aeration properties. Most sphagnum peat sold in Australia is imported. It is ideal for the propagation of both seedlings and cuttings, and is still by far the most important material for propagation. Sedge peats are more

Mist propagation in operation.

Propagating Materials — Sand; peat moss; mixture.

granular and have a pH of about 5.5. They are satisfactory for seedling germination, but inferior to sphagnum peat for cuttings.

(b) Perlite is a naturally occurring silicate material of volcanic origin. It is mined and heated to 725°C to produce very light, sponge-like, sterile particles of greyish-white colour. These are screened into various grades from fine to coarse. It has moderate water holding capacity, and is excellent as an aerating medium. Perlite is best used in mixtures with other materials such as peat moss or vermiculite, although it has proved to be an excellent rooting medium on its own, for mist propagation.

(c) Pine bark. Finely ground bark of *Pinus radiata* (particles less than 6 mm diameter) has proved a useful peat moss substitute, for seed germination. Fresh bark contains toxins which inhibit plant growth, and bark should be aged before use, by storing moist, in a heap for 6-8 weeks. Pine bark has not proved satisfactory for cuttings. Pine bark is also called pine peat.

(d) Sand. This is composed of small silica granules, derived from the weathering of solid rock. For propagation purposes, it is best to use a coarse sharp sand, derived from quartz. This will not pack too tightly, and therefore provides good aeration. It is commonly available as 'river sand'. Do not use beach sand, even if washed thoroughly, as the granules are rounded and can pack tightly. Sand can contain many weed seeds, and often fungal diseases, so it is wise to carry out sterilisation before use. Sand does not hold water, nor does it have any nutrient value, but it provides excellent drainage and aeration.

(e) Sawdust. This has been used to a very limited extent as a substitute for peat moss. It has good moisture retention and aeration properties. All types of sawdust must be aged, as they can contain toxins when fresh. Aging consists of storing the sawdust, moist, in a heap for 6-8 weeks. Most sawdusts are not recommended for cuttings, but good results have been obtained by using sawdust of *Pinus radiata* as a substitute for peat. Most aged sawdusts are extremely useful for germination of large seeds such as *Banksia* species. Sawdust that has come from timber known to be treated with any form of preservatives should not be used.

(f) Scoria gravel. This material is a light-weight aggregate, derived from crushed basalt. It is dull reddish in colour. It contains internal pores and has properties intermediate between soil and sand. It holds both water and nutrients in a form available to plants. Its pH is 7-10. Because it is mechanically crushed, there can be excessive fine particles, and samples with more than 30% fines should not be used without sieving. Scoria has not proved successful as a propagating medium for cuttings, but it is excellent for raising ferns from spores.

(g) Topsoil. Some propagators use a small amount (0.5% to 20%) of good quality topsoil in their propagating mixes. High quality loam with plenty of organic material is becoming difficult to obtain in many areas. What is available usually has a high clay content, and therefore is not recommended for propagation purposes. Soils must be sterilized, as they frequently contain disease organisms.

(h) Vermiculite. A naturally occurring mica, which has been expanded by exposure to temperatures of 1110°C. It is a hydrated magnesium-aluminium iron silicate material, and the heat treatment results in a very light material with excellent water-holding and aeration characteristics. The pH varies from 6.5-7.5. It is sterile because of the heating process, and can retain nutrients for extended periods before releasing them. It is available in coarse and fine grades. Excellent for propagation of both seedlings and cuttings, but must be handled very carefully as it is easily over-watered. It is important not to compact this material when wet, as the pores are easily clogged. Useful and safe mixes are 1 part vermiculite : 2 parts coarse sand (by volume), or equal parts vermiculite and perlite.

Propagating Mixtures

Seed

A basic mix, usually sufficient for good germination is —

  3 parts sand
  1 part peat moss or aged sawdust.

A small amount of blood and bone fertilizer can be added to provide nutrients.

A mix of 1 part vermiculite and 1 part sawdust is also excellent for the germination of many species.

Cuttings

A basic mixture that has proved to be successful is —

  3 parts coarse sharp river sand
  1 part peat moss.

Many variations of the above are used. In some cases ½ to 1 part of good quality loam has been added. This produces a good mixture for use when cuttings are placed in individual tubes.

Other successful cutting mixes include equal parts by volume of perlite and vermiculite, or 2 parts perlite : 1 part peat moss.

Sterilisation of Propagating Mixes

To produce healthy plants, it is essential to provide a healthy growing medium. Any mixtures that contain soil, sand or other materials that are not guaranteed to be sterile, will need treatment prior to use, to control soil-borne diseases, pests and weeds.

Steam Treatment

In this technique a batch of soil is treated with steam for 30 minutes, after the soil has reached a temperature of 100°C. Steam only moves evenly through friable open soil mixes, and is not successful for heavy or over-wet soils. Steam has the disadvantage that it can be difficult to handle, and it wets the soil, which means that the mixture must be allowed to dry out before it can be used for potting. Suitable equipment for steam treatment is occasionally available to a home gardener, and a useful steaming container based on an 18 litre drum can be constructed.

Steam-Air Treatment

In this system, soil is raised to 60°C and held there for 30 minutes by means of a mixture of steam and air. For best results the medium needs to be moist, but not wet. If possible it should be moist for more than 3 days before treatment. This renders organisms more heat sensitive. Once treated, the mixture should not be allowed to come in contact with untreated mixture, benches, pots or tools, as re-infestation can occur readily with serious consequences. Steaming is an efficient and relatively inexpensive treatment once the equipment is installed.

The steam-air treatment is superior to steam for the following reasons —

(i) Sterilization at 60°C removes most pathogens and kills most weed seeds, but does not effect beneficial organisms that can help to control pathogen outbreaks.

(ii) Sterilization is more rapid, because of penetration gained by the use of an air blower.

(iii) Soil temperature is held at 60°C for 30 minutes, and when cooled it is ready for immediate use.

(iv) Penetration and effectiveness are easily measured, as thermometer readings can be taken without fear of steam burns.

(v) Toxic effects are minimal.

(vi) Steam-air mixtures can be used safely near plants, or people.

(vii) Plastic containers can be treated, at temperatures of up to 65°C.

Heat Treatment

Some control of pathogens can be obtained by heating small quantities of potting mix in an oven, at 95°C for 30 minutes. This is a useful technique for the home gardener or amateur enthusiast without the benefit of expensive equipment. Results are improved if the soil mix is held moist in a heap for about 3 days before treatment.

Chemical Treatment

Toxic chemicals which vaporize readily can be used to sterilize soil mixes. Chemicals of this type are known as fumigants. They can be very effective. The main disadvantages are as follows:

1. Most fumigants are extremely poisonous, and should be used only by trained operators.
2. The chemicals cannot be used safely in confined areas.
3. Some chemicals cannot be used in residential areas.
4. Toxic residues may remain in the soil, (e.g. bromide). These can damage sensitive species, especially young seedlings.
5. An aeration period is needed prior to planting.
6. The chemicals are ineffective at low temperatures, and cannot be used on wet soil.

Chloropicrin is an effective fumigant against most soil pathogens, insects and weeds. Soil temperature should be at least 15°C before chloropicrin can be used. Treated areas are covered by a plastic sheet for 3 days, and cannot be used for at least 14 days.

Methyl Bromide is odourless and very poisonous, and usually contains about 2% chloropicrin as a warning agent. The gas is released under a plastic sheet which remains for 2 days. A further 3 days should be allowed for aeration before using. Bromide residues may remain, and these can be toxic to plants.

Chloropicrin — Methyl Bromide mixtures of 55% -45% or 66% -34% are more effective than either chemical used alone. Soil must be covered by a plastic sheet for 2-3 days, then allowed to aerate for at least 14 days.

Formalin is the most suitable of the chemicals for general use. It has a low toxicity when compared with the above compounds. Commercial formalin is best mixed in the ratio of 1 part to 20-24 parts of water. The solution is watered into the soil at the rate of 1 litre per 100 square cm. The soil should then be watered heavily and covered with a plastic sheet for 2 days, after which the soil is aerated. Aeration is helped by working the mixture, when dry enough, using tools previously washed in formalin. The mixture should not be used until no odour of formalin can be detected.

Propagation

Fungicides

The application of fungicidal drenches such as Coban, Terrazole etc., can be very beneficial in preventing or controlling outbreaks of pathogens. They can be distributed as powder through the soil mix before potting, or applied as drenches after potting.

PROPAGATING CONTAINERS

Many types of containers can be used successfully for the propagation of Australian plants. The main prerequisite is for a sufficient number of open drainage holes. Clear containers of glass

Seedlings in different size containers
Left *Acmena smithii*, Centre *Syzygium coolminianum*, Right *Podocarpus elatus*. — density of *Syzgium* seedlings due to polyembryony.

or plastic are not recommended, because algae are formed between the medium and the container, and can often prevent good drainage. It is best to use new containers, especially for rare or valued species. With pots that are to be re-used, it is imperative that they be thoroughly washed and preferably soaked in a germicide or disinfectant, then re-washed and aired. This will prevent the spread of any pests or diseases.

Seedling Containers

1. Trays or flats

These are usually wooden or plastic, and are variable in size. They need to have a depth of 5 cm to 7.5 cm. Plastic containers are recommended, as they have less chance of disease carry-over because of the non-absorbent and smooth surface. They are also much lighter than wood, and need less storage room.

2. Styrene-foam cups and trays

These are most useful containers, provided there are ample drainage holes.

3. Peat or fibre pots

Seed can be sown directly into these pots, filled with soil, and after germination left to develop until ready to plant out — pot and all. Pots must be kept moist, otherwise roots will not penetrate the pot walls, and may spiral.

4. Plastic pots

Small plastic pots can be used for direct sowing. Larger pots are often used for community sowing, but are not as good as trays because the seedlings are usually harder to transplant.

Palm seedlings in different containers.

Community pot containing cuttings of *Banksia ericifolia.*

Small tubes, each containing a separate cutting — a simple and efficient way of handling quantities of cuttings.

Containers for Cuttings

1. Plastic pots

These are the most commonly used, in varying sizes, and may be either round or square. A widespread practice is to use pots of about 10-15 cm diameter, in which a number of cuttings are placed. In some cases 5 cm diameter pots are used for single cuttings.

2. Plastic trays

Trays of the same size as seedling trays (about 35 cm x 30 cm x 5 cm) are gaining greater use by some nurseries. They are frequently used for mist propagation. Each tray takes about 200 cuttings.

3. Peat or fibre pots

Useful for cuttings, as long as the propagation medium does not become too wet.

4. Clay pots

Prior to the introduction of plastics, clay or terracotta pots were used extensively, and they are still used by many people today. The main disadvantage is their porosity, which aids both drying out, and depositing of salts. They can also harbour pests and diseases, and are heavy. After each use they should be soaked thoroughly to remove the salts, and sterilized to kill any pests and diseases.

18   Propagation from Seed

Seeds are the end product of the flowering of plants. During the flowering period, pollination and fertilization take place, with the resultant transfer of genes.

Propagation from seed, or sexual propagation, is used more than any other method of propagation. The two main reasons are that it is the simplest, and therefore also the cheapest way of producing plants.

With human sexual reproduction there is variation within the progeny, and this also occurs with plants. Propagation from seed therefore has the disadvantage of not always being able to reproduce plants with identical characteristics as the parent plant from which seed was collected, e.g. *Eucalyptus ficifolia.* Variation occurs due to hybridization and segregation, and this is often seen with species of *Callistemon, Grevillea* and *Eucalyptus.* Other genera such as *Acacia, Banksia, Eugenia* and *Melaleuca* are much more stable, and variation because of hybridization occurs rarely.

Vegetative propagation has the advantage that it ensures the perpetuation of the species without variation. In many cases at present, species can only be grown from seed, due to the failure of other propagation methods, but this situation could change in the future, with success in meristem culture propagation.

Propagation from seed can be valuable because new forms for cultivation can be selected from the seedlings. Seedlings also play an important role as rootstock for grafting and budding, although to date there has only been limited work in this regard using Australian plants.

SEED COLLECTION

Seed of a range of native plants is collected and sold by various government bodies and private collectors throughout Australia. Most of the seed goes to commercial nurseries and government departments such as forestry, and a considerable amount is also exported to other countries. Seed collection is a thriving and very specialised business.

Seed of many species is very difficult or almost impossible to obtain. This is due to a variety of causes, including
  (i) rarity of some species such as *Banksia goodii,*
 (ii) over zealous collecting of some species, such as *Eucalyptus nicholii,*
 (iii) sporadic flowering in many species, often associated with poor seasons,
 (iv) inaccessibility of many species in isolated areas,
  (v) the fruiting habits and characteristics of some species make commercial collecting impractical. This is particularly applicable to many rainforest plants, which fruit sporadically and the seeds have a very short-lived viability period.

The harder the seed is to obtain, or the rarer the species, the more costly is the seed.

Home gardens are a reservoir of seed of a wide range of species, and enthusiasts are encouraged to collect and make use of this seed. Seeds should only be collected from healthy plants that are considered to be true to type, unless seedlings produced from hybrids are to be used for experimental and plant selection purposes.

Fruit Categories

The term fruit in this context refers to the organ containing the seed, and has no reference to its edible qualities. For seed collecting purposes, fruits can be broadly divided into 3 categories.

1. Those which remain on the plant for many seasons and are only shed after severe stress such as plant death, after a branch is broken, or after scorching by fire. This type is very common in Australia, particularly in the heathlands, sandplains, dry sclerophyll forest and inland areas. In the majority of cases the fruit are hard woody capsules. Examples are species of *Banksia, Beaufortia, Callistemon, Dryandra, Eucalyptus, Hakea, Leptospermum* and *Melaleuca.*

A selection of woody seed capsules of Australian plants.

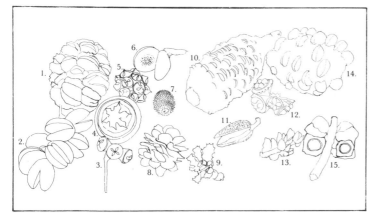

Key to above photo
 1. *Banksia nutans*
 2. *Grevillea glauca*
 3. *Eucalyptus megacornuta*
 4. *Eucalyptus macrocarpa*
 5. *Eucalyptus lehmannii*
 6. *Hakea platysperma*
 7. *Casuarina stricta*
 8. *Banksia laricina*
 9. *Dryandra praemorsa*
10. *Banksia grandis*
11. *Xylomelum angustifolium*
12. *Eucalyptus coronata*
13. *Hakea francisiana*
14. *Banksia lemanniana*
15. *Eucalyptus tetraptera*

Mature seed capsules of *Callistemon citrinus* are retained on the plant for many years.

2. Those which shed the seed annually, with the fruit usually remaining on the tree for a short period after seed dispersal. These are also very common in Australia, and are widely distributed throughout a variety of vegetation types. Seed dispersal varies from a passive opening of the fruit, with the seed dispersed by plant movement and wind, e.g. *Angophora* spp., to active dispersal by techniques such as the pods exploding, e.g. *Acacia* spp. and many members of the family Fabaceae.

3. Those which shed the whole fruit containing the seed. These are usually shed annually, and the fruit often contains only a single seed, although some contain many, e.g. *Ficus* spp. and *Passiflora* spp. The fruits are often fleshy and fed upon by a variety of creatures such as

Variation in Banksia seed cones.
Left *Banksia lemanniana* — follicles prominent among withered flowers. Centre *Banksia laricina* — note absence of flower parts around follicles. Right *Banksia serrata* — follicles partially hidden among withered flowers.

possums, bats and birds. Seeds of this type often have some unusual pre-germination requirements such as fermentation in the fruit, or partial digestion in an animal's gut. Fruits of this type are commonly found in rainforests, e.g. *Elaeodendron* spp., *Endiandra* spp., *Elaeocarpus* spp., *Planchonella* spp., *Garcinia* spp., *Syzygium* spp., *Acmena* spp., *Castanospermum australe*, but also include some from dry areas, such as *Santalum* spp., *Billardiera* spp., *Persoonia* spp., and *Owenia acidula*.

Collection of Fruits

Seeds of plants from category (i) above pose few problems for collection. The seeds are retained on the bushes and can be collected at any time of the year. With all genera that retain their seed on the plant in hard woody capsules, it is best to not collect capsules that are less than 12 months old. Younger capsules open very tardily if at all, and the seed is probably immature and will not germinate.

Collection of seed from species in category (ii), which shed their seeds, poses considerable problems, and constant observation is required if the seed is to be collected. The period of seed ripening varies with the season and the species. Species of herbs such as *Pelargonium* and *Erodium*, and many grasses, mature and are dispersed in a matter of a few weeks, whereas species of wattles and grevilleas may take 2-4 months to ripen. Often seeds ripen very rapidly, and are dispersed in periods of very hot weather. Generally fruits change colour from green to brown before the seeds are dispersed. They can be collected at this stage, and the seeds left to mature in the fruit.

Alternatively clusters of fruit can be covered while still on the plant. Old stockings or muslin are suitable materials for covering, as they allow air movement around the fruit and seeds. A further method is to spread tarpaulins or plastic sheeting on the ground beneath the bushes, to collect dispersed seed.

Fruits of species in category (iii) above can be collected from the ground beneath the tree. The fruits on the ground indicate that others will be ripe, and these can be collected by climbing or shaking the plant. The main problem in collecting seeds of this type is that the fruits may ripen over a considerable period, and it is difficult to judge when they are mature. They also may not ripen at the same time each year, varying with the climatic conditions.

Variation

Seeds of any species vary considerably in size, and it has been found that the larger seeds consistently germinate better, and produce larger and more vigorous seedlings than small seeds.

Considerable variation exists within some genera, as to the retention or dispersal of seed, and so it is often difficult to generalise for a genus. For example, in the very large genus *Eucalyptus*, the vast majority of species retain their seed for many years in woody capsules. Some species however, particularly those in tropical areas, shed their seed annually when it is mature. Examples are *E. alba*, *E. confertiflora*, *E. miniata*, *E. papuana*, *E. peltata* and *E. tessellaris*. In the genus *Callistemon*, all species retain their seed with the exception of *C. viminalis*, which sheds it annually. Most species of *Grevillea* shed their seeds 2-4 months after flowering, however those of *G. glauca* and *G. annulifera* are retained in hard woody capsules until the plant dies, or branches are broken. The majority of species of *Banksia* retain their seeds in woody cones, however a few species such as *B. coccinea*, *B. dentata*, *B. integrifolia* and *B. marginata*, shed their seeds annually.

Problems Encountered in Seed Collection

One of the most difficult problems faced is to collect mature seed. Where seed is retained on the plant it should be at least 12 months old before collection. If in doubt, collect material from very old wood. Where seed is shed, a change in colour of the fruit is a good indication that maturity is close. If some seeds have already been shed, then the others are probably mature enough for collection. This is especially a good guide for species of eucalypts, which shed their seeds, because some capsules always mature a few days earlier than the bulk.

Seed and seed pods of *Acacia myrtifolia*.

Some simple techniques can provide a useful guide, and may prevent the collection of immature seed. A sample bunch of eucalypt capsules, or *Callistemon viminalis*, can be collected and placed in a bag in a warm position. If seed is shed rapidly (within a couple of days), the capsules are ready for collection. If the capsules open tardily and the seed is difficult to extract, the capsules are probably not mature. Scratching the surface of the seed follicles of *Banksia* cones provides a good indication of maturity. If they are brown and hard the cones are ready for collection, whereas if they are soft and green the seeds are immature. In a number of plant species the hardening and change in colour of the seed coat is a good guide to seed maturity. Some fruits can be sliced open with a knife to examine the seeds.

Colouring of fruit is usually a good guide to seed maturity, but this is not always so for some rainforest species such as *Elaeodendron australe*, *Elaeocarpus reticulatus*, and *E. grandis*. The fruits of these species may colour very early, while the seed is quite immature, and hang on the tree for several months before finally ripening. Often the feeding activity of native animals will indicate when the fruits are finally ripe.

The seeds or fruits of some species are unpleasant to collect for various reasons. Irritant hairs are to be found surrounding the seeds or scattered around the outside of the capsule of some species. If these penetrate the skin they can cause itching or a burning sensation, which may last for several hours. Examples are *Brachychiton*

acerifolium, *Hibiscus heterophyllus*, *H. splendens*, *Lagunaria patersonii*, and *Mucuna gigantea*. The fleshy coats of some fruit and seeds contain toxic chemicals which may burn or damage the skin. The best example is the palm *Caryota rumphiana*, the fruits of which, if handled, produce an intense burning sensation which lasts for hours. Seeds of some species produce deep long lasting stains on skin if handled, e.g. *Jasminum* spp. Many seeds are poisonous, but are not dangerous unless eaten, e.g. *Abrus precatorius*, *Cycas* spp., and *Macrozamia* spp. The fruits of some plants smell so strongly when ripe that they are off-putting, e.g. *Morinda citrifolia*. Some seeds are difficult to collect because the foliage is prickly, or even very pungent, e.g. *Hakea sericea*, *H. victoriae*, *Isopogon ceratophyllus*. Strong, thick gloves are very useful.

Parthenocarpy

Seedless fruits are not uncommon in some species such as *Acmena australis*, *Cupaniopsis* spp., *Harpullia pendula*, *Pittosporum phillyreoides* and *Syzygium leuhmannii*. This condition is known as parthenocarpy, and results from the hormone levels in the plant at flowering time. If fertilization has been ineffective, the seeds abort, and in normal trees these undeveloped fruit fall soon after flowering. Sometimes however the placenta of the fruit acts as a site of hormone activity, and an apparently normal fruit develops. Usually normal fruits are present on a tree along with parthenocarpic fruits, but some trees of *Syzygium leuhmannii* produce only parthenocarpic fruit. On a tree with mixed normal and parthenocarpic fruits, the parthenocarpic fruits can usually be distinguished because they ripen earlier, are smaller, and are usually less brightly coloured.

SEED EXTRACTION

The extraction of ripe seed from fruits that do not release the seed whilst still retained on the plant, can be done in varying ways.

These species can be divided into two groups.

1. Species that release seed when fruits are dry.

Included in this group are some of the Proteaceae family, e.g. *Hakea*, *Isopogon*, *Petrophile* and *Xylomelum*, and many genera of the Myrtaceae family, e.g. *Callistemon*, *Calothamnus*, *Eucalyptus*, *Leptospermum*, *Melaleuca* and *Regelia*.

Procedure for seed extraction —

(a) Place capsules in a container such as a paper or cloth bag. Open plastic containers can be used for small quantities, provided the capsules are spread out in one or two layers,

Propagation

Capsules, seeds and buds of *Eucalyptus* species.

allowing for ample aeration. The capsules usually contain a fair degree of moisture, and as drying takes place, condensation can occur on the container and seed if aeration is inadequate. The increase in humidity can provide ideal conditions for fungus or mould growth that will ruin the seed. Do not use plastic bags.

(b) Place container in a warm dry location, e.g. on a sunny window ledge, near a heater, or in a boiler room etc.

(c) Capsules usually open within 1-6 weeks. The seed will be expelled, or can be removed by shaking.

(d) Sow seed, or store in an air-tight, moisture-free container.

2. Species that retain seeds, even though fruits are dry.

Members of the Proteaceae family form the majority of this group. With genera such as *Isopogon* and *Petrophile*, the seeds of some species are released, whilst in others they are embedded in a woody cone in which case they can be picked out readily by hand. Fertile seeds are distinguished by the hard nut-like base. Some species of *Banksia* and *Dryandra* readily release their seed, however others will need special treatment if seed is to be obtained from the cones or capsules.

Procedure for seed extraction:

(a) Banksia

(i) Cones are scorched on an open fire, or placed in an oven with temperature at about 180°C to 200°C.

(ii) Remove cones when follicles begin to open wide enough for seeds to fall out.

(iii) Place in container of water to cool.

(iv) Remove from water to dry.

(v) Shake when dry, or use tweezers to remove seeds. A wood-like separator will also be present. Seeds can be identified by their black colour, and papery wings attached. A strong tool such as a screwdriver can be used as a lever to open follicles and to remove the seed.

(vi) If the seed is difficult to remove, the above procedures can be repeated.

(vii) With some species such as *B. coccinea* and *B. laricina*, it can be extremely difficult to remove the seed. It is recommended that after (ii), the cones be left to soak for 7-14 days, and removed for drying.

(viii) Sow seed, or store in air-tight, moisture-free container.

(b) Dryandra

(i) The hard, shiny, wedge-shaped seed capsules can be easily removed from the spent flower-heads, by cutting at the base of the flower-heads, making sure to not damage the capsules.

(ii) Capsules can then be placed in a saucepan over an open fire, in a frypan, or in a tray in

Cones of *Banksia spinulosa.*
Background — untreated cone
Foreground — treated cone showing opened follicles
Front — Left — separator
        Centre — seed with wing
        Right — seed with wing removed

Cones of *Banksia serrata.*
Left — mature, as on tree
Centre — after drying, with follicles starting to open
Right — after fire treatment to release seed

an oven with temperature at about 180°C to 200°C. If seed is fully mature, the capsules will open, releasing the winged seed. Care must be taken to not overheat during this treatment, as it can damage the seed. Some species such as *D. formosa, D. praemorsa* and *D. sessilis* will release their ripe seed whilst still on the plant.

There are some species, e.g. *Ficus* spp. that have seed enclosed in the ripe fruit when it is shed, and retained within the fruit even after drying. There is no need to extract the seed, as it will germinate after the outer portion of the fruit rots and breaks down.

Close-up of cone of *Banksia serrata*, showing opened follicle surrounded by withered flowers. A separator is visible in the upper follicle.
Foreground — Left 2 winged seeds
Right 2 separators.

SEED VIABILITY AND SEED STORAGE

Viability is the ability of a seed to remain alive and retain the ability to germinate in time. Length of viability varies tremendously with the species, some being viable for only a few days, e.g. *Pothos longipes, Schefflera actinophylla*, while others have been successfully germinated after 100 years, e.g. *Acacia* spp. Viability of seed is greatly influenced by the conditions under which the seed is stored.

Seed viability decreases with increases in the moisture content of the seed, humidity, and temperature. Commercial seed is stored at low temperatures, in sealed chambers of low humidity. Good viability can be retained with seeds of many Australian species by storing them in airtight glass or plastic containers, in a cool dry location (temperature range 10-20°C.) All containers should be carefully labelled with the species name and date of collection. Many pests feed on stored seed, so the addition of a combination fungicide and pesticide is a wise precaution. This should not be over applied however, as many fungicides can reduce seed viability. Cloth, plastic or paper bags should not be used for long term storage.

Viability Tests

A number of tests are available for measuring the viability of seeds. The simplest is to slice the seed across transversely and examine the tissue. If white and healthy the seed is probably viable, whereas if it is wizened and brownish, the seed is dead.

A more accurate test is to soak seeds for a couple of hours and then slice them in half. The part containing the embryo is placed on moist blotting paper in a dish, and the dish placed in a warm position in subdued light. The cotyledons of viable seeds turn green, whereas non viable seeds rot quickly.

The most accurate method of testing seed viability is the tetrazolium test, however this is not a simple, quick test. The seeds are soaked in water for 24 hours, and then for 1-2 days in a 0.25% solution of 2,3,5 — triphenyl tetrazolium chloride in water. While in the tetrazolium solution they are kept in the dark and at a temperature between 23 and 32°C. After soaking, the seed can be examined immediately or stored in water in a refrigerator until testing. The tissues of viable seeds stain red strongly, while dead tissues are white. Weak or old tissues are mottled red or pink. The uptake of tetrazolium can be improved by first slicing some seeds in half.

201

Propagation

SOWING OF SEED

Procedure for sowing seed:

1. Fill container with propagating mixture, leaving room for a water catchment.

2. Firm mixture evenly, but not too tightly, allowing for good drainage and aeration.

3. Water from above, until thoroughly moist, or alternatively stand seed container in shallow water, allowing the mixture to absorb water through the drainage holes.

4. Sow seed.

5. Cover seed with a fine mixture about 1 or 2 times the thickness of the seed.

6. Water top of propagating mixture lightly, making sure to not disperse seeds. Alternative methods of watering after sowing are discussed later in this chapter.

7. Place container in a warm, sheltered position.

Seed Size

For convenience in handling, seed can be grouped into three categories: fine seed, medium seed and large seed, depending on size.

1. Fine Seed

The seeds of this group are small to minute. When sowing it is important to only spread the seed sparsely. This is especially relevant to genera such as *Agonis, Beaufortia, Callistemon, Calothamnus, Eucalyptus, Leptospermum* and *Melaleuca*, all of which usually have a high germination percentage. Oversowing can result in a dense forest of seedlings that do not grow strongly, because of excessive competition. If germination is very dense, it is a good idea to remove some of the seedlings early on, so as to allow better development of those remaining. This is referred to as 'thinning out'.

The following methods help to ensure that seed is not sown too thickly:

(a) Use a salt or pepper shaker, or similar receptacle with small holes.

(b) Mix dry, fine sand with the seed before sowing.

With fine seed, care must be taken to not cover the seed too deeply, as this could retard or prevent germination.

Fine seed must be watered carefully. Heavy watering can disperse the seed, or wash it to the surface, which can result in poor germination if the propagating medium becomes dry. This is usually serious when seed is just beginning to germinate. A very fine spray should be used at all times, and the mixture damped down but not soaked. (See also, Alternative Germination Methods, page 204.)

Variation in seed size of legumes.
Left — *Chorizema cordatum*
Right — *Hardenbergia violacea.*

Variation of seed size between *Grevillea johnsonii* (LHS) and *Grevillea glauca* (RHS)

2. Medium Seed

With seeds of larger size, it is very important to sow sparsely, as each seedling has larger cotyledons than the fine seed, and therefore needs more room to develop. In some cases seed can be planted in individual containers; this facilitates handling and also removes the need for transplanting and the possibility of damage to tender root systems.

Species of *Banksia, Dryandra* and *Hakea* etc. usually have papery wings attached to the seed. It is best to remove these prior to sowing. This is easily done in the hand, by taking a quantity of the winged seeds, and lightly pressing the seed against fingers and palm. The wings will disintegrate without any damage to the seed, and can be dispersed by blowing or winnowing.

3. Large Seed

These can be sown singly in individual containers, or placed in groups in large containers, with about 7-10 cm of sand, or sand and peat, at the base. The layer of seed can be covered with up to 7 cm of sand above, however seeds of some species such as *Castanospermum, Cycas, Macadamia* and *Macrozamia*, germinate quite successfully if only half buried on the surface. As germination

Sowing seed of *Banksia spinulosa*. Seed should not be sown too densely.

Seed and Seed Pod of *Castanospermum australe*. A single seed sown in a pot of propagation mixture. Note level of seed in pot.

occurs, seedlings can be removed to individual containers.

Plants with large seed include species of *Archontophoenix, Castanospermum, Cycas, Elaeocarpus, Floydia, Garcinia, Lepidozamia, Macadamia, Macrozamia, Normanbya, Planchonia* etc.

Germination Period

The time between the sowing of seed and the appearance of the seedlings above ground (germination), varies greatly between genera and even within a genus. It is obviously affected by temperature and also by the moisture content of the propagating medium.

The quickest seeds to germinate are usually

Germinating seeds of *Macrozamia communis* — note level of seeds in pot.

Covering seed of *Banksia spinulosa*, with propagating medium, to a depth of approximately 1-2 times the thickness of the seed.

203

those of ephemerals or annuals, e.g. species of the family Apiaceae, also Asteraceae, in which germination can occur in a few days. Species of *Acacia, Callistemon, Eucalyptus, Melaleuca* etc., usually germinate within one month. *Banksia* and *Hakea* species usually take 1-2 months, although some species may appear more quickly. Palms usually take 6-12 months, while cycads may take 1-2 years. Some genera such as *Billardiera* and *Patersonia* can be planted in spring in southern Australia, but germination will not occur until autumn, after rains have broken the summer drought and the weather is generally cooler.

The time for germination can also be greatly influenced by pre-sowing treatments such as stratification, soaking and peeling of the seed coat.

Alternative Germination Methods

Capillary Beds

Capillarity is the movement of water up through the soil above a water surface, such as a water table. The same effect can be obtained by placing a pot of soil in a container of shallow water. Capillary beds employ this principle, and are very useful for retaining an even moisture content in the propagation mixture. Most seeds can be germinated by this method. The great advantage is that damping off is kept to a minimum because of the conditions created. The mixture is just damp, and not over-wet. This means there is also ample aeration. There is also no need for overhead watering, which eliminates one of the major means of the spread of fungi by splashing. Excess water on leaves and stems is also eliminated. The capillary method can be applied on a very small or a large scale. Its major disadvantage on a large scale is that if a disease organism gets into the system, it is readily spread from pot to pot.

1. Seeds are sown in a container, in a mixture of 1 part washed sand to 1 part perlite, or a similar freely draining medium.

2. A tray is filled with coarse sand.
3. The tray is half filled with water.
4. Seedling container is placed on the coarse sand, but above the level of the water.
5. Constant water level can be maintained by using an inverted bottle or similar container holding water. The neck is placed at the required water level.
6. The tray is placed in a warm protected position, a bottom heat bed, or alternatively in a box heated with electric light bulbs. A fairly constant temperature of 20 to 25°C is ideal for germination. The number of light bulbs required will depend on the size of the area to be heated.

Bog Method

The bog method gains its name from the waterlogged or bog-like conditions that are created for germination. This method is very similar to capillary beds, except that the tray in which the seedling container is placed has only water, and no sand. There is also no need to cover the seeds with soil, because the whole surface is continually moist. As with capillary beds, overhead watering is not necessary, which means there is no dispersion of the seed.

This method is highly recommended for fine-seeded species of *Agonis, Astartea, Baeckea, Beaufortia, Callistemon, Calothamnus, Dracophyllum, Drosera, Eucalyptus, Kunzea, Leptospermum, Melaleuca, Regelia, Sinoga, Tristania* and other moisture-loving species.

Procedure:

1. Seeds are sown on a well drained mixture of 3 parts washed sand, 1 part peat moss, and 1 part good quality loam.
2. The seedling container is placed in a container of water, so that after absorption, the water-level is about half the depth of the propagating mixture.
3. This water-level is maintained, without spilling water onto the seeds.
4. When the seedlings are about 0.5 cm tall,

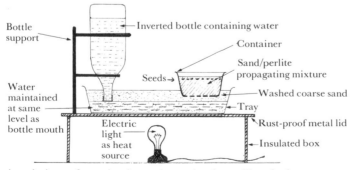

A technique of germination, using a simple capillary bed.

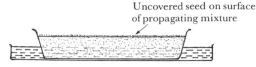

Uncovered seed on surface of propagating mixture

The Bog-method of seed germination.

remove the seedling container from the water, and treat as seedlings grown under normal conditions. It is a good idea to harden off the seedlings for about 5 days before pricking out. If seedlings are left in the water tray too long, the roots that have penetrated to the base of the container will be constantly waterlogged, and can rot.

Problems during Germination

Disease prevention and control during germination.

The following points should help to combat any disease problems.

1. Use new or sterilized containers.

2. Use sterilized mixture if possible. Do not use soil that has previously been used for the germination of seedlings, or for the recent growth of plants, unless it has been sterilized. Some benefit can be gained by pouring boiling water over the soil, or by lighting a small fire on the soil.

3. Treat seed with a fungicide before sowing.

4. Sow seed sparsely. This allows for stronger growth, and air movement between the seedlings. Dense seedlings, combined with high moisture content and no air movement, are ideal conditions for an outbreak of fungal disease such as 'Damping Off'.

5. A good practice is to wash the propagation area with a disinfectant to kill any existing diseases, before the seedling containers are placed in their final position.

6. The first watering after sowing the seed can contain a fungicide such as captan.

Damping Off

This is the main disease that occurs during seed germination, and may be caused by different pathogens. Seeds and seedlings can be affected, often resulting in the death of a large number of plants.

If 'damping off' occurs, it can be very difficult to control unless treated in the initial stages. The symptoms are wilting and toppling of young seedlings, as the attack usually occurs on the stems, near ground level. On some occasions the top growth can still appear healthy, due to the humid growing conditions, but the lower stem and root growth is dead.

For control methods, see Pests and Diseases, page 172.

TREATMENTS AND TECHNIQUES TO GERMINATE DIFFICULT SPECIES

The seeds of some species are difficult to germinate without special pre-sowing treatments. The usual response from untreated seed is no germination or a very low percentage or sporadic germination over a long period. The seeds of many of these species have inbuilt mechanisms designed to prevent mass germination until a particular set of favourable circumstances occurs. Some of these mechanisms are not well understood, and research is needed to elucidate the mechanisms and produce treatments which will give consistent results. The treatments may be applied to a general group of plants such as a genus or family however within these groups there are species or genera which may not respond because they have a different mechanism.

Mechanisms

Hard Seeds: a high proportion of the seeds of many species have hard waxy testa which is impervious to water penetration and gas exchange and so effectively keeps the seed in a dormant condition (about 2% are soft initially). This testa is purely a physical barrier and if it is broken and conditions are favourable the seed germinates rapidly. Species with this type of seed coat mainly belong to the families Caesalpiniaceae (e.g. the genera *Lysiphyllum, Caesalpinia, Cassia, Labichea, Petalostylis* etc), Fabaceae (most of the pea flowers have this mechanism but not all e.g. *Castanospermum australe*) and Mimosaceae (e.g. the genera *Acacia* and some *Albizia*).

Woody Seeds: the seeds of some species are retained within a woody coat which is actually part of the fruit. This is usually impervious to water penetration although gas exchange may occur. If the woody coat is broken and conditions are favourable, the seed germinates rapidly. Species with this type of seed are common in the family Convolvulaceae (e.g. the genera *Convolvulus, Ipomea, Bonamia, Merremia*) and in some rainforest plants such as *Rhodosphaera rhodanthema*.

Inhibitors: these are naturally occurring chemicals which prevent the germination of seed. They are usually present in the seed coat (testa) but may also be found in the material around the seed embryo (endosperm). The inhibitors may be simple chemicals such as common salt (sodium chloride) which is frequent in seeds from inland areas, or complex chemicals. More than one chemical may be involved in the inhibition. Seeds containing inhibitors are found in species of the genera *Crowea, Correa,*

Propagation

Eriostemon, Boronia, Phebalium, Asterolasia, Drummondita, Billardiera, Cycas, Macrozamia, Livistona, Caryota, Elaeocarpus.

Dormancy: seeds of some species have a dormant period after they mature. During this period they will not germinate even if all conditions are favourable for germination. With most species this dormant period is transitory usually lasting 1-4 months. Examples are species of *Acacia, Billardiera, Kennedia* and *Patersonia.*

Specific Temperature Requirements: research has shown that seeds of some exotic species respond to different day/night temperature combinations and fluctuations. These requirements may be so specific that the seeds will not germinate unless subjected to the particular combination required. Such responses probably occur with some native species but they remain unknown at present.

Tropical species especially those from coastal areas, will not germinate satisfactorily at temperatures less than 25°C.

Combination Mechanisms: in the seeds of a number of species it is a combination of mechanisms which prevent germination. For example the seeds of many species of the family Rutaceae (e.g. the genera *Crowea, Eriostemon, Correa* and *Boronia*) are hard and impervious but when the testa is broken the seed still will not germinate due to the presence of inhibitors which must first be leached out. In other genera such as *Billardiera* the seeds contain inhibitors which must first be removed but also require the presence of growth promoting chemicals which are formed after exposure to some conditions in the environment. When this balance of inhibitors/promoters tips in favour of the promoters, then the seeds can germinate. Many legumes have a dormancy mechanism which lasts about 2 months after they mature and are shed.

Short Viability: the seeds of many tropical species have a short life of 2 to 20 days and unless sown during this period lose viability and die. The seed itself does not appear any different physically but is incapable of germination. Seeds of this type are found in species of such genera as *Schefflera, Linospadix, Laccospadix, Pothos, Hollandea* and *Scindapsus.*

Treatment

Hard and Woody Seeds

As the barrier for germination of these species is purely physical it can be overcome by using simple techniques which will allow water to penetrate into the seed and gas exchange to occur.

Methods that can be used are as follows:

1. Boiling Water: this is the method most

The hard coats of some seeds need softening before sowing — pouring boiling water on Acacia seeds.

commonly used. The seeds are placed in a container, covered with boiling water, left to soak for 12 to 24 hours. The softened seeds will swell and can be separated for sowing. The remainder can be retreated. It may be necessary for species with very hard testa, to repeat the process 2 to 3 **or more times. Boiling may damage some seed.**

2. Abrasion: place the seed between sheets of sand-paper. By rubbing the sheets together the abrasive action will remove part of the outer coating. Care needs to be taken to prevent the seed being damaged by excessive abrasion. Large quantities of seed can be tumbled in a drum lined with sand-paper. Seed should then be sown immediately after abrading.

3. Filing or Cutting: the outer coating of seeds large enough to handle with some ease, can be broken by using a small three cornered file or sharp knife. Care must be taken to not damage the embryo of the seed and to avoid this it is a good idea to determine the exact layout of the seed before cutting. Seeds with woody coats are readily handled in this way, a shallow slice being taken off the woody coat to just expose the seed inside.

4. Sulphuric Acid: *Acacia* seeds respond very well to soaking in concentrated sulphuric acid for a period of between 10 and 20 minutes. Use only a glass or earthenware container, and wear protective clothing, gloves, and preferably glasses also. Other hard-coated seeds should also respond to this method, but little is known regarding the length of soaking time. Light stirring is needed to ensure good contact between the acid and the seed coat. Do not stir vigorously as this may create too much heat. After treatment the acid must be drained off as thoroughly as possible before washing the seed with water to remove any remaining acid. Care must be exer-

206

cised with this treatment, because of the tremendous heat release when water is added to the acid. This can result in splattering. A better policy is to add the treated seed gradually to a container of water, whilst continually stirring to disperse the acid. Seed can then be washed under flowing water in a plastic strainer for about 5 minutes. Sow seed immediately.

5. Hydrogen peroxide: recent experiments have found that this compound could be very useful for improving the germination of seed of many species. Little is to date known regarding its application to Australian species. The treatment process is the same as for Sulphuric acid.

6. Dry Heat: recent experiments have shown that exposure to periods of dry heat can overcome the problem of an impermeable seed coat and allow germination to occur. Each species has a threshold temperature above which the seed responds to the heat treatment and also a thermal death point at which it is killed. Exposure to temperatures above the threshold and below the thermal death point for very short periods is sufficient to allow germination to occur. The threshold temperature varies with the particular species and even within a genus e.g. in the genus *Acacia* some species respond to a threshold as low as 50°C whereas others need at least 70°C. A common successful technique is to expose the seeds for temperatures between 70-80°C for 30-60 seconds. The seeds are then sown as usual.

7. Immature Seeds: the seeds of some legumes can be germinated satisfactorily if they are taken from the fruit and sown just as the seed coat is hardening and changing colour from green to brown. At this stage they need no treatment but require optimum conditions so that germination is rapid. Not many species have been tested by this technique and it is possible that it can be more widely used to overcome the problems of dormancy and an impermeable coat. This technique has proved successful with *Hardenbergia violacea, H. comptoniana, Cassia odorata, C. artemisioides, Acacia* spp. and *Lysiphyllum hookeri, Barklya syringifolia.*

Treatments to overcome Inhibitors and Dormancy

Leaching: most of the inhibitors are water soluble and can be leached from the testa however the amount of leaching required varies considerably with the species and in some cases with the batch of seed. Leaching times vary from 1 week to 10 weeks. Simple chemicals like common salt are readily washed out by soaking with successive changes of water. Soaking however is not recommended for long periods and a better procedure is continuous leaching under running water. The seeds are held in muslin bags to prevent dispersal. As the inhibitors are leached out the seeds germinate and can be removed and planted. This technique has been successfully used with species of *Crowea, Eriostemon* and *Correa.* Leaching with warm water improves the process but requires the use of specialized equipment. Leaching with alkaline solutions (pH about 9) also has been shown to overcome inhibitors in some members of the family Rutaceae.

Stratification: the seeds of a number of species respond to exposure to periods of low temperature. This is known as a chilling response and for success it must be undertaken in the presence of moisture. The chilling is responsible for the initiation of promoting systems within the seeds and the moisture for leaching inhibitors. This process is commonly employed for the germination of exotic species but little is known about the responses of Australian natives although some success has been achieved with species of *Anigozanthos, Billardiera, Rubus, Grevillea, Banksia* and *Boronia.*

The components of stratification are chilling temperature and length of chilling period. The temperatures commonly used for stratification are between 1°C and 5°C and for periods between 1 and 8 weeks. Much research is needed to determine the best combinations for various species. Seeds should never be frozen as tissue damage will occur. Presoaking for 24 hours before stratification may improve the response.

Techniques of stratification vary. The simplest method is to sow the seeds in pots or trays of moist, coarse sand and place outside for the winter. Alternatively the pot can be put in a refrigerator provided the seeds are moistened from time to time. Another technique is to mix the seed with premoistened sand and peat moss, seal in a plastic bag and place in the bottom of a refrigerator until ready to be sown. Seeds can also be sandwiched between layers of moistened sheets of blotting paper, inserted in a plastic bag or between plastic sheeting and placed in the refrigerator. The seeds must be kept moist at all times and after stratification they should be sown and placed in a warm sheltered position to induce rapid germination.

Soaking: the seeds of some species of eucalypts have been found to germinate better if soaked in water for 1 to 3 days before sowing. This does not appear to be a response to leaching but apparently is simply due to improved water uptake.

Alternate Wetting and Drying: periods of soaking interspersed with periods of drying have been found to improve germination of some difficult species such as *Boronia* and *Grevillea.*

Propagation

Fermentation: germination of a few species has been improved by allowing the seed to ferment in the fruit before sowing. This group includes species of *Passiflora, Billardiera scandens, B. cymosa* and some palms such as *Caryota rumphiana.*

Partial Digestion: the seeds of many rainforest species germinate very well after they have been partially digested by animals and large birds. The cassowary is particularly significant in this respect and it is believed that this bird has played an important role in the distribution and ecology of some plants. So far this digestive effect has not been reproduced experimentally. Seeds that germinate well after partial digestion include species of *Aristotelia, Aceratium, Elaeocarpus* and *Astroloma.*

Peeling the Testa: the seeds of some species which germinate slowly can be speeded up by pre-soaking for 24 hours and carefully peeling off the testa. This technique is particularly effective with many species of *Grevillea* such as *G. leucopteris, G. juncifolia* and *G. petrophiloides* and also many species in the family Liliaceae.

Chilling and Fire: some response has been obtained in species of *Boronia* and *Crowea* by stratifying the seeds then sowing in a terra cotta pot and burning a pile of leaves on the surface. The seeds should be watered as soon as the ashes cool.

Alternate Day/Night Temperatures: seeds of species from inland areas are subjected to large temperature fluctuations and it is believed that these changes play a major role in softening hard seeds and/or overcoming inhibitors, e.g. it has been found that seeds of some legumes soften and are able to germinate after exposure to fluctuating temperatures and dryness for 4 to 5 weeks in hot areas.

Soil temperatures in arid areas range from 20°C at night to 65°C in the day. Seeds of a range of species have been exposed to similar temperature fluctuations and some species respond by an improvement in germination e.g. *Hibiscus trionum.*

Improvement by Storage: the germination of seed of species which have a dormancy mechanism can be improved simply by storage. The length of storage ranges from 2 months to 2 years. In the case of legumes, storage for 2 months before the seed coat is disrupted and the seed is sown will improve germination over seed sown straight after harvest. Many grasses have a very low percent germination if fresh seed is sown but the numbers increase gradually with time and germination is best after 1-2 years storage, e.g. *Aristida* spp., *Astrebla* spp., *Bothriochloa* spp., *Cymbopogon* spp., *Dichanthium* spp., *Digitaria* spp., *Eulalia* spp., *Themeda australis* and *Thyridolepis* spp.

Seedlings of *Callitris rhomboidea*, showing a desirable density, and ideal stage for potting on.

Seedlings of *Banksia serrata* which have been left too long in the seedling container. When transplanted at this stage, damage to root systems is likely to occur.

Cordyline stricta seedlings.

POST GERMINATION PROCEDURE

A general rule with seedlings of Australian plants is to transplant them to their growing-on containers, as soon as they can be handled. In some cases this can mean just as they are pushing their way through the soil, e.g. *Banksia*, *Grevillea*, *Hakea* and *Telopea* species. Most other species, including *Eucalyptus*, *Melaleuca*, and many of the pea plants, will be suitable when they are 0.5-1 cm tall.

If seedlings have been grown in a sheltered location such as a propagation house or frame, they must be 'hardened off' for 3 to 5 days before transplanting, otherwise many deaths can occur.

When transplanting, do not be afraid to pinch-prune the roots if they are too long to fit into the container without bending. If roots are bent or twisted when potting, it usually means that they will keep growing this way when the plant is placed into its permanent location. Research has shown that to prune the roots of young seedlings, including *Eucalyptus* species, helps produce stronger, healthier plants.

After transplanting, thoroughly water the plants. The addition of a root stimulant and fungicide is usually beneficial at this time. Place the containers in a mild, sheltered location, or cover them with shade cloth until the plants are established. This can be for a period of up to 2 weeks. They can then be placed in a sunny location where they will grow into strong young plants. One method to save labour is to place a portable shade frame over the pots. This can be removed easily when required.

The Swiss Roll Method

This is an unusual technique of handling seedlings which was developed in Finland and is well suited to systems of mechanization. It is also known as the 'Nisula' method. It is a very economical method of using space since many small plants can develop in a limited area.

A strip of polythene about 4 m x 30 cm is spread out on a bench and a potting mixture is spread in a layer over the polythene to about 1 cm thick. The seedlings are laid out about 10 cm apart along each edge with the roots facing inwards and the tops on the outside. The polythene is then carefully rolled keeping the bundle tight and when finished it is tied tightly. The bundle is then cut in half between the two rows of root systems giving 2 bundles each of about 30 plants. A similar technique can be used for cuttings that are easy to strike e.g. *Prostanthera nivea*, *Westringia fruticosa*.

Choice of Growing Container

There is a wide range of different types and

Root pruning of Acacia seedling, prior to potting, by pinching with fingers.

Acacia seedlings showing the reduction of the root systems after root pruning. Left — Not pruned. Right — pruned.

3   Firming soil around the stem and roots of
    Eucalyptus seedling, keeping the soil level
    around the stem, the same as when in the
    seedling tray.

1   Root pruning of Eucalyptus seedling, prior to
    potting, by pinching with fingers.

2   Eucalyptus seedling, ready for potting. Make sure
    that roots are not twisted or coiled.

4   Although only having 1 or 2 pairs of leaves, Banksias
    can have a well developed root system, and seedlings
    will need to be separated with care.

5   Root pruning of Banksia seedling, by pinching with
    fingers.

6   Young Banksia seedling after root pruning.

9   Removing *Banksia spinulosa* seedling from tube, prior to potting on.

7   Preparing to place Banksia seedling into potting medium. Make sure roots are not twisted or coiled.

8   Firming soil around Banksia seedling, keeping the soil at the same level as the original seedling tray.

10   Teasing and uncoiling roots of *Banksia spinulosa* seedling, prior to potting on.

11   Potting on *Banksia spinulosa* — filling new container with soil mixture to a slightly higher level than finally desired, to allow for settling.

Propagation

A selection of plastic containers suitable for growing Australian plants.

sizes of containers suitable for growing-on Australian plants until they are ready for planting in a permanent situation.

Some of the commonly used containers are:

1. Wood veneer or polythene tubes. Although larger sizes are obtainable, tubes of 15 cm x 5 cm are usually used, primarily for growing large shrubs or trees. The wood veneer needs to be soaked, and then rolled to the desired diameter and secured by a rubber band or metal staple. The polythene tubes have been extruded, and no extra labour is needed to prepare them in readiness for planting.

This type of container helps promote vertical roots. As the tubes are open-ended, the roots are not restricted, and therefore coiling is non-existent, or greatly limited. Once plants are established, early planting is recommended.

2. Polyethylene Bags. Available in a range of sizes, this type of container is very suitable. Research has shown that the roots of plants grown in such containers do not readily coil, as occurs in rigid, tapered, plastic containers.

The main disadvantages of bags, are that the soft sides restrict ease of handling and filling, and the bags break down after a time (usually when about 12-24 months old). They are ideal for short-term growing of plants.

3. Rigid Plastic Pots. These are by far the most commonly used containers for growing-on of Australian plants. They are very easy to handle and fill with growing medium, but have the disadvantage of promoting root coiling, which is detrimental to plant growth, unless corrected at the time of planting.

4. Terracotta Pots are not now commonly used, except for specimen plants of epiphytic orchids. One of the main disadvantages with terracotta pots is the build up of salts on the porous sides, which can affect plant growth.

Selection of Growing Medium

See Cultivation of Container Grown Plants — Potting Mixes, page 102.

SPECIALISED SEXUAL PROPAGATION

Orchid Seed Propagation

Orchid seeds lack any stored food and must be raised under sterile conditions if large quantities are to be grown successfully. Smaller quantities can be grown by a couple of simple techniques. However these systems are not always reliable.

Sterile Technique

The technique of raising orchid seed under sterile conditions is complicated when compared with normal seed-raising techniques. The procedure however is logical and fairly straightforward, and quickly mastered after a few practice runs.

Sowing Media

The seed must be sown on an agar medium

Orchid seedlings in flask — native *Dendrobium* hybrid.

which has been fortified by nutrient salts. This medium sets to the consistency of jelly but retains a thin film of water over the surface in which the orchid seeds germinate. The medium also provides an ideal substrate for the growth of fungi and bacteria. If present these will smother the orchid seeds and hence the medium and growing flasks must be sterilized before sowing.

All media consist of basic nutrient salts, sugar and agar but various additives such as vitamins and growth regulators are added by experimenters. Fruit products such as green coconut milk and ripe bananas are also used. These are not generally needed and the basic formula developed by Dr Knudson early this century is still the most successful. This formula is given in the accompanying table.

Knudson's Orchid Formula 'C'

Chemical	Symbol	Quantity
Sucrose	$C_{12}H_{22}O_{11}$	20.0 g
Agar		15.0 g
Calcium nitrate	$Ca(NO_3)_2 \cdot 4H_2O$	1.0 g
Ammonium sulphate	$(NH_4)_2SO_4$	500 mgm
Monobasic potassium phosphate	KH_2PO_4	250 mgm
Magnesium sulphate	$MgSO_4 : 7H_2O$	250 mgm
Ferrous sulphate	$FeSO_4 : 7H_2O$	25 mgm
Manganese sulphate	$MnSO_4 : 4H_2O$	7.5 mgm

All of these chemicals can be purchased from chemists or chemical supply companies. The chemicals must be weighed accurately using a sensitive balance because the concentrations of each element are critical.

Preparation of Media

Take 1 litre of water and warm it gently. Add the ingredients one at a time and stir until each is dissolved before adding the next. Add the agar last and stir thoroughly until it is dissolved. The medium is now mixed but must be adjusted to the correct pH of 5-5.2.

A small sample is tested by a colour indicator or litmus paper. If too acid a drop of 0.1 normal potassium hydroxide is added to the bulk solution, mixed and the pH retested. Further additions may be necessary although the pH usually changes rapidly with the addition of small quantities. If the solution is too alkaline it is adjusted with drops of 0.1 normal hydrochloric acid in a similar manner to that outlined above.

Seed Flasks

Orchid seeds are commonly sown in wide mouthed bottles such as cream bottles or flat bottles such as those used for whisky and spirits. Erlenmeyer flasks are also excellent for the purpose. Whatever type is used must be of glass and be capable of being sterilized.

The opening of the bottle or flask is sealed with a tight fitting rubber stopper. The stopper has a hole in the centre through which is inserted a piece of glass tubing for ventilation. The tubing is bent over near the middle and the end closed with a plug of cotton wool. This allows ventilation but prevents contamination by fungi and bacteria. The setup is shown in the accompanying photograph of orchid seedlings in a cream bottle.

All bottles and stoppers must be washed thoroughly and rinsed several times before use. After the agar is prepared it is poured into the flasks using a funnel to avoid splashing the neck and sides. The agar can be allowed to set horizontally or on a slant if the bottles are tilted. The stoppers are inserted and the bottles are ready for sterilization.

Sterilization

The prepared flasks are best sterilized in an autoclave however a pressure cooker serves the purpose well. The flasks are sterilized for 20 minutes at 15 psi.

Sterilizing the Seed

Orchid seed may be contaminated with fungal spores and hence must be sterilized before sowing. Some spores are resistant to sterilization and these can be readily killed if the orchid seed is first soaked in a weak sugar solution (2 teaspoons to a cup of water) for 12-24 hours.

Orchid seed is sterilized in solutions of calcium hypochlorite (10 g calcium hypochlorite with 140 ml water). A small quantity of seed is shaken in a small bottle about two thirds full of the calcium hypochlorite solution for about 20 minutes. The excess calcium hypochlorite solution is drained off and replaced with sterile water. The orchid seed can now be picked up and sown in the flasks with a sterile eye dropper (4 drops per flask).

Cleanliness is essential throughout the whole sowing operation as contamination can readily occur. Contaminated flasks will show up within a few days of sowing and must be discarded. A special sowing area or simple cabinet will greatly reduce the risk of infection.

Seedling Development

If the seed is fertile it begins to swell and within 6 weeks turns green. The first leaves appear within 3-6 months and the roots within 10-12 months. The seedlings can be transplanted into community pots when they are sufficiently well developed.

Propagation

Transplanting

The seedlings are washed from the flask with warm water and all traces of agar removed by washing. They should then be dipped in a mild fungicide and are ready for planting into community pots.

A simple and very effective community pot can be made from a clean used ice cream container or 9 litre bucket. Chopped live sphagnum moss is placed in a layer about 5 cm thick over the bottom. The moss is moistened and the seedlings placed about 3 cm apart in the moss with the roots just covered. A sheet of glass is placed over the top of the container to create humidity and the whole is placed in a partially lighted protected situation. After a couple of weeks the glass can be removed and the seedlings can be potted when sufficiently well developed.

Simple Techniques

The simplest technique is to sprinkle the ripe orchid seed on the surface of the potting medium around the base of the plant. The plants are kept watered normally and with luck in about 12 months small seedlings will be visible.

This technique has proved successful for some species of Australian terrestrial orchids which are very difficult to raise by sterile techniques e.g. species of *Thelymitra, Diuris* and *Caladenia*. It has also proved successful for tropical terrestrials such as *Calanthe triplicata, Malaxis latifolia* and *Spathoglottis paulinae*. Some epiphytes that can be propagated by this technique include *Dendrobium kingianum, D. speciosum, Liparis reflexa* and *L. nugentae*.

Towelling Technique

This is a fairly simple technique for raising

Dendrobium speciosum is a hardy orchid that can be grown in a garden situation.

small numbers of orchid seedlings. It is a very old technique that was developed before the techniques of sterile culture were perfected. It is only satisfactory for epiphytic species.

A new terracotta pot (15-20 cm across) is boiled in water for about 15 minutes. While it is boiling a mixture of chopped sphagnum moss, peat moss and tree fern fibre is made up and moistened. After the pot has been sterilized it is filled to about one third with the above mixture. Another quantity of the mixture is then compacted into a tight ball, partially wrapped with a piece of new towelling and forced into the top of the pot with the towelling uppermost. A gap of 2-3 cm is left between the top of the towelling and the top of the pot. Some sphagnum moss is forced around the edge of the pot to reduce evaporation. The towelling and mixture are then sterilized by pouring boiling water over the whole lot.

When cool enough orchid seed can be sprinkled over the surface of the towelling. A few tips of live orchid roots are scattered among the seeds to provide the important myccorrhizal fungi necessary for successful germination. A glass cover is then placed over the surface of the pot and the pot stood in a container of boiled water which is maintained at about 3 cm high. The pots are placed in a shady, protected position.

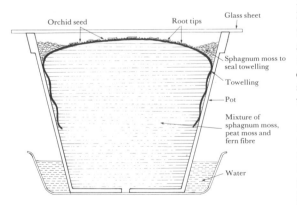

Towelling method of sowing Orchid Seed.

Germination takes 6-8 weeks and is first indicated by the presence of fine fungal threads around the seeds. The seedlings are ready for pricking out after 12-24 months. Transplanting and aftercare are the same as outlined under the sterile techniques.

Propagation of Fern Spores

The production of ferns by spores is the most efficient way of raising large numbers of any species. Unfortunately the process is not always easy and the results are never predictable. It is this unreliability which has caused nurseries to neglect the vast range of ferns available, and to concentrate on the hardy species which are easy to propagate.

Technique of Spore Sowing
1. Prepare the sowing medium making sure that it is moist.
2. Wash second hand pots or use new pots.
3. Fill the pots to one third with coarse propagating sand.
4. Fill the remainder of the pot with sowing medium, press it down to make it firm and leave a catchment of at least 3 cm below the rim of the pot.
5. Pour boiling water over the pot and sowing medium until the top part of the mixture has been thoroughly moistened. An alternative is to place the pot containing the medium in an oven at 93°C (200°F) for at least 30 minutes.
6. Allow to cool until the mixture is just warm.
7. Sow the spores thinly using a spoon or the blade of a knife.
8. Dampen the freshly sown spores with a fine mist (such as from the type of hand pump used in ironing).
9. Cover immediately with a sheet of glass or polythene (see below).
10. Stand the pot to about one third its depth in clean water.
11. Cover the glass or plastic with a sheet of newspaper for 2-3 weeks. This ensures more uniform germination in some species.
12. Maintain water level until germination has completed and the first true fronds are beginning to appear.
13. Remove the glass or polythene and allow the plants to harden off.

After hardening the sporelings can be pricked out into trays or pots. They are usually pricked out in clumps or groups. When these have developed into a mass of healthy plants they can be further split up. Once they have reached 5-10 cm high they are hardy little plants that are quite easily handled.

Fern sporelings contaminated with mosses.

Notes on Spore Raising
The use of boiling water or oven heating is to kill the spores of algae, liverworts, mosses or alien ferns which may be present in the medium. These spores germinate faster than the sown fern spores and unless destroyed smother the young ferns before they have developed.

If the spores are fertile the prothalli appear on the surface of the medium as a green scum. These continue to develop and eventually end up as distinct moon-shaped prothalli.

The time of development varies considerably with the species. Fast growing species such as *Christella dentata* or *Athyrium japonicum* may develop the first true leaves within 8 months of sowing and be established plants within 18 months of sowing. Slow growing species such as *Blechnum patersonii* or *Asplenium nidus* may take 12-18 months before developing the first true leaf and 2-3 years to become established small plants.

Collection of Spores
Spores are collected by placing a mature frond in folded paper or an envelope or paper bag and storing in a warm dry place. The spores are shed after a few days and appear as a fine dust on the

Propagation

Fern sporelings showing good germination.

and must be mixed constantly while being wetted to achieve uniform uptake and distribution of water. Once wet it remains so for a considerable time as it can absorb up to ten times its weight in water.

Chopped tree fern fibres provide an excellent medium for raising spores. These are commonly fibres of *Dicksonia antarctica* or *Cyathea australis*. Their pH is 4.7 and they have good moisture holding properties. Because of their fibrous nature, air circulation is better around the spores than in peat moss. Mixtures of these materials with coarse propagating sand have proved good for raising fern spores.

paper. They should not be collected in plastic bags as moulds may develop in the humid atmosphere. Collection of viable spores is one of the major requisites for successful raising of spores.

Media used for Spore Raising

Fern spores are sown on a variety of media. Some of these have been selected because specific requirements have been noticed by growers while others are based on personal preferences or factors such as ease of handling or ease of acquisition of the material. Most species require a pH of about 4.5-6.0 for successful germination.

Peat moss is the commonest material used for raising fern spores. Sphagnum peat moss has a pH of about 4.5 and this seems to suit many ferns although it may need to be raised by the addition of lime for some species. Most importantly it is virtually sterile and does not provide a good growing medium for pathogenic bacteria and fungi. It is difficult to wet initially

216

19 Cuttings

INTRODUCTION TO VEGETATIVE PROPAGATION

Vegetative propagation is the multiplication of an individual plant into a series of plants, genetically identical with the parent and with each other. There are a number of systems available for vegetative propagation, but each involves the use of vegetative tissue of the plant to be multiplied. Vegetative propagation is opposed to sexual propagation, which involves pollination, fertilization and the transfer of genes.

Vegetative propagation offers the following advantages:

1. The features of the species, form or cultivar, will be accurately reproduced and perpetuated. This means that superior forms which have been selected or hybrids which have been raised, can be multiplied and distributed. This overcomes one of the major disadvantages of seedlings, which is variability, in both flower and vegetative characteristics.

2. Vegetatively propagated plants flower while much younger than seedlings. This is especially important for commercial ventures such as flower growing, fruit production (e.g. *Macadamia* nuts), and also the sale of container-grown plants in nurseries.

Systems of Vegetative Propagation

Plants may be propagated by a variety of vegetative methods that include —

Cuttings, Layering, Division, Grafting, Budding, and many specialized techniques, such as micro propagation.

CUTTINGS

Cuttings are pieces of plants which, when separated from the plants and maintained under good conditions, produce new roots and growth to become separate plants. They may be treated in various ways to encourage the production of a new plant, but basically their requirements are:

1. An adequate water supply.

2. Adequate aeration at the base of the cutting for the formation of roots.

3. An optimum temperature at the base of the cutting for the formation of roots.

4. The avoidance of stress caused by extremes of temperature or by low humidity.

In practical terms, cuttings may consist of pieces of root, stem, large branches or trunk, a single leaf or pieces of leaf, pieces of stem each with a single bud, and with or without leaf. Theoretically plants can be propagated from single cells, but in practice this has proved impractical, being most closely approached by meristem and tissue culture.

Cutting propagation is widely employed for dicotyledons, but is rare in monocotyledons although successful in such woody genera as *Dracaena* and *Cordyline*.

With plants that do not readily produce seeds, cuttings can be a successful method of propagation. In some species, plants can be produced much more easily from cuttings than from seed, e.g. species of *Correa*, *Crowea*, *Dampiera*, *Grevillea* and *Lechenaultia*.

The selection of suitable cutting material, the timing, and method of collection, can be of critical importance in the survival and successful rooting of cuttings, especially those species that are difficult to propagate.

Types of Cuttings

Stem Cuttings

Stem cuttings are the most common type of cuttings used for plant propagation. The stems are cut into sections, and treated on the basis of the firmness of the growth needed.

This firmness is related to stage of growth. As a new shoot develops from a flush of growth, it is at first soft, then hardens off as it matures. Cuttings from soft growth are known as softwood cuttings; those from semi-mature growth, semi-hardwood cuttings; and those from hardened or mature growth, hardwood cuttings. As the shoot passes through these stages of maturity, rooting potential decreases, with softwood cuttings having the highest rooting ability. However, very young soft shoots need careful nursing, and are only suited to propagation under intermittent mist, or very humid conditions such as under a jar or plastic bag. The semi-mature shoots, while having a lower rooting potential, are hardier, and better suited to general propagating conditions. The fully mature shoots are woody, slower to root, and are also more tolerant of less than ideal propagating conditions.

Leaf Cuttings

In some species, whole leaves or parts of leaves can form roots and initiate new plants, if put in as cuttings. This method is not used for many Australian plants, however *Boea hygroscopica* is readily propagated by using a mature leaf with 2-5 cm of leaf stalk. The stalk and basal part of the leaf are buried in the medium, and kept moist, and warm. The leaf cuttings can be placed in separate pots or community containers. With constant temperature of about 25°C and high humidity, new plants form fairly quickly on the stalk or at the leaf base.

If the main veins are also cut near the surface of the propagating medium, new plants can form at the cuts, giving more than one plant per leaf.

Single Node Cuttings

In this technique, selected shoots are cut off, across the internodes, to give small stem sections, each bearing a leaf and a single bud. This method can produce more plants than the stem cuttings, because theoretically each bud is capable of producing a new plant. The new plant is formed at the node, and cuttings need only to comprise a leaf, stalk and stem with node.

The cuttings are placed in the propagating medium, the node being level with the surface of the medium. In species with large leaves a stake is used to support the cutting until roots are formed. Often the leaves may be rolled and held by a rubber band. This method is suitable for species of *Clematis, Dischidia, Dracaena, Ficus, Hoya, Raphidophora, Rubus* and *Scindapsus*.

Leaf Bud Cuttings

In this type of propagation, a bud and supporting leaf are cut from the stem with a shield of wood 2-4 cm long. The cut should be shallow and not penetrate too deeply into the wood of the stem. This method of taking cuttings is very similar to cutting a bud for budding, however the entire leaf is left intact on the cutting.

After taking the leaf bud cutting, the entire basal shield of wood is buried 1-2 cm deep in the propagating medium. Roots are formed from the basal shield, and new growth is produced from the bud. These shoots should be allowed to develop until they are large enough for potting as separate plants.

This type of propagation has the advantage that the leaf bud cuttings can be removed from the parent plant without the need to cut off the stems. It is essential that the buds should be sufficiently developed and mature enough to form shoots, otherwise roots but not growth will result.

Leaf bud cuttings are best taken during the warm months of the year. The technique has proved successful with species of *Cissus, Hoya* and *Rubus*.

Root Cuttings

The roots of many species will initiate buds and develop into new plants, when cut from the root system and placed in propagating conditions. This is not a widely used method of propagation, but has application with species that do not set seed readily and are difficult to grow from stem cuttings. As a general rule, those species which produce suckers can often be propagated from root cuttings.

It is preferable to use young roots, and they should be cut before plants start vigorous new growth, as there will be a large amount of food stored in the roots at that time. The best roots are obtained from young plants 2-4 years of age. The roots are cut into sections, which vary in size, depending on the species, but usually the smaller the species of plant, the smaller the section. Root cuttings are commonly 7-10 cm long, but may be up to 30 cm, e.g. *Bombax*.

Root cuttings dehydrate very easily, especially the smaller roots. They should be moistened soon after collection, and kept moist until planted in the propagating medium.

The cuttings can be planted vertically or horizontally in the propagating medium. If planted vertically, care must be exercised to ensure the cuttings are not upside down. This can be easily avoided by always cutting straight across the top of a root section, and making a slanting cut at the base. Small cuttings can be scattered over the medium, and just covered with fine sand or sawdust. Larger cuttings are buried deeper.

The pots containing root cuttings are best placed in a shaded location, and must not be allowed to dry out. Bottom heat propagating units are good for root cuttings, as the cuttings are often taken in the colder months of the year when plants are dormant.

Some species of the following genera can be propagated by this method. *Acacia, Atalaya, Austromyrtus, Banksia, Bombax, Cochlospermum,*

Cutting material should be stored in plastic bags before processing, to prevent dehydration.

Commersonia, Dampiera, Denhamia, Exocarpos, Melaleuca, Pelargonium, Rubus, Rulingia and *Scaevola.*

Branch and Trunk Cuttings

Large stems, branches, and even sections of trunks of some species can be successfully used for propagation. These cuttings are commonly 1-3 m long, and may be 4-20 cm in diameter. They have the advantage of quickly developing into a sizeable plant, and reducing the waiting period necessary when planting a small plant. Because they are large however, they may take 1-2 years to produce a sufficiently strong root system to support the trunk and new growth. Because of this, they need to be well-staked in the early years.

Branch and trunk cuttings are mainly used in tropical regions, and they are only successful for a few species. They are taken at the onset of, or during, the wet season, and are usually propagated in the position where they are to be grown.

Both trunk and branch cuttings can be used to successfully propagate *Erythrina indica*, and branch cuttings are successful for *Brachychiton acerifolium* and *Bombax ceiba* var. *leiocarpa.*

Collection of Cuttings

The following aspects relating to the collection of cuttings should help ensure success.

1. The best time to collect material is in the early morning, before the sun has been on plants. The reason is that the sap flow is at its peak at this time, having been replenished during the cool of the night. The material will then be in peak condition, and if prepared as cuttings as soon as possible, there is the greatest likelihood of success in propagation.

2. Best results are obtained if cuttings are put in as soon as possible after collection. If however it is necessary for them to be transported any distance, make sure that no dehydration occurs, and that the cuttings are kept cool at all times, to maintain them in first class condition. For short distances, plastic bags are ideal, but there can be some generation of heat. Bags should be covered by a blanket, rug or similar material. Never leave a plastic bag of cuttings in full sunshine. For long distance transportation, a good method is to wrap the slightly moist cuttings in several layers of moist newspaper, and then place in a plastic bag.

An important aspect of transporting cuttings is to not keep them too moist, as this can have two bad side effects, First, ideal conditions are created for moulds and fungi, which spread very quickly in a confined area, and cause defoliation of the cuttings. The second problem that occurs with over-wet cuttings is known as sweating. This is caused by high moisture, lack of oxygen, and some generation of heat. The leaves blacken and may shed from the cutting material while it is still in the bag. Similar problems can occur by crowding too many cuttings into a plastic bag.

Ideally, the cutting material needs to be only slightly moist, and it is better for it to be a little too dry, rather than too wet.

The use of portable insulated coolers can be of assistance on extended trips, however small fridges such as are used for camping, or in caravans and campmobiles, should be used with care. These are very efficient units, but they can get to below freezing point. If this happens, plant material is rendered useless, and the results may not be evident until the cuttings have been in the propagating area for a few days.

3. Collection of cuttings can be an excellent method of pruning. Take care when removing any material so that the plants are not mis-shapen by inappropriate pruning. Particularly when collecting from plants other than your own, try to take cuttings without leaving visible evidence of indiscriminant pruning, or unsightly butts that could allow for the entrance of disease organisms.

Juvenile and Adult Growth Phases

Plants have both juvenile and adult phases of growth. In some species this is well exemplified by different leaf patterns, such as are familiar in many of the eucalypts, but in most plants it is not obvious. Flowering is generally restricted to plants which are in the adult stage of growth.

Propagation

The juvenile phase of growth is referred to as juvenility.

One significance of juvenility lies in the ability of cuttings to form roots. In general, cuttings of seedlings form roots readily and this capacity decreases with the age of the plant, and in some species cuttings from old plants are impossible to strike. Knowing that a plant is in a juvenile phase can make rooting of a difficult species possible, and this has been proved in some eucalypts e.g. *E. grandis* and *E. ficifolia*, but it is not used commercially.

The major problem with propagating from the juvenile phase is that a species is likely to vary from seed, in factors such as flower colour or growth habit. Under these circumstances the flower colour or other adult characteristics of the parent will be unknown when the cuttings are taken.

Once a plant has passed into the adult phase, it is doubtful if it can ever be re-induced back into the juvenile phase. Some procedures however can induce an apparent temporary return to juvenility, resulting in more ready rooting of cuttings. These treatments include severe pruning, such as in the formation of a hedge or a stool bed type system, whereby the shoots are continually cut back to old wood, and the resulting new growth is used as cuttings.

Ringing or Girdling

The percentage rooting can sometimes be increased by taking the cuttings from shoots which have been ringed or girdled 2-3 weeks before collection. The procedure is very quick and simple, and consists of running a knife blade in a complete circle around the shoot, so as to cut the bark to the depth of the wood. This allows accumulation of food material in the shoot, and it has been shown that cuttings taken from such material on shy rooting species, root better than untreated material. The girdle can be placed on a shoot that contains material sufficient for several cuttings, or on a single small shoot. In the latter case, the basal cut of the cutting is made across the stem just below the girdle.

Girdling has been used successfully to aid in the grafting of commercial strains of *Macadamia* nuts. Shoots suitable for graft scions are girdled 2-3 months before they are grafted and this process greatly increases the final take.

Selection of Cutting Material

The selection of suitable cutting material varies from species to species, and there is no definite rule. It is also affected by the propagation structure used, and the type of propagation to be undertaken. A guideline for general propagation is to use material that is supple, but not too soft. This is known as semi-hardwood. A quick test to select suitable material is to bend it to a right angle. If it bends easily and then springs back fairly quickly to its original position, it can be classed as semi-hardwood.

Best results will be gained by using material from young plants. In general, cuttings from young plants produce roots much more readily than if taken from old specimens. Certain mature plants of various species are extremely difficult to propagate from cuttings, e.g. *Persoonia pinifolia*, whilst successful rooting is achieved by using material from very young plants. (See **Juvenile and Adult Growth Phases, page 219**).

A good general policy is to collect firm, fairly new material, as this strikes quickly, with fewer problems than old material. The growth rate usually decreases on older branches, and the material is woody and hard to strike. This is particularly obvious on the older, lower parts of a tall bush or small tree. Suitable material however may be collected from such a plant, by using material with a high growth activity, which is usually found near the top. As growth activity moves up a plant, the best cutting material is to be found at higher and higher levels.

On bushy species, whole terminal branch sections may be collected, and prepared later into a series of terminal and side shoot cuttings. In species with long sparsely branched growth, the tips (8-15 cm long) may be taken and prepared as cuttings, or the whole terminal removed and cut up into a series of cuttings.

Select material that is healthy, and free from obvious disease, or distortion. This is particularly important, because if the plant is infected when the cuttings are taken, rooting will be difficult, and the percentage strike greatly reduced. Frequently if a disease is present on cuttings at preparation time, it will flare up in the conditions of the propagating house, and cause severe losses. Distorted growth may be the result of virus infection, and propagation will only perpetuate the virus and help its spread. New growth will have had less chance to come in contact with disease than old growth, and provides the best source of cutting material. If possible, never take cuttings from branches that have been in contact with the ground. In the event of *Phytophthora* being present in the area, low branches could be contaminated with spores, through brushing the soil, or by splashing of water caused by rain or artificial watering. *Phytophthora* has been found in plants at a height of up to 2 m above ground level. When collecting cuttings of ground-covers and low growing

1 Selected branch of *Grevillea rosmarinifolia*, with suitable growth for cuttings.

2 Selection of suitable material for cuttings.

3 Selected shoot suitable for cuttings.

4 Shoot cut to produce 2 cuttings.

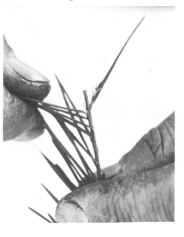

5 Two cuttings of *Grevillea rosmarinifolia*.

6 Lower of the 2 cuttings needs shortening to node.

7 Cuttings with soft tip removed from cutting on left, and cutting on right shortened to node.

8 Lower foliage removed from cutting by pulling upwards, to minimize damage to bark.

9 Completed cuttings ready for placing in propagating medium.

Cutting of *Grevillea rosmarinifolia*, placed into propagating medium, and firmed.

Cutting ready for placement in propagating structure.

plants, try to get material that is on the top layer of the plant, as this is less likely to be contaminated.

Plants grown in cultivation usually provide better material than 'bush' plants, because they grow more vigorously under usually more favourable conditions. Bush material is in many cases much harder, and therefore will take longer to strike. Also it is easier to observe the garden grown plants, and to judge when is the best time for collecting cuttings.

There are some guides used in relation to the suitability of growth for propagation by cuttings. One of these is the leaf/shoot ratio. The number of leaves on cutting material, compared to the length of that material, is known as the leaf/shoot ratio. It can be easily assessed, and can provide a useful guide to the suitability of plant material for cuttings. The higher the ratio, the better the material. In general, short leafy cuttings strike more readily than large sparsely leaved material, which has few internodes. As an example, terminal shoots of main branches are generally too coarse for use as cuttings. Such branches have long internodes, large leaves, and a low leaf/shoot ratio. Side branches provide much better material, having closer internodes, smaller leaves, and a higher leaf/shoot ratio. Leaf/shoot ratio should only be used as a general guide, as the results can be complicated by factors such as the stem thickness, and leaf size.

The above is a general guide to the selection of suitable cutting material, however there are always plants which do not conform to the rules. Such plants may need careful study, before suitable material can be selected for their propagation. Two such groups can be mentioned as an illustration of this problem.

1. If the species to be propagated exhibits distinct erect and lateral growths, such as in species of *Araucaria*, cuttings should only be taken from erect shoots. Such cuttings strike more rapidly and develop into normal erect trees. Cuttings from the side shoots are more difficult to strike, and develop into floppy atypical plants, which lack the ability for normal erect growth.

2. With large leaved species, such as *Hibiscus tiliaceus*, *Macaranga* spp., and some *Abutilon* spp., it is best to avoid vigorous shoots with large leaves, and select weaker side shoots which have smaller leaves. Shoots with large leaves are not only difficult to handle, but also dry out more readily.

Processing of Cuttings

Basic Procedure for Processing of Cuttings

1. Collect plant material, and maintain under optimum conditions until ready for processing.

2. Cut plant material into cuttings. Wound (see p.228) the base of the cutting if necessary.

3. Remove the leaves on the lower half to two thirds of the cutting, without damaging the bark.

4. Dip the base of the cutting in hormone solution or powder.

5. Insert the basal half to two thirds of the cutting into the propagating medium.

6. Water thoroughly, and place the cuttings in a propagating structure.

Tools

A number of different tools may be used for the preparation of cuttings, incuding knives, scissors, razor blades and secateurs. Regardless of preference, tools must be kept in a sharp condition so the blade can make a smooth cut. If the cuttings are torn, bruised or otherwise damaged by blunt tools, the damaged tissue can provide a point of entry for disease organisms. Cleanliness of tools is also of utmost importance. Regular washing with a germicide or disinfectant will reduce the possibility of disease organisms being introduced onto the cuttings.

For ease of working and efficiency, secateurs are recommended. There is less likelihood of damage to hands, as can happen with razor blades and knives. Usually cheap secateurs have not been designed for precise work, such as the preparation of cuttings. A good quality pair is therefore a wise investment, reducing cutting losses due to tissue damage, and saving time.

Care of Cutting Material

In order to keep the plant material in good condition, after collection, the following points are recommended.

(i) At all times during processing, material must not be allowed to dry out, but at the same time it should not be too wet.

(ii) For the processing of cuttings, choose a situation which is not in direct sunlight or wind.

(iii) It is preferable if the room temperature does not exceed 25°C.

(iv) Once processed, insert cuttings in the propagation medium as soon as possible, and place the pots etc., in the propagating structure.

(v) To obtain good results with some species, it is necessary that they be processed as soon as they have been gathered. If left for a time in a moist atmosphere, such as a plastic bag or wet newspaper, the outer layer of bark is very prone to damage by ripping when lower leaves are being removed. Plants affected in this way include species of *Darwinia*, *Hibbertia* and *Pimelea*.

Lateral or Terminal Cuttings

It has been found that cuttings from lateral growth will produce roots sooner than cuttings from terminal growth, in some non-Australian plants. Whether this is so with Australian plants is not known, because of the lack of research on the subject, but it is certainly most likely.

Often it is necessary to take whatever cutting material is available, however if selection is possible, better results are usually achieved by using tip cuttings rather than those from farther down on the old wood. In some cases however, 2, 3, or 4 consecutive cuttings can be obtained from the one piece of stem if in good condition. This technique of cutting preparation is common in ground covers such as *Dampiera diversifolia*, *Grevillea thelemanniana* and *Myoporum parvifolium*, but can also be used for shrubs which produce long shoots, e.g. *Acacia varia*, *Grevillea lavandulacea*, *G. rosmarinifolia*.

Where to Cut

As a general rule, the basal cut should be made just below a node. Exceptions to this rule are discussed later in this section. Some propagators recommend cutting at right angles to the stem, others at an angle which will allow a larger area for the penetration of root producing hormones if they are used. The upper cut is usually as near as possible to a node, and at an angle so that water will run off rather than sit on the top. If both cuts are close to nodes, this will restrict dying back of any excess wood, and therefore diminish the possibility of disease organisms entering and spreading throughout the cutting.

In some species however, dieback always occurs at the top of the cutting, and if the cut is made too close to the node, then dieback can proceed down through the top bud. This eliminates any possibility of growth from the top bud, and new shoots must be produced from lower buds or dormant stem buds. These shoots always develop at a lower angle than the top shoot, and are usually less vigorous. Examples where such dieback may be a problem, are species of *Ardisia*, *Cayratia*, *Cissus*, *Clematis* and *Pandorea*, also *Grevillea* spp. such as *G. hookerana*. To obviate this problem, the upper cut should in these cases be made through the internode, to allow for an area of dieback before the upper bud is reached. This dieback can be of particular importance in cuttings consisting of two nodes, such as are common in *Cissus* and *Clematis* spp.

It is not always necessary to make the basal cut immediately below a node, as in some species roots can be produced along the length

Propagation

3 Cutting of *Acacia lasiocarpa*, showing heel.

6 Selected branch of *Grevillea hookerana*, with suitable growth for cuttings.

1 Selected branch of *Acacia lasiocarpa* with suitable growth for cuttings.

4 Removal of soft tip growth from cutting.

7 Trimming cutting below a node.

2 Pulling off lateral growth with heel at base.

5 Cutting after removal of lower foliage. The cutting is ready for placement in propagating medium.

8 Untrimmed cutting.

9 Removal of flower-head from
Grevillea hookerana cutting.

10 Damage to bark occurs if
sideshoots are pulled downwards.

11 Removing side shoot from
cutting.

12 Removal of lower side growth
from cutting of *Grevillea
hookerana*.

13 Removal of soft tips and flower
bud from cutting.

14 Shortening of long foliage of cutting.

15 Cutting of *Grevillea hookerana*,
showing trimmed foliage.

16 Cutting ready for placement in
propagation media.

17 Dipping cutting in hormone
powder.

18 Cutting ready for placement in
propagating structure.

Propagation

of the internode. This is common in sappy species of genera such as *Hoya, Pothos, Piper, Scindapsus* and *Raphidophora*, but also occurs in woody genera such as *Hibbertia, Kennedia, Rhododendron* and *Stephania*. For these plants, the position of the basal cut is unimportant, and equally good results can be obtained by cutting through an internode.

Length of cuttings

The length of cuttings is usually dictated by the type of material available. Generally cuttings from 7.5 cm to 15 cm are used. Propagation with longer cuttings has been successful, and there is some evidence that longer cuttings produce roots faster than small ones. Longer cuttings have in some cases proved more successful for harder wood, and small cuttings for soft wood. Very long cuttings are sometimes used for tropical species (see Branch and Trunk Cuttings, page 219).

Cuttings with or without heels

A heel is a portion of older wood, left at the base of a side shoot when that side shoot is torn off by a downward motion.

There is much romantic lore about the benefits of heeled cuttings, however with most species of Australian plants it has been found that heels are of no benefit in the production of roots. The basal region of a shoot is the site of hormone activity and accumulation, and it is best to take the cutting with the basal cut at the origin of the new growth. The advantage of heeled cuttings is to ensure that this important basal part is included in the cutting. Equally good results can be obtained by making the basal cut through the buds of the basal region where the side shoot joins the branch. In some species such as *Grevillea hookerana*, cuttings with heels often produce a very large callus that continues to enlarge without forming roots. This is known as overcallusing (see page 234).

Removal of lower foliage

Research has shown that if cuttings can be kept in good condition, with the maximum amount of foliage retained, roots will be produced in a shorter time. With most species it is recommended that foliage on the lower half to two thirds of the cutting be removed. This should be removed carefully, without damaging the outer stem tissue and bark. A simple technique, successful for many species, is to simply pull the foliage downwards with one smooth motion. For some cuttings however, this technique can be detrimental, as stripping of the bark may readily occur. The alternative

1 Removing leaf of *Boea hygroscopica* for propagation.

2 Placing leaf in propagating medium.

3 Leaf cutting ready for placement in propagating structure.

226

1   Propagation of *Ficus* by single bud cutting — cutting stem below node.

4   Single-bud cutting potted up in propagating medium.

2   Propagation of *Ficus* by single bud cutting — cutting stem above node.

5   Leaf of single-bud cutting supported by small stake and rubber band.

3   Dipping base of single-bud cutting into rooting hormone powder.

6   Single-bud cutting of *Ficus*, showing root system and developing shoot.

227

Propagation

technique is to remove the foliage by pulling up-wards. Experimentation with one or two cuttings in each batch will provide the answer as to which method is appropriate. If leaves cannot be pulled in either direction without damage to the bark, or if there are large side shoots that cannot be pulled manually, it will be necessary to cut the leaves and/or shoots, as close to the stem as possible. The cuts should be neat and clean to allow quick healing.

Cuttings with large leaves

Some species, e.g. *Grevillea barklyana, G. bipin-natifida, G. hookerana, Hibiscus tiliaceus,* and *Stenocarpus sinuatus,* have long leaves, which can cause problems in two ways if they are left intact on cuttings:

(i) The cutting is put under stress in trying to supply sufficient moisture to keep the leaves alive, and dehydration can occur rapidly.

(ii) The large leaves may prevent moisture from penetrating the propagation mixture, and if this is not corrected, the very small buds in the leaf axils may die. If this happens, although the leaves may still be alive, and even if the cutting roots, there may be no growth buds left to shoot.

The easiest way to overcome the above difficulties is to reduce the leaf area, by cutting off the top third or half of each of the remaining leaves. The cuts must be clean and not ragged, and the leaves not bruised, again to reduce the chance of entry of disease organisms. Some propagators believe that the production of roots is slower if the leaves are cut, and that this should only be done in extreme circumstances.

Wounding

It is often beneficial with difficult-to-root species, to wound the base of the cutting. This technique provides a larger area for callusing and the formation of roots.

The simplest method of wounding is to pull the lowest leaf or lateral shoot downwards, to leave a tear. Another method is to cut the outer

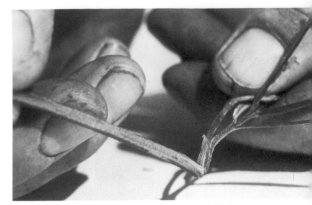

Wounding base by pulling off sideshoot. This increases the area available for root formation.

surface at the base of the cutting, with sharp secateurs or a knife. (See also Ringing or Gir-dling, page 220.)

Rooting Hormones

The use of hormone rooting powders and liquids aids the formation of roots in cuttings. The hormones usually promote quicker rooting of cuttings, and can also stimulate roots in larger quantity, with a better and more uniform quality.

The root promoting materials, or hormones, are readily available in commercial preparations of powders, the hormones being dispersed in talc. The chemical most commonly used is IBA (Indole butyric acid), which is not a naturally occurring material, but is synthetically manufac-tured. Its chemical structure is very similar to auxin (Indole acetic acid) which is a naturally occurring hormone found in all plants. IBA lacks many of the properties of auxin but has a definite promoting effect on the formation and growth of roots. Another synthetic auxin relative, NAA (Naphthalene acetic acid) has proved to have some promoting effects on root formation with certain species, when used either separately or mixed with IBA. At this stage NAA is used on a very small scale, mainly experimentally, and IBA

Materials needed to make up commonly used concentrations of IBA rooting powders:

Final concentration	Weight of IBA	Volume of alcohol	Weight of talc	Application
1,000 ppm	100 mg	40 ml	100 g	Softwood
2,500 ppm	250 mg	40 ml	100 g	Softwood
3,000 ppm	300 mg	40 ml	100 g	Semi-hardwood
5,000 ppm	500 mg	40 ml	100 g	Semi-hardwood
7,500 ppm	750 mg	40 ml	100 g	Hardwood
8,000 ppm	800 mg	40 ml	100 g	Hardwood
10,000 ppm	1g	40 ml	100 g	Hardwood

is widely used. IBA is a crystalline substance, but for cuttings it is used as either powder preparations or in solutions.

Powders

Commercial preparations of powders are available in 3 strengths, for softwood, semi-hardwood, and hardwood cuttings. For most species semi-hardwood powder is suitable.

Preparation: All preparation should be carried out in a dimly lit room, as IBA will break down on exposure to light. The required quantity of IBA is weighed out and dissolved in a small volume of alcohol (ethyl alcohol, methyl alcohol or methylated spirit). The solution is then stirred into good quality fine talc to form a smooth paste. The paste is stirred and dried until it becomes a fine dry powder. The accompanying table gives the quantities of the various materials needed to make up commonly used concentrations. Larger batches can be mixed if required, using the same ratio of materials.

3 Placing single node cutting in propagating medium.

1 Preparation of single node cutting of *Hoya australis* — cutting stem below node.

4 Single node cutting ready for placement in propagating structure.

2 Trimming leaves of single node cutting.

5 Plants of *Hoya australis*, 12 months after being propagated from single node cuttings.

Propagation

Use: Dip the lower 1-2 cm of the prepared, moist cutting, in the powder. Withdraw, and tap to get rid of excess, then place the cutting in the propagation material, taking care to not remove too much powder.

Storage: Powders should be stored in an airtight, dark or opaque container, in the refrigerator. Properly prepared and stored they will remain active for 6-12 months.

Comments on the use of hormone powders:

(i) Make sure excess is removed from the base of cutting. A large mass of moist talc can restrict the availability of air to the base of the cutting.

(ii) It has been found in some species that excess application can promote excess growth of the callus, without the formation of roots (overcallusing), e.g. *Grevillea hookerana* and other large-leaved *Grevillea* species.

(iii) Uniform applications of powder can be difficult to achieve because of the different amounts of moisture on the base of the cuttings. This can be overcome by dipping the bases of cuttings in water first, and shaking off excess. Also cuttings with a hairy or silky texture will retain more powder than those with a smooth surface.

(iv) It is recommended that powder be placed in a small container holding enough for one batch of cuttings, rather than use it direct from the storage container. This will help prevent the deterioration of the compound from moisture, and contamination by fungi or bacteria that can be transferred from the cuttings.

(v) An improved penetration of the hormone can be achieved by a quick dip of the bases of the cuttings into 50% alcohol before dipping in the powder.

Liquid Mixtures

These mixtures are mainly used by commercial nurseryman, but can also be used by enthusiasts. IBA is the hormone most commonly used, but NAA and IAA can be handled in the same way. Recent research has shown that combinations of hormones in the liquid state may produce better results than either hormone used by itself. One very successful combination is IBA 1,000 ppm and NAA 1,000 ppm in 50% alcohol.

Preparation: The required quantity of IBA is weighed out, and added to either ethyl alcohol, methyl acohol, or methylated spirit. When the IBA crystals have all dissolved in the alcohol, an equal quantity of water is added to give the final concentration. The accompanying table gives the quantities of the various materials needed to make up commonly used concentrations.

Use: Concentrated solutions are commonly applied as a quick dip. The cutting base (1-2 cm) is dipped into the solution for 5 seconds, and the cuttings can either be planted immediately, or after the base has dried. Some cuttings can be damaged by the alcohol, and it has been found beneficial to allow the bases of these to dry out after dipping, and before insertion in the cutting medium.

It has been found that concentrations above 2,500 ppm may cause damage to the outer bark of some cuttings, and this effect is worse, the deeper the cutting is dipped into the solution. In this case it is recommended that a slanting cut be made at the base of the cutting to increase the surface area, and only the very basal part of the cutting be dipped into the solution.

Dilute solutions of low concentrations (5-100 ppm) are sometimes used, and the bases of the cuttings are left to soak in them for 10-15 hours. These solutions are made up in water, after

Materials needed to make up commonly used concentrations of IBA solution:

Final concentration	Weight of IBA	Volume of alcohol	Volume of water	Final volume	Application
50 ppm	50 mg	500 ml	500 ml	1 litre	Softwood
100 ppm	100 mg	500 ml	500 ml	1 litre	Softwood
500 ppm	500 mg	500 ml	500 ml	1 litre	Softwood
1,000 ppm	1 g	500 ml	500 ml	1 litre	Softwood
2,000 ppm	2 g	500 ml	500 ml	1 litre	Semi-hardwood
2,500 ppm	2.5 g	500 ml	500 ml	1 litre	Semi-hardwood
3,000 ppm	3 g	500 ml	500 ml	1 litre	Semi-hardwood
4,000 ppm	2 g	250 ml	250 ml	500 ml	Hardwood
5,000 ppm	2.5 g	250 ml	250 ml	500 ml	Hardwood

dissolving the IBA in a very small quantity of alcohol.

Storage: Liquid mixtures of IBA should be placed in dark brown or opaque glass bottles, and stored in a refrigerator. They should only be removed from the refrigerator immediately prior to use, and should be returned immediately after use. Used in this manner the solutions will retain their activity indefinitely.

Solutions are rendered inactive by bright sunlight, high temperatures, or being left in warm lighted situations for periods of more than 10 hours. Solutions subjected to these conditions take on a brownish tinge, and are best discarded.

Comments on the use of liquid mixtures:

(i) Cuttings can be treated in bundles, thus saving much time in the process.

(ii) Application is more uniform than with powders, therefore more uniform results can be expected.

(iii) The same solution can be re-used for the treatment of many cuttings, provided it is stored correctly.

(iv) Evaporation of the alcohol will result in increase of the concentration, hence the solution should be kept in an airtight container at all times when not in use.

(v) Dosage at too high a concentration, or dipping for too long, can inhibit growth, cause yellowing of foliage or blackening of stems, and usually results in the death of the cutting.

Lanolin Pastes

Rooting hormones can also be applied in lanolin paste, but this method of application is now rarely used, except for air layering. (See page 258.) In general, higher concentrations of rooting hormone are needed for air layering than are used for cuttings (8,000-10,000 ppm is common). The lanolin is heated until it is molten, and the weighed amount of rooting hormone is stirred in. The paste is then allowed to cool.

Quantities needed to make various concentrations are given in the accompanying table.

Concentration	Weight of lanolin	Weight of IBA	Final quantity
5,000 ppm	200 g	1 g	200 g
7,500 ppm	200 g	1.5 g	200 g
10,000 ppm	200 g	2 g	200 g
12,500 ppm	200 g	2.5 g	200 g
15,000 ppm	200 g	3 g	200 g

Storage: Lanolin pastes will keep indefinitely if stored in a sealed, brown glass bottle, and kept in a refrigerator.

CONDITIONS REQUIRED FOR THE ROOTING OF CUTTINGS

Cuttings need external conditions free of stresses if they are to survive and form roots. An easy interpretation to remember is to provide conditions that will keep the cuttings in more or less the same condition as they would be on growing plants. These conditions involve water (for cooling, evaporation and transpiration and humidity) temperature, light and air.

Water

The air surrounding the cuttings should be as humid as possible, to reduce the stress that occurs with transpiration from leaves, and evaporation from the surface of the propagating medium. The presence of leaves on cuttings helps in the initial root formation. With excessive leaves however, there can be the reverse effect, with transpiration reducing the water content of the cutting to a stage where the cutting will die before any roots are formed.

As well as humidity, it is also important to keep the propagating medium moist, but not over-wet, so that moisture can be absorbed through the stem. The moisture content of the propagating medium and the humidity, can be maintained manually by spraying the cuttings, the floor, and walls of the propagating structure regularly, with water, or by having an automatic misting system. There are many such systems from which to choose.

The use of mist irrigation maintains a film of moisture on the leaves, which creates a humid atmosphere and also reduces the temperature of the cuttings. This helps lower the transpiration rate, and benefits the rooting process (see Temperature).

If transpiration can be reduced, the degree of light can be increased, to increase the photosynthetic process, thus promoting better conditions for the rooting of the cuttings. With high humidity and the foliage so often covered in water, there can be the danger of infestation by fungi. This is most likely to happen in poorly ventilated propagating areas. (See discussion regarding the importance of Air page 232.)

Temperature

The optimum temperature for the propagation of most species is a daytime temperature of 20°C-27°C, with a night temperature of about 15°C. It is however difficult in practice to maintain these temperatures, because of varying weather conditions. Good results are obtained if the base of the cutting can be maintained 5°C-10°C warmer than the top, with an upper limit of about 20°C. The reason is that root development will take precedence over the leaf buds. If bud growth starts before roots, it can be detrimental to root development. Thus use is made of bottom heat propagating units (see **Propagating Structures**, page 187), especially during the winter months in southern Australia.

Most species will root without any artificial heating or cooling. Careful control of ventilation, and adequate shading of propagating structures are required for successful results. Ventilation should be used when conditions become still and humid, and the plants can benefit from the air movement and fresh air.

Shading is particularly important, because it is very easy to dehydrate or burn cuttings by exposure to sun through clear glass or plastic. This can be particularly troublesome on cloudy days, as temperatures can rise rapidly under clear glass if sunny periods occur.

Light

Leafy cuttings must have light to carry out photosynthesis as a normal part of their metabolism. As a general rule, the greater the amount of light, the quicker there will be root formation. High light intensity can however lead to undesirable effects, such as a rise in temperature which may dry out the cuttings because of increased evaporation and transpiration. High light intensity also leads to greater nitrogen use, and leaves may become pale and bleached.

A balance must be achieved, whereby the cuttings receive an optimum amount of light for photosynthesis, but of an intensity which will not cause damage.

The length of exposure to light each day is known as the photoperiod. This is generally shorter in winter than in summer, and this may be a critical factor in the rooting of cuttings during winter in southern Australia, when days are short and cloudy and dull weather is frequent. Under these conditions the use of fluorescent lamps over cuttings, to increase both light intensity and photoperiod, has been found to be beneficial for rooting.

Air

Oxygen is essential for the formation of callus and root at or near the base of a cutting. Unless air can readily penetrate the propagating medium, it is most likely that root formation will be retarded. Aeration can be impeded in two ways.

(i) The use of a propagating medium that contains a large percentage of very small granules that compact readily.

(ii) Waterlogging. The medium should be kept moist, not over-wet, as waterlogging will lead to the death of the cutting stem tissue. Excessive amounts of water-retaining materials such as peat moss can be a major cause of waterlogging (see Propagating Media, page 190).

Oxygen is also essential for respiration to occur in the leafy part of the cutting, and for numerous oxidation reactions inside the plant.

The movement of air is most important for the prevention or reduction of fungal and mould growth. Humidity and lack of air movement when combined, provide ideal conditions for fungal organisms to multiply quickly. Adequate ventilation of propagating structures is therefore most important.

Hardening Off

Cuttings are usually propagated in humid, warm conditions, resulting in soft, tender growth. If suddenly exposed to conditions such as dryness, bright sunshine, wind, heat or cold, damage to the new growth can occur. The soft plants must first be gradually hardened off before they are placed outside.

There are several alternatives for the 'hardening off' of rooted cuttings —

If propagated with a mist system:

1. Leave them in the propagating structure for a few days, and turn off the mist, or gradually decrease the misting periods. Water only to keep moist. Remove them to a sheltered location outside for a further 'hardening off' before potting into the growing medium.

If propagated without bottom heat or mist:

2. Remove rooted cuttings into a sheltered location, such as a cold frame or shade house, to provide protection.

3. Pot on rooted cuttings immediately, but leave them in the propagating structure, or some other humid atmosphere, for a few days, until suitable for removal to a more open location.

4. If propagation is done with individual cuttings in small containers (e.g. 50 mm tubes), rooted cuttings can be moved directly to the 'hardening off' area, provided it is not an extremely hot or windy day. They should be watered immediately, and if desired, can be potted on.

5. Glass screens out ultra violet from the sun's rays. Plants that have produced new growth in glasshouses should never be put straight outside into bright sunshine, as the foliage will burn from the ultra violet rays. They should be first placed in a shade house or some sheltered location, where they can harden off before being placed into sun.

If using a bottom heat unit:

6. The heat should be turned off for a few days before potting if the cuttings are inserted direct into the medium. If the cuttings are placed in pots, then the heat can be left on, but after rooting the pot of rooted cuttings is lifted and placed onto the surface of the unit to harden for a few days before potting.

Potting On

After hardening off, the struck cuttings are ready for potting. A recommended procedure is to drench plants, 7-10 days prior to potting, with a fungal drench such as Coban or Terrazole, and root stimulant. The root stimulant will promote better development of the root system, while the fungicide will control any soil borne diseases which may be present.

Cuttings rooted in a community pot should be potted as soon as possible. If left too long, roots can become entangled, which leads to damage during the potting process.

Rooted cuttings should be thoroughly watered before potting. This ensures that the roots and leaves are in good condition whilst potting, and if roots are broken, the plant is better able to cope than if dry. The root system of cuttings

2   Separation of cuttings. Care must be taken not to damage root systems.

3   Place rooted cutting into growing medium. The hole must be wide enough to accommodate the root system, without bending or restricting.

4   Firming soil around the roots or rooted cutting, keeping the soil level around the stem, as in the propagating mix.

1   Community pot of rooted cuttings, ready for potting — *Brachycome multifida*.

propagated in a community pot must not be allowed to dry out during the potting process.

If the roots are too long to fit vertically in the new containers, they should be pruned, making sure that other parts of the plant are not damaged. It is imperative that roots of trees and shrubs be placed straight, to allow for proper root development. Bends or twists weaken the root system, and may cause the plant to blow over after being planted out.

After potting, plants should be thoroughly watered until soaked. This can be followed with a fungal drench and root stimulant if desired. The pots should be placed in a sheltered area until the plants have recovered from the disturbance of roots, and new root growth is underway. Growing areas can be temporarily covered with shade cloth or similar material, to provide some protection until the plants are growing. A period of 4-7 days is most desirable.

Cuttings rooted individually in small containers, can be potted soon after rooting, with no disturbance or damage to the roots. If however roots have been left to develop for a considerable period prior to potting, coiling may have occurred. The long roots should be uncoiled and pruned, without damaging the remaining roots, and plants then potted. Thoroughly soak the plant and medium as mentioned earlier, and place the plant in the growing area. There is usually no need to provide shade or protection for plants from individual containers if they have been well hardened off, as there will have been negligible root disturbance. In very hot weather, shelter for a few days would be beneficial.

Soil Mixes
For recommended mixes, see Cultivation of Container Grown Plants, Potting Mixes, page 102.

PROBLEMS IN ROOTING CUTTINGS

Fungus Damage
Cuttings can be subject to fungal attacks, and unless these are controlled, damage or death will result. Initial sterilisation of the propagating medium will greatly reduce the likelihood of attacks by soil borne fungi such as *Pythium* and *Phytophthora*. (See Soil Sterilisation Techniques, page 193.)

Botrytis cinerea (Grey Mould) is one of the most common fungal diseases to attack plant tissue in propagating structures. It is spread by air-borne spores, and multiplies rapidly. Control can be effected by the use of a fungicide such as captan or benomyl. Cuttings can be dipped into a solution of the fungicide before being placed into propagation containers. Alternatively captan can be added to the rooting powder to save time in application. It has been found that in some cases rooting is promoted with such a combination.

Fungal attacks can break out in the propagating structure, and constant observation is required so that outbreaks can be controlled. It is a wise practice to remove all dead cuttings and leaves from the propagation area, as these are ideal hosts for fungal organisms.

Overcallusing
Cuttings of some species and cultivars suffer from a problem known as overcallusing. The callus which forms at the base of the cutting continues expansion and becomes quite large and unwieldy. Roots are often not formed, but it is unclear whether the large callus is inhibiting root formation, or whether there is some other cause.

Overcallusing can result from the excess application of rooting hormones, however this does not occur consistently. It is also more likely to occur on non-vigorous cutting material. Cuttings suffering from overcallusing may survive for up to 2 years before their reserves run out and they die. Nurserymen usually discard such cuttings, however some rooting can be obtained by removing the majority of the callus, dipping the cutting in hormone powder, and replacing it in the propagating medium.

Cuttings of many species of the family Proteaceae suffer from overcallusing, including *Buckinghamia celsissima*, *Grevillea hookerana*, *G.* 'Ivanhoe', *G. longifolia*, *Hakea laurina*, and *Stenocarpus sinuatus*.

Difficult-to-root Cuttings
Cuttings of some species have proved difficult to root e.g. *Persoonia pinifolia*, *Ricinocarpos* spp. and many *Eucalyptus* spp. The general tendency is for such cuttings to languish in an apparently dormant condition until they run out of food supplies and die. Frequently callus is produced at the base of the cutting and this may develop into large formations (see Overcallusing). Some cuttings may survive for as long as 2 years before dying.

Research has found that the difficulty of forming roots may be related to a sheath of woody cells and fibres on the outside of the phloem. Where this sheath is thick and continuous, rooting is difficult, whereas where it is incomplete or absent, rooting occurs readily. In general, the sheath is thicker on older plants and thinner on younger plants, but it also varies with the species.

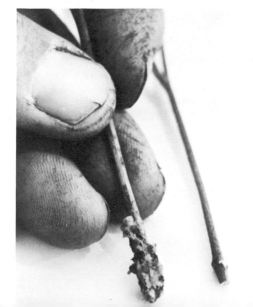

1 Massive development of callus (overcallusing) of *Grevillea* 'Ivanhoe'. RHS — Prepared cutting.

2 Trimming of excess callus of unrooted cutting.

3 Unrooted cutting of *Grevillea* 'Ivanhoe' after excess callus trimmed off — ready for repotting in propagating medium.

The selection of cutting material is of critical importance in increasing the percentage take, in shy rooting or difficult-to-root species. Shoots from young plants, from juvenile seedlings (see Juvenile and Adult Growth Phases), from adventitious growths emanating from the trunk or large branches, or from root suckers provide the type of material needed for better rooting. This type of material generally contains a thinner woody sheath than do the older shoots.

Slow Formation of Roots

Cuttings of some species which usually root readily, may be slow to produce roots, taking up to 1-2 years, e.g. species of *Acrotriche*, *Alyxia*, *Astroloma*, *Epacris*, *Eriostemon*, *Geleznowia*, some *Grevillea*, *Synaphaea*, and *Woollsia*.

There are various reasons for this —

1. One of the most common factors is the initial use of poor cutting material, due either to unavailability of good material, or wrong selection. An example is *Epacris longiflora* — by using old woody growth, cuttings will sit for a long time, however by using firm new tip growth, roots can be formed in 4-8 weeks.

2. The propagation technique being used may be wrong. Some species respond well to constant bottom heat, e.g. species of *Eriostemon*, such as *E. australasius*, *E. buxifolius*, *E. hispidula* and *E. myoporoides*. Other genera include *Acradenia*, *Boronia*, *Helicia*, *Persoonia* and *Stenocarpus*.

3. The ferny-leaved and large-leaved *Grevillea* spp. often form large calluses at the expense of roots. The callus can be removed and the cutting re-potted. (See Overcallusing.)

Poor Formation of Roots

Some species may produce only one root from the callus, e.g. some *Grevillea* spp. This is common when overcallusing occurs. By having only one root, development may be retarded after potting on.

A stronger root system may be produced by the application of rooting hormones.

Poor root development can also occur when the propagation medium is too fine, and becomes waterlogged, thus not allowing for proper aeration.

Root nematodes will also restrict proper root production.

Root Nematodes

Unless sterilized soil is used for propagation of cuttings, various organisms can be prevalent and may reduce the efficiency of propagation. Nematodes, which are minute worm-like animals, can restrict both the initial formation of roots from the callus, and the ensuing root

A selection of rooted cuttings in pots and below comparing root systems.

L *to* R *Grevillea x gaudichaudii, Dampiera diversifolia, Hibbertia scandens, Epacris longiflora.*

Rooted cuttings — comparison of root systems. Left — *Grevillea × gaudichaudii* Right — *Dampiera diversifolia.*

Rooted cuttings — comparison of roots systems. Left — *Hibbertia scandens.* Right — *Epacris longiflora.*

growth. A notable example is the genus. *Eremaea.* See Nematodes, Pest and Disease section, page 161.

There are specific nematocides available, but they need to be used with great care, as side effects such as death of plant tissue can result.

Identification of Roots

To the experienced eye it is not difficult to identify roots, but to the new enthusiast there can be some pitfalls. Often the propagation medium can contain root-like material that has been incorporated in components such as riversand or peat moss, or in soil if it has been used. On some occasions this will be fine dead roots.

One of the difficult groups for the inexperienced propagator to identify, is the Epacridaceae family. Species of *Astroloma* and *Epacris* etc., produce extremely fine roots. Initially they are translucent, and later they become the same colour as the propagating medium. Members of the closely related Ericaceae family produce similar roots, e.g. *Agapetes, Gaultheria* and *Rhododendron.*

The majority of Australian plants grown from cuttings have roots which are fleshy and white, and therefore are easy to identify, e.g. species of *Acacia, Boronia, Correa, Grevillea, Leptospermum* and *Melaleuca.*

Brittle Roots

Some plants produce brittle roots that can be easily damaged during the potting up process, e.g. species of *Boronia, Correa* and *Epacris.* Damage is most likely to occur if cuttings are placed in a community container. If this method is used, it is best to remove propagation medium before the roots have become too entangled. Damage is least likely to occur if single cuttings are initially placed in small containers for propagation. When rooted, they can be removed and potted, without any problem.

Rooted cutting of *Dampiera cauloptera*, showing
emergence of a sucker.

Rooted cutting with soil washed away, showing root
system and sucker.

20 Grafting and Budding

GRAFTING

Grafting is a technique of propagation commonly used for the production of commercial fruit varieties, many deciduous ornamentals and some evergreens such as selected forms of camellias, rhododendrons and conifers. It is not widely used in the production of Australian plants at present but will probably be more commonly used in the future. It is interesting to note that the first recorded graft involving an Australian plant was as early as 1846 in France when *Lechenaultia formosa* was grafted onto *L. biloba* to produce a mixture of blue and red flowers.

Grafting is carried out for 2 major reasons.

1. To put roots or a root system onto the difficult to propagate species or selected forms and cultivars.

2. To supply a rootstock which has some beneficial effects on the grafted variety. Examples of such beneficial effects are:

(a) a change in the growth habit such as dwarfness or compactness

(b) resistance to specific soil conditions such as salt, lime and waterlogging

(c) resistance to root diseases such as cinnamon fungus. Canberra Botanic Gardens has successfully used *Westringia fruticosa* as a rootstock resistant to cinnamon fungus, for the establishment of selected species and cultivars of *Prostanthera* and *Westringia*.

Terms

Grafting is a specialised subject and involves the use of many specialised terms, the more significant of which are:

Callus: crystalline tissue which is produced by exposed cambium such as in wounds.

Cambium: a layer of active cells between the wood and the bark.

Compatible: a term used when plants grafted together produce a strong permanent union (cf. incompatible).

Left — Budding Knife.
Right — Grafting Knife.

Double-worked: twice grafted, as when an interstock is used.

Incompatible: a term used when plants which have been grafted together, fail to form a strong, permanent union.

Interstock: a scion interposed between the stock and the desired scion to overcome incompatibility problems.

Rootstock: root bearing part onto which the scion is grafted.

Scion: part of the plant which is desired to be propagated and which is grafted onto the rootstock.

Scion Rooting: development of roots from the scion. The grafted plant then has roots from both the stock and the scion.

Stock: the basal part onto which the scion is grafted. It may not necessarily have roots e.g., cutting graft (see also root-stock).

Union: where the scion meets the stock.

Worked: a term often used meaning the same as grafted.

Propagation

Cambial Contact

Contact between the cambium layers of the stock and scion is essential if a satisfactory graft union is to be formed. Only a small area of contact is necessary for a graft to establish, however, a large area of contact means that a satisfactory union establishes more quickly.

The cambium is a thin layer of active cells found between the bark and the wood. In young shoots the bark is thin and the cambium lies near the outside of the stem. As the stem ages the bark thickens and in old stems the cambium may be 0.5-1 cm in from the outside.

When grafting, it is the cambium layer of the stock and scion which must be matched, not the bark. This is no problem where wood of the same species and age is being grafted but the two must be matched carefully when handling different species or wood of different ages.

Compatibility

The formation of a permanent graft union depends on the compatibility of the 2 species involved. Compatibility is a complex phenomenon and is affected by genetic factors.

As a general rule only closely related species can be successfully grafted. This rule is a good guide but does not always hold true as it is known that within some species, strains may be incompatible with other strains. Often species with similar vegetative characters can be successfully grafted even though they may be dissimilar botanically e.g., *Clianthus formosus* onto *Colutea arborescens*, *Crowea saligna* onto *Correa alba*. Incompatibility occurs when grafts fail to establish because of insurmountable genetic differences between the stock and the scion. It usually shows up as failure to form a union followed by death of the scion or a clean break at the graft union some years later. Degrees of incompatibility can occur resulting in weak or stunted trees. Trees may also grow, apparently well, for many years but incompatibility may be delayed and show up late, even after periods of 10 years or more.

Grafting with an Interstock

In some cases incompatibility between stock and scion can be overcome by using a piece of a species as an intermediate stock. This species is compatible with both the stock and the final scion variety and overcomes the barrier between the two. The procedure is more difficult to carry out than a single graft but is necessary to obtain the beneficial effect from a rootstock which is incompatible with a scion.

The system is fairly commonly used with deciduous species but is, as yet, little known in natives. As an example of the use of an interstock most *Prostanthera* species and cultivars can be grafted directly onto *Westringia fruticosa* which is resistant to attacks by cinnamon fungus. The small-leafed species of *Prostanthera* such as *P. aspalathoides* and *P. chlorantha*, however, are incompatible with the *Westringia* stock. This incompatibility has been overcome at the Canberra Botanic Gardens by using a piece of *Prostanthera nivea* as an interstock. This species is compatible with both the *Westringia* and the small-leafed *Prostanthera* and overcomes the incompatibility barrier. The double grafting system is slow but can be improved by first preparing the *Westringia fruticosa*/*Prostanthera nivea* section as a cutting graft. After this has rooted the small-leafed *Prostanthera* can be top-grafted onto the growing *P. nivea*.

General Rules for Grafting

All cuts should be clean and with neat edges. They should be made with decisive strokes using a very sharp instrument such as a grafting knife, razor blade or scalpel.

The height of grafting is arbitrary although most grafts are made 10-40 cm above soil level. It is important not to graft disease sensitive species too low, as scion rooting can occur with the consequent loss of the scion if the roots come into contact with the pathogen.

Disbudding of the stock is necessary after grafting. All stock shoots should be removed as soon as noticed for if they become vigorous they can compete with the scion variety. The higher the graft the more stock that will have to be disbudded.

Time of Grafting

It is impossible to give a time of year which is optimum for grafting throughout Australia as conditions vary tremendously. As a general rule for grafting it is best to avoid climatic extremes. The winter of southern Australia is too cold and callusing of the union is slow. Even in heated glasshouses results are not good because of day/night temperature fluctuations and short day length slowing down plant responses. In very hot weather the scion desiccates readily and may die before callusing can occur.

Grafting of evergreens is best carried out just before a growth flush, and while both the stock and the scion are in a quiescent state. It pays to observe the growth habits of the species to be grafted before attempting the grafting. If the plant makes short spurts of growth which enter a dormant period before the next flush then the idcal time to graft is just before the buds swell for the new flush.

Many species have a continual growth habit which speeds up or slows down depending on weather conditions. As the growing tip elongates, the axillary buds lower down break dormancy and grow to form side shoots. For plants with this type of growth, the older wood makes the most suitable scions and is best cut and used just as the axillary buds swell.

Preparation and Care of Scionwood

Every care must be taken to keep scionwood in good condition. Evergreen wood often deteriorates rapidly and is best grafted as soon as possible after collection. When grafting under warm conditions, collect wood in batches sufficient to last a couple of hours and protect it from sun and desiccation. Discard any that is not used, and collect a fresh batch before the next grafting session.

Scions should be cut from the tree, preferably in early morning, and put straight into plastic bags out of the sun. Leaves should be removed from woody scions but should be left on young soft scions to help maintain the graft until the union is established.

The wood of some evergreen species can be held for a few months if wrapped and stored correctly. It should be collected while in a dormant state, the leaves removed and the scions dipped in a fungicide and excess shaken off. Sheets of moistened newspaper are wrapped around the scions and the whole lot sealed in a bag or sheet of polythene film. Wrapped this way scions can be stored in a cool chamber at 1°C for a week to a few months depending on the species (variegated *Tristania conferta* scions have been successfully stored for 3 weeks at 1°C).

Preparation of the Stock

For top grafts the stock should be cut off with secateurs at the height to be grafted and the edges of the cut trimmed with a knife. Shoots and leaves 4-5 cm below the cut should be removed. Lower branches can be left to act as nurse limbs but must be shortened back if they appear to be competing with the graft.

For stocks which are to be side grafted, the leaves and branches are cleared for 4-8 cm from the trunk in the region where the graft is to be inserted.

Aftercare

Aftercare of grafts is important to ensure a good take. The root system of the stock must not be allowed to dry out nor must the scion. The grafted plants are best placed in a humid glasshouse or frame, but if these are unavailable then some warm sheltered position out of the wind may be acceptable. Pests and diseases must be controlled.

Growth of the rootstock must not be allowed to compete with the scion although some growth may actually aid in its take e.g., the use of nurse limbs.

The tape should be left covering the graft until well after it takes. If removed too early the callus tissue can dehydrate and the graft may fail. The tape should be removed 2-3 months after the graft has taken and well before it causes any constriction to the growth.

Grafting Aids

Some techniques can be very useful aids to evergreen grafting, and for difficult to graft species may mean the difference between success and failure.

A plastic bag inverted over the scion helps maintain humidity around the scion. For leafless grafts the bags need only be loosely draped over the scion but for scions bearing leaves, and especially for young soft growth, the bags should be partially sealed at the bottom. The bags are left over the scion until the graft has taken. They should be removed when new growth commences otherwise the growth becomes too soft and is susceptible to disease or may sweat.

Leafy grafts can be placed under mist propagating systems and this will aid the take. Mist is especially beneficial for grafts involving very young tissue such as micro-grafts or cotyledon grafts. Grafts should not be held under mist for too long after taking, otherwise hardening off can become a major problem.

Small leafless scions can be completely covered after grafting by winding budding tape over the whole scion. This prevents the scion from drying out and preserves the axillary buds in a viable condition. The scion is observed for growth at intervals and when bud movement is noticed the tape is removed.

Treatment of plants of the scion variety, before grafting, can dramatically influence the take. Cincturing 4-6 weeks before grafting, by ringing the bark of a selected branch in a complete circle with a knife or by removing a small band of bark, can be of considerable benefit. The use of cinctured wood has become a standard technique now for the propagation of commercial cultivars of macadamia nuts.

Another technique is to remove the leaves from the selected scion shoot 1-2 weeks before grafting. This is particularly beneficial for those species which grow in flushes with a dormant

Propagation

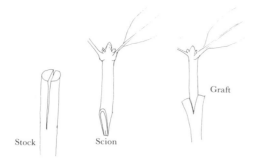

Wedge or Cleft graft.

period in between. The leaves should be removed from the scion while it is dormant and the graft made 1-2 weeks later.

Chemicals known as anti-transpirants reduce water loss from leaves by reducing evaporation and transpiration. These can aid leafy grafts if sprayed onto branches of the scion 1-2 days before they are cut for grafting. The sprays must be used at recommended strength otherwise they can have toxic side effects.

Choice of Graft

Basically there are not many different types of grafts which can be used. Each, however, has numerous modifications which have been developed to satisfy specific conditions. Grafting tends to be influenced by personal prejudices and also by factors such as climatic conditions, stage of growth and species.

The choice of the type of graft to use is relatively unimportant for easy to graft species but may be very important for difficult types. The choice depends on such factors as:
1. relative size of stock and scion
2. texture and character of wood i.e., whether hard, pithy, soft or sappy
3. stage of growth of the stock and scion
4. experience and personal preference.

TYPES OF GRAFT

Graft names are not standardized and vary between countries, states and people. Names may be misapplied and ambiguous names are often used. Drawings are included to illustrate the techniques involved.

Wedge or Cleft Graft

The most commonly used graft and one which has proved successful for grafting species of *Grevillea*, *Banksia*, *Prostanthera*, *Eriostemon* and *Correa*.

This is a very easy method of grafting and can be quickly learned by inexperienced people. It is most commonly used where there is a disparity in size between the stock and the scion but can also be used successfully where they are of equal size. It can also be used in place of a whip/tongue graft where the wood is pithy and difficulty is experienced in cutting a tongue. It is also a useful graft to use on species with soft bark which may tear easily.

Herbaceous Cleft Graft

A modified wedge graft used on soft herbaceous tissue which splits easily or is too sappy to maintain the scion after tying. A wedge of tissue is removed from the stock and the scion cut to match. Tying must be done carefully as the scion may slip out. Cutting is carried out with a sharp instrument such as a scalpel or razor blade. This type of graft has been used to successfully graft sturts desert pea (*Clianthus formosus*) onto the New Zealand species (*C. puniceus*).

Whip and Whip/Tongue Graft

One of the commonest grafts used, and very suitable when the stock and scion are of similar size and not more than 2.5 cm in diameter. A very strong union is formed and the method is very quick.

For a whip graft, a slanting cut is made on both the stock and the scion, and the cambiums of the two matched together and tied.

A whip/tongue graft is a modified whip graft with a tongue cut into the sloping cut of both the stock and the scion. The tongue aids the union, and is especially useful for holding the grafts together before and during tying.

The slanting cut for both types of graft should be about six times the thickness of the scion. The tongue for the whip/tongue graft is made about one-third of the way down the cut in both the stock and the scion.

Side Grafts

As the name implies, the scion is grafted into the side of a growing plant. The mother plant (stock) is left growing until the graft has taken and is cut off in stages until only the graft and basal part of the stock are left. This type of graft is useful where the stock is much larger in diameter than the scion and is especially useful for thin scions (as in *Agonis flexuosa* 'Variegata').

A number of variations can be used but in all cases care must be taken to match the cambiums of the stock and scion. The graft is inserted into the trunk of the stock usually 5-8 cm above soil level.

1 Trimming up rootstock of *Grevillea robusta*, prior to top grafting.

7 Cutting wedge on the base of the scion of *Grevillea johnsonii*.

4 Matching scion of *Grevillea johnsonii* with rootstock, to determine point of grafting.

2 Trimmed *Grevillea robusta*, ready for top grafting.

8 Inserting scion of *Grevillea johnsonii* into *G. robusta* stock.

3 Cutting off *Grevillea robusta* rootstock at point to be grafted.

5 Trimming leaves from *Grevillea johnsonii* scion.

9 Completed *Grevillea* graft before tying.

6 Splitting cleft in *Grevillea robusta* rootstock.

10 Tying completed graft with plastic tape.

11 A plastic bag is draped loosely over the completed graft.

The commonest methods of side grafting used are:

1. the bark of the stock is cut in a T the same as when budding. The scion is cut like a wedge with a longer sloping cut on the side nearest the stock. The base of the scion is inserted into the T and forced down between the bark and the wood thus lifting the bark. This is one of the easiest types of side graft to carry out and is very useful for species which have thick bark. It can only be done when the sap is running freely in the stock and the bark lifts easily.

2. a shallow oblique cut is made downward through the bark and part of the wood and left attached by the base to the stock. The scion is

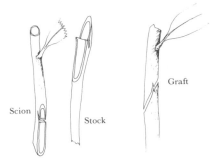

Whip-tongue graft.

prepared in a similar manner to the preceding one and inserted into the slice. This type of graft can be used on species with thin bark and does not rely on the bark lifting for success.

3. a shallow slice 3-4 cm long is removed from the stock with a short wedge cut at the base. The scion is prepared in a similar manner, inserted, and taped to the stock. The cuts necessary for this graft are similar to those for a chip bud. It is an easy graft to perform and can be used on species with thin bark and at any time of the year. This graft has been successfully used by research workers to graft selections of the desert lime (*Eremocitrus glauca*) onto citrus rootstocks.

For all types of side grafts, the scions, after insertion, must be sealed securely with budding tape. If sealing is a problem in the upper angle between the stock and scion a small ball of grafting wax can be inserted and pushed in to fill the gap.

Approach Graft

A very simple basic technique, used mainly for extremely difficult species or very valuable plants which are in short supply and where 100% success is essential e.g., variegated *Eucalyptus*.

The stock and the scion are placed in close proximity while still growing, and a slice of tissue is taken out of each in the area where they are to be joined. The cut surfaces are tied together and the plants are left united for 3-6 months. After callus has formed the stock is cut back in a few stages before the scion is finally severed.

This system is best carried out after growth flushes have finished on the scion variety, as vigorous growth after grafting can lessen callus formation and delay the formation of the union. It is sometimes beneficial to remove the leaves from the scion before severing, or hang a plastic

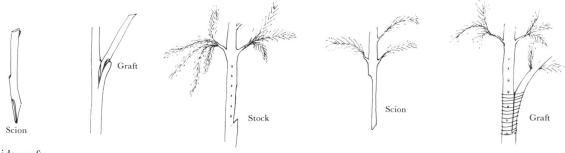

Side grafts.

bag over it afterwards, as there can be considerable shock to the plant's system after the final cut is made. There are a number of variations of the shape of the cuts which can be made but these do not greatly influence the result and are mostly a matter of personal preference. A large area of contact is not necessary to ensure a good union.

Irrigated Approach Graft

The graft is prepared in a way similar to an approach graft but the base of the scion is severed and maintained by a bottle of water taped to the stock. It is an easy graft to carry out and usually gives a good percentage take. It is useful for rare species or those whose material is in short supply.

The water level must be maintained in the bottle especially in the early stages of the. graft. An improved effect can be obtained by using a cut flower preservative in the bottle such as

8-hydroxyquinoline citrate at 200 ppm. A plastic bag initially draped loosely over the scion also helps.

This graft has been successfully employed on grevilleas, eucalypts and hakeas.

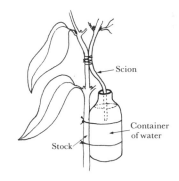

Irrigated approach graft.

Approach graft.

Plants to be approach grafted

Stems joined together and sealed

Saddle Graft

This graft is virtually a reverse of the wedge graft. It is used for those species where splitting of the rootstock is a problem resulting in damage and possible infection. It is particularly useful for root grafts.

A wedge is cut on the stock instead of the scion and the pointed tip is cut off. A corresponding split is made in the scion and the two are matched and tied.

Saddle graft.

245

1 Irrigated approach grafting of
   Grevillea johnsonii — cutting a
   slice from the rootstock *Grevillea
   robusta.*

2 Matching cuts on the stock and
   scion.

3 Placing scion against stock
   prior to tying.

4 Placing a bottle over the base
   of the scion.

5 Finished irrigated approach
   graft.

6 *Grevillea johnsonii* grafted onto
   G. robusta by irrigated approach
   — the stock has been cut off
   above the graft.

7 Irrigated approach graft on
   eucalypt. *D.V. Beardsell photo*

8 *Hakea bucculenta* top grafted onto
   H.suaveolens.

9 *Hakea francisiana* grafted onto *H.
   salicifolia* by irrigated approach
   graft.

Micrografts

In this type of graft small pieces of very young tissues are involved. Cutting is carried out using very sharp instruments such as scalpels or razor blades. Vigorous healthy seedlings are used as stocks and are prepared as for a cleft graft. All leaves in the immediate vicinity of the cleft are removed. Tips of fast growing shoots are used as scions and are usually only 1-2 cm long. Folded leaves on the scion and around the apex are left untouched and the basal part cut to a slender wedge.

The graft is matched and held together and sealed by a piece of self-adhesive medical bandage. The graft is kept under a mist system or a bell jar until a union is formed (often only about 2 weeks). After the graft has taken, the plants must be hardened off carefully as the tissues are very soft.

Micrografts require care, for the tissues used are soft and delicate. They have been used with some limited success on eucalypts.

Cotyledon Graft

As the name suggests very young tissues are used for this type of graft. Seedlings of the plants to be used as stock and scion are germinated so that they reach the grafting stage together. When the seedlings of the stock have developed 2-3 true leaves, the stem is cut across above the cotyledons and split longitudinally between them. A very young scion is cut off (usually the growing tip of a seedling) and the base is shaped into a narrow wedge and inserted into the split.

The graft is held together and sealed with self-adhesive medical tape or grafting wax and

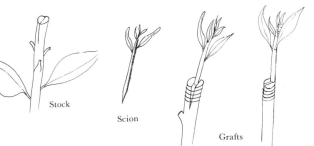

Micrograft.

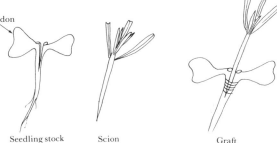

Cotyledon graft.

kept under a bell jar or mist system until a union is formed.

In England sturts desert pea (*Clianthus formosus*) is commonly grafted onto *Colutea arborescens* by this system. The graft is not commonly used in Australia, however, some success has been achieved grafting *Eucalyptus ficifolia* onto *E. calophylla* by this method.

Seed Grafts

A novel type of graft developed to propagate commercial strains of chinese chestnut and adapted for commercial varieties of macadamia nuts. The seeds are germinated and when the shoot is 8-20 cm tall it is cut off and a scion with a wedge-shaped cut at the base is forced into the fleshy cotyledons. The scion is about 6-8 cm long and leafless. For best results it is cut from wood which has been cinctured 4-6 weeks previously.

After the scion is inserted into the cotyledons the nut and basal half of the scion are buried in the potting mixture and the pots preferably placed on bottom heat. Union between the cotyledon tissues and the scion takes place over 4-8 weeks and roots are produced from the base

Hakea scoparia, top grafted onto *H. suaveolens*.

Propagation

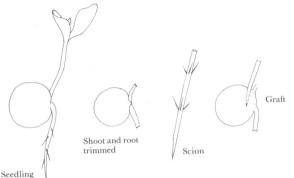

Seedling

Shoot and root trimmed

Scion

Graft

Seed graft.

of the scion. Plants usually become well established after 4-6 months and are ready for planting out after 15-18 months. As well as selected strains of *Macadamia*, the closely related bopple nut (*Floydia praealta*) can also be propagated in this way. Other plants with large fleshy seeds such as the mangosteens (*Garcinia* spp.) would also be worth trying.

Cutting Grafts

As the name suggests the graft is made onto an unrooted piece of stock and both are put in as a single cutting. The system is only successful where the stock is very easy to strike from cuttings as roots must form quickly to help form the union and support the scion. It has been successfully employed for grafting *Westringia* and *Prostanthera* species and hybrids, onto the hardy *Westringia fruticosa* which is resistant to cinnamon fungus. Whip/tongue or cleft grafts are commonly used to make the union.

The stock is prepared as a cutting and is usually 8-10 cm long. Some leaves are left on the stock to aid rooting and it is also beneficial to treat the base with rooting hormone.

The scions, about 6 cm long and bearing leaves, are grafted onto the stock (as bench grafts) and the whole unit is then put in as a cutting. These may be put in under mist but hardy species at optimum times of the year need only bottom heat or even unheated conditions to achieve callusing of the union and rooting.

Root Grafts

In this type of graft scions from the top of the plant are grafted onto pieces of roots or whole root systems. It is not commonly practised on Australian natives but can be used where potted root systems are available or thick stubby root pieces can be obtained. Whip/tongue, cleft or saddle grafts are most commonly the grafts used.

1 Cutting grafts of *Prostanthera nivea* on *Westringia fruticosa*, ready for placing in propagating medium.

2 Cutting grafts ready for placing into propagating structure.

In a modification of the root graft the whole root system of a potted seedling may be used. The seedling is cut off at, or just above ground level, the stem split and a wedge graft inserted. The wound is best sealed with grafting wax and soil mounded over the graft until a union is formed. Scions of eucalypts can be inserted into the lignotubers of seedlings in a similar manner.

Nurse Graft

As the name implies, a temporary graft is made to sustain the desired scion species or variety until it develops its own root system. This type of graft is primarily used for those species which are difficult-to-root from cuttings or very slow to form roots. The technique is used occasionally for commercial crops such as apples and pears but does not appear to have been used for natives.

A piece of root or a rooted cutting is used as the stock and the desired scion variety is grafted on by a whip/tongue or cleft graft. A piece of copper wire is wound tightly around just above the graft union and the graft is buried in soil or propagating medium to about half the length of the scion. The graft maintains the scion in good condition until it forms its own roots. The copper wire constricts development of the rootstock and eventually it dies away leaving the scion variety on its own roots.

BUDDING

Budding is a technique of propagation that employs the same principles and plant processes as grafting but only single buds are used. It is often termed bud-grafting because of the close relationship between the two techniques.

Budding is a common technique of propagation for various deciduous exotic species but is not widely used for evergreens. It is rarely used for the propagation of Australian plants but could have potential for wider application. The techniques involved are simple and can be easily learned.

Budding is carried out for the same reasons as grafting but is used as an alternative to grafting when

1. for various reasons grafting is not satisfactory or possible

2. when only a limited quantity of propagating material is available. Each mature bud on a stick can be used to produce a new plant.

The factors of cambial contact, compatability and aftercare apply to budding the same as they do for grafting. These are discussed in more detail under Grafting.

3 Cutting grafts of *Prostanthera nivea* on *Westringia fruticosa* showing struck rootstock and callused graft.

Roots may be susceptible to splitting and in these cases saddle grafts have been more successful than cleft grafts.

The roots and scions are best collected during a dormant period in the plant's growth cycle and preferably just before a flush of growth. The grafts should be made as soon as possible after the material is collected as roots dehydrate rapidly if not kept in a moist environment. After grafting the grafts are tied with tape and buried in soil above the union. It is beneficial if they are potted and placed in a bottom heat unit.

Root grafts.

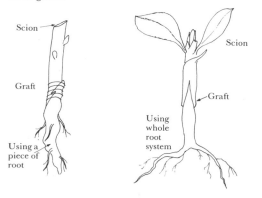

Propagation

Timing

Budding is best carried out while the rootstock is growing and there is good sap flow. This can be at various times during the year but the safest time is probably spring.

Selection of Buds

Buds should be healthy, mature and well developed. Usually those on 1-2 year old wood are quite satisfactory. Preferably collect the buds before growth flush occurs. The best buds on a stick are those in the middle and towards the base. Avoid the upper buds as they may be immature.

Storage of Budwood

Budwood is often at the most suitable stage for budding while dormant during winter, but the rootstocks are not ready at this time. The budwood can be cut and stored for 1-3 months or until the stocks are ready, if proper precautions are taken. The budsticks should be cut and the leaves removed to leave a petiole about 1 cm long. The budsticks should then be labelled, wrapped in layers of moist newspaper, then sealed in polythene sheeting. They can then be placed on the bottom of a refrigerator for storage.

Tying

After budding, the cut area is covered with polythene budding tape. This should be overlapped and wound tightly to exclude water from the bud. On small buds the tape can be wound right over the top of the bud whereas plump buds are left protruding.

Preparation of the Stock

Budding is carried out on the stock 15-20 cm above ground level. As a general guide the stock should be of at least pencil thickness at this height before it is suitable for budding. All leaves and sideshoots are removed for 4-6 cm around the area to be budded.

Staking

The young growths from buds are brittle and very easily broken by wind. They should be staked and tied continually until they are strong enough to support themselves.

TYPES OF BUDDING

Variations in techniques of budding are not as great as they are in grafting and only about three techniques have been used on Australian plants. The commonest technique of budding deciduous species is known as 'T' budding. This is not usually practical for evergreen species because it relies on the bark being easily separated from the wood (termed slipping). The technique known as chip budding does not rely on the condition of the bark for success, and is most commonly used for evergreens. Microbudding is also sometimes used for the citrus group of plants among which are some native species. Punch budding is used by commercial nurseries to produce strains of macadamia nuts.

Chip Budding

This type of budding derives its name from the way that the bud is cut along with a chip of bark and wood. A chip of similar shape and size is removed from the stock and the piece containing the bud is inserted, matched and tied.

Both the chips from the stock and the budstick are cut in the same manner. The budstick is held with the buds upright or facing away from the handler and the first cut is made below a bud and down into the wood at an angle of 45°. The second cut is made 1-2 cm above the bud and is angled inwards and down until it intersects the first cut. A similar chip is cut from the stock and the chip containing the bud is inserted, matched and tied. It is important that the cambium of both the bud and stock should be carefully matched even if this is only possible on one side. After budding the whole area is sealed carefully with plastic budding tape.

The buds usually take from 2-4 weeks to form a strong union, but this depends on variable factors such as the prevailing weather conditions and the growth of the stock. The bud should be examined at regular intervals and if it is still green and healthy after 3-4 weeks about one third of the growth can be removed from the stock. This should start the bud into growth and another one third of the stock can be removed after a further 7 days. The remainder of the stock can be cut off about 2 cm above the bud and the tape removed when the bud has started into strong growth.

Examples: this type of bud is used to propagate the various variegated forms of *Tristania conferta* onto green-leaved seedlings.

Microbudding

This type of budding is essentially the same as inverted 'T' budding except that, as the name suggests, very small buds are used. A bud stock is cut from the tree to be propagated and the leaves trimmed off just above the bud leaving a short length of petiole. For bud cutting the budstick is held with the buds facing toward the handler and the bud is removed by a flat cut which passes just beneath the bud.

1 Trimming *Tristania conferta* in preparation for budding variegated cultivar.

2 Matching stem of the variegated cultivar with the rootstock of *Tristania conferta*.

3 Trimmed budstick of variegated cultivar, matched for size with *Tristania conferta*.

4 Cutting bud from budstick of variegated cultivar of *Tristania conferta* — first cut.

5 Cutting bud from budstick of variegated cultivar of *Tristania conferta* — second cut.

6 Inserting bud of variegated cultivar in stock of *Tristania conferta*.

7 Completed bud tied with plastic budding tape.

8 Variegated cultivar of *Tristania conferta*, showing bud union 15 months after budding.

Propagation

In the rootstock a transverse and a vertical cut is made to form an inverted 'T'. The flaps of bark on the 'T' are opened and the bud slipped in. Care must be taken to ensure that the bud is placed the right way up. The area is then taped over tightly with budding tape.

After 14 days the tape can be removed and if the bud has taken the rootstock can be removed progressively over 2 weeks to force the bud into growth.

Examples: this type of bud has been used to propagate the native *Microcitrus* species onto citrus rootstocks such as sweet orange and trifoliata.

Punch Budding

This is a relatively new technique developed to propagate commercial strains of macadamia nut trees. The buds are removed with an oval punch which has an internal diameter on the long axis of 1-1.5 cm. The punch is made of tubular steel and the edges are ground and filed until very sharp. To remove a bud the punch is placed over the bud with the bud at the centre. The punch is forced down through the bark into the wood and the bud lifted with a small twist. A similar cut is made in the bark of the stock and the bud inserted and tied with plastic budding tape. Punch budding is best carried out in the spring and early summer as the stocks come into growth. Matured buds 1-2 years old give best results.

21 Other Propagation Techniques

DIVISION AND SEPARATION

Division is a means of vegetative propagation, and has the advantage of being able to perpetuate the characteristics of the parent plant. Propagation by division is mainly restricted to the monocotyledons such as lilies, grasses, palms and orchids, although it can be used for groups such as ferns and fern allies, and creeping dicotyledons which root along the stems. Species of *Anigozanthos*, *Conostylis*, *Lomandra*, *Orthrosanthos* and *Patersonia* are commonly propagated from division, together with lilies such as *Dianella*, *Dichopogon*, *Johnsonia*, *Thysanotus* etc. Dicotyledons that can be divided include some species of *Isotoma*, *Mazus*, *Mentha*, *Mitrasacme*, *Pratia*, *Ranunculus* and *Scleranthus*.

Division is a simple method, with no special expertise necessary.

The main requirements for success are as follows:
1. Damage to plant tissue should be kept to a minimum.
2. There should be ample healthy, young roots, to be able to support the foliage.
3. The divisions must have buds or growing points, to produce new growth and new roots. The top growth must be reduced to balance with the reduced root system.

A beneficial procedure is to drench the plant and soil with a fungal drench and root stimulant, about 5-7 days before division is attempted. This will control fungal organisms that might be present in the soil, and at the same time help to promote strong healthy roots.

Time to Divide

The optimum time for division is when roots are being formed, usually after a growth flush, or at the end of the dormancy period. This is particularly applicable to some of the species which are difficult to establish after division, such as some species of *Conostylis*. In subtropical and tropical areas, plants need to be kept under observation, and can be divided at the onset of new shoot growth, which is usually an indication of new root growth. In temperate regions, late winter is the ideal period for a wide range of species. This means that the divisions do not have to experience cold wet weather, which retards the formation of new roots and foliage. If heated propagating structures are available, many species can be divided in late autumn or winter. Bottom heat units are very useful for stimulating new root growth in potted divisions.

Transplanting and Potting of Divisions

The divisions need to be kept moist at all times, to prevent dehydration of the roots and leaves. With large divisions such as can be done with *Anigozanthos*, these can be transferred from their growing position to another location in the ground, without much disruption to growth. Water the plant well, and it is recommended to follow with a fungal drench and root stimulant. Regular observation is needed to maintain moist soils around the divisions. Do not over water, as this can lead to waterlogging and rotting of roots.

With small divisions, it is advisable to pot the divisions into containers, so that they can re-establish their root systems and develop new foliage before planting out to permanent locations. This is the practice commonly adopted by commercial nurseries.

Method of Division

1. Select the plant for division. It may be a plant growing in the ground, or in a container.
2. Thoroughly drench the plant, 7-10 days prior to division, with a fungal drench and root stimulant.
3. Remove the plant from the ground or container.
4. Loosen soil from around the roots. This is hastened by lightly agitating the plant in water. This technique will remove excess soil, and should minimise damage to healthy roots.

253

5. The clumps of some species can be separated with the hands. In other instances, clean, sharp secateurs or a knife should be used. It is unwise to divide plants into a large number of divisions, as small divisions will have a struggle to survive.
6. Dead roots should be removed, and living roots, especially any damaged ones, trimmed, to enable easy potting.
7. Portion of the foliage should be removed to compensate for loss of roots.
8. The division is ready for potting. (See Cultivation of Container Grown Plants, Potting Mixes, page 102.)
9. Fill container with growing medium, to a level which will allow the division to be repotted to the same depth as previously. If planted too deeply, rotting may occur.
10. It is important that roots be spread evenly, and placed pointing downwards, to allow for proper development.
11. Fill container with soil, to the original level of the plant, firm the mix, and water well.
12. Drench with a root stimulant and fungicide.
13. Place the container in a warm, sheltered position, until root and foliage growth takes place.
14. Within 2-6 months, plants should be ready for planting.

Plants Suitable for Division

Plants suitable for division may be species which form (1) Clumps; (2) Rhizomes; (3) Crowns; (4) Pseudo bulbs.

1. Clumps

Included in this group are grasses and lilies. Some species, e.g. *Sowerbaea juncea* and *Themeda australis*, can be easily separated with the hands, without any need for cutting instruments.

2. Rhizomes

A rhizome is a specialised underground stem, which resembles a root, but bears nodes and buds. Rhizomes are often fleshy, and are generally segmented in appearance. They may be straight, but frequently branch at the nodes.

Rhizomes are extremely variable in size and shape, and three groups can be distinguished. Long slender symmetrical rhizomes with sparse nodes are known as leptomorph type, while the thickened fleshy type with crowded nodes is known as the pachymorph type. Intermediate forms are known as the mesomorph type. It is important to know what type of rhizome a plant has, for it affects the method of propagation to be used.

Leptomorph Rhizomes: Propagation of plants with this type of rhizome is carried out by cutting the rhizome at the internodes, ensuring that each section has a bud. The cut sections are laid horizontally in propagating medium or sphagnum moss and new shoots develop from the nodes. As these shoots enlarge, roots are produced at the base, and at this stage the sections can be potted as separated plants. Propagation is best carried out in the warm months, and after the rhizomes have ceased growth.

Species which can be propagated in this way include *Aneilema acuminatum, A. biflorum, Cordyline* spp., and most grasses with runners.

Pachymorph Rhizomes: These are generally very irregular in shape, and the points of division are readily apparent. Each section bears a stem at its apex which has leaves and/or flowers. Division is carried out when the growths have finished, and just as active new growth is beginning in the rhizome. The rhizome is severed at each major constriction, so that each section bears a stem. This stem is cut off just above the rhizome, and the rhizome section placed in propagating medium or sphagnum moss until new shoots and roots are formed. Care should be taken to place the rhizome section upright.

Species which can be propagated in this way include most members of the ginger family, Zingiberaceae (*Alpinia* spp., *Amomum* spp., *Curcuma* spp., *Zingiber* spp.).

Mesomorph Rhizomes: These rhizomes branch freely, and each branch bears a growth at its apex. The points of division are readily apparent, and the rhizomes can be divided into single pieces or branched sections, depending on the number required. The smaller sections will take longer to become established than the larger sections. Division is best carried out in late winter or early spring, just as the plants are coming into growth. Small sections should be potted up and established before being planted out, however larger sections can be planted directly into the garden.

Species which can be propagated in this way include *Anigozanthos* spp., *Blancoa canescens, Colocasia esculenta, Conostylis* spp. and *Haemodorum* spp.

Plants in this group produce new rhizomes as the old ones die. It is most important when dividing, to make sure that new rhizomes are selected for potting. *Anigozanthos* species are readily divided using a sharp knife or secateurs. The old rhizomes are easily recognised and can be discarded. Some species of *Conostylis* have proved difficult to establish after division, e.g. *C. bealiana, C. setigera* and *C. teretifolia*.

Usually new roots start to form from the base

4 Division ready for potting.

1 Well established clump of *Blandfordia grandiflora* ready for division.

5 Division with roots spread evenly, prior to potting.

6 Plant in soil to same depth as prior to repotting.

2 Removing clump from pot — note dense root system.

3 Separation of clump into divisions.

Propagation

of leaves near the stem. When these are about 1 cm long, plants are ready for division. Always use sections from near or on the outside of the clump. This is the youngest part of the plant, and the material will be the most likely to successfully establish again after division. Species such as *Conostylis stylidioides*, and *C. aculeata* ssp. *preissii* are stoloniferous, and can be readily divided as the new aerial roots form, before they contact the soil.

3. Crown Divisions

The crown of herbaceous plants is situated near ground level, and it expands and enlarges as the plant gets older. After a while natural divisions occur within the crowns, although the plants continue to grow together as a clump, and in fact are often still joined by old woody tissue. These crowns can be divided with a sharp knife, and the divisions potted as separate plants.

Species which can be divided in this way include *Acrostichum aureum, A. speciosum, Asplenium falcatum, A. laserpitiifolium, Blechnum camfieldii, B. patersonii, Boea hygroscopica, Polystichum fallax, P. formosum, Pteris pacifica, P. tremula, P. tripartita, P. umbrosa* and *P. vittata.*

4. Pseudo Bulbs

Pseudo bulbs are specialised storage organs produced by some orchids. They are actually swollen stems, and are joined together by rhizomes. During the growing season, new pseudo bulbs are formed, with leaves at the apex, and some of the older pseudo bulbs lose their leaves and become dormant. In some

2   Removing fibrous sheath from backbulb of *Cymbidium madidum.*

3   Potting up of *Cymbidium madidum* in sphagnum moss.

4   Potted backbulb of *Cymbidium madidum.*

1   Trimming dead roots from backbulb of *Cymbidium madidum.*

6 Divisions of elkhorn (*Platycerium bifurcatum*) can be established on slabs of dead treefern. The sphagnum moss helps to establish the plant.

5 Growth of *Cymbidium madidum* from backbulb ready for potting.

7 Division of elkhorn must be wired securely to support future growth.

8 A small division of elkhorn, securely attached to a slab of dead treefern.

species (e.g. *Dendrobium 'kingianum*), offshoots develop at the nodes. These form into small plantlets which develop roots and leaves, and can be readily transplanted when mature (see Aerial Growths, page 261).

With most species, the usual method of division is to cut the rhizome into sections, each with at least 2-3 dormant pseudo bulbs, and separate from the new growth. This stimulates new shoots or 'back breaks' from the old bulbs. These can be left in the clump to grow for a season and then removed and potted as separate plants. Alternatively, the clump can be divided and the dormant pseudo bulbs removed, potted in sphagnum moss and placed on bottom heat. Each section of rhizome and pseudo bulbs will eventually shoot and grow into a separate plant.

Dividing Elkhorns

Most species of the group of ferns commonly known as elkhorns (*Platycerium* spp.) can be propagated by division. Because their rhizomes are hidden within the leaves and root system the technique of division is described separately.

Three of the four Australian species (the exception is *P. superbum*) produce suckers and build up into large clumps consisting of many plantlets. These clumps are easily divided and the plantlets can be mounted on a slab to form separate plants.

Each plantlet is capable of surviving on its own provided that it is not too small. They can be separated from the main clump by running a sharp knife around the back of the plantlet and severing the rhizome and roots. The piece can then be wired securely onto a support usually with a pad of moist material such as sphagnum moss underneath. The plants are best grown on pieces of hardwood, tree-fern or a dead tree. They should not be wired to live trees as they can allow the entry of pests such as borers. The clumps should be watered regularly until they become established as separate plants.

Serpentine layering of a long slender stem.

LAYERING

The technique of layering is generally employed for species that are difficult to propagate from cuttings. It is however often used by enthusiasts for a wide range of species because the technique requires little skill and gives good success. Its main disadvantages are that the technique is laborious and time consuming and that only a few layers can be put on each plant at a time.

Although not widely used for the propagation of Australian plants a few different techniques of layering are used on occasions including simple layering, tip layering, serpentine layering and air layering.

Simple Layering

In this technique branches near the ground, of shrubs or trees, are bent down to the ground and a portion of the stem is covered with soil. The stems are usually pegged to prevent lifting and movement by wind. Roots are formed from along the buried section of stem and when established the layers can be separated and potted.

Rooting of layers can be improved by wounding the section of stem before it is buried. The stem can be slit upwards for a short distance or a notch cut out or the stem girdled and a complete circle of bark removed. The branches can also be twisted upwards so as to tear some of the bark. The application of rooting hormones to the wound assists further in the formation of roots.

Layering can be carried out at any time during the growing season. Most layers can be separated from the parent plant 6-12 months after the layer has been set. Inspections should be carried out at fairly regular intervals to follow the development of the root system so as to determine when the layer can be severed. If possible it should be severed during cool cloudy weather. The soil for layering should be in good tilth with plenty of organic matter to prevent drying out.

Layering can also be carried out by pegging a stem into a pot containing a suitable growing medium. After rooting the layer can be severed and removed without disturbance to the root system. The pot must be watered at frequent intervals as the growing medium can dry out more quickly than soil in the ground. For the same reason a larger pot is more suitable than a small one.

Suitable Species: layering can be carried out on any species which has suitable branches growing near ground level. It is particularly easy to carry out on ground covers and procumbent plants.

Serpentine Layering

A simple technique which is only suitable for climbers or plants with long willowy stems. The stems are bent in a series of undulating curves and simple layers are made on each lower curve where it touches the ground. These are covered with soil and the upper curves are left unburied and provide the shoots for the new plants. After rooting each layer is severed and potted to be established as a separate plant.

Suitable Species: the technique has been carried out on species of jasmine such as *Jasminum aemulum* which is very difficult to strike from cuttings. It could probably be applied to species of other genera such as *Cissus, Clematis, Gymnanthera, Ipomoea, Merremia, Morinda, Pandorea* and *Trichosanthes.*

Tip Layering

This is the simplest form of layering but is restricted to a few species which are capable of rooting and forming new plants from the tips of shoots. Firm young shoots are bent down in the summer months and their tips are buried 8-10 cm deep in the soil or in a pot. Rooting occurs within a few weeks and new shoots are initiated from the buds near the tip. The new plants may be severed and established when root and top growth of the layers is well underway.

Suitable Species: the native species of *Rubus* are readily propagated by this method.

Air Layering

Air layering, also commonly called marcottage, is a useful technique for the propagation of a range of plants including natives. It is a specialised technique that is not commonly used but should be more widely tested on difficult-to-propagate species and cultivars. The results are generally better in humid situations such as in a glasshouse but the technique can be very successful outside. The technique is not difficult to carry out and a certain degree of skill is gained after a few layers have been made. The essentials of the treatment are to partially isolate a shoot by girdling or wounding, surround the wound with moist material until roots form, and then cover the shoot and establish it as a separate plant.

Procedure

1. Remove all leaves from the stem, 5-10 cm on either side of where the wound is to be made.

2. Wound the stem by making an upward cut 5 cm long or girdling the stem by removing a circle of bark about 1 cm wide.

3. Scrape the surface of the wound to remove any remaining phloem.

4. Apply rooting hormone to the wound. This can be applied as liquid, powder or in lanoline paste. The last form is the most successful for aerial layering.

5. Place a handful of damp sphagnum moss around the wound and compact.

6. Wrap polythene film around the sphagnum moss and tie tightly at each end, and in the middle if necessary.

7. Tie a light support across the layer and secure at each end so that it reduces the chance of the layer breaking off at the wound.

8. When roots are well established and clearly visible the layer can be severed and potted as a separate plant.

Selection of a Suitable Stem

Young shoots 1-2 years old which have short internodes, and healthy leaves and leaf buds, have been found to be most suitable for aerial layering. They should be in a well lighted position preferably on the outer canopy of the bush or tree. Large branches are difficult to establish as separate plants and small to medium size stems perform more satisfactorily.

Type of Wound

Girdling the stem by removing a circle of bark

1   Aerial layering of *Acacia baileyana* — stripping leaves from area to be layered.

2   The stem is girdled by removing a section of bark.

3   Close-up of girdled section.

259

4   Aerial layering of *Acacia baileyana* — sphagnum moss wrapped around girdled section.

5   Tying up aerial layer of *Acacia baileyana*.

6   Finished aerial layer of *Acacia baileyana*.

1-4 cm wide is the best type of wound to make for aerial layers. It consistently gives better results than the upward cut because the latter type often does not wound sufficient tissue to induce rooting. A double bladed knife may be used to make the cut. The girdle must be at least 1 cm wide. Smaller girdles will heal too quickly for root formation to take place, especially with the slower or difficult-to-root species. The cut should not penetrate the wood as this will weaken the stems.

Wrapping Material

Aerial layers may take from 6 months to 2 years to become sufficiently well established for removal. The polythene film used must be of sufficient durability to last this length of time and preferably should be of a type stabilized against breakdown by ultra violet rays from the sun. The polythene should not be too thick as it must be sufficiently pliable to be wrapped easily and tied. Aluminium foil has also been used successfully as a wrapping material.

Timing

Aerial layering can be carried out at any time of the year provided that the shoots are at the right stage of growth. This stage is when the shoots have just hardened-off after a flush of growth. In southern Australia winter may be too cold for root formation and aerial layering is best carried out in the warmer months. In tropical regions it can be an advantage to time aerial layers so that they are ready for severing during the wet season as this will help the plants become established.

Rooting Medium

Live sphagnum moss is very suitable as a rooting material because it has all of the necessary requirements viz:

1. It is open in structure and allows sufficient air movement.

2. It retains sufficient water for root development

3. It does not break down in the life of the layer.

4. It adheres and is easy to hold in place while tying.

Other materials have been successfully used including coconut fibre, vermiculite and peat moss. The material should be moist but not overwet when it is used.

Wrapping

A handful of the rooting medium is placed in the centre of a sheet of polythene of dimensions about 18 x 25 cm. The rooting medium is held around the stem and the polythene folded over and sealed at each end with string or adhesive tape. The layer must be sealed thoroughly so that water cannot penetrate otherwise the rooting medium will become waterlogged. If the layer is in full sunshine a paper covering over the polythene will prevent overheating.

Establishing the Layer

The main difficulties of aerial layering occur during the transference and establishment of the layer. It should be potted into an open well drained mix (see Potting Mixtures) and placed into a cool shady position protected from the wind. It is best held in such a position for at least a fortnight before gradually being exposed to sunlight. If excessive growth has been made before root formation, then some of this may have to be removed to aid transplanting. This should be removed after due consideration has been given to the future shape of the plant. Alternatively some leaves can be removed to aid establishment of the layer.

Suitable Species

Many species can probably be propagated by this method but those for which the technique has proved successful include *Acacia baileyana, Canarium australianum, Castanospermum australe, Casuarina equisetiifolia, Dillenia indica, Ficus rubiginosa* 'Variegata', *F. macrophylla, F. benjamina, Macadamia integrifolia, Schefflera actinophylla, Stenocarpus sinuatus*.

SPECIALISED PROPAGATION

A number of plants produce growths from their roots, leaves or flower stems, which can be used for propagation. These growths are variously termed gemmae, offsets, plantlets, suckers, aerials, keikis, tubercles or bulbils. When sufficiently large they can be established as separate plants. Each system is a means of vegetative reproduction and the resultant plants are identical with their parents.

Aerial Growths

Some indigenous species of orchids of the genus *Dendrobium* produce aerial growths or keikis from nodes near the top of the pseudobulbs. These mature into a miniature pseudobulb with leaves at the top and roots at the bottom. They also produce new pseudobulbs from the base and eventually develop into a small clump of bulbs on the top of the parent pseudobulb. They can be broken off the parent pseudobulb when mature and can be established as separate

1   Aerial growths of *Dendrobium kingianum*.

2   Potting up aerial growths in sphagnum moss.

3   Aerial growths potted up.

plants. They should not be removed until roots are produced from the base of the aerial. They establish well if potted in orchid mix or sphagnum moss.

Species which reproduce freely by this method include *Dendrobium kingianum*, *D. × delicatum* and *D. fleckeri*. Species which produce occasional aerial growths are *D. tetragonum*, *D. speciosum* and *D. ruppianum*.

Aerial growths are also produced on the stems of bamboos and some other coarse grasses. These tend to be more conspicuous on horizontal stems and they rarely produce roots except when in close proximity to the ground. For propagation purposes they should not be broken off the stem, but rather a whole section of stem cut off and laid horizontally in well prepared soil, with the base of the aerial growth just covered. The soil should be kept well watered and the growth can be transplanted when roots are formed. Aerials can be induced to form on bamboos if lengths of stem about 2 m long are laid horizontally, lightly covered with soil and kept moist.

Auricles

Auricles are thick, fleshy, ear-like structures which surround the base of the fronds in the fern genera *Angiopteris* and *Marattia*. They can be a very useful means of propagating those species which have not been successfully raised from spores. The stem is cut off above and below the auricles to give a stem section with the auricles attached. This is then buried in propagating medium with the tops of the auricles just exposed. The auricles eventually produce a plant from the base and this can be potted separately when well enough developed. The auricles generally take 6-12 months to form plants. The auricles are best put in as cuttings during the warm months. A bottom heat propagating bed speeds up the formation of plants.

Basal Offsets

These are like sucker growths produced from the base of the trunk at ground level of semi-woody or pithy plants. Frequently they will not develop fully and remain partially dormant or growing slowly unless something happens to damage the main stem. Often they have a few roots developed at their base and if carefully separated from the parent they can be established as separate plants. They are best removed in cool weather and must be placed in a sheltered position until their root system becomes well enough established to support the growth. Species which can be propagated in this way include the palms *Laccospadix australasicus*,

Basal offsets on stem of *Laccospadix australasicus*.

Ptychosperma macarthuri and *Linospadix* spp. and some species of *Pandanus* and *Cordyline* and the tree ferns *Cyathea baileyana*, *C. rebeccae* and *Dicksonia youngiae*.

Bulbils

Bulbils or plantlets are produced on the fronds of certain ferns. They are usually produced at the junctions of veins, in particular along the major midrib. The bulbil starts off as a small tuberous structure which increases in size and eventually develops small fronds. If the frond is near ground level or the atmosphere is sufficiently humid, roots are also formed and the bulbil becomes a plantlet. These will increase in size as the frond ages. When sufficiently developed they can be removed and established as separate plants. The larger and more developed the plantlet the easier it will be to establish.

Species commonly propagated by this method are *Asplenium attenuatum*, *A. bulbiferum*, *A. paleaceum*, *Athrium accedens*, *Polystichum australiense*, *P. proliferum* and *Ampelopteris prolifera*.

Bulbs

A bulb is a specialised underground storage organ which contains a dormant bud surrounded by thick, fleshy scales. The dormant bud contains the growth for the following season (leaves and/or flowers) and the fleshy scales are in fact modified leaf bases. Bulbs of Australian plants are all of the tunicate type, i.e. they are covered with a dry papery covering (tunic) which protects the bulb from drying and mechanical injury.

As bulbs increase in size they divide naturally. These divisions may grow together for a couple of years but after a while become completely separate plants. Small offsets are also produced from the base of the parent bulbs and these also develop and eventually become separate bulbs. Natural increase is often slow and the numbers can be increased by a couple of simple propagation techniques.

Scaling

In this technique the outer 2-3 layers of thick fleshy scales are removed from the bulb and planted in trays of propagating medium about 5 cm deep. The scales are inserted vertically to about half their length and small bulblets and roots form on the basal damaged parts in 4-10 weeks. The process is speeded up if the trays are placed on a bottom heat unit. Dipping the scales in 1 ppm naphthalene acetic acid will also stimulate bulblet formation. Sphagnum moss is an ideal medium in which to set the scales.

The scales can also be placed in a partially inflated polythene bag containing sphagnum moss. After the bulblets are well developed they can be removed and potted up or rowed out in shallow trays to develop further. Scaling can be carried out on dormant bulbs although results may be better if the bulbs are lifted while growing, the scales removed and the bulbs replanted. This technique has been carried out on *Crinum asiaticum, C. flaccidum* and *Eurycles amboinensis.*

Bulb Cutting

In this technique a mature bulb is cut vertically into 8 sections, each section containing segments of scales and a portion of the thickened base. The sections are planted vertically in propagating medium with their tips just showing. New bulblets develop from the scales near the base and when sufficiently large can be separated and planted in trays and allowed to develop. The process is speeded up if the pots containing the sections are placed on a bottom heat unit. This technique has been carried out on *Crinum flaccidum* and *Eurycles amboinensis.*

Flower Stem Propagation

The fleshy stems of some monocotyledons are long lasting after flowering has finished, and occasionally produce plantlets from nodes along their length. This is sometimes conspicuous in species of the orchid genus *Phalaenopsis*, e.g. *P. amabilis.* The plantlets can be pinned into a pot while still attached to the flower stems and separated when they develop their own roots. An alternative technique is to wrap some moist sphagnum moss around the flower stem near the plantlet to induce root formation. Various attempts have been made to induce plantlet formation from dormant nodes of *Phalaenopsis*

flower stems by the application of plant hormones and growth regulators but results have been variable. Some success has been achieved by excising the buds and growing them in a flask of nutrient medium under sterile conditions (see Meristem Culture). The orchid *Bromheadia venusta* produces plantlets from the base of its flower stems and occasional plantlets are produced on the stems of other orchids such as *Sarcochilus ceciliae* and *S. roseus.*

The flower stems of the orchid *Phaius tancarvilliae* can be used for propagation although they rarely produce plantlets in nature. If the flower stems are cut up into lengths 10-15 cm long and laid in sphagnum moss in a bottom heat unit or propagation frame, plantlets sprout from some of the nodes. These may take 6-12 months to form but when they have developed their own roots they can be potted as separate plants. The lilies *Tricoryne elatior* and *Thysanotus multiflorus* also produce plantlets on the flower stems.

Other species can possibly be propagated by this technique but these are unknown to the authors.

Gemmae

A few species of plants are known to produce small vegetative buds or gemmae on their root systems. These become readily detached and under favourable conditions can be established as separate plants. This technique is probably more widespread than is known at present. The terrestrial orchid *Spiranthes sinensis* produces gemmae along its tuberous roots and these can be grown if planted in small pots of sphagnum moss. Tiny offsets which may be gemmae are produced from aroid species such as *Typhonium brownii* and *Amorphophallus variabilis.*

Micro Propagation

Micro propagation is as the name suggests the propagation of plants from very small pieces (termed explants) of tissue or even single cells. The technique requires very careful procedures and the use of fairly expensive equipment but large numbers of uniform plants can be produced. There are many plant tissues which can be grown by a variety of techniques but in all cases the tissue is grown under sterile (or aseptic) conditions on cultures containing essential nutrients and hormones. Micro propagation has the potential for very rapid multiplication of superior clones of plants and is very valuable for species which are difficult to propagate. It can also be used to produce and establish disease-free plants. Micro propagation requires

Tissue culture of Ferns.
Left — *Adiantum aethiopicum.* Right — *Platycerium bifurcatum.*

specialized equipment and techniques out of reach of the average hobbyist, however it is gaining wide acceptance and application in the nursery industry.

Meristem Culture

In this technique a shoot apex or meristem is removed from a plant, grown on sterile medium and induced to produce other shoots. As these other shoots proliferate they can be cut from the original meristem and transferred to new culture flasks containing sterile medium. By manipulating the contents of the medium it is possible to either cause the meristems to keep dividing or else to develop leaves and roots and become independent small plants. The addition of hormones such as naphthalene acetic acid (NAA) to the culture medium stimulates root formation on some species. Thus the process can be divided into 2 stages the first for multiplication of the plants and the second for plant development. After the plantlet has developed leaves and roots it can be transferred from the culture flask to a soil medium where it can be grown as a normal plant.

Meristem culture has been used very successfully for propagation of orchids particularly cultivars of the genus *Cymbidium*. It has also been used to propagate some native ferns such as *Adiantum aethiopicum*, *Platycerium bifurcatum*, *Doodia caudata*, as well as species and hybrids of the kangaroo paws (*Anigozanthos rufus*, *A. pulcherrimus*, *A.* 'Pink Joey' and *Macropidia fuliginosa*).

Embryo Culture

In this technique the embryo is removed from a seed and grown on nutrient medium under sterile conditions. The technique is very useful for overcoming seed dormancy and inhibitor problems but as yet it does not have wide practical application.

A similar technique is used for propagation of orchids. The pods are removed when about two thirds mature, sterilized on the outside by dipping in sodium or calcium hypochlorite, and cut open to obtain the green immature seeds which are sown onto agar in sterile conditions. This technique has the advantage of speed and simplifies the sowing process since only the outside of the pod needs to be sterilized.

Polyembryony

The seeds of some species contain more than one embryo and when germinated produce more than one seedling from what is apparently a single seed. Only one of these seedlings (sometimes none) is sexual in origin, the others arising vegetatively from cells outside the embryo. The vegetative seedlings are thus identical with the parent plant and, if the sexual seedlings can be eliminated, a pure line will result. A few rainforest plants are polyembryonic including *Davidsonia pruriens* but one of the best examples is provided by *Syzygium coolminianum*. This species is commonly grown in south-eastern Australia and the seeds each produce 3-8 seedlings. This explains the lack of variation in cultivated plants of this species because the majority of seedlings are identical to the parent.

Suckers

A sucker is a shoot which arises from an adventitious bud on a root and eventually develops into a separate plant. Suckers can be dug out, cut from the parent roots (often with a section of the root attached) and established as separate plants. They are best dug during cool weather and if possible before the parent plant makes active growth. If the sucker has not formed roots of its own it should be potted and treated as a cutting. In general those species which produce

Section of a root showing development of suckers.

264

Suckering of *Wahlenbergia gloriosa*, suitable for division into individual plants.

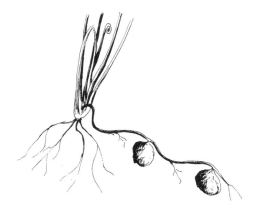

Tubers developing on stolon of *Nephrolepis cordifolia.*

suckers can also be propagated by root cuttings (see also Root Cuttings page 218).

Species which can be propagated by suckers include *Atalaya hemiglauca, Banksia marginata, Dampiera cuneata, D. lanceolata, D. rosmarinifolia, Eremocitrus glauca, Rubus probus, Wahlenbergia gloriosa.*

Tubercles

Small aerial tubers are produced in the leaf axils of some *Dioscorea* species notably *D. sativa*. These mature as the stems begin to die off and can be removed and planted immediately or stored for a couple of months. They should be planted shallowly with the top of the tubercle just at ground level. They develop quickly and after 12 months are sturdy young plants.

The aroid *Remusatia vivipara* produces aerial stems which bear small prickly tubercles at each node. These mature as the stems wither off and can be treated as for the tubercles of *D. sativa* above.

Tubers and Tuberoids

Tubers are swellings which develop near the apex of underground stems or stolons. They are a modified stem structure and act as both a storage organ and a reproductive unit. True tubers are rare in Australian plants e.g.

Nephrolepis cordifolia. Tuberoids however are quite common in terrestrial orchids which form colonies in nature e.g. *Pterostylis nutans, P. curta, P. pedunculata, P. concinna, P. baptistii, Corybas diemenicus, C. dilatatus, C. fimbriatus, Acianthus exsertus, A. reniformis,* and *Lyperanthus nigricans.* The tuberoids also act as a storage and reproductive unit but are produced on the apex of specialised roots not on stolons or underground stems as are true tubers.

When mature the root connecting the parent plant with the progeny tuberoid withers leaving the tuberoid as a separate unit. This grows into a new plant and develops a new tuberoid when conditions are right for growth. The tuberoids can be separated when mature and used to establish new plants or colonies. Some species such as *P. nutans* and *P. concinna* will produce up to 5 new tuberoids from each parent plant in a single growing season.

Tuberous Roots

The roots of some plants are thickened and act as storage organs (e.g. *Arthropodium* spp., *Asparagus racemosus, Dichopogon strictus, Eustrephus latifolius* and *Geitonoplesium cymosum*) while others have thickened tuberous structures attached (e.g. *Cissus opaca, Dioscorea* spp., *Nephrolepis cordifolia* and *Stemona australiana*).

Species of the former group usually have the thickened roots clustered near the base of the stem. Each one of the thickened roots has the potential to become a separate plant but it must be cut from the parent with a small portion of the stem attached. It should be then potted and

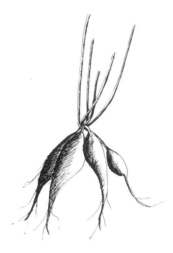

Tuberous root system of *Eustrephus latifolius.*

with proper conditions and care will develop into a separate plant.

Species of the latter group have the tuberous swellings scattered along the root system usually attached by a lateral root. These organs can be removed and potted, and if mature will develop into separate plants.

Tuberous Stems

Certain plants have thickened structures at or just below ground level which have arisen from stem tissue. These are mostly herbaceous type plants which produce growth while conditions are favourable, and die back to the tuberous stem in times of stress. These tuberous stems can be dug up while dormant and divided by longitudinal cuts into pieces. The cut surfaces should be dusted with an insecticide and provided the piece contains one or more vegetative buds it will shoot and develop into a new plant.

Plants which can be propagated in this way are species of *Abelmoschus, Aristolochia pubera, Bonamia, Cayratia, Dioscorea, Ipomoea* and *Stephania.*

Hardy ferns in a natural setting.

W.R. Elliot

Part Five

Plant Lists and
Supplementary Information

22   Plants for Various Purposes

The plants in the following lists are suitable for specific conditions, or problem positions in the garden. They also may have certain attributes which make them suitable for specific uses. By placing such plants together in a list, it is hoped that this will facilitate selection of suitable species.

These lists should only be regarded as a guide. The absence of a species from a list does not necessarily mean that it is unsuitable for the purpose. More detailed information will be given under each species in the volumes to follow.

Up-to-date species names are used wherever known.

DIFFICULT SOIL TYPES

CALCAREOUS SOILS

* — withstands heavy, wet, calcareous soils

Abutilon geranioides
  theophrastii
Acacia acuminata
  aneura
  argyrophylla
  brachybotrya
  burkittii
  calamifolia
  calcicola
  cana
  cardiophylla
  chalkeri
  colletioides
  cyanophylla
  cyclops
  dodonaeifolia
  euthycarpa
  farinosa
  glandulicarpa
  hakeoides
  harpophylla
  heteroclita
  iteaphylla
  ligulata
  lineata
 * longifolia var. sophorae

 * melanoxylon
  merrallii
  microbotrya
  montana
  notabilis
  oswaldii
  pendula
  prolifera
  pycnantha
 * retinodes
  rhetinocarpa
  rigens
  rostellifera
  rotundifolia
  salicina
 * saligna
  sowdenii
  strongylophylla
  trineura
  vernicuflua
  victoriae
  wattsiana
  wilhelmina
* Agonis flexuosa
Alyogyne hakeifolia
  huegelii

Angophora costata
  floribunda
Araucaria bidwillii
  heterophylla
Baeckea behri
* Banksia integrifolia
 * marginata
Billardiera cymosa
Bossiaea cinerea
  prostrata
Brachychiton populneum
Callistemon brachyandrus
 * 'Harkness'
  macropunctatus
 * rigidus
  teretifolius
  viminalis
Callitris hugelii
  preissii
Calytrix tetragona
Cassia artemisioides
  nemophila
  sturtii
Casuarina cristata
  cunninghamiana
 * glauca
  leuhmannii
  stricta
Clematis microphylla
Correa reflexa
Darwinia micropetala
Dodonaea angustissima
  boroniifolia
  humilis
  lobulata
Eremaea beaufortioides
  rosea
  violacea
Eremophila alternifolia
  crassifolia
  denticulata
  freelingii
  glabra
  longifolia
  maculata
  polyclada
  scoparia
Eucalyptus albens
  astringens
 * botryoides

  brockwayii
  burracoppinensis
  campaspe
  cinerea
 * cornuta
 * cosmophylla
  crucis
  dielsii
  diptera
  diversifolia
  dumosa
  eremophila
  erythrocorys
  erythronema
  flocktoniae
  foecunda
  forrestiana
  gardneri
  gillii
 * gomphocephala
  goniantha
  gracilis
  grossa
  kruseana
  lansdowneana
 * leucoxylon
 * macrandra
  nutans
  oleosa
 * platypus
  pyriformis
  salmonophloia
  salubris
  sargentii
  spathulata
  steedmanii
  stoatei
  stricklandii
  torquata
  viminalis var. racemosa
Eutaxia microphylla
Geijera parviflora
Grevillea aspera
  ilicifolia
  lavandulacea
  leucopteris
  pinaster
  rosmarinifolia
  thelemanniana

269

Hakea adnata
bucculenta
francisiana
leucoptera
multilineata
nitida
nodosa
petiolaris
purpurea
rugosa
scoparia
suaveolens
sulcata
vittata
Halgania cyanea
lavandulacea
Hibiscus farragei
Kunzea baxteri
*Lagunaria patersonii
Lasiopetalum baueri
behrii
schulzenii
*Leptospermum laevigatum
*lanigerum
Melaleuca acuminata
*armillaris
cordata
*decussata
*ericifolia
gibbosa
*halmaturorum

*lanceolata
megacephala
*nesophila
squarrosa
uncinata
Melia azedarach
Myoporum desertii
floribundum
*insulare
oppositifolium
parvifolium
viscosum
Olearia ciliata
magniflora
muelleri
pimelioides
pteridifolia
rudis
Phebalium bullatum
glandulosum
stenophyllum
Pittosporum phillyreoides
Pomaderris oraria
Prostanthera baxteri
behriana
calycina
chlorantha
microphylla
nivea
Templetonia retusa
Viminaria juncea

microtheca
miniata
peltata
polycarpa
pruinosa
ptychocarpa
tectifera
tereticornis
tessellaris
Erythrina indica
verspertilio
Ficus benjamina
macrophylla
obliqua
platypoda
rubiginosa
Grevillea dryandri
glauca
goodii
heliosperma
mimosoides
parallela
pteridifolia
robusta
striata
Hakea chordophylla
lorea
purpurea
Hibiscus tiliaceus
Hymenosporum flavum
Jacksonia scoparia
Kennedia rubicunda
Lagerstroemia archerana
Leptospermum brachyandrum
fabricia

flavescens
Macrozamia communis
diplomera
heteromera
moorei
pauli-guilielmi
spiralis
Melaleuca argentea
bracteata
cajuputii
dealbata
decora
hypericifolia
leucadendron
linariifolia
minutifolia
nervosa
nodosa
quinquenervia
saligna
symphiocarpa
tamarascina
viridiflora
Melastoma polyanthum
Melia azedarach
Parinari nonda
Peltophorum pterocarpum
Petalostigma banksii
Pittosporum revolutum
undulatum
Pongamia pinnata
Schefflera actinophylla
Stenocarpus sinuatus
Syzygium suborbiculare
Thryptomene oligandra

HEAVY CLAY SOILS

Tropical and Subtropical Regions

Abutilon auritum
Acacia aulacocarpa
calyculata
fimbriata
gnidium
holosericea
latescens
leptostachya
podalyriifolia
salicina
simsii
stenophylla
torulosa
Acmena smithii
Adansonia gregorii
Baeckea virgata
Banksia dentata
robur
Bombax ceiba var. leiocarpa
Brachychiton acerifolium
bidwillii
discolor
diversifolium
paradoxum
populneum

Bursaria incana
tenuifolia
Callistemon chisholmii
pachyphyllus
polandii
rigidus
salignus
viminalis
Callitris intratropica
Capparis lasiantha
mitchellii
Castanospermum australe
Casuarina cristata
cunninghamiana
inophloia
Cochlospermum fraseri
gillivraei
Cycas cairnsiana
media
Eucalyptus apodophylla
bigalerita
camaldulensis
confertiflora
crebra
maculata

HEAVY CLAY SOILS

Temperate Region

Acacia acinacea
acuminata
adunca
baileyana
boormanii
brachybotrya
buxifolia
calamifolia
cardiophylla
cultriformis
cyclops
fimbriata
floribunda
howittii
iteaphylla
melanoxylon
notabilis
pravissima
prominens
retinodes
riceana
rigens
salicina

saligna
spectabilis
stricta
subulata
verniciflua
Agonis flexuosa
juniperina
parviceps
Angophora costata
Anigozanthos flavidus
Astartea fascicularis
Astroloma humifusum
Baeckea linifolia
virgata
Banksia ericifolia
spinulosa
Bauera rubioides
Beaufortia incana
orbifolia
Billardiera scandens
Bossiaea prostrata
Brachychiton acerifolium
populneum

Large shrubs are very useful for screening in public areas.
'Your Garden' photo

Excellent screening effect, by making use of plants with
differing growth habits.
'Your Garden' photo

Melaleuca squamea withstands both waterlogged
or dry soils.
W.R. Elliot photo

The prostrate form of *Grevillea aquifolium* is ideal for
cascading over rocks, embankments, etc.
W.R. Elliot photo

271

Brachyscome multifida
Brachysema lanceolatum
  praemorsum
Callistemon brachyandrus
  'Burgundy'
  citrinus
  linearis
  macropunctatus
  'Mauve Mist'
  pallidus
  phoeniceus
  pinifolius
  'Reeves Pink'
  salignus
  speciosus
  viminalis
  viridiflorus
Callitris huegelii
Calothamnus quadrifidus
  sanguineus
Casuarina cunninghamiana
  littoralis
  rigida
  stricta
  thuyoides
  torulosa
Correa baeuerlenii
  glabra
  lawrenciana
Dampiera linearis
  rosmarinifolia
Darwinia fascicularis
Dodonaea procumbens
Eremophila longifolia
  maculata
Eriostemon myoporoides
Eucalyptus alpina
  astringens
  bancroftii
  botryoides
  caesia
  camaldulensis
  cephalocarpa
  cinerea
  coccifera
  cordata
  cornuta
  cosmophylla
  crenulata
  deanei
  eremophila
  erythrocorys
  erythronema
  forrestiana
  gardneri
  globulus
  grandis
  haemastoma
  kitsoniana
  lehmannii
  leucoxylon
  macrandra
  maculata
  mannifera

  megacornuta
  nicholii
  occidentalis
  pauciflora
  platypus
  preissiana
  robusta
  saligna
  scoparia
  sideroxylon
  spathulata
  stellulata
  tetraptera
  viridis
Eutaxia microphylla
Frankenia pauciflora
Goodenia lanata
  ovata
Goodia lotifolia
Grevillea acanthifolia
  asplenifolia
  arenaria
  'Audrey'
  barklyana
  brevicuspis
  'Canberra Gem'
  'Clearview David'
  confertifolia
  'Crosbie Morrison'
  'Dargan Hill'
  dimorpha
  floribunda
  ×*gaudichaudii*
  glabella
  glabrata
  'Ivanhoe'
  jephcottii
  juniperina
  lanigera
  miqueliana
  mucronulata
  'Pink Pearl'
  'Poorinda Constance'
  'Poorinda Elegance'
  'Poorinda Firebird'
  'Poorinda Peter'
  'Poorinda Queen'
  robusta
  rosmarinifolia
  sericea
  shiressii
  sp. 'Glut'
  tridentifera
  triloba
  tripartita
  victoriae
Hakea elliptica
  nodosa
  orthorrhyncha
  petiolaris
  salicifolia
  suaveolens
  teretifolia
Hardenbergia violacea

Helichrysum apiculatum
  semipapposum
Homoranthus flavescens
Hymenosporum flavum
Hypocalymma angustifolium
  cordifolium
Indigofera australis
Isopogon anethifolius
Jacksonia scoparia
Kennedia beckxiana
  macrophylla
  nigricans
  retrorsa
  rubicunda
Kunzea ambigua
  parvifolia
  pomifera
Lagunaria patersonii
Lambertia formosa
Leptospermum flavescens
  'Horizontalis'
  humifusum
  juniperinum
  lanigerum
  nitidum 'Copper Sheen'
Lomatia ilicifolia
Mazus pumilio
Melaleuca armillaris
  decussata
  diosmiifolia
  ericifolia

  halmaturorum
  hypericifolia
  incana
  lanceolata
  linariifolia
  nesophila
  spathulata
  squarrosa
  styphelioides
  thymifolia
  violacea
Melia azedarach
Mentha diemenica
Myoporum insulare
  parvifolium
Pandorea pandorana
Patersonia occidentalis
Phyla nodiflora
Pittosporum phillyreoides
  undulatum
Pratia pedunculata
Pultenaea pedunculata
Regelia ciliata
Sollya heterophylla
Thryptomene saxicola
Tristania conferta
  laurina
Veronica perfoliata
Viminaria juncea
Viola hederacea
Westringia fruticosa

SALINE SOILS

c — coastal
i — inland

Abutilon halophilum i
Acacia cyclops c
  iteaphylla i
  ligulata ci
  longifolia var *sophorae* c
  oswaldii i
  pycnantha i
  retinodes ci
  rostellifera c
  salicina ci
  sowdenii i
  stenophylla i
  victoriae i
Acanthus ilicifolius c
Actinostrobus pyramidalis ci
Aegialitis annulata c
Aegiceras corniculatum c
Alyogyne hakeifolia i
Antidesma bunius c
Arthrocnemum arbusculum i
  halocnemoides i
  lecostachyum i
  lylei i
Atriplex isatidea ci
  cinerea ci
  nummularia ci

  rhagodioides ci
Avicennia eucalyptifolia c
  marina c
Banksia integrifolia c
  marginata c
Brachychiton gregorii i
  populneum i
  rupestre i
Brachycome graminea c
  parvula c
Bruguiera cylindrica c
  exaristata c
  gymnorhiza c
  parviflora c
Callistemon citrinus c
  pachyphyllus c
  rigidus c
  salignus ci
Callitris columellaris ci
  rhomboidea i
Camptostemon schultzii c
Carpobrotus modestus ci
  rossii ci
Cassia artemisioides i
Casuarina cristata ci
  cunninghamiana ci

equisetifolia c
glauca ci
leuhmannii i
littoralis ci
obesa ci
stricta ci
torulosa c
Ceriops decandra c
tagal c
Cynometra ramiflora c
Disphyma clavellatum
Eucalyptus astringens i
botryoides ci
brachycorys i
brockwayii i
calycogona i
camaldulensis i
campaspe i
cladocalyx i
cornuta ci
dielsii i
diptera i
doratoxylon i
dumosa i
eremophila ci
erythrocorys ci
flocktoniae i
gomphocephala ci
griffithsii i
incrassata ci
kondininensis ci
largiflorens i
lehmannii c
le souefii i
longicornis i
loxophleba ci
macrandra i
occidentalis ci
oleosa i
ovularis i
pileata i
platycorys i
platypus var.
  heterophylla ci
pterocarpa i
robusta c
salmonophloia i
salubris i
sargentii i
spathulata ci
striaticalyx i
tereticornis i
tessellaris i

torquata i
woodwardii i
Excoecaria agallucha c
Ficus macrophylla ci
Grevillea nematophylla i
Hakea leucoptera i
Heritiera littoralis c
Hibbertia cuneiformis c
  scandens c
Hibiscus tiliaceus c
Lagunaria patersonii ci
Leptospermum flavescens c
Lumnitzera littorea c
  racemosa c
Melaleuca armillaris ci
  cuticularis ci
  cymbifolia i
  ericifolia c
  globifera c
  glomerata i
  halmaturorum ci
  hamulosa i
  huegelii c
  lanceolata ci
  linariifolia c
  microphylla ci
  nesophila c
  pentagona c
  preissiana ci
  quinquenervia c
  squarrosa c
  styphelioides ci
  thymoides i
Melia azedarach i
Myoporum insulare ci
  montanum i
  platycarpum i
  viscosum ci
Nitraria schoberi i
Nypa fruticans c
Osbornea octodonta c
Pittosporum phillyreoides i
Rhizophora apiculata c
  mucronata c
  stylosa c
Salicornia quinqueflora ci
Santalum lanceolatum i
Scaevola calendulacea c
  crassifolia c
Scyphiphora hydrophylacea c
Viminaria juncea c
Xylocarpus australasicum c
  ×granatum c

gracilifolia
hakeoides
iteaphylla
linifolia
longifolia var. sophorae
montana
pravissima
prominens
pycnantha
retinodes
salicina
saligna
suaveolens
trineura
uncinata
Actinotus helianthii
Adenanthos obovata
  sericea
Agonis flexuosa
  juniperina
Alyogyne huegelii
Angophora costata
  hispida
Anigozanthos bicolor
  flavidus
  humilis
  manglesii
  pulcherrimus
  rufus
  viridis
Astroloma conostephioides
  pinifolium
Baeckea astarteoides
  behri
Banksia attenuata
  baueri
  baxteri
  brownii
  burdettii
  coccinea
  elderana
  ericifolia
  grandis
  integrifolia
  marginata
  media
  occidentalis
  ornata
  pilostylis
  praemorsa
  prionotes
  prostrata
  quercifolia
  repens
  serrata
  speciosa
  sphaerocarpa
  verticillata
Beaufortia decussata
  elegans
  sparsa
  squarrosa
Billardiera cymosa
  ringens

variifolia
Blandfordia grandiflora
  nobilis
Boronia fraseri
  pilosa
  serrulata
Bossiaea heterophylla
Brachysema latifolium
  sericeum
Burtonia scabra
Callistemon brachyandrus
  citrinus
  linearis
  macropunctatus
  phoeniceus
  pinifolius
  viminalis
Callitris columellaris
  rhomboidea
Calocephalus brownii
Calothamnus chrysantherus
  gilesii
  homalophyllus
  pinifolius
  quadrifidus
  sanguineus
  villosus
Calytrix alpestris
  depressa
  fraseri
  glutinosa
Cassia artemisioides
  nemophila
  sturtii
Casuarina glauca
  microstachya
  muellerana
  ramosissima
  stricta
Chamelaucium sp. Walpole
  uncinatum
Conospermum mitchellii
  triplinervium
Conostylis aculeata
  seorsiflora
Correa alba
  pulchella
  reflexa
Dampiera cuneata
  linearis
  rosmarinifolia
Darwinia citriodora
  fascicularis
  leiostyla
  taxifolia
Daviesia brevifolia
  incrassata
Dillwynia sericea
Dodonaea lobulata
Doryanthes excelsa
Dryandra baxteri
  calophylla
  formosa
  fraseri

SANDY SOILS

Acacia acinacea
  anceps
  baileyana
  brachybotrya
  buxifolia
  calamifolia

cardiophylla
colletioides
cultriformis
cyclops
floribunda
glandulicarpa

nobilis
polycephala
praemorsa
Epacris impressa
longiflora
microphylla
pulchella
Eremaea beaufortioides
violacea
Eremophila calorhabdos
dichroantha
divaricata
glabra
maculata
oppositifolia
Eriostemon spicatus
Eucalyptus caesia
calycogona
camaldulensis
cladocalyx
crucis
desmondensis
diversifolia
eremophila
erythrocorys
erythronema
ficifolia
gardneri
gomphocephala
gracilis
grossa
incrassata
kruseana
lansdowneana
lehmannii
leucoxylon
macrandra
macrocarpa
megacornuta
nutans
orbifolia
platypus
pyriformis
rhodantha
scoparia
sepulcralis
steedmanii
stricklandii
tetragona
tetraptera
torquata
viridis
woodwardii
Gompholobium grandiflorum
huegelii
Gossypium sturtianum
Grevillea aquifolium
asparagoides
banksii
buxifolia
confertifolia
endlicherana
floribunda
glabella

hookerana
ilicifolia
intricata
lanigera
lavandulacea
pinaster
rosmarinifolia
sericea
speciosa
stenomera
thelemanniana
tripartita
vestita
victoriae
Hakea baxteri
bucculenta
cinerea
corymbosa
cucullata
francisiana
laurina
multilineata
orthorrhyncha
purpurea
scoparia
victoriae
Halgania cyanea
lavandulacea
Helichrysum apiculatum
baxteri
bracteatum
leucopsidium
Hemiandra pungens
Hibbertia cuneiformis
fasciculata
scandens
stricta
virgata
Hibiscus splendens
Homoranthus flavescens
Howittia trilocularis
Hymenosporum flavum
Hypocalymma angustifolium
robustum
tetrapterum
Isopogon buxifolius
cuneatus
dubius
formosus
Jacksonia furcellata
Kennedia beckxiana
coccinea
eximia
glabrata
macrophylla
microphylla
nigricans
prostrata
rubicunda
Kunzea affinis
baxteri
ericifolia
parvifolia
pauciflora

pomifera
Lagunaria patersonii
Lambertia formosa
Lasiopetalum behri
discolor
schulzenii
Leptospermum flavescens
'Horizontalis'
laevigatum
nitidum
petersonii
squarrosum
Lechenaultia biloba
floribunda
formosa
Melaleuca armillaris
decussata
elliptica
fulgens
halmaturorum
hypericifolia
incana
lateritia
lanceolata
micromera
nematophylla
pulchella
pungens
spathulata
squamea
squarrosa
steedmanii
thymifolia
violacea
wilsonii
Melia azedarach
Micromyrtus ciliata
Myoporum insulare
viscosum
Olearia dentata
phlogopappa
Orthrosanthus laxus
multiflorus
Patersonia fragilis
occidentalis
Persoonia nutans
pinifolia

Petrophile biloba
sessilis
squamata
Phebalium glandulosum
Pimelea ferruginea
Pittosporum phillyreoides
Pomaderris lanigera
Pratia pedunculata
Pronaya fraseri
Prostanthera aspalathoides
denticulata
lasianthos
melissifolia
ovalifolia
rotundifolia
spinosa
Pultenaea daphnoides
humilis
pedunculata
Regelia ciliata
cymbifolia
inops
megacephala
velutina
Scaevola striata
Sollya heterophylla
Sowerbaea juncea
Stylidium graminifolium
Stypandra caespitosa
glauca
Swainsonia galegifolia
greyana
Telopea oreades
speciosissima
Templetonia retusa
Tetratheca ciliata
thymifolia
Thomasia petalocalyx
Thryptomene baeckeacea
calycina
saxicola
Thysanotus multiflorus
Verticordia densiflora
plumosa
Wahlenbergia gloriosa
Westringia fruticosa
Xanthorrhoea australis

WATERLOGGED SOILS

Tropical and Subtropical Regions

Baeckea diosmifolia
imbricata
virgata
Banksia paludosa
robur
Blechnum indicum
Callistemon citrinus
chisholmii
comboynensis
polandii

salignus
sieberi
viminalis
Casuarina cristata
cunninghamiana
glauca
leuhmannii
littoralis
Clerodendrum inerme
Cordyline stricta

Disphyma blackii makes a good groundcover, and has fire retardant properties.
W.R. Elliot photo

The woody fruits of *Pandanus pedunculatus* hang on the tree for some years before ripening.
D.L. Jones photo

Elaeodendron australe has brightly coloured fruits.
D.L. Jones photo

The climber, *Stephania japonica*, has attractive leaves, and decorative fruits.
D.L. Jones photo

275

Plants Lists and Glossary

Cyclosorus interruptus
Epacris microphylla
Eucalyptus alba
  largiflorens
  phoenicea
  robusta
  tereticornis
Gleichenia dicarpa
  microphylla
  rupestris
Grevillea pteridifolia
Hakea gibbosa
  pedunculata
Kunzea ambigua
Leptospermum arachnoideum
  attenuatum
  fabricia
  flavescens
  lanigerum
  longifolium
  phylicoides
  wooroonooran

Melaleuca acacioides
  armillaris
  bracteata
  cajuputii
  decora
  hypericifolia
  leucadendron
  linariifolia
  magnifica
  minutifolia
  nodosa
  quinquenervia
  styphelioides
  symphiocarpa
  thymifolia
  uncinata
  viridiflora
Sinoga lysicephala
Tristania conferta
  exiliflora
  laurina
  suaveolens

decussata
ericifolia
halmaturorum
incana
lateritia
leucadendron
lanceolata
linariifolia
nesophila
quinquenervia
spathulata
squarrosa
styphelioides
suberosa
thymifolia

violacea
Patersonia fragilis
  occidentalis
Pratia pedunculata
Ranunculus collinus
  gunnianus
  inundatus
Scaevola hookeri
Sollya heterophylla
Sprengelia incarnata
Todea barbara
Tristania conferta
  laurina
Viminaria juncea
Wittsteinia vacciniacea

WATERLOGGED SOILS

Temperate Region

Acacia cyclops
  riceana
  salicina
  stenophylla
Agonis juniperina
  parviceps
Astartea fascicularis
Baeckea imbricata
  virgata
Banksia robur
Bauera rubioides
Blandfordia nobilis
Blechnum indicum
  minus
  nudum
Boronia megastigma
Callistemon citrinus
  macropunctatus
  paludosus
  salignus
  sieberi
  speciosus
  viminalis
  viridiflorus
Casuarina cristata
  cunninghamiana
  glauca
  leuhmannii
  obesa
  paludosa
  stricta
  thuyoides
Cyclosorus interruptus
Epacris impressa
  microphylla
  obtusifolia

Eucalyptus aggregata
  alpina
  astringens
  camaldulensis
  camphora
  cosmophylla
  crenulata
  kitsoniana
  largiflorens
  microcarpa
  muellerana
  neglecta
  occidentalis
  ovata
  ovularis
  pauciflora
  robusta
  spathulata
  stellulata
Gleichenia dicarpa
  microphylla
Grevillea acanthifolia
  confertifolia
Hakea nodosa
Hypolepis muelleri
  rugosula
Kunzea ambigua
  parvifolia
Leptospermum juniperinum
  lanigerum
  phylicoides
  scoparium
Mazus pumilio
Melaleuca acuminata
  armillaris
  cuticularis

The wheel-like flower-heads of Stenocarpus sinuatus are long lasting and showy. Although a rain forest tree, it has proved adaptable to a wide range of climates.

CLIMATIC CONDITIONS

ARID CLIMATES

Acacia adunca
  acinacea
  baileyana
  beckleri
  boormanii
  brachybotrya
  brachystachya
  calamifolia
  cambagei
  colletioides
  coriacea
  cyperophylla
  decora
  doratoxylon
  flexifolia
  gladiiformis
  glandulicarpa
  gracilifolia
  hakeoides
  harpophylla
  iteaphylla
  lasiocalyx
  notabilis
  omalophylla
  oswaldii
  pendula
  peuce
  rigens
  salicina
  sowdenii
  spectabilis
  stenophylla
  tetragonophylla
  uncinata
  victoriae
Actinostrobus acuminatus
  arenarius
Adansonia gregorii
Agonis flexuosa
Albizia basaltica
  procera
Apophyllum anomalum
Atalaya hemiglauca
Atriplex angulata
  acutibractea
  eardleyae
  inflata
  limbata
  nummularia
  rhagodioides
  semibaccata
  spongiosa
  stipitata
  vesicaria
Baeckea behri
Banksia baueri
  caleyi
  elderana
  hookerana
  laevigata ssp. fuscolutea

repens
victoriae
Bassia biflora
  eriacantha
  paradoxa
Beaufortia orbifolia
Bombax ceiba
Brachychiton acerifolium
  discolor
  diversifolium
  gregorii
  paradoxum
  populneum
  rupestre
Callistemon viminalis
Callitris huegelii
  endlicheri
  rhomboidea
  verrucosa
Calocephalus brownii
Calothamnus chrysantherus
  gilesii
  homalophyllus
  quadrifidus
  rupestris
  validus
Capparis lasiantha
  mitchellii
Cassia artemisioides
  nemophila
  sturtii
Casuarina cristata
  decaisneana
  muellerana
  pinaster
Chamaelaucium uncinatum
Cheiranthera cyanea
Clematis microphylla
Clianthus formosus
Cochlospermum fraseri
  gregorii
Conospermum triplinervium
Crinum flaccidum
Cynanchum floribundum
Dodonaea lobulata
Dryandra foliolata
  nobilis
  patens
  quercifolia
Enchylaena tomentosa
Eremaea beaufortioides
  fimbriata
  violacea
Eremophila denticulata
  freelingii
  gilesii
  glabra
  granitica
  latrobei
  longifolia

macdonellii
maculata
mitchellii
pantonii
scoparia
sturtii
Eucalyptus alba
  albens
  angulosa
  annulata
  astringens
  behriana
  brockwayii
  calycogona
  campaspe
  cladocalyx
  clelandii
  cornuta
  crebra
  dichromophloia
  dumosa
  dundasii
  eremophila
  exserta
  flocktoniae
  foecunda
  forrestiana
  froggattii
  gamophylla
  gardneri
  gillii
  gracilis
  incrassata
  kitsoniana
  lansdowneana
  largiflorens
  leucoxylon
  longicornis
  loxophleba
  macrandra
  melanophloia
  melliodora
  microtheca
  occidentalis
  ochrophloia
  odorata
  oleosa
  papuana
  pilligaensis
  platypus
  polybractea
  populnea
  preissiana
  redunca
  salmonophloia
  salubris
  sargentii
  sideroxylon
  spathulata
  steedmanii
  stricklandii
  tessellaris
  tetraptera
  thozetiana

torquata
'Torwood'
viridis
wandoo
websterana
woollsiana
woodwardii
Flindersia maculosa
Frankenia pauciflora
Geijera parviflora
Glischrocaryon behrii
Gossypium sturtianum
Grevillea bracteosa
  eriostachya
  eryngioides
  excelsior
  floribunda
  glauca
  juniperina
  lavandulacea
  macrostylis
  pinaster
  pteridifolia
  robusta
  striata
  tripartita
  vestita
Hakea adnata
  bucculenta
  cinerea
  divaricata
  ednieana
  francisiana
  leucoptera
  multilineata
  orthorrhyncha
  petiolaris
  platysperma
  ruscifolia
  scoparia
  trifurcata
  vittata
Heterodendron oleifolium
Hymenosporum flavum
Isopogon divergens
  formosus
Jasminum lineare
Kunzea affinis
  pauciflora
  preissiana
Lambertia ericifolia
  multiflora
Lasiopetalum behri
  discolor
  schulzenii
Lysiphyllum carronii
Maireana georgei
  sedifolia
  tomentosa
Melaleuca armillaris
  bracteata
  glomerata
  halmaturorum
  lanceolata

277

linophylla
megacephala
nematophylla
pauperiflora
pungens
seriata
uncinata
wilsonii
Melastoma polyanthum
Melia azedarach
Myoporum insulare
montanum
platycarpum
viscosum
Olearia magniflora
pimeleoides
rudis
Owenia acidula
Petalostigma quadriloculare
Petrophile longifolia
serruriae
teretifolia
Phylla nodiflora
Pittosporum phillyreoides
Prostanthera striatiflora
Psoralea patens

Ptilotus manglesii
obovatus
Regelia ciliata
cymbifolia
inops
velutina
Rhagodia nutans
Santalum lanceolatum
Sarcostemma australe
Scaevola ovalifolia
spinescens
Senecio anethifolius
gregorii
magnificus
Solanum sturtianum
Swainsona canescens
galegifolia
greyana
phacoides
stipularis
Templetonia egena
retusa
Teucrium racemosum
Ventilago viminalis
Westringia fruticosa

ferruginea
intermedia
leptophleba
melanophloia
nesophila
pellita
peltata
phoenicea
platyphylla
polycarpa
resinifera
seeana
setosa
shirleyi
tectifera
tereticornis
tessellaris
torelliana
Euodia elleryana
Flindersia australis
brayleana
pubescens
Grevillea hookerana
lanigera
robusta
Hakea gibbosa
lorea
salicifolia
Harpullia pendula
Hibiscus diversifolius
heterophyllus
splendens
Jacksonia scoparia
Kennedia rubicunda
Leptospermum brachyandrum
brevipes
fabricia
flavescens
longifolium

liversidgei
speciosum
squarrosum
Melaleuca argentea
bracteata
decora
hypericifolia
linariifolia
quinquenervia
saligna
symphiocarpa
Melastoma denticulatum
polyanthum
Melia azedarach
Notelaea ovata
Persoonia falcata
Pittosporum revolutum
rhombifolium
undulatum
Pleiogynium solandri
Schefflera actinophylla
Semecarpus australiensis
Sinoga lysicephala
Stenocarpus salignus
sinuatus
Syzygium coolminianum
fibrosum
floribundum
leuhmannii
moorei
Terminalia ferdinandii
melanocarpa
muelleri
sericocarpa
Tristania conferta
laurina
pachysperma
suaveolens

COASTAL AREAS

The following plants are suitable for coastal conditions but will not tolerate severe exposure to salt spray. Those species listed as tolerant of salt spray will also grow under these conditions.

Tropical and Subtropical Regions

Acacia calyculata
holosericea
leptostachya
podalyriifolia
simsii
Acmena smithii
Aleurites moluccana
Alphitonia excelsa
Baeckea camphorata
citriodora
linearis
stenophylla
virgata
Banksia dentata
marginata
robur
serratifolia
spinulosa
Barklya syringifolia
Brachychiton acerifolium
bidwillii
discolor
diversifolium
paradoxum
populneum
Buckinghamia celsissima

Bursaria tenuifolia
Callistemon pachyphyllus
polandii
rigidus
salignus
viminalis
'Tinaroo Hills'
Callitris columellaris
intratropica
Casuarina littoralis
torulosa
Clerodendrum floribundum
tomentosum
Cochlospermum fraseri
gillivraei
Commersonia bartramia
Cordyline stricta
Crotalaria laburnifolia
trifoliastrum
Elaeocarpus reticulatus
Eucalyptus acmenioides
alba
apodophylla
crebra
curtisii
dichromophloia

COASTAL AREAS

Temperate Region

Acacia acinacea
aculeatissima
baileyana
bivenosa
brownii
calamifolia
cochlearis
cognata
continua
cupularis
decipiens
elongata
glaucescens
iteaphylla
ligulata
longifolia
melanoxylon
myrtifolia
nitidula
notabilis

oxycedrus
podalyriifolia
pravissima
prominens
pycnantha
retinodes
saligna
stricta
suaveolens
verticillata
Acrotriche affinis
ramiflora
Actinostrobus pyramidalis
Actinotus helianthii
minor
Adenanthos cuneata
sericea
Agonis floribunda
juniperina
linearifolia

marginata
parviceps
Albizia lophantha
Angophora costata
 floribunda
 hispida
Anigozanthos flavidus
Anthocercis littorea
Apium prostratum
Astroloma conostephioides
 humifusum
 pinifolium
Baeckea astarteoides
 densifolia
 linifolia
 ramosissima
 virgata
Banksia aspleniifolia
 attenuata
 baueri
 baxteri
 coccinea
 dryandroides
 ericifolia
 grandis
 ilicifolia
 lemanniana
 marginata
 nutans
 occidentalis
 prionotes
 pulchella
 quercifolia
 serratifolia
 solandri
 speciosa
 verticillata
Bauera rubioides
Beaufortia schaueri
Billardiera cymosa
 longiflora
 scandens
Boronia clavata
 denticulata
 filifolia
 megastigma
 tetrandra
Bossiaea cinerea
 dentata
Brachysema lanceolatum
 praemorsum
Burtonia conferta
Callistemon citrinus
 linearis
 macropunctatus
 pinifolius
 rigidus
 salignus
 speciosus
 viminalis
Callitris oblonga
 rhomboidea
Calothamnus gilesii
 gracilis

quadrifidus
pinifolius
sanguineus
validus
Calytrix alpestris
 sullivanii
 tetragona
Cassia aciphylla
 artemisioides
Casuarina cristata
 cunninghamiana
 littoralis
 monolifera
 paludosa
 rigida
Chamelaucium sp. Walpole
 ciliatum
 uncinatum
Chorizema cordatum
 diversifolium
 trigonum
Clematis microphylla
 pubescens
Correa baeuerlenii
 lawrenciana
 mannii
 pulchella
Crowea dentata
 exalata
 saligna
Cyathodes juniperina
Dampiera cuneata
 stricta
Darwinia camptostylis
 citriodora
 diosmoides
 fascicularis
 vestita
Dianella revoluta
Dichondra repens
Dillwynia sericea
Dodonaea angustissima
 multijuga
 triquetra
 viscosa
Dryandra cuneata
 formosa
 pteridifolia
 quercifolia
 sessilis
 tenuifolia
Epacris exserta
 impressa
 longiflora
 microphylla
 myrtifolia
 pulchella
Eremophila glabra
Eriostemon myoporoides
 verrucosus
Eucalyptus anceps
 botryoides
 brachycalyx
 burdettiana

calophylla
citriodora
cneorifolia
conglobata
cornuta
cosmophylla
crucis
decurva
desmondensis
diptera
diversifolia
dumosa
eremophila
erythrocorys
eximia
falcata
ficifolia
forrestiana
globulus
grossa
gummifera
haemastoma
incrassata
insularis
kitsoniana
kruseana
lansdowneana
leucoxylon
macrandra
maculata
megacarpa
megacornuta
muellerana
occidentalis
odorata
ovata
pauciflora
perriniana
platypus
polyanthemos
preissiana
pulchella
pulverulenta
rugosa
saligna
scoparia
sepulcralis
sideroxylon
spathulata
steedmanii
stricklandii
tasmanica
tetragona
torquata
viminalis var. racemosa
Eutaxia obovata
 microphylla
Ficus macrophylla
 rubiginosa
Geranium pilosum
Grevillea banksii
 brownii
 buxifolia
 glabrata

juniperina
lanigera
lavandulacea
longifolia
mucronulata
nudiflora
robusta
rosmarinifolia
thelemanniana
tridentifera
tripartita
Hakea bakerana
 ceratophylla
 crassifolia
 cucullata
 elliptica
 ferruginea
 gibbosa
 hookerana
 laurina
 leucoptera
 petiolaris
 purpurea
 rostrata
 rugosa
 salicifolia
 sericea
 trifurcata
 varia
 victoriae
Hardenbergia comptoniana
 violacea
Helichrysum scorpioides
Hibbertia cuneiformis
 cunninghamii
 fasciculata
 sericea
 stricta
Kennedia eximia
 nigricans
 rubicunda
Kunzea parvifolia
Lambertia formosa
Leptospermum flavescens
 juniperina
 petersonii
 scoparium
 squarrosum
Logania crassifolia
 ovata
Melaleuca citrina
 decussata
 densa
 diosmifolia
 elliptica
 fulgens
 globifera
 hypericifolia
 incana
 micromera
 quinquenervia
 thymoides
 violacea
 wilsonii

279

Plant Lists and Glossary

Muehlenbeckia gunnii
Nematolepis phebalioides
Olearia ciliata
  glutinosa
  ramulosa
Patersonia fragilis
  occidentalis
Pelargonium australe
  rodneyanum
Phyla nodiflora
Pimelea rosea
  serpyllifolia
Pittosporum rhombifolium
  undulatum
Pomaderris racemosa
Pultenaea acerosa

obcordata
Regelia ciliata
  velutina
Ricinocarpos glaucus
  pinifolius
Rulingia hermanniifolia
Sollya heterophylla
Spyridum vexilliferum
Stylidium graminifolium
Thryptomene micrantha
  saxicola
Verticordia plumosa
Viminaria juncea
Xanthosia rotundifolia
Zygophyllum billardieri

FROST HARDY

Acacia aculeatissima
  baileyana
  beckleri
  boormanii
  buxifolia
  continua
  cultriformis
  dealbata
  decora
  decurrens
  floribunda
  flexifolia
  howittii
  leptospermoides
  linifolia
  obliquinervia
  oxycedrus
  pravissima
  prominens
  rubida
  spectabilis
  triptera
  verniciflua
  verticillata
  vestita
Asterolasia trymalioides
Astroloma conostephioides
  humifusum
Atriplex nummularia
  rhagodioides
  semibaccata
Baeckea gunniana
  imbricata
  ramosissima
  virgata
Banksia caleyi
  blechnifolia
  ericifolia
  lemanniana
  marginata
  media
  petiolaris
  spinulosa
Bauera rubioides
  sessiliflora

Billardiera longiflora
  scandens
Blandfordia grandiflora
Boronia filifolia
  megastigma
  muelleri
  pinnata
Brachyscome multifida
Callistemon brachyandrus
  citrinus
  macropunctatus
  pallidus
  paludosus
  rigidus
  salignus
  sieberi
  viridiflorus
Callitris oblonga
Calothamnus gilesii
  sanguineus
Calytrix alpestris
  sullivanii
  tetragona
Cassia artemisioides
  nemophila
  sturtii
Casuarina cunninghamiana
  glauca
  littoralis
  microstachya
  muellerana
  paludosa
  pinaster
  stricta
  torulosa
Celmisia asteliifolia
Cheiranthera cyanea
Claytonia australasica
Clematis aristata
Correa alba
  backhousiana
  baeuerlenii
  decumbens
  'Mannii'
  lawrenciana

pulchella
reflexa
sp. 'Pink'
Craspedia glauca
Crowea exalata
Dampiera cuneata
  lanceolata
  rosmarinifolia
  stricta
Darwinia fascicularis
Daviesia latifolia
  virgata
Dianella caerulea
  revoluta
  tasmanica
Dillwynia sericea
Dodonaea boroniifolia
  viscosa
Dryandra baxteri
  calophylla
  formosa
  nobilis
  patens
  polycephala
  runcinata
  sessilis
  tenuifolia
Epacris apiculata
  impressa
  longiflora
  microphylla
  pulchella
Eremophila denticulata
  dichroantha
  gibbifolia
  glabra
  maculata
Eriostemon myoporoides
  verrucosus
Eucalyptus alpina
  behriana
  caesia
  cinerea
  cladocalyx
  coccifera
  cordata
  crenulata
  crucis
  forrestiana
  gardneri
  gillii
  glaucescens
  gracilis
  gunnii
  haemastoma
  kitsoniana
  kruseana
  leucoxylon
  macrandra
  mannifera
  melliodora
  nicholii
  orbifolia
  pauciflora

perriniana
polyanthemos
polybractea
preissiana
pulchella
risdonii
sargentii
scoparia
sideroxylon
spathulata
steedmanii
stellulata
stricklandii
tetragona
tetraptera
torquata
vernicosa
viridis
woodwardii
Goodenia geniculata
  hederacea
  humilis
Goodia lotifolia
Grevillea alpina
  aquifolium
  arenaria
  australis
  barklyana
  baueri
  buxifolia
  'Canberra Gem'
  capitellata
  'Clearview David'
  confertifolia
  'Crosbie Morrison'
  diminuta
  dimorpha
  dryophylla
  floribunda
  ×gaudichaudii
  hookerana
  ilicifolia
  jephcottii
  juniperina
  lanigera
  laurifolia
  lavandulacea
  longifolia
  miqueliana
  oleoides
  parviflora
  'Pink Pearl'
  'Poorinda Constance'
  'Poorinda Elegance'
  'Poorinda Firebird'
  'Poorinda Queen'
  ramosissima
  repens
  rivularis
  rosmarinifolia
  sericea
  speciosa
  steiglitziana
  tridentifera

tripartita
victoriae
Hakea bucculenta
  cinerea
  corymbosa
  elliptica
  eriantha
  francisiana
  lissocarpha
  multilineata
  nodosa
  orthorrhyncha
  petiolaris
  purpurea
  rostrata
  salicifolia
  scoparia
  sericea
  suaveolens
  teretifolia
Hardenbergia violacea
Helichrysum apiculatum
  baxteri
  bracteatum
  semipapposum
Herpolirion novae-zealandiae
Hibbertia aspera
  cistiflora
  empetrifolia
  procumbens
  stricta
  virgata
Hovea lanceolata
Indigofera australis
Isopogon anemonifolius
  anethifolius
Jacksonia scoparia
Kunzea capitata
  parvifolia
  pomifera
Lambertia ericifolia
Leptospermum flavescens
  humifusum
  juniperinum
  lanigerum
  nitidum
  phylicoides
  scoparium
  squarrosum
Lobelia alata
Lomandra filiformis
  glauca
  longifolia
Lomatia fraseri
  ilicifolia
Melaleuca armillaris
  cuticularis
  decussata
  elliptica
  fulgens
  halmaturorum
  incana
  linariifolia
  pungens

squamea
squarrosa
styphelioides
thymifolia
uncinata
wilsonii
Micromyrtus ciliata
Myoporum debile
  parvifolium
Nothofagus cunninghamii
Olearia floribunda
  phlogopappa
Pandorea pandorana
Parahebe derwentiana
  perfoliata
Patersonia fragilis
  occidentalis
Persoonia nutans
  pinifolia
Petrophile sessilis
  squamata
Phebalium glandulosum
  lamprophyllum
Pimelea flava
  glauca
  nivea
Pittosporum phillyreoides
Polyscias sambucifolius
Podocarpus lawrencei
Pomaderris lanigera
Pratia pedunculata
Prostanthera aspalathoides
  cuneata
  denticulata
  lasianthos
  melissifolia
  microphylla
  nivea
  rotundifolia
  spinosa
  walteri
Pultenaea daphnoides
  humilis
  pedunculata
  subalpina
Ranunculus lappaceus
Regelia ciliata
Rhagodia nutans
Scaevola hookeri
Scleranthus biflorus
Stylidium graminifolium
Stypandra caespitosa
  glauca
Telopea oreades
  speciosissima
  truncata
Tetratheca ciliata
  thymifolia
Themeda australis
Thomasia petalocalyx
Thryptomene calycina
  saxicola
Thysanotus tuberosus
Veronica nivea

Viola betonicifolia
  hederacea
Wahlenbergia gloriosa

stricta
Westringia fruticosa
  seniifolia

SALT SPRAY RESISTANT

The following plants are very useful for exposed coastal conditions.

Tropical and Subtropical Regions

Acacia aulacocarpa var.
  macrocarpa
  auriculiformis
  longifolia var. *sophorae*
  mountfordiae
  torulosa
Acanthus ilicifolius
Acronychia imperforata
Adenanthera pavonina
Aegiceras corniculatum
Albizia procera
Alectryon subcinereus
Alstonia actinophylla
  scholaris
Alyogyne pinonianus
Alyxia buxifolia
Araucaria bidwillii
  cunninghamii
Bambusa arnhemica
Banksia ericifolia
  integrifolia
  paludosa
Banksia serrata
Barringtonia asiatica
  speciosa
Bombax ceiba var. *leiocarpa*
Calocephalus brownii
Calophyllum inophyllum
Canarium australianum
Canavalia maritima
Capparis spinosa var. *num-mularia*
Carallia brachiata
Cassia brewsteri
Casuarina equisetifolia
  glauca
  stricta
Cerbera odollam
Clerodendrum inerme
Cocos nucifera
Cordia subcordata
Correa alba
Crinum pedunculatum
Crotalaria cunninghamii
Cupaniopsis anarcardioides
Dillenia alata
Elaeocarpus grandis
Eucalyptus bleeseri
  camaldulensis
  clavigera
  confertiflora
  miniata
  papuana

porrecta
ptychocarpa
robusta
Ficus benjamina
  macrophylla
  microcarpa var. *hillii*
  obliqua
  rubiginosa
  virens
Grevillea banksii
Hibbertia scandens
Hibiscus tiliaceus
Ipomoea pes-caprae
Lagunaria patersonii
Leptospermum laevigatum
Melaleuca armillaris
  dealbata
  lanceolata
  leucadendron
  nervosa
  viridiflora
Mimusops elengii
Morinda citrifolia
Nauclea coadunata
Ochrosia elliptica
Pandanus aquaticus
  pacificus
  pedunculatus
  spiralis
Peltophorum pterocarpum
Pittosporum melanospermum
Planchonia careya
Pongamia pinnata
Scaevola calendulacea
  taccada
Sophora tomentosa
Spinifex hirsutus
Stackhousia spathulata
Stephania japonica var.
  discolor
Sterculia quadrifida
Syncarpia glomulifera
Terminalia catappa
Thespesia populnea
Trichodesma zeylanicum
Triumfettia chaetocarpa
  procumbens
Vigna marina
Vitex ovata 'Purpurea'
  trifolia
Westringia fruticosa

Plant Lists and Glossary

SALT SPRAY RESISTANT

Temperate Region

Acacia cedroides
  cultriformis
  cyclops
  heteroclita
  longifolia var. sophorae
  retinodes
  rostellifera
Acaena anserinifolia
Acrotriche cordata
Adriana klotzschii
  quadripartita
Agonis flexuosa
Alyxia buxifolia
Andersonia sprengelioides
Anthocercis viscosa
Araucaria bidwillii
Astartea fascicularis
Atriplex cinerea
  isatidea
  nummularia
  patula
Banksia integrifolia
  media
  paludosa
  praemorsa
  robur
  serrata
  speciosa
Boronia alata
  albiflora
  tetrandra
Bursaria spinosa
Callistemon pallidus
Callitris columellaris
Calocephalus brownii
Calothamnus villosus
Calystegia soldanella
Carpobrotus modestus
  rossii
Casuarina equisetifolia
  glauca
  humilis
  lehmanniana
  pusilla
  stricta
  thuyoides
Correa alba
  backhousiana
  reflexa
Dianella revoluta
Diplolaena dampieri
Disphyma blackii
Eucalyptus gomphocephala
  lehmannii
  platypus var. heterophylla
  robusta
Ficus macrophylla
  rubiginosa
Hakea clavata
  nitida

oleifolia
  prostrata
  suaveolens
Helichrysum paralium
  scutellifolium
Hibbertia scandens
Ipomoea pes-caprae
Kunzea ambigua
  baxteri
  pomifera
Lagunaria patersonii
Lasiopetalum discolor
  schulzenii
Leptospermum laevigatum
  sericeum
Leucopogon parviflorus
  revolutus
Lhotzkya ericoides
Melaleuca armillaris
  cuticularis
  ericifolia
  halmaturorum
  huegelii
  hypericifolia
  lanceolata
  leucadendron
  nesophila
  pentagona
  polygaloides
  (coastal form)
  squarrosa
Muehlenbeckia adpressa
Myoporum insulare
  parvifolium
  serratum
  viscosum
Olearia axillaris
Pimelea dichotoma
  ferruginea
Phebalium rude
Rhagodia baccata
  radiata
  spinescens
Salicornia australis
Samolus repens
Scaevola calendulacea
  crassifolia
Selliera radicans
Senecio lautus
Spinifex hirsutus
Stackhousia spathulata
Stephania japonica
Swainsonia lessertifolia
Tetragonia implexicoma
Templetonia retusa
Thomasia petalocalyx
Vitex ovata 'Purpurea'
Westringia dampieri
  fruticosa

The papery fruits of *Dodonaea lobulata* are borne on female plants.

W.R. Elliot photo

SHADY, DRY POSITIONS

Acacia acinacea
  aculeatissima
  alata
  aspera
  baileyana
  boormanii
  brownii
  buxifolia
  cardiophylla
  cultriformis
  decora
  fimbriata
  glaucoptera
  gracilifolia
  howittii
  iteaphylla
  linearis
  longifolia
  longifolia var. sophorae
  mitchellii
  mucronata
  pentadenia
  pravissima
  retinodes
  riceana
  steedmanii
  stricta
  suaveolens
  triptera
  ulicifolia
  venulosa
  verniciflua
  verticillata
Acrotriche prostrata
  serrulata

Actinostrobus acuminatus
  pyramidalis
Angophora hispida
Asplenium australasicum
  bulbiferum
  nidus
Astroloma humifusum
  pallidum
Baeckea behrii
  densiflora
  virgata
Banksia asplenifolia
  caleyi
  dryandroides
  integrifolia
  lemanniana
  marginata
  media
  robur
  spinulosa
Billardiera cymosa
  longiflora
  scandens
Blechnum cartilagineum
Boronia anemonifolia
  crenulata
  filifolia
  fraseri
  gracilipes
  molloyae
  muelleri
  pinnata
Bossiaea disticha
  linophylla
Brachyloma ericoides

282

Pittosporum rhombifolium has sweetly perfumed flowers, followed by masses of small orange berries.

W.R. Elliot photo

Australia has several species of *Gardenia*, all of which have sweetly perfumed flowers — **Gardenia** species Cape York.

D.L. Jones photo

Cycads bear large interesting woody fruits — *Lepidozamia peroffskyana*.

D.L. Jones photo

The light climbing *Billardiera* from King Island, Tasmania has succulent berries.

W.R. Elliot photo

Plant Lists and Glossary

Brachysema aphyllum
  lanceolatum
  praemorsum
Bursaria spinosa
Callitris columellaris
  oblonga
  rhomboidea
  verrucosa
Calothamnus quadrifidus
  sanguineus
Calytrix alpestris
  sullivanii
  tetragona
Cassia aciphylla
Casuarina humilis
  lehmanniana
  littoralis
  muellerana
  paludosa
  pusilla
Chorizema cordatum
Christella dentata
Comesperma ericinum
  volubile
Cordyline stricta
Correa alba
  backhousiana
  baeuerlenii
  calycina
  decumbens
  glabra
  lawrenciana
  reflexa
  schlechtendalii
Crowea exalata
Culcita dubia
Cyathea australis
Darwinia fascicularis
  taxifolia
Daviesia acicularis
  brevifolia
  latifolia
  virgata
Dianella caerulea
  revoluta
Dichondra repens
Dichopogon fimbriatus
  strictus
Dillwynia hispida
  sericea
Dodonaea adenophora
Doodia aspera
  caudata
  media
Dryandra drummondii
  nivea
  pteridifolia
Eremophila calorhabdos
  glabra (prostrate forms)
Eriostemon buxifolius
  hispidulus
  myoporoides
  nodiflorus
  pungens

verrucosus
Eucalyptus alpina
  cneorifolia
  cosmophylla
  deformis
  haemastoma
  kitsoniana
  ligustrina
  pauciflora
  pulverulenta
  radiata
  stellulata
Eutaxia cuneata
  microphylla
  obovata
Gahnia sieberana
Gompholobium huegelii
  latifolium
Goodenia amplexans
  lanata
  ovata
  varia
Goodia lotifolia
Grevillea alpina
  anethifolius
  aquifolium
  arenaria
  buxifolia
  brevicuspis
  capitellata
  crithmifolia
  diminuta
  dimorpha
  dryophylla
  evansii
  floribunda
  glabrata
  ilicifolia
  insignis
  jephcottii
  juniperina
  lanigera
  microstegia
  miqueliana
  mucronulata
  occidentalis
  pauciflora
  pilulifera
  polybractea
  ramosissima
  repens
  rogersii
  rosmarinifolia
  sericea
  shiressii
  sphacelata
  steiglitziana
  triloba
  victoriae
Hakea baxteri
  costata
  cristata
  cyclocarpa
  dactyloides

erinacea
gibbosa
invaginata
lissocarpha
nitida
nodosa
orthorrhyncha
prostrata
pycnoneura
rostrata
salicifolia
scoparia
sericea
suaveolens
subsulcata
sulcata
trifurcata
ulicina
undulata
varia
Hardenbergia violacea
Helichrysum diotophyllum
  obcordatum
Hibbertia cistiflora
  cuneiformis
  dentata
  empetrifolia
  exutiacies
  fasciculata
  scandens
  stricta
Histiopteris incisa
Homoranthus flavescens
Hovea heterophylla
  lanceolata
Indigofera australis
Isopogon anemonifolius
  anethifolius
Jacksonia furcellata
  scoparia
  sericea
Kennedia beckxiana
  macrophylla
  nigricans
  rubicunda
Kunzea capitata
  pomifera
Lambertia formosa
  uniflora
Lasiopetalum behri
  discolor
  schultzenii
Lastreopsis acuminata
  microsora
Lepidosperma elatius
Lomandra filiformis
  glauca
  longifolia
Lomatia ilicifolia
  silaifolia
Melaleuca armillaris
  decussata
  diosmifolia
  hypericifolia

radula
wilsonii
Mirbelia oxyloboides
Morinda jasminoides
Myoporum debile
  floribundum
  insulare
  parvifolium
  viscosum
Olearia teretifolia
Oxylobium lanceolatum
Pandorea pandorana
Pelargonium rodneyanum
Persoonia nutans
  pinifolium
Petrophile serruriae
  sessilis
Phebalium bilobum
  bullatum
  glandulosum
  lamprophyllum
  squameum
  squamulosum
Pimelea ferruginea
  nivea
Polystichum proliferum
Pomaderris aspera
  ferruginea
  lanigera
  pilifera
Prostanthera aspalathoides
  baxteri
  behriana
  calycina
  chlorantha
  denticulata
  lanceolata
  microphylla
  spinosa
  stricta
  violacea
  walteri
Pterostylis concinna
  nutans
  pedunculata
Pultenaea costata
  flexilis
  graveolens
  gunnii
  humilis
  laxiflora
  pedunculata
  weindorferi
Regelia ciliata
  cymbifolia
  inops
  megacephala
Rhagodia nutans
Sollya heterophylla
Sphaerolobium vimineum
Templetonia retusa
Thomasia macrocarpa
  petalocalyx
Viola hederacea

Westringia crassifolia	*linifolia*
fruticosa	*rigida*

SHADY, WET POSITIONS

Acacia axillaris
cognata
elongata
extensa
fimbriata
floribunda
howittii
leprosa
pravissima
riceana
verniciflua
verticillata
Actinostrobus pyramidalis
Adriana glabrata
Agonis hypericifolia
juniperina
parviceps
spathulata
Archontophoenix cunninghamii
Astartea fascicularis
heteranthera
Atherosperma moschatum
Athyrium assimile
australe
Baeckea crenatifolia
linifolia
utilis
virgata
Banksia robur
spinulosa
Bauera rubioides
sessiliflora
Baumea juncea
Beaufortia decussata
sparsa
Bedfordia arborescens
salicina
Billardiera bignoniacea
longiflora
scandens
Blechnum camfieldii
chambersii
fluviatile
minus
nudum
patersonii
wattsii
Boronia megastigma
muelleri
parviflora
Bursaria spinosa
Callicoma serratifolia
Callistemon citrinus
comboynensis
pallidus
paludosus
salignus
shiressii

sieberi
viminalis
viridiflorus
Callitris macleayana
Calothamnus quadrifidus
Calytrix alpestris
Carex fascicularis
Casuarina humilis
paludosa
pusilla
rigida
Celastrus australis
Ceratopetalum apetalum
gummiferum
Chorizandra enodis
Claytonia australasica
Clematis aristata
glycinioides
pubescens
Coprosma quadrifida
Cordyline stricta
Correa aemula
calycina
lawrenciana
reflexa
Cyathea australis
celebica
leichhardtiana
Darwinia diosmoides
Dennstaedtia davallioides
Dianella coerulea
revoluta
tasmanica
Dichopogon strictus
Dicksonia antarctica
youngiae
Diplarrena moraea
Dodonaea humifusa
procumbens
viscosa
Doryphora sassafrass
Elaeocarpus reticulatus
Epacris apiculata
breviflora
gracialis
lanuginosa
microphylla
obtusifolia
paludosa
virgata
Eriostemon myoporoides
Eucalyptus bancroftii
camphora
coccifera
crenulata
elata
globulus
grandis

kitsoniana
obliqua
ovata
parvifolia
pulchella
regnans
risdonii
spathulata
stellulata
tasmanica
urnigera
viminalis
Eucryphia lucida
milliganii
Eupomatia laurina
Ficus stephanocarpa
Gahnia clarkei
radula
sieberana
trifida
Goodenia elongata
hederacea
humilis
ovata
Goodia lotifolia
Grevillea barklyana
rivularis
shiressii
victoriae
Hakea eriantha
nodosa
Hedycarya angustifolia
Helmholtzia acorifolia
Hibbertia dentata
scandens
Histiopteris incisa
Howittia trilocularis
Hypolepis australis
muelleri
rugosula
Indigofera australis
Isotoma fluviatilis
Juncus spp.
Kennedia rubicunda
Kunzea ericifolia
muelleri
parvifolia
recurva
Lastreopsis acuminata
decomposita
hispida
marginans
microsora
munita
smithiana
Leptopteris fraseri
Leptospermum flavescens
humifusum
juniperinum
lanigerum
nitidum
petersonii
phylicoides
rotundifolium

scoparium
squarrosum
Libertia pulchella
Livistona chinensis
Lobelia alata
Lomatia fraseri
myricoides
Mazus pumilio
Melaleuca armillaris
decora
decussata
ericifolia
hamulosa
hypericifolia
leucadendron
linariifolia
nesophila
nodosa
ovaria
raphiophylla
spicigera
squamea
squarrosa
styphelioides
thymifolia
violacea
Mentha australis
diemenica
Micromyrtus ciliata
Morinda jasminoides
Nothofagus cunninghamii
Olearia argophylla
argophylla 'Variegata'
astrotricha
dentata
floribunda
iodochroa
lirata
obcordata
phlogopappa
teretifolia
Orthrosanthus laxus
multiflorus
Pandorea jasminoides
pandorana
Parsonsia brownii
Passiflora cinnabarina
Patersonia occidentalis
Phebalium lamprophyllum
Pimelea axiflora
Pittosporum bicolor
undulatum
Polyscias elegans
sambucifolius
Polystichum proliferum
Pomaderris aspera
Pratia pedunculata
Prostanthera hirtula
lasianthos
Pteris tremula
umbrosa
Ranunculus lappaceus
robertsonii
Rumohra adiantiformis

Plant Lists and Glossary

Scaevola aemula
  hookeri
  pallida
Scirpus nodosus
Selliera radicans
Smilax australis
  glyciphylla
Stenocarpus sinuatus
Stephania japonica

Syzygium coolminianum
  paniculata
Todea barbara
Tristania conferta
  laurina
Viola betonicifolia
  hederacea
  sieberana
Westringia fruticosa

WIND RESISTANT

The following plants have proved to be valuable for resisting strong winds and some have even survived cyclones successfully.

Tropical and Subtropical Areas

Acmena smithii
Alectryon subcinereus
Alstonia scholaris
Archontophoenix alexandrae
  cunninghamii
Baeckea virgata
Barringtonia speciosa
Callistemon formosus
  polandii
  viminalis
  'Tinaroo Hills'
Callitris columellaris
Calophyllum inophyllum
Castanospermum australe
Casuarina cunninghamiana
  equisetifolia
  inophloia
  littoralis
Cerbera odollam
Cocos nucifera
Cordia subcordata
Cupaniopsis anarcardioides
Eucalyptus tereticornis

tessellaris
Hibiscus tiliaceus
Leptospermum brachyandrum
  fabricia
  flavescens
  longifolium
Livistona australis
  benthamii
  drudei
  muelleri
Melaleuca argentea
  bracteata
  leucadendron
  linariifolia
Melia azedarach
Normanbya normanbyana
Ochrosia elliptica
Pandanus pedunculatus
Stenocarpus sinuatus
Sterculia quadrifida
Terminalia catappa
Vitex ovata

WIND RESISTANT

Temperate Region

Acacia adunca
  boormanii
  calamifolia
  cedroides
  cochlearis
  cupularis
  cyclops
  decipiens
  elata
  floribunda
  heteroclita
  howittii
  longifolia
  longifolia var. sophorae

  pendula
  penninervis
  pravissima
  prominens
  rigens
  rostellifera
  rubida
  salicina
  saligna
Acrotriche cordata
  ramiflora
Agonis flexuosa
  marginata
Alyxia buxifolia

Andersonia sprengelioides
Angophora costata
  floribunda
  hispida
  melanoxylon
Araucaria bidwillii
Astartea fascicularis
Atriplex cinerea
  nummularia
Baeckea diosmoides
Banksia attenuata
  integrifolia
  lemanniana
  marginata
  media
  praemorsa
  prostrata
  quercifolia var. integrifolia
  repens
  serrata
Boronia alata
  albiflora
  tetrandra
Bossiaea dentata
Burtonia conferta
Callistemon brachyandrus
  citrinus
  macropunctatus
  pallidus
  paludosus
  phoeniceus
  salignus
  shiressii
  sieberi
  viridiflorus
Callitris columellaris
  oblonga
  rhomboidea
  verrucosa
Calothamnus gilesii
  pinifolius
  quadrifidus
  rupestris
  sanguineus
  villosus
Carpobrotus modestus
  rossii
Casuarina cristata
  cunninghamiana
  glauca
  paludosa
  rigida
  stricta
Chorizema trigonum
Correa alba
  backhousiana
  glabra
  reflexa
Darwinia citriodora
  diosmoides
Dillwynia pungens
Disphyma clavellatum
Dodonaea adenophora
  ceratocarpa

Dryandra formosa
  pteridifolia
  quercifolia
  sessilis
  tenuifolia
Eucalyptus acaciaeformis
  alpina
  aggregata
  annulata
  archeri
  astringens
  behriana
  blakelyi
  botryoides
  burdettiana
  calycogona
  camaldulensis
  cinerea
  cladocalyx
  cneorifolia
  cornuta
  cosmophylla
  crebra
  crenulata
  dawsonii
  dealbata
  deanei
  decurva
  delegatensis
  dumosa
  dundasii
  elata
  eremophila
  flocktoniae
  foecunda
  forrestiana
  gardneri
  glaucescens
  globulus
  gomphocephala
  gracilis
  grossa
  gummifera
  incrassata
  johnstonii
  kitsoniana
  lansdowneana
  largiflorens
  lehmannii
  leucoxylon
  longicornis
  loxophleba
  macrandra
  macrorhyncha
  maculata
  megacarpa
  melliodora
  microcarpa
  mitrata
  muellerana
  neglecta
  nutans
  obliqua
  occidentalis

Ferns are renowned for their decorative foliage, and the new fronds of some species are bright pink — *Blechnum wattsii*.

W.R. Elliot photo

A variegated form of *Agonis flexuosa* is highly prized as a foliage plant.

D.L. Jones photo

Many rainforest plants have decorative foliage, and flushes of colourful new growth — *Brackenridgea nitida*.

D.L. Jones photo

The colourful foliage of *Hakea victoriae* is only apparent on mature plants.

W.R. Elliot photo

Plant Lists and Glossary

Eucalyptus orbifolia
  ovata
  paniculata
  parvifolia
  pauciflora
  pellita
  perriniana
  platypus
  polyanthemos
  polybractea
  porosa
  preissiana
  pulchella
  pulverulenta
  pyriformis
  radiata
  rhodantha
  risdonii
  robusta
  rubida
  rupicola
  saligna
  salmonophloia
  salubris
  sargentii
  scoparia
  sideroxylon
  sieberi
  socialis
  spathulata
  steedmanii
  stellulata
  stoatei
  striaticalyx
  stricta
  tasmanica
  tetragona
  urnigera
  viminalis
  viridis
  wandoo
  youngiana
Eutaxia obovata
Ficus macrophylla
  rubiginosa
Geijera parviflora
Grevillea concinna
  confertifolia
  glabella
  lavandulacea
  nudiflora
  paniculata
  robusta
  rosmarinifolia
  tripartita
Hakea ceratophylla
  corymbosa
  crassifolia
  elliptica
  eriantha
  nitida
  nodosa
  prostrata
  pycnoneura

  salicifolia
  suaveolens
  ulicina
  victoriae
  vittata
Hibbertia cuneiformis
  cunninghamii
Jacksonia compressa
  scoparia
Kennedia coccinea
  eximia
  nigricans
  rubicunda
Kunzea ambigua
  baxteri
  muelleri
  pauciflora
  pomifera
Lagunaria patersonii
Lambertia ericifolia
  formosa
Lasiopetalum baueri
  discolor
  schulzenii
Leptospermum flavescens
  'Horizontalis'
  humifusum
  laevigatum
  lanigerum
  nitidum
  phylicoides
  scoparium
  sericeum
Leucopogon parviflorus
  revolutus
Lhotzkya ericoides
Melaleuca acuminata
  alternifolia
  armillaris
  bracteata
  citrina
  crassifolia
  decussata
  diosmifolia
  elliptica
  ericifolia
  fulgens
  gibbosa
  globifera
  glomerata
  halmaturorum
  huegelii
  hypericifolia
  lanceolata
  lateritia
  linariifolia
  neglecta
  nesophila
  pentagona
  polygaloides
  quinquenervia
  radula
  squarrosa
  styphelioides

  wilsonii
Myoporum insulare
  montanum
  platycarpum
  viscosum
Phebalium rude
  squameum
Pittosporum bicolor
  phillyreoides
  undulatum
Podocarpus elatus
  lawrencei
Pultenaea obcordata

Regelia ciliata
  velutina
Rhagodia spinescens
Ricinocarpos glaucus
Scaevola crassifolia
Sollya heterophylla
Syncarpia glomulifera
Templetonia retusa
Tristania conferta
  laurina
Westringia dampieri
  fruticosa

Melaleuca styphelioides, with its papery bark.

288

SPECIFIC USES AND FEATURES

AVENUE TREES

Tropical and Subtropical Regions

Acacia auriculiformis
  bakeri
  elata
  torulosa
Acmena australis
  graveolens
  hemilampra
  smithii
Acronychia acidula
Adansonia gregorii
Agathis microstachya
  robusta
Albizia canescens
  procera
  thozetiana
  toona
  xanthoxylon
Aleurites moluccana
Alstonia actinophylla
  scholaris
Araucaria bidwillii
  cunninghamii
Archontophoenix alexandrae
  cunninghamii
Argyrodendron actinophyllum
  peralatum
  polyandrum
  trifoliolatum
Austromyrtus bidwillii
Backhousia anisata
  bancroftii
  hughesii
Banksia integrifolia
Barringtonia asiatica
Beilschmiedia bancroftii
  elliptica
  obtusifolia
Brachychiton acerifolium
  discolor
  diversifolium
  populneum
Callistemon salignus
  viminalis
Callitris columellaris
  macleayana
  intratropica
Calophyllum inophyllum
Canarium australianum
Castanospermum australe
Casuarina cunninghamii
  equisetifolia
  glauca
  inophloia
  torulosa
Ceratopetalum apetalum
Cryptocarya obovata
Doryphora sassafrass

Elaeocarpus bancroftii
  grandis
Erythrina indica
  verspertilio
Erythrophleum chlorostachys
Eucalyptus alba
  bancroftii
  bigalerita
  bleeseri
  citriodora
  clavigera
  confertiflora
  grandis
  maculata
  miniata
  papuana
  sideroxylon
  tereticornis
  tessellaris
  torelliana
Eugenia eucalyptoides
Ficus benjamina
  destruens
  macrophylla
  microcarpa var. hillii
  obliqua
  rubiginosa
  watkinsiana
Flindersia australis
  bourjotiana
  brayleana
  schottiana
Grevillea hilliana
  pinnatifida
  robusta
Harpullia pendula
Melaleuca argentea
  leucadendron
  linariifolia
  quinquenervia
  styphelioides
  symphiocarpa
  viridiflora
Livistona australis
  benthamii
Melia azedarach
Nauclea coadunata
Oreocallis wickhamii
Podocarpus amarus
  elatus
Rhodosphaera rhodanthema
Stenocarpus sinuatus
Sterculia quadrifida
Syncarpia procera
Syzygium cormiflorum
  floribundum
  moorei

Terminalia catappa
Toona australis

Tristania conferta
  neriifolia
Xanthostemon chrysanthus

AVENUE TREES

Temperate Regions

Acacia dealbata
  decurrens
  elata
  melanoxylon
  salicina
Acmena smithii
Agathis robusta
Angophora costata
  floribunda
  melanoxylon
  woodsiana
Araucaria bidwillii
  cunninghamii
Archontophoenix
  cunninghamii
Argyrodendron actinophyllum
Banksia integrifolia
Brachychiton acerifolium
  discolor
  populneum
Callitris columellaris
  huegelii
  endlicheri
Casuarina cunninghamii
  fraserana
  huegeliana
  luehmannii
  stricta
  torulosa
Eucalyptus amygdalina
  astringens
  bancroftii
  camaldulensis
  chapmaniana
  citriodora
  cladocalyx
  crenulata

  dawsonii
  globulus
  grandis
  gummifera
  largiflorens
  leucoxylon
  maculata
  maculosa
  maidenii
  melliodora
  nicholii
  nitens
  pauciflora
  pulchella
  radiata
  regnans
  risdonii
  rubida
  saligna
  sideroxylon
  sieberana
  smithii
  spathulata
  tereticornis
  viminalis
Ficus macrophylla
  rubiginosa
  watkinsiana
Grevillea robusta
Melaleuca decora
  linariifolia
  styphelioides
Livistona australis
Melia azedarach
Syzygium floribundum
Tristania conferta

BOG GARDENS

Acacia elongata
  extensa
  riceana
  verticillata
Abrotanella spp.
Agonis juniperina
  parviceps
Alisma plantago-aquatica
Asperula conferta
Asplenium flabellifolium
Arthropodium milleflorum
Astelia alpina
  nervosa

Athyrium australe
  japonicum
Baeckea crenatifolia
  gunniana
  utilis
Banksia robur
Bauera rubioides
Blandfordia grandiflora
  nobilis
  punicea
Blechnum camfieldii
  cartilagineum
  fluviatile

289

Plant Lists and Glossary

Blechnum indicum
  minus
  nudum
  penna-marina
  wattsii
Boronia megastigma
  muelleri
  parviflora
  polygalifolia
Bossiaea foliosa
  riparia
Brachycome aculeata
  cardiocarpa
  multifida
  scapigera
Brasenia schreberi
Bulbine bulbosa
Burchardia umbellata
Callicoma serratifolia
Callistemon citrinus
  linearis
  paludosus
  salignus
  viminalis
Caltha introloba
Calytrix tetragona
Carex fascicularis
  gaudichaudiana
  inversa
Casuarina cunninghamiana
  cristata
  equisetifolia
  glauca
  lehmanniana
  obesa
  paludosa
  pusilla
  thuyoides
Celmisia asteliifolia
Ceratopteris thalictroides
Chamaescilla corymbosa
Christella dentata
Claytonia australasica
Cotula alpina
  coronopifolia
  filicula
  reptans
Craspedia glauca
  globifera
Cyathea australis
  celebica
Cynoglossum australe
Cyperus exaltatus
Dianella caerulea
  tasmanica
Dichondra repens
Diplarrena moraea
Dodonaea humifusa
  procumbens
Dracophyllum secundum
Drosera auriculata
  binata
  peltata
  whittakeri

Elaeocarpus reticulatus
Eleocharis sphacelata
Epacris brevifolia
  exserta
  gunnii
  impressa
  lanuginosa
  microphylla
  obtusifolia
  paludosa
  petrophila
  pulchella
  robusta
  serpyllifolia
Eucalyptus aggregata
  bancroftii
  botryoides
  camaldulensis
  camphora
  cordata
  cosmophylla
  crenulata
  globulus
  grandis
  gunnii
  kitsoniana
  largiflorens
  occidentalis
  ovata
  pauciflora
  pulchella
  robusta
  spathulata
  tenuiramis
  urnigera
Eucryphia lucida
  milliganii
Eupomatia laurina
Frankenia pauciflora
Gentianella diemensis
Gleichenia dicarpa
  microphylla
  rupestris
Gnaphalium argentifolium
Goodenia elongata
  hederacea
  humilis
  ovata
Goodia lotifolia
Grevillea acanthifolia
  australis
  confertifolia
  rivularis
  shiressii
Hakea bakerana
  nodosa
  salicifolia
  sericea
  ulicina
Herpolirion novae-zealandiae
Hibbertia procumbens
  serpyllifolia
Histiopteris incisa
Howittia trilocularis

The smooth white bark of *Eucalyptus citriodora*.

The flaking bark of *Eucalyptus maculata*.

290

Hypolepis distans
  muelleri
  punctata
  rugosula
Hypoxis glabella
Isophysis tasmanica
Isotoma fluviatilis
Juncus australis
  pallidus
  polyanthemos
Kunzea capitata
  ericifolia
  micromera
  muelleri
  parvifolia
  recurva
Leptospermum juniperinum
  lanigerum
  phylicoides
Libertia paniculata
  pulchella
Lindsaea linearis
Lobelia alata
  quadrangularis
Ludwigia peploides
Lycopodium laterale
Marsilea drummondii
  mutica
Mazus pumilio
Melaleuca alternifolia
  armillaris
  bracteata
  cuticularis
  decora
  decussata
  densa
  ericifolia
  gibbosa
  halmaturorum
  hamulosa
  hypericifolia
  lanceolata
  lateritia
  leucadendron
  linariifolia
  microphylla
  minutifolia
  nesophila
  nodosa
  preissiana
  pustulata
  quinquenervia
  radula
  rhaphiophylla
  squamea
  squarrosa
  styphelioides
  suberosa
  thymifolia
  viminea
  violacea
  viridiflora
  wilsonii
Mentha australis

  diemenica
  laxiflora
Myriophyllum elatinoides
  propinquum
Nothofagus cunninghamii
  gunnii
Olearia asterotricha
  dentata
  glandulosa
  iodochroa
  lirata
  myrsinoides
  phlogopappa
  ramulosa
  stellulata
Oreomyrrhis argentea
Orthrosanthus laxus
  multiflorus
Oxalis lactea
Parahebe derwentiana
  nivea
Patersonia fragilis
  occidentalis
Pimelea glauca
  humilis
Platylobium formosum
Polyscias sambucifolius
Polystichum formosum
  proliferum
Pomaderris apetala
  aspera
Pratia pedunculata
  purpurascens
  surrepens
Prostanthera decussata
  hirtula
  lasianthos
  melissifolia
  phylicifolia
  rhombea
  rugosa
  stricta
  walteri
Pteris tremula
  umbrosa
Pultenaea fasciculata
  juniperina
  subumbellata
  weindorferi
Ranunculus collinus
  gunnianus
  monticola
  rivularis
  trichophyllus
Restio australis
  tetraphyllus
Richea continentis
  dracophylla
  scoparia
Sambucus australasica
Samolus repens
Scaevola aemula
  albida
  hookeri

Scleranthus biflorus
  singuliflorus
Selaginella australiensis
  uliginosa
Selliera radicans
Senecio linearifolius
Sowerbaea juncea
Sprengelia incarnata
Spyridium parvifolium
Stylidium graminifolium
Symphionema montanum
Todea barbara
Triglochin procera
  striata
Tristania laurina
  neriifolia

Typha angustifolia
Utricularia aurea
  dichotoma
Villarsia exaltata
  reniformis
Viola betonicifolia
  hederacea
  sieberana
Wahlenbergia communis
  gloriosa
  saxicola
Westringia rubiifolia
  seniifolia
Wittsteinia vacciniacea
Xyris operculata

CONTAINER PLANTS

Acacia aculeatissima
  alata
  amblygona
  ericifolia
  flexifolia
  glaucoptera
  pravissima
  'Golden Carpet'
  pulchella
  varia var. affinis
Actinodium cunninghamii
Actinotus helianthi
Agapetes meiniana
Agonis flexuosa 'Variegata'
Alocasia macrorrhiza
Anigozanthos bicolor
  flavidus
  humilis
  manglesii
  pulcherrimus
  rufus
  viridis
Anopterus glandulosus
  macleayanus
Archontophoenix alexandrae
  cunninghamii
Asplenium australasicum
  bulbiferum
  nidus
  simplicifrons
Asterolasia trymalioides
Astroloma ciliatum
  conostephioides
  humifusum
Baeckea crassifolia
Banksia brownii
  canei
  laricina
  petiolaris
  prostrata
  pulchella
  repens
  sphaerocarpa
  violacea

Beaufortia elegans
  heterophylla
  purpurea
  schaueri
Blandfordia flammea
  nobilis
Blechnum camfieldii
  nudum
  wurunuran
Boronia anemonifolia
  crenulata
  filifolia
  megastigma
  molloyae
  pilosa
  serrulata
Billardiera cymosa
  longiflora
Bossiaea aquifolium
  dentata
Brachyscome multifida
Brachychiton populneum
  rupestre
Brachysema latifolium
  sericeum
Buckinghamia celsissima
Calamus australis
  caryotoides
Calectasia cyanea
Callistemon 'Mauve Mist'
  'Reeves Pink'
  sieberi
  subulatus
  viminalis
  'Captain Cook'
  viridiflorus
Callitris huegelii
  intratropica
  oblonga
  rhomboidea
Calothamnus gibbosus
  gracilis
  planifolius
  sanguineus

The thick, brown, scaly bark of *Casuarina cunninghamiana*.

villosus
Calytrix aurea
 fraseri
 glutinosa
 sapphirina
 tenuifolia
Carpentaria acuminata
Caryota rumphiana
Cassia artemisioides
Celmisia asteliifolia
Chamelaucium sp. Walpole
 megalopetalum
 uncinatum
Cheiranthera cyanea
Chorizema aciculare
 dicksonii
 reticulatum
Conospermum amoenum
 stoechadis
Conostylis bealiana
 juncea
 setigera
 stylidioides
Cordyline stricta
Correa baeuerlenii
 decumbens
 'Mannii'
 pulchella
 reflexa
Crowea dentata
 exalata
 saligna
Cyathea australis
 cooperi
 woollsiana

Cyathodes juniperina
Cymbidium madidum
Dampiera diversifolia
 fasciculata
 glabriflora
 linearis
 rosmarinifolia
 teres
Danthonia pallida
Darwinia citriodora
 collina
 lejostyla
 meeboldii
 rhadinophylla
 taxifolia
Dendrobium delicatum
 kingianum
 speciosum
Dianella tasmanica
Dichopogon strictus
Dicksonia antarctica
 youngiae
Dodonaea boroniifolia
 humifusum
 procumbens
Doodia aspera
 media
Doryanthes excelsa
 palmeri
Dryandra calophylla
 foliosissima
 pteridifolia
 speciosa
 tenuifolia
Epacris impressa

longiflora
pulchella
reclinata
Eremaea beaufortioides
 violacea
Eremophila dichroantha
 gibbifolia
 granitica
 oppositifolia
Eriostemon australasius
 nodiflorus
 pungens
 spicatus
Eucalyptus caesia
 erythrocorys
 forrestiana
 grossa
 kruseana
 orbifolia
 perriniana
 preissiana
 torquata
 vernicosa
Eucryphia lucida
Eupomatia laurina
Ficus rubiginosa
 'Variegata'
Gompholobium ecostatum
 huegelii
Goodenia geniculata
 lanata
Gossypium sturtianum
Grevillea alpina
 banksii
 baueri
 bipinnatifida
 brownii
 chrysophaea
 confertifolia
 dimorpha
 dryandri
 endlicherana
 floribunda
 flexuosa
 ×gaudichaudii
 glabella
 intricata
 lanigera
 laurifolia
 lavandulacea
 miqueliana
 muelleri
 nudiflora
 pilulifera
 pulchella
 sericea
 speciosa
 steiglitziana
 thyrsoides
 wilsonii
Hakea costata
 lehmanniana
 myrtoides
 pupurea

Halgania cyanea
Helichrysum baxteri
 bracteatum
 leucopsidium
Helipterum roseum
Helmholtzia acorifolia
Hemiandra pungens
Hibbertia dentata
 empetrifolia
 fascicularis
 obtusifolia
 procumbens
 stellaris
 virgata
Homoranthus flavescens
Hovea chorizemifolia
 heterophylla
 longipes
 pungens
 trisperma
Hymenosporum flavum
Hypocalymma angustifolium
 cordifolium 'Golden Veil'
 puniceum
 robustum
 speciosum
Isopogon cuneatus
 divergens
 formosus
 latifolius
Isotoma axillaris
Kennedia microphylla
Kunzea affinis
 parvifolia
 preissiana
Laccospadix australasicus
Lambertia inermis
 multiflora
Lastreopsis marginans
 microsora
 smithiana
Lasiopetalum behrii
Lechenaultia biloba
 formosa
 laricina
 tubiflora
Leptospermum nitidum
 'Copper Sheen'
 scoparium var.
 rotundifolium
Libertia paniculata
 pulchella
Licuala ramsayi
Livistona australis
 drudei
 muelleri
Lomandra glauca
 longifolia
Melaleuca cordata
 incana
 micromera
 nematophylla
 polycephala
 pulchella

spathulata
thymifolia
violacea
wilsonii
Micromyrtus ciliata
Myoporum debile
floribundum
parvifolium
Olearia ciliata
iodochroa
phlogopappa
Orthrosanthus laxus
multiflorus
Patersonia fragilis
occidentalis
Petrophile biloba
squamata
Phebalium bullatum
lamprophyllum
Philotheca salsolifolia
Pimelea ferruginea
spectabilis
Platytheca verticillata
Podocarpus lawrencei
spinosus
Polystichum proliferum
Prostanthera aspalathoides
calycina
cuneata
incana
microphylla
spinosa
violacea
Pteris tremula
tripartita
umbrosa
Ptilotus obovatus
Ptychosperma elegans
Pultenaea cunninghamii
graveolens
humilis

pedunculata
polifolia
Regelia inops
Restio tetraphyllus
Rhododendron lochae
Scaevola hookeri
striata
Schefflera actinophylla
versteegii
Scleranthus biflorus
Sowerbaea juncea
Spyridium cinereum
parvifolium
vexilliferum
Stylidium graminifolium
humilis
laricifolium
preissii
spathulatum
uniflorum
Stypandra caespitosa
Symphionema montanum
Syzygium leuhmannii
Telopea speciosissima
Tetratheca ciliata
thymifolia
Themeda australis
Thryptomene baeckeacea
strongylophylla
Thysanotus multiflorus
Verticordia chrysantha
insignis
mitchelliana
monodelpha
plumosa
Viola hederacea
sieberana
Wahlenbergia gloriosa
saxicola
Xanthorrhoea australis
Xanthosia rotundifolia

rhetinocarpa
spectabilis
terminalis
trigonophylla
triptera
verniciflua
Acrotriche serrulata
Actinostrobus pyramidalis
Actinotus helianthi

†Adiantum
cunninghamii
formosum
hispidulum
Agonis juniperina
Ailanthus triphysa
Aleurites moluccana
Alyogyne huegelii
*Angiopteris evecta

The Bird's Nest Fern, *Asplenium australasicum*, is hardy and adaptable to a variety of situations.

Ferns are suited to small shady areas.

DECORATIVE FOLIAGE

* = species with spectacular foliage.
† = species with attractive new growth flushes.
(See also, list of species with variegated foliage.)

Acacia amblygona
argyrophylla
brachybotrya
cardiophylla
cognata
cultriformis
dawsonii
denticulosa
dimidiata
drummondii
*dunnii
ericifolia
flexifolia
†glaucoptera
gracilifolia

gunnii
harpophylla
†iteaphylla
lanigera
lasiocalyx
lasiocarpa
leucoclada
merinthophora
muellerana
obliquinervia
*o'shanessyi
pendula
podalyriifolia
pravissima
prominens

Plant Lists and Glossary

†Angophora costata
Arachniodes aristata
Asplenium australasicum
  bulbiferum
  falcatum
  nidus
  simplicifrons
Astroloma ciliatum
Atriplex nummularia
  rhagodioides
†Banksia baxteri
  brownii
  †dryandroides
  elderana
  †grandis
  petiolaris
  prostrata
  quercifolia
  repens
  solandri
Beaufortia decussata
  incana
Blechnum camfieldii
  fluviatile
  nudum
  wurunuran
Boronia filifolia
  fraseri
  molloyae
Bossiaea linifolia
  (bronze foliage form)
Brachychiton acerifolium
  rupestre
Brachysema lanceolatum
  sericeum
†Callistemon salignus
Callitris columellaris
  huegelii
  intratropica
  oblonga
Calocephalus brownii
Calothamnus lehmannii
  quadrifidus
  (grey-leaf form)
Cassia artemisioides
  nemophila
  sturtii
Castanospermum australe
Casuarina equisetifolia
  pinaster
  ramosissima
  torulosa
Celmisia asteliifolia
Christella dentata
Cissus antarctica
  *repens
Chorizema ilicifolium
Cordyline stricta
  terminalis
Cyathea baileyana
  celebica
  cooperi
  rebeccae
  robertsiana

woollsiana
Darlingia darlingiana
  ferruginea
Darwinia citriodora
Daviesia brevifolia
  pectinata
*Deplanchea tetraphylla
Dicksonia antarctica
  youngiae
Dillenia alata
Dodonaea adenophora
  lobulata
  multijuga
†Doodia aspera
  caudata
  media
Dracaena angustifolia
Dryandra armata
  baxteri
  calophylla
  drummondii
  foliosissima
  formosa
  fraseri
  nobilis
  patens
  polycephala
  praemorsa
  proteoides
  pteridifolia
  quercifolia
  sessilis
  tenuifolia
Eremophila bowmanii
  gibbifolia
  hillii
Eucalyptus campaspe
  †cinerea
  †cordata
  †crenulata
  elata
  gardneri
  grossa
  gunnii
  kruseana
  macrocarpa
  orbifolia
  perriniana
    (juvenile foliage)
  pulverulenta
  rhodantha
  †risdonii
  spathulata
  tetragona
  tetraptera
  viridis
  woodwardii
†Eupomatia laurina
Eutaxia microphylla
Ficus destruens
Frankenia pauciflora
†Geissois benthamii
  biagiana
Goodia lotifolia

Grevillea acanthifolia
  †aquifolium
  asparagoides
  asplenifolia
  arenaria
  banksii
  barklyana
  bipinnatifida
  brevicuspis
  candelabroides
  dielsiana
  dryophylla
  endlicherana
  †×gaudichaudii
  glabrata
  hilliana
  hookerana
  ilicifolia
  insignis
  'Ivanhoe'
  intricata
  johnsonii
  †laurifolia
  lavandulacea
  leucopteris
  longistyla
  macrostylis
  microstegia
  pectinata
  petrophiloides
  phanerophlebia
  pinnatifida
  platypoda
  †'Poorinda Peter'
  †repens
  rivularis
  robusta
  'Robyn Gordon'
  sp. 'Glut'
  steiglitziana
  synapheae
  thelemanniana
  trifida
  triloba
  tripartita
  vestita
  willisii
  wilsonii
Hakea baxteri
  †bucculenta
  cinerea
  conchifolia
  corymbosa
  cucullata
  †elliptica
  myrtoides
  petiolaris
  trifurcata
  †undulata
  victoriae
Hardenbergia comptoniana
Helichrysum apiculatum
  semipapposum
Hibbertia fasciculata

  stellaris
Hibiscus splendens
  tiliaceus
*Hicksbeachia pinnatifolia
Homoranthus darwinioides
  flavescens
†Hoya australis
  macgillivrayi
  nicholsoniae
Hypocalymma cordifolium
  tetrapterum
Indigofera australis
Isopogon anemonifolius
  anethifolius
  †ceratophyllus
  divergens
  dubius
  formosus
  trilobus
Jacksonia furcellata
  scoparia
Kunzea pulchella
Lambertia echinata
  ilicifolia
  orbifolia
†Lasiopetalum dasyphyllum
  schulzenii
Lastreopsis hispida
  marginans
  microsora
  smithiana
  grayi
†Leptospermum nitidum
  'Copper Sheen'
  †phylicoides
  (bronze forms)
Lomatia ilicifolia
  silaifolia
*Macaranga tanarius
Mackinlaya macrosciadia
†Maniltoa schefferi
Marattia salicina
Maytenus bilocularis
Melaleuca diosmifolia
  elliptica
  hypericifolia
  incana
  micromera
  seriata
Melia azedarach
Microsorium diversifolium
  punctatum
  scandens
Mirbelia dilatata
Morinda jasminoides
  reticulata
Musa banksii
  fitzalanii
  hillii
Myoporum floribundum
Nothofagus cunninghamii
Olearia teretifolia
  (compact form)
Oxylobium tricuspidatum

294

Many hakeas have decorative foliage, and one such species is *Hakea undulata*.

Many *Casuarina* species have decorative fruits. An example is *C.pusilla.*

Pandorea jasminoides
  pandorana
Paraceterach muelleri
†*Persoonia pinifolia*
†*Petrophile longifolia*
  serruriae
  squamata
Phebalium bullatum
  stenophyllum
Phymatocarpus
  porphyrocephalus
Pimelea ferruginea
  nivea
Piper caninum
  mestonii
  novae-hollandiae
  rothianum
Plectranthus argentatus
Podocarpus lawrencei
Polyscias elegans
  sambucifolius
  murrayii
Polystichum formosum
Pomaderris lanigera
Prostanthera baxteri
  nivea var. *induta*
  rhombea
  violacea
Pteris pacifica
  tremula

  tripartita
  umbrosa
Ptilotus obovatus
Pultenaea cunninghamii
  †*hispidula*
Raphidophora australasica
  pachyphylla
  pinnata
Regelia megacephala
  velutina
**Schefflera actinophylla*
  *versteegii
**Scindapsus altissimus*
Scleranthus biflorus
**Stemona australiana*
†*Stenocarpus sinuatus*
Stephania japonica
Sticherus flabellatus
Swainsonia greyana
†*Syzygium leuhmannii*
Tetrastigma nitens
Thomasia macrocarpa
Toona australis
†*Tristania laurina*
Verticordia mitchelliana
  plumosa
†*Vesselowskya rubifolia*
Xanthorrhoea australis
Xanthosia rotundifolia

DECORATIVE FRUIT

Tropical and Subtropical Regions

Abarema grandiflora
  hendersonii
Abrus precatorius
Aceratium ferrugineum
  megalospermum
  sericolepsis
Acmena australis
  graveolens
  hemilampra
  smithii
Acronychia acidula
  acronychioides
  imperforata
  oblongifolia
Adenanthera abrosperma
  pavonina
Adenia heterophylla
Alectryon subcinereus
  tomentosus
Aleurites moluccana
Alocasia macrorrhiza
Alyxia ruscifolia
Antidesma bunius
  dallachyanum
  erostre
  ghaesembilla

  parvifolium
Archidendron lucyi
  vaillantii
Archontophoenix alexandrae
  cunninghamii
Ardisia brevipedata
  pseudojambosa
Aristotelia megalosperma
Arytera lautererana
Austromyrtus acmenioides
  dulcis
  hillii
  lucida
  rhytisperma
Beilschmiedia bancroftii
Blepharocarya involucrigera
Bombax ceiba
Brachychiton acerifolium
  discolor
  paradoxum
Brackenridgea australiana
Breynia oblongifolia
Bridelia exaltata
Bubbia whiteana
Buchanania arborescens
  muelleri

295

The buds, flowers and fruits of *Eucalyptus forrestiana*, are decorative.

Buchanania obovata
Calamus australis
  caryotoides
Callicarpa longifolia
  pedunculata
Calophyllum inophyllum
Capparis arborea
Canthium coprosmoides
  lucidum
Cardiospermum halicababum
Carissa ovata
Celtis paniculata
Ceratopetalum apetalum
  gummiferum
Cerbera inflata
Chrysophyllum pruniferum
Citriobatus lancifolius
  multiflorus
  pauciflorus
Clematis aristata
  glycinoides
Clerodendrum floribundum
  tomentòsum
Cochlospermum gregorii
  gillivraei
Codonocarpus cotinifolius
Commersonia batramia
Connarus conchocarpus
Cordia myxa
Cordyline cannaefolia
  haageana
  stricta
Cryptocarya triplinervis
Cupaniopsis anarcardioides
Davidsonia parvifolia
  pruriens

Deeringia amaranthoides
Delabrea michieana
Dillenia alata
Dioscorea sativa
  transversa
Diospyros ferrea
  mabacea
  pentamera
Diplocylos palmatus
Diploglottis australis
Dodonea adenophora
  attenuata
  boroniifolia
  viscosa
Drypetes australasica
Eleagnus latifolia
Elaeocarpus bancroftii
  grandis
  reticulatus
Elaeodendron australe
Endiandra sieberi
Entada scandens
Ervatamia angustisepala
Eucalyptus miniata
  peltata
  ptychocarpa
Eupomatia laurina
Eustrephus latifolius
Euodia elleryana
Fagraea racemosa
Faradaya splendida
Ficus benjamina
  crassipes
  destruens
  fraseri
  henneana

macrophylla
obliqua
rubiginosa
triradiata
watkinsiana
Floydia praelta
Flindersia australis
  bourjotiana
  pubescens
  schottiana
  xanthoxyla
Glochidion ferdinandii
Grevillea glauca
Halfordia drupifera
Harpullia pendula
Hicksbeachia pinnatifolia
Hypserpa laurina
Laccospadix australasica
Linospadix monostachya
Macadamia integrifolia
  tetraphylla
  whelanii
Medinella balls-headleyi
Microcitrus australasica
  australis
  inodora
Morinda salomonensis
Notelaea longifolia
Ochrosia elliptica
  moorei
Operculina riedeliana
Owenia acidula

venosa
Pandanus pedunculata
Parsonsia velutina
Parinari nonda
Pilidiostigma rhytispermum
Planchonella australis
Pleiogynium timorense
Podocarpus amarus
  elatus
Psychotria loniceroides
Rapanea howittiana
  variabilis
Randia fitzalanii
Rauwenhoffia leichhardtii
Rhodamnia spongiosa
  trinervia
Rhodomyrtus macrocarpa
Rhodosphaera rhodanthema
Salacia chinensis
Smilax australis
Sterculia quadrifida
Syzygium coolminianum
  cormiflorum
  corynanthum
  fibrosum
  floribundum
  leuhmannii
  moorei
  paniculatum
Ternstroema cherryi
Tetrastigma nitens
Trichosanthos pentaphylla

DECORATIVE FRUIT

Temperate Regions

Acacia baileyana 'Purpurea'
  melanoxylon
  suaveolens
  uncinata
Acmena smithii
Acronychia acidula
Acrotriche prostrata
  serrulata
Actinostrobus pyramidalis
Alectryon tomentosus
Alyxia buxifolia
Angophora costata
  hispida
Astroloma humifusum
  pinifolium
Atriplex holocarpa
  spongiosa
Banksia caleyi
  candolleana
  dryandroides
  grandis
  laricina
  lemanniana
  menziesii
  nutans

prionotes
serrata
spinulosa
violacea
Billardiera cymosa
  longiflora
  scandens
Brachychiton acerifolium
  populneum
Callitris oblonga
  rhomboidea
  verrucosa
Cardiospermum halicacabum
Casuarina corniculata
  luehmannii
  microstachya
  muellerana
  pinaster
  pusilla
  stricta
Cenarrhenes nitida
Ceratopetalum apetalum
  gummiferum
Choricarpa leptopetala
Cissus antarctica

hypoglauca
Citriobatus multiflorus
Clematis aristata
  glycinoides
  microphylla
Coprosma hirtella
  nitida
  quadrifida
Cordyline stricta
Cryptocarya triplinervis
Cupaniopsis anarcardioides
Cyathodes acerosa
  dealbata
  glauca
  juniperina
Dianella caerulea
  revoluta
  tasmanica
Dodonaea adenophora
  boroniifolia
  lobulata
Doryanthes excelsa
Dryandra polycephala
  proteoides
Drymophila cyanocarpa
Elaeocarpus grandis
  reticulatus
Elaeodendron australe
Enchylaena tomentosa
Eremocitrus glauca
Eucalyptus bupestrium
  burdettiana
  burracoppinensis
  caesia
  cooperana
  coronata
  crucis
  erythrocorys
  ficifolia
  forrestiana
  globulus
  goniantha
  gummifera
  incrassata
  kingsmillii
  lehmannii
  macrocarpa
  megacornuta
  orbifolia
  pachyphylla
  preissiana
  pyriformis
  rhodantha
  sepulcralis
  steedmanii
  stoatei
  stowardii
  tetragona
  tetraptera
  todtiana
  torquata
  urnigera
  youngiana
Eupomatia laurina

Eustrephus latifolius
Exocarpos cupressiformis
  latifolius
Ficus coronata
  macrophylla
  obliqua
  rubiginosa
  watkinsiana
Floydia praelta
Gahnia sieberana
Gaultheria appressa
  hispida
Grevillea annulifera
  glauca
Hakea bucculenta
  elliptica
  francisiana
  laurina
  multilineata
  orthorrhyncha
  pandanicarpa
  petiolaris
  platysperma
  suaveolens
Hibbertia scandens
Hymenosporum flavum
Isopogon anethifolius
  cuneatus
  divergens
  formosus
  trilobus
Kunzea pomifera
Lambertia formosa
Leichhardtia leptophylla
Leucopogon lanceolatus
  montanus
  parviflorus
Linospadix monostachya
Macadamia integrifolia
  tetraphylla
Melia azedarach
Microcitrus australasica
  australis
Mirbelia oxyloboides
Myoporum debile
  desertii
  insulare
Nitraria schoberi
Notelaea ligustrina
Owenia acidula
Passiflora herbertiana
Pentachondra pumila
Pernettya lanceolata
  tasmanica
Persoonia pinifolia
Petrophile diversifolia
  sessilis
  teretifolia
Pipturus argenteus
Pittosporum bicolor
  phillyreoides
  revolutum
  rhombifolium
  undulatum

The buds and fruits of *Isopogon trilobus* are intricately patterned, and decorative.

The fruits of the quandong, (*Santalum accuminatum*) are recognised as being among the tastiest of Australian plants.

Plant Lists and Glossary

Planchonella australis
Pleiogynium timorense
Pleiococca wilcoxiana
Podocarpus elatus
  spinulosus
Polyscias sambucifolius
Rapanea howittiana
Rubus gunnianus
  hillii
  moorei
  parvifolius
  rosifolius
Santalum acuminatum
  lanceolatum
Scaevola calendulacea
Scirpus nodosus

Solanum aviculare
  laciniatum
Stephania japonica
Syzygium coolminianum
  floribundum
  leuhmannii
Tasmannia lanceolata
  insipida
Telopea speciosissima
Themeda australis
Trochocarpa gunnii
  thymifolia
Ximenia americana
Xylomelum angustifolium
  pyriforme

The large woody fruits of *Xylomelum angustifolium* are most decorative.

EROSION CONTROL

Acacia aneura
  bivenosa
  boormanii
  calamifolia
  colletioides
  cyclops
  dealbata
  difformis
  floribunda
  hakeoides
  harpophylla
  implexa
  longifolia
  longifolia var sophorae
  melanoxylon
  pravissima
  rubida
  salicina
  saligna
  sentis
  stenophylla
  tetragonophylla
Actinostrobus arenarius
Adenanthos pungens
Agonis flexuosa
Araucaria cunninghamii
Atalaya hemiglauca
Atriplex cinerea
  vesicaria
Banksia baueri
  caleyi
  candolleana
  elegans
  integrifolia
  marginata
  media
  petiolaris
  pulchella
  repens
Brachysema sericeum
Bursaria spinosa
Callistemon citrinus
  'Harkness'
  salignus

  viminalis
Callitris rhomboidea
  verrucosa
Calocephalus brownii
Calothamnus gilesii
  homalophyllus
  sanguineus
Calystegia soldanella
Canavalia maritima
Carpobrotus modestus
  rossii
Cassia artemesioides
  nemophila
Casuarina cristata
  cunninghamiana
  equisetifolia
  glauca
  leuhmannii
  muellerana
  rigida
  stricta
Culcita dubia
Dampiera cuneata
  linearis
Disphyma blackii
Dryandra nivea
  obtusa
  pteridifolia
  tenuifolia
Eremocitrus glauca
Eremophila glabra
  (prostrate forms)
  longifolia
Eucalyptus behriana
  camaldulensis
  foecunda
  gracilis
  incrassata
  microcarpa
  oleosa
  platypus
  populnea
  socialis
  spathulata

  todtiana
  viridis
  yalataensis
Goodenia ovata
Grevillea asplenifolia
  fasciculata
  longifolia
  nudiflora
Hakea hookerana
  lissocarpha
  trifurcata
Hibbertia scandens
Ipomoea pes-caprae
Jacksonia scoparia
Kennedia beckxiana
  macrophylla
  nigricans
  rubicunda
Kunzea parvifolia
Leptospermum
  'Horizontalis'
  laevigatum
  lanigerum
  myrsinoides
  phylicoides
Maireana aphylla
  sedifolia
Mazus pumilio
Melaleuca alternifolia

  armillaris
  ericifolia
  huegelii
  lanceolata
  lateralis
  leucadendron
  nesophila
  nodosa
  pentagona
  thyoides
  uncinata
  wilsonii
Microlaena stipoides
Myoporum insulare
  viscosum
Olearia argophylla
Pittosporum phillyreoides
  undulatum
Pteridium esculentum
Regelia ciliata
Scaevola calendulacea
Spinifex hirsutus
Stephania japonica
Tristania conferta
  laurina
Ventilago viminalis
Viola hederacea
  sieberana
Vitex trifolia

FIRE RETARDANT PROPERTIES

Arthrocnemum halocnemoides
  lylei
Atriplex angulata
  cinerea
  halimoides
  holocarpa
  leptocarpa
  limbata
  muelleri
  nummularia
  rhagodioides
  semibaccata
  stipitata
  vesicaria
Carpobrotus glaucescens
  modestus
  rossii
  virescens
Chenopodium cristatum
Claytonia australasica
Dichondra repens
Disphyma blackii
Enchylaena tomentosa
Eremophila glabra
  maculata

Frankenia densa
  pauciflora
Muireana aphylla
  brevifolia
  erioclada
  georgei
  pyramidata
  sedifolia
  triptera
Myoporum debile
  parvifolium
Nitraria schoberi
Pachycornia tenuis
  triandra
Phyla nodiflora
Rhagodia baccata
  hastata
  nutans
  spinescens
Salicornia quinqueflora
Scaevola hookeri
Scleranthus biflorus
Selliera radicans
Suaeda australis

Geijera parviflora, an excellent shade and fodder tree. Note how lower foliage has been grazed by stock.

D.L. Jones photo

TREES FOR FIREWOOD

The following trees produce good to excellent fuel for firewood.

Acacia acuminata
  aneura
  bidwillii
  brachystachya
  burrowii
  cambagei
  coriacea
  excelsa
  filicifolia
  glaucescens
  harpophylla
  homalophylla
  implexa
  mabellae
  melanoxylon
  notabilis
  pendula
  peuce
  pycnantha
  salicina
  stenophylla
Albizia procera
Angophora costata
  floribunda
Banksia grandis
  integrifolia
  marginata
  serrata
Callitris endlicheri
  glauca

huegelii
intratropica
Casuarina cristata
  cunninghamii
  decaisneana
  dielsiana
  equisetiifolia
  littoralis
  leuhmannii
  stricta
  torulosa
Davidsonia pruriens
Eremophila mitchellii
Erythrophloeum
  chlorostachys
Eucalyptus albens
  aromaphloia
  argophloia
  astringens
  behriana
  blakelyi
  bosistoana
  brockwayii
  caleyi
  camaldulensis
  campaspe
  crebra
  consideniana
  dealbata
  dichromophloia

dives
drepanophylla
exserta
fasciculosa
gillii
gummifera
haemastoma
hemiphloia
intermedia
largiflorens
leucoxylon
melanophloia
melliodora
microcarpa
microtheca
moluccana
occidentalis
odorata
paniculata
pauciflora
pilligaensis
polycarpa

polyanthemos
punctata
radiata
rubida
rudis
salmonophloia
shirleyi
siderophloia
sideroxylon
stellulata
tectifera
tereticornis
trachyphloia
viminalis
wandoo
woollsiana
Leptospermum laevigatum
Melaleuca armillaris
Santalum acuminatum
Xanthostemon chrysanthus
  paradoxus
  whitei

FODDER PLANTS

The following species have foliage which can be eaten by stock. Such plants can be very useful as stock feed during drought situations.

Acacia aneura
  argyrodendron
  aulacocarpa
  bidwillii
  brachystachya
  cana
  cheelii
  coriacea
  doratoxylon
  estrophiolata
  excelsa

harpophylla
kempeana
loderi
omalophylla
oswaldii
pendula
peuce
salicina
sentis
Albizia basaltica
  lophantha

299

Plant Lists and Glossary

Alphitonia excelsa
Angophora subvelutina
Apophyllum anomalum
Atalaya hemiglauca
Atriplex angulata
 cinerea
 halimoides
 holocarpa
 leptocarpa
 limbata
 muelleri
 nummularia
 rhagodioides
 semibaccata
 stipitata
 vesicaria
Avicennia officianalis
Brachychiton gregori
 populneum
 rupestre
Bursaria spinosa
Canthium latifolium
 odoratum
 oleifolium
Capparis mitchellii
 umbonata
Carissa lanceolata
Cassia artemisioides
 circinnata
 desolata
 nemophila
 phyllodinea
Casuarina campestris
 cristata
 cunninghamiana
 decaisneana
 glauca
 littoralis
 stricta
Chenopodium nitrariaceum
Codonocarpus cotiniifolius
Dodonea attenuata
 lobulata
 viscosa
Ehretia membranifolia
Enchylaena tomentosa
Eremophila bignoniiflora

latrobei
longifolia
maculata
oppositifolia
Eucalyptus albens
 camaldulensis
 cladocalyx
 gamophylla
 gummifera
 gunnii
 largiflorens
 melliodora
 pauciflora
Ficus macrophylla
 rubiginosa
Flindersia maculosa
 strzeleckiana
Geijera parviflora
Gossypium sturtii
Grevillea striata
Hakea leucoptera
 vittata
Heterodendrum oleifolium
Hibiscus heterophyllus
Jasminum lineare
Lavatera plebeia
Lysiphyllum carronii
Maireana brevifolia
 pyramidata
 sedifolia
Marsdenia leichhardtiana
Maytenus cunninghamii
Melaleuca ericifolia
Muehlenbeckia
 cunninghamiana
Myoporum insulare
 platycarpum
Owenia acidula
Pittosporum phillyreoides
Rhagodia billardieri
 hastata
 nutans
 parabolica
 spinesens
Santalum acuminatum
 lanceolatum
Ventilago viminalis

anceps
annulata
astringens
blakelyi
bosistoana
botryoides
bridgesiana
caleyi
calophylla
calycogona
camaldulensis
celastroides
conica
cornuta
crebra
cypellocarpa
delegatensis
diversifolia
drepanophylla
eremophila
fastigiata
ficifolia
foecunda
gardneri
globulus
gracilis
incrassata
intermedia
largiflorens
leucoxylon
loxophleba
maidenii
melanophloia
melanoxylon
melliodora
microcarpa
microtheca
obliqua
ochrophloia

oleosa
panda
papuana
pauciflora
pellita
platypus
polycarpa
resinifera
rubida
rudis
seeana
sideroxylon
socialis
tereticornis
tessellaris
torquata
viminalis
Eucryphia billardieri
Heterodendron oleifolium
Jagera pseudorhus
Leptospermum flavescens
 juniperinum
 laevigatum
 lanigerum
 myrsinoides
 nitidum
Leucopogon parviflorus
 virgatus
Melaleuca bracteata
 ericifolia
 lanceolata
 leucadendron
 quinquenervia
 squarrosa
Myoporum platycarpum
Pittosporum undulatum
Tristania conferta
 suaveolens

HONEY PRODUCING PLANTS

The following species produce sufficient quantities of nectar for honey production. See also list of Pollen Producing Plants.

Acacia colletioides
Aegiceras corniculatum
Alphitonia excelsa
 petriei
 whitei
Anopterus glandulosus
 macleayanus
Atherosperma moschatum
Banksia integrifolia

marginata
serrata
Bursaria spinosa
Clematis aristata
 glycinoides
 microphylla
Eucalyptus acmenoides
 alba
 albens

INDOOR PLANTS

Acmena smithii
Agathis microstachya
 robusta
Araucaria bidwillii
 cunninghamii
Archontophoenix alexandrae
 cunninghamii
Asplenium australasicum
 bulbiferum
 nidus
Bowenia serrulata
 spectabilis
Brachychiton acerifolium
 discolor
 populneum
 rupestre
Buckinghamia celsissima
Calamus australis
 caryotoides
 motii
Carpentaria acuminata
Caryota rumphiana

Castanospermum australe
Cissus antarctica
 hypoglauca
 repens
Cordyline cannifolia
 rubra
 stricta
Cyathea australis
 cooperi
 woollsiana
Cycas media
Darlingia darlingiana
 ferruginea
Davallia pyxidata
 solida
Dendrobium delicatum
 gracilicaule
 kingianum
 speciosum
Dicksonia antarctica
 youngiae
Doryanthes excelsa

Schefflera actinophylla, an ideal indoor plant.

palmeri
Elaeocarpus reticulatus
Eucryphia lucida
Eupomatia laurina
Ficus benjamina
  crassipes
  destruens
  macrophylla
  microcarpa var hillii
  obliqua
  rubiginosa 'Variegata'
  stephanocarpa
  triradiata
  watkinsiana
Geissois benthamii
Goodia lotifolia
Grevillea robusta
  shiressii
Gronophyllum ramsayi
Hicksbeachia pinnatifolia
Hoya australis
  keysii
  nicholsoniae
Hymenosporum flavum
Jagera pseudorhus
Laccospadix australasicus
Lepidozamia hopei
  peroffskyana
Licuala ramsayi
Linospadix minor
  monostachyus
Livistona australis
  benthamii
  muelleri
Macrozamia communis
  diplomera

lucida
miquelii
moorei
pauli-guilielmi
riedlei
spiralis
Medicosma cunninghamii
Melastoma denticulatum
  polyanthum
Nephrolepis cordifolia
Nothofagus cunninghamii
Pandorea pandorana
Piper caninum
  mestonii
  rothianum
Podocarpus elatus
  lawrencei
  spinosus
Polyscias elegans
Pothos longipes
Pteris umbrosa
Ptychosperma elegans
Raphidophora australasica
  pinnata
Rhododendron lochae
Rhodosphaera rhodanthema
Schefflera actinophylla
  versteegii
Scindapsus altissimus
Solanum aviculare
  laciniatum
Stenocarpus sinuatus
Stephania japonica
Syzygium leuhmannii
Tasmannia lanceolata
Vesselowskya rubifolia

MAT PLANTS AND GROUNDCOVERS
Light covers — to 1 m tall.

Acacia aculeatissima
  amblygona
  laricina
  pilosa
Acrotriche serrulata
Asterolasia trymalioides
Astroloma compactum
  humifusum
  pallidum
Banksia goodii
  prostrata
Baeckea ramosissima
Blechnum penna-marina
Bossiaea cordigera
  foliosa
  prostrata
Brachycome multifida
Brachysema latifolium
  praemorsum
Claytonia australasica
Correa decumbens
  pulchella
  reflexa (prostrate
  forms)
Cotula filicula
Dampiera cauloptera
  cuneata
  diversifolia
  fasciculata
  glabriflora
  lanceolata
  lavandulacea
  linearis
  rosmarinifolia
Darwinia camptostylis
  glaucophylla

  grandiflora
  rhadinophylla,
  taxifolia ssp. macrolaena
Disphyma blackii
Dodonaea humifusum
  procumbens
Eutaxia microphylla
Frankenia pauciflora
Goodenia corynocarpa
  hederacea
  humilis
  lanata
Grevillea capitellata
  (Holsworthy form)
  juniperina var. trinerva
Helichrysum baxteri
  bracteatum 'Diamond
  Head'
  leucopsidium
  scorpioides
Hemiandra pungens
Hibbertia obtusifolia
  procumbens
Homoranthus flavescens
Isotoma fluviatilis
Kennedia eximia
  microphylla
Kunzea muelleri
Lechenaultia formosa
  (prostrate forms)
Lobelia alata
  quadrangularis
Mazus pumilio
Melaleuca violacea
  (prostrate form)
Micromyrtus ciliata

Helichrysum leucopsidium is an excellent rockery plant, and spreads by suckers.

Groundcovers are excellent for suppressing weed growth, and for reducing fluctuation in temperature at the soil surface. *Kennedia rubicunda* is an excellent example.

MAT PLANTS AND GROUNDCOVERS

Vigorous and Rampant; Wide spreading;
To about 1 m tall

Acacia baileyana (prostrate
  form)
  glaucoptera
  pravissima 'Golden
    Carpet'
  redolens (prostrate
    form)
Banksia petiolaris
  repens
  sp. Lake King WA
Bauera rubioides
Brachysema sericeum
Carpobrotus modestus
  rossii
Callistemon phoeniceus
    (prostrate form)
Dichondra repens
Eremophila glabra
    (prostrate forms)
Grevillea acanthifolia
    (prostrate form)
  alpina (Grampians
    forms)
  aquifolium (prostrate
    forms)
  australis
  brownii
  confertifolia (prostrate
    form)
  diminuta
  ×*gaudichaudii*
  ilicifolia (prostrate
    form)
  juniperina 'Molonglo'
  laurifolia
  microstegia
  nudiflora
  pilosa

'Poorinda Royal
    Mantle'
  repens
  sp. Ben Major Vic.
  sp. Black Range Vic.
  sp. Enfield Vic.
  sp. Fryerstown Vic.
  synapheae
  thelemanniana (various
    forms)
  tridentifera (prostrate
    form)
Hardenbergia violacea
Helichrysum apiculatum
Hibbertia empetrifolia
  scandens
Kennedia coccinea
  glabrata
  macrophylla
  nigricans
  procurrens
  prostrata
  retrorsa
  rubicunda
Kunzea pomifera
Leptospermum
  'Horizontalis'
  humifusum
Melaleuca glaberrima
    (prostrate form)
Mentha diemenica
Oxylobium alpestre
    (low forms)
Phyla nodiflora
Platylobium formosum
Prostanthera walteri
Rhagodia spinescens

Myoporum debile
  parvifolium
Oxylobium tricuspidatum
Persoonia chamaepitys
  chamaepeuce
Petrophile longifolia
    (prostrate form)
Pimelea filiformis
Platylobium alternifolium
Pratia pedunculata
Prostanthera hirtula
    (prostrate form)
  saxicola var. *montana*
    spinosa
Ptilotus obovatus
Pultenaea fascicularis
  pedunculata

  polifolia
  prostrata
Scaevola hookeri
  pallida
  ramosissima
  striata
Scleranthus biflorus
  singuliflorus
Spyridium cinereum
  parvifolium 'Austraflora
    Nimbus'
Symphionema montanum
Viola hederacea
  sieberana
Wahlenbergia gloriosa
Xanthosia rotundifolia

POLLEN PRODUCING PLANTS

Acacia aulacocarpa
  baileyana
  dealbata
  doratoxylon
  fimbriata
  genistifolia
  mearnsii
  melanoxylon
  pulchella
  pycnantha
  verticillata
Aegiceras corniculatum
Alphitonia excelsa
Angophora costata
  subvelutina
  woodsiana
Atherospermum moschatum
Avicennia marina

Baeckea virgata
Banksia integrifolia
  marginata
  serrata
Boronia rosmarinifolia
Bursaria spinosa
Callistemon brachyandrus
  citrinus
  macropunctatus
  paludosus
  pycnantha
  salignus
  viminalis
Callitris calcarata
  columellaris
  huegelii
  intratropica
Casuarina cunninghamiana

littoralis
Eucalyptus acmenoides
  anceps
  aromaphloia
  behriana
  bosistoana
  botryoides
  bridgesiana
  camaldulensis
  cinerea
  crebra
  cypellocarpa
  dealbata
  diversifolia
  dumosa
  eremophila
  fastigiata
  foecunda
  gardneri
  globulus
  goniocalyx
  gummifera
  incrassata
  intermedia
  largiflorens
  maculata
  maidenii
  mannifera
  melanophloia
  microtheca
  nitens
  obliqua
  oleosa

  platypus
  regnans
  resinifera
  salubris
  seeana
  sieberi
  smithii
  socialis
  tereticornis
  torquata
  viminalis
Eucryphia billardieri
Grevillea robusta
Heterodendrum oleifolium
Melaleuca decussata
  ericifolia
  gibbosa
  hypericifolia
  lanceolata
  linariifolia
  nodosa
  quinquenervia
  squarrosa
  viridiflora
Muehlenbeckia cunninghamii
Myoporum insulare
  platycarpum
Nitraria schoberi
Pittosporum phillyreoides
Pultenea villosa
Xanthorrhoea australis
  minor
  resinosa

Species of *Boronia* are renowned for their delicate perfumes — *Boronia megastigma*

PERFUMED FLOWERS

Boronia serrulata.

Acacia calamifolia
  cardiophylla
  dealbata
  floribunda
  genistifolia
  mearnsii
  obtusata
  prominens
  howittii
  spectabilis
  suaveolens
  subulata
Aegiceras corniculatum
Albizia retusa
Alocasia macrorrhiza
Alstonia constricta
  scholaris
Amorphophallus glabra
Anopterus glandulosus
  macleayanus
Anthocercis viscosa
Arthropodium milleflorum
Atherosperma moschatum
Boronia citriodora
  clavata
  floribunda
  heterophylla

  megastigma
  muelleri
  pinnata
  purdieana
  tetrandra
  serrulata
Bursaria spinosa
Calomeria amaranthoides
Calophyllum inophyllum
Calytrix aurea
Capillipedium spicigerum
Carissa lanceolata
  ovata
Cassia brewsteri
  nemophila
Clerodendron floribundum
  inerme
  tomentosum
Commersonia bartramia
Corymborkis veratrifolia
Crinum angustifolium
  asiaticum
  brachyandrum
  brevistylum
  brisbanicum
  douglasii
  flaccidum

Crinum pedunculatum is one of the few bulbs found in Australia. It is very easily grown, and the large white flowers are stongly scented.

Pittosporum undulatum is widely grown in Australia and overseas, because of its delightful perfume.

Small flowers of *Cynoglossum suaveolens* release a strong spicy perfume on warm days.

Crinum pedunculatum
Cymbidium canaliculatum
  madidum
  suave
Cynoglossum suaveolens
Dendrobium aemulum
  canaliculatum
  ×*delicatum*
  discolor
  falcorostrum
  johannis
  kingianum
  monophyllum
  ruppianum
  speciosum
  teretifolium
  tetragonum
Dichopogon fimbriatus
  strictus
Drosera whittakeri
Eucalyptus clavigera
  kitsoniana
  obliqua
  porrecta
Faradaya splendida
Garcinia mestonii
  warrenii
Gardenia edulis
  fucata
  jardinei

  macgillivrayii
  megasperma
  merikin
  ochreata
  pyriformis
  resinosa
  suffruticosa
Gymnanthera nitida
Hakea rostrata
Hoya australis
  keysii
  macgillivrayii
Hymenanthera dentata
Hymenosporum flavum
Isotoma axillaris
Jacksonia scoparia
Jasminum aemulum
  didymum
  lineare
  simplicifolium
  suavissimum
Kennedia glabrata
  stirlingii
Lechenaultia floribunda
Lomandra effusa
  endlicheri
Mallotus discolor
Medicosma cunninghamii
Melaleuca argentea
  squarrosa

Melodinus australis
Morinda jasminoides
  umbellata
Myosotis suaveolens
Olearia adenophora
  ramulosa
Parsonsia plaesiophylla
  straminea
Persoonia arborea
Pimelea physodes
Pittosporum revolutum
  rhombifolium
  undulatum
Plectorrhiza brevilabris
Randia benthamiana
  fitzalani
  moorei

  subsessilis
Ricinocarpus pinifolius
  tuberculatus
Sambucus gaudichaudiana
Sarcochilus falcatus
  hartmannii
  fitzgeraldii
  olivaceus
Scaevola crassifolia
  glandulifera
  microphylla
Sowerbaea juncea
Stackhousia monogyna
Tetracera nordtiana var.
  wuthiana
Tricoryne elatior

PERFUMED FOLIAGE

Acacia leprosa
  redolens
  retinocarpa
  verniciflua
Acmena smithii
Actinostrobus pyramidalis
Agonis flexuosa
  juniperina
  parviceps

Angophora costata
  hispida
Astartea fascicularis
  heteranthera
Backhousia anisata
  citriodora
Baeckea astarteoides
  citriodora
  densifolia

Flowers of *Medicosma cunninghamii* have a sweet scent similar to that of orange blossoms.

The foliage of *Backhousia citriodora* has an outstanding lemon fragrance.

The foliage of *Plectranthus argentatus* emits a pleasant fragrance.

linifolia
virgata
Beaufortia decussata
  incana
  schaueri
Boronia anemonifolia
  citriodora
  denticulata
  floribunda
  heterophylla
  mollis
  molloyae
  muelleri
  pinnata
Callistemon citrinus
  pallidus
  phoeniceus
  viminalis
Callitris columellaris
  hugelii
  intratropica
  macleayana
  oblonga
  roei
  verrucosa
Calothamnus asper
  gibbosus
  homalophyllus
  quadrifidus
  sanguineus
  villosus
Calytrix alpestris
  brachyphylla
  depressa
  sullivanii
  tetragona
Cassinia aculeata
  arcuata
  longifolia
Chamelaucium sp. Walpole
  ciliatum
  uncinatum
Correa calycina
  schlechtendalii
Crowea exalata
  saligna
Cymbopogon exaltatus
  obtectus
  refractus
Darwinia citriodora
  diosmoides
  fascicularis
  lejostyla
  neildiana
  rhadinophylla
  vestita
Dodonaea adenophora
  boroniifolia
Eremaea violacea
Eriostemon myoporoides
  verrucosus
Eucalyptus alpina
  caleyi
  cephalocarpa

cinerea
citriodora
coccifera
cordata
crenulata
dawsonii
dives
doratoxylon
gardneri
glaucescens
globulus
gunnii
haemastoma
ligustrina
maculata
melliodora
nicholii
odorata
polyanthemos
polybractea
pulchella
radiata
sclerophylla
scoparia
sideroxylon
spathulata
stellulata
tenuiramis
viminalis
viridis
Eupomatia laurina
Helichrysum dendroideum
  diosmifolium
  paralium
  secundiflorum
  thyrsoideum
Homoranthus darwinioides
  flavescens
Hypocalymma angustifolium
  cordifolium
Ixodia achilleoides
Kunzea ambigua
  parvifolia
  recurva
Leptospermum epacridoideum
  lanigerum
  liversidgei
  petersonii
  phylicoides
Melaleuca armillaris
  calothamnoides
  diosmifolia
  fulgens
  globifera
  hypericifolia
  leucadendron
  saligna
Mentha australis
  diemenica
  laxiflora
Micromyrtus ciliata
Microsorium scandens
Olearia dentata
  iodochroa

Some species of *Hakea* have prickly foliage, and provide excellent refuge for birds. — *Hakea sericea.*

glabra
'Mannii'
pulchella
reflexa
schlechtendalii
Crowea exalata
  saligna
Dampiera cuneata
  diversifolia
Epacris impressa
  longiflora
  microphylla
Eremophila gibbifolia
  glabra
  maculata
Eriostemon myoporoides
  verrucosus
Eutaxia microphylla
Grevillea alpina
  baueri
  buxifolia
  capitellata
  chrysophaea
  confertifolia
  dimorpha
  evansii
  floribunda
  lanigera
  lavandulacea
  miqueliana
  pilulifera
  sericea
  speciosa
  steiglitziana
  victoriae
Hakea costata
  erinacea
  lehmanniana
  myrtoides
  purpurea
Halgania cyanea
Helichrysum apiculatum
  baxteri

bracteatum
elatum
semipapposum
Hibbertia empetrifolia
Hovea elliptica
  lanceolata
Isopogon anethifolius
Lechenaultia biloba
  formosa
Myoporum debile
  parvifolium
Olearia dentata
  floribunda
  iodochroa
  phlogopappa
  teretifolia
Orthrosanthus multiflorus
Patersonia fragilis
  occidentalis
Phebalium lamprophyllum
  stenophyllum
Pimelea ferruginea
Prostanthera aspalathoides
  cuneata
  denticulata
  incana
  lasianthos
  melissifolia
  microphylla
  ovalifolia
  rotundifolia
  violacea
  walteri
Scaevola aemula
  striata
Stypandra caespitosa
  glauca
Symphionema montanum
Thomasia grandiflora
  petalocalyx
Veronica formosa
Westringia glabra
  seniifolia

Pelargonium australe
Phebalium bilobum
  lamprophyllum
  glandulosum
Pittosporum undulatum
Plectranthus argentatus
  graveolens
  parviflorus
Prostanthera aspalathoides
  chlorantha
  cineolifera
  cuneata
  denticulata
  hirtula
  incisa
  lanceolata
  lasianthos
  leichhardtii
  melissifolia
  microphylla

odoratissima
ovalifolia
rotundifolia
staurophylla
stricta
violacea
Pultenaea graveolens
Regelia ciliata
  megacephala
Scholtzia parviflora
Senecio linearifolius
  odoratus
Syncarpia glomulifera
Syzygium coolminianum
  paniculatum
Thryptomene calycina
  saxicola
Verticordia plumosa
Zieria cytisoides
  veronicea

SAFE NEAR UNDERGROUND PIPES

Acacia buxifolia
  conferta
  drummondii
  leptospermoides
  myrtifolia
  pulchella
Asterolasia asteriscophora
Bauera rubioides
  sessiliflora
Billardiera scandens
  longiflora

Boronia crenulata
  denticulata
  fraseri
  heterophylla
  megastigma
  pinnata
Brachysema lanceolatum
Chorizema cordatum
Correa alba
  baeuerlenii
  decumbens

PRICKLY LEAVES OR THORNS

Such plants can provide a refuge for birds, and can be useful for the prevention of unwanted traffic by human beings and animals.

Acacia aculeatissima
  brownii
  colletioides
  continua
  farnesiana
  genistifolia
  juniperina
  oxycedrus
  paradoxa
  pugioniformis
  pulchella
  riceana
  rupicola

sentis
siculiformis
spinescens
tetragonophylla
triptera
ulicifolia
verticillata
victoriae
Alyxia ruscifolia
Bursaria spinosa
Caesalpinia scortechinii
Callistemon brachyandrus
Capparis lasiantha

306

spinosa
Carissa ovata
  lanceolata
Casuarina pinaster
Citriobatus linearis
  pauciflorus
  spinescens
Cudrania cochinchinensis
Cyathodes juniperina
Daviesia brevifolia
  genistifolia
  horrida
  preissii
Dryandra armata
  patens
  polycephala
Epacris apiculata
Eryngium rostratum
Grevillea acanthifolia
  acerosa
  asparagoides
  bipinnatifida
  brevicuspis
  'Canberra Gem'
  confertifolia
  dielsiana
  glabrata
  insignis
  juniperina
  lavandulacea
  macrostylis
  microstegia
  phanerophlebia
  'Pink Pearl'
  platypoda
  rivularis

sp. 'Glut'
  steiglitziana
  trifida
  tripartita
  vestita
  wilsonii
Hakea cinerea
  corymbosa
  erinacea
  lissocarpha
  myrtoides
  preissii
  purpurea
  ruscifolia
  sericea
  suaveolens
  teretifolia
Hemiandra pungens
Hovea pungens
Isopogon ceratophyllus
Lambertia echinata
  formosa
Leptospermum spinescens
Lomatia ilicifolia
Melaleuca pungens
Mirbelia dilatata
Pandanus aquaticus
  monticola
  pedunculatus
Petrophile diversifolia
  serruriae
  teretifolia
Prostanthera spinosa
Pultenaea juniperina
Richea continentis
  scoparia

Excellent screening can be obtained by mass planting. Note the differing heights of plants used.

SCREENING PLANTS

To create an effective screen, it is advisable to plant species that will grow to a range of heights. If tall plants only are used, they will thin out at the base in a few years, and will not provide an effective screen. It is then difficult to establish young plants in competition with the roots of the trees.

Three vegetation layers are usually the most suitable,

e.g. (1) to 2 m high
      (2) 2-5 m high
      (3) 5 m plus.

In some situations, even a further low layer may be required.

An effective screen can be obtained quickly by planting in raised mounds of local soil.

Tropical and Subtropical Regions

Abutilon auritum 1
  indicum 1
Acacia amoena 2
  aulacocarpa 2
  baueri 1

  binervata 2
  brunioides 1
  complanata 1
  cultriformis 2
  gonoclada 1

Plant Lists and Glossary

Acacia hispidula 1
  holosericea 1
  humifusa 1
  leptostachya 1
  tetragonophylla 1
  viscidula 1
Acmena smithii var. minor 2
Backhousia anisata 2
  citriodora 2
  myrtifolia 2
Baeckea diosmifolia 1
  linifolia 1
  virgata 2
Banksia dentata 2
  ericifolia 2
  integrifolia 2
  spinulosa 2
Barklya syringifolia 2
Bursaria incana 1
  spinosa 2
Callicoma serratifolia 2
Callistemon chisholmii 1
  citrinus 2
  comboynensis 2
  polandii 2
  salignus 2
  shiressii 2
  viminalis 2
Ceratopetalum apetalum 3
  gummiferum 2
Carissa lanceolata 2
Cassia artemisioides 1
  brewsteri 2
  nemophila 1
  venusta 1
Citriobatus lancifolius 2
Clerodendrum tomentosum 1
Commersonia echinata 2
Cupaniopsis anarcardioides 3
Elaeocarpus reticulatus 3
Elaeodendron australe 3
Eupomatia laurina 2
Fenzlia obtusa 1
  retusa 1
Ficus stephanocarpa 1
Gardenia megasperma 1
  ochreata 1
Grevillea banksii 2
  decora 1
  floribunda 1
  glauca·2
  glossostigma 1
  heliosperma 2

hookerana 2
'Ivanhoe' 2
johnsonii 2
juncifolia 2
longifolia 2
longistyla 2
mimosoides 1
pinnatifida 1
striata 1
wickhamii 1
Hakea bakerana 1
  dactyloides 1
  pedunculata 1
  purpurea 1
  salicifolia 2
Hibbertia banksii 1
  candicans 1
  longifolia 1
Hibiscus diversifolius 2
  heterophyllus 2
  tiliaceus 2
Hicksbeachia pinnatifolia 2
Hovea acutifolia 1
  elliptica 1
  longifolia 1
  longipes 1
Jacksonia scoparia 2
  thesioides 1
Kunzea ambigua 2
Lagerstroemia archerana 1
Leptospermum
  arachnoideum 1
  fabricia 1
  flavescens 2
  lanigerum 2
  longifolium 1
  wooroonooran 1
Macaranga tanarius 2
Mallotus discolor 2
Medicosma cunninghamii 1
Melaleuca armillaris 2
  diosmifolia 2
  erubescens 1
  hypericifolia 2
  nodosa 1
  symphiocarpa 2
Melastoma polyanthum 2
Myoporum platycarpum 2
Pittosporum revolutum 2
  rhombifolium 2
Rhodamnia trinerva 2
Westringia fruticosa 1
  'Wynabbie Gem' 1

Acacia flexifolia effectively screening a brick wall.

SCREENING PLANTS

Temperate Regions

Acacia adunca 3
  baileyana 3
  boormanii 2
  calamifolia 2
  cardiophylla 2

conferta 2
cultriformis 2
cyclops 2
decora 2
fimbriata 3

flexifolia 1
floribunda 3
howittii 3
iteaphylla 2
longifolia 3
longifolia var. sophorae 2
paradoxa 2
pendula 2-3
penninervis 3
pravissima 2-3
prominens 3
pycnantha 2
retinodes 2
riceana 2
verniciflua 2
Acmena smithii 3
Angophora costata 3
  hispida 2-3
Baeckea virgata 2
Banksia baxteri 2
  caleyi 1
  dryandroides 1
  ericifolia 2-3
  lemanniana 2
  marginata 2
  media 2
  praemorsa 2
  spinulosa 2
Bauera rubioides 1
  sessiliflora 1
Beaufortia incana 1
  orbifolia 1
Boronia fraseri 1
  pinnata 1
Bossiaea linophylla 1
Brachysema lanceolatum 1
Callistemon 'Burgundy' 2
  citrinus 2

'Harkness' 2-3
linearifolius 2
'Mauve Mist' 2
pallidus 2
paludosus 2
'Reeves Pink' 2
salignus 2-3
shiressii 2-3
viminalis 2-3
'Violaceus' 2
Callitris columellaris 3
  oblonga 2
  rhomboidea 3
Calothamnus quadrifidus 2
  villosus 1-2
Ceratopetalum
  gummiferum 2
Chorizema cordatum 1
Correa aemula 1
  backhousiana 1-2
  baeuerlenii 1-2
  calycina 1-2
  glabra 1-2
  'Mannii' 1-2
  lawrenciana 2
  pulchella 1
  reflexa 1
  schlechtendalii 1-2
Crowea exalata 1
Darwinia citriodora 1
  diosmoides 2
Dryandra baxteri 2
  foliosissima 1-2
  nobilis 2
  praemorsa 2
  pteridifolia 1
Eremophila glabra 1
  maculata 1

Hardenbergia comptoniana, effectively screening a brick wall.

Landscaping by Paul Thompson.

Screening of a wall, using *Melaleuca incana* as the main screening plant.

Eriostemon myoporoides 1	*lanigera* 1-2
Eucalyptus bancroftii 3	*lavandulacea* 1-2
calycogona 3	*miqueliana* 2
cinerea 3	*pinaster* 2
coccifera 3	'Poorinda Constance' 2
cordata 3	'Poorinda Elegance' 2
crenulata 3	'Poorinda Queen' 2
diversifolia 3	*rivularis* 2
elata 3	*rosmarinifolia* 1-2
eremophila 3	*sericea* 2
ficifolia 3	*shiressii* 2
forrestiana 3	*speciosa* 2
gardneri 3	*steiglitziana* 1-2
globulus 3	*stenomera* 1
grossa 2	*triloba* 1-2
gunnii 3	*vestita* 2
kitsoniana 3	*victoriae* 1-2
lehmannii 2-3	*Hakea bucculenta* 2
leucoxylon 3	*corymbosa* 2
ligustrina 3	*elliptica* 2
macrandra 3	*eriantha* 2
maculata 3	*laurina* 2
megacornuta 3	*multilineata* 2
melliodora 3	*petiolaris* 2
neglecta 3	*salicifolia* 2-3
nicholii 3	*suaveolens* 2-3
nutans 2	*trifurcata* 2
pauciflora 3	*undulata* 2
perriniana 3	*Hibbertia empetrifolia* 1
platypus 2-3	*Homoranthus flavescens* 1
risdonii 3	*Hovea elliptica* 2
rupicola 2	*lanceolata* 2
scoparia 3	*Hypocalymma*
sideroxylon 3	*angustifolium* 1
spathulata 3	*cordifolium* 1
steedmanii 3	*Isopogon anemonifolius* 1
stellulata 3	*anethifolius* 2
tenuiramis 3	*Kunzea ambigua* 2
Eupomatia laurina 2-3	*ericifolia* 2
Eutaxia cuneata 1	*micromera* 1
obovata 1	*recurva* 1-2
Goodia lotifolia 2	*Lasiopetalum behrii* 1
Grevillea aquifolium 1-2	*discolor* 1
arenaria 2	*schulzenii* 1
'Audrey' 2	*Leptospermum flavescens* 2
baueri 1	'Horizontalis' 1
brevicuspis 1	*laevigatum* 2-3
buxifolia 1	*lanigerum* 2
capitellata 1	*nitidum* 1-2
'Clearview David' 2	*nitidum* 'Copper
'Crosbie Morrison' 1	Sheen' 1
crithmifolia 1-2	*petersonii* 2
dimorpha 1	*scoparium* var. *rotundifolium* 1
endlicherana 2	*Melaleuca armillaris* 2-3
evansii 1	*decussata* 2
glabella 1-2	*diosmifolia* 2
glabrata 2	*elliptica* 2
hookerana 2	*ericifolia* 2-3
ilicifolia 1	*glaberrima* 2
'Ivanhoe' 2	*halmaturorum* 2
intricata 1-2	*hypericifolia* 2
jephcottii 1-2	*incana* 2
johnsonii 2	*linariifolia* 2-3
juniperina 2	*megacephala* 2

Plant Lists and Glossary

Melaleuca micromera 1-2
  nesophila 2
  pulchella 1
  scabra 1
  seriata 1-2
  spathulata 1-2
  squamea 2
  squarrosa 2
  thymifolia 1
  violacea 1
  wilsonii 1-2
Mirbelia dilatata 1-2
  oxyloboides 1
Myoporum insulare 2
  viscosum 1-2
Olearia argophylla 2
  iodochroa 1
  phlogopappa 2
  teretifolia
    (compact form) 1
Persoonia pinifolia 2
Phebalium lamprophyllum 1
Pimelea ferruginea 1

Pittosporum undulatum 2-3
Prostanthera incana 1
  lasianthos 2
  melissifolia 1-2
  nivea 1-2
  ovalifolia 2
  'Poorinda David' 2
  rotundifolium 1-2
  stricta 1-2
  violacea 1
  walteri 1
Pultenaea graveolens 1
Regelia ciliata 1-2
  cymbifolia 1-2
  inops 1-2
  megacephala 1-2
  velutina 2
Thomasia macrocarpa 1
Thryptomene saxicola 1
Tristania conferta 3
Westringia fruticosa 2
  glabra 1
  seniifolia 1

Acmena australis is an excellent dense-foliaged tree for tropical regions.

SMOG TOLERANT

* = highly resistant

Acacia brachybotrya
  burkittii
  buxifolia
  calamifolia
  decurrens
  * *dodonaeifolia*
  drummondii
  elata
  * *glandulicarpa*
  * *heteroclita*
  * *iteaphylla*
  * *jonesii*
  longifolia
  longifolia var. *sophorae*
  * *melanoxylon*
  microbotrya
  myrtifolia
  * *notabilis*
  pravissima
  * *prominens*
  pycnantha
  * *retinodes*
  schinoides
  stricta
  * *subulata*
  terminalis
  trineura
  * *triptera*
  verniciflua
  * *vestita*
  * *wattsiana*
* *Actinostrobus pyramidalis*
Agathis robusta
Agonis flexuosa
Angophora costata
Boronia megastigma

Brachychiton acerifolium x
  populneum
  * *populneum*
Bursaria spinosa
* *Callistemon brachyandrus*
  citrinus
  pallidus
  rigidus
  * *salignus*
  shiressii
  viminalis
Callitris preissii
* *Calothamnus quadrifidus*
  * *sanguineus*
  * *schaueri*
Casuarina campestris
  cristata
  cunninghamiana
  * *glauca*
  * *huegeliana*
  * *muellerana*
  * *pusilla*
  stricta
* *Dodonaea angustissima*
  viscosa
Eucalyptus aggregata
  * *alpina*
  astringens
  bosistoana
  botryoides
  * *brockwayii*
  burdettiana
  caesia
  calophylla
  camaldulensis
  * *campaspe*

  * *citriodora*
  * *cladocalyx*
  cornuta
  corrugata
  cosmophylla
  crebra
  crenulata
  dielsii
  elata
  * *eremophila*
  erythrocorys
  eudesmioides
  * *fasciculosa*
  fibrosa
  ficifolia
  * *flocktoniae*
  globulus
  gomphocephala
  * *gracilis*
  * *gummifera*
  incrassata
  * *kitsoniana*
  * *kondininensis*
  lehmannii
  leucoxylon
  lindleyana
  longicornis
  * *macrorhyncha*
  maculata
  mannifera
  melliodora
  microcarpa
  microtheca
  muellerana
  * *neglecta*
  obliqua

  occidentalis
  oleosa
  * *orbifolia* ssp
    websterana
  * *ovata*
  * *parvifolia*
  pauciflora
  pellita
  * *perriniana*
  * *platypus*
  preissiana
  pruinosa
  * *pulverulenta*
  * *rubida*
  sepulcralis
  sieberi
  * *sideroxylon*
  * *stoatei*
  stricklandii
  stuartiana
  * *tasmanica*
  tetraptera
  torquata
  viminalis
  viridis
  * *woodwardii*
Eutaxia microphylla
Grevillea 'Pink Pearl'
  robusta
  rosmarinifolia
* *Hakea elliptica*
  laurina
  * *salicifolia*
  * *sericea*
  * *suaveolens*
  * *victoriae*

*Hardenbergia violacea
Lagunaria patersonii
Leptospermum flavescens
   laevigatum
   lanigerum
Melaleuca armillaris
   bracteata
   decussata
   halmaturorum
   hypericifolia
   incana
   lateritia
   lanceolata

*linariifolia
  nesophila
  squamea
  squarrosa
  styphelioides
  teretifolia
  thymifolia
*wilsonii
*Myoporum insulare
  montanum
*Pittosporum phillyreoides
Tristania conferta
  laurina

SPECIMEN TREES

Tropical and Subtropical Regions

Acacia auriculiformis
  bakeri
  bidwillii
  torulosa
Acmena australis
  graveolens
  hemilampra
  smithii
Acronychia acidula
  oblongifolia
Adansonia gregorii
Adenanthera pavonina
Agathis microstachya
  robusta
Albizia canescens
  procera
  thozetiana
  toona
  xanthoxylon
Aleurites moluccana
Alstonia actinophylla
  scholaris
Araucaria bidwillii
  cunninghamii
Archontophoenix alexandrae
  cunninghamii
Argyrodendron actinophyllum
  peralatum
  polyandrum
  trifoliolatum
Austromyrtus bidwillii
Banksia integrifolia
Backhousia anisata
  bancroftii
  citriodora
  hughesii
Baloghia marmorata
Barringtonia acutangula
  asiatica
  calyptra
  racemosa
Beilschmiedia bancroftii
  elliptica
  obtusifolia
Brachychiton acerifolium

  bidwillii
  discolor
  diversifolium
  populneum
Buckinghamia celsissima
Callistemon salignus
  viminalis
Callitris columellaris
  macleayana
  intratropica
Calophyllum inophyllum
Canarium australianum
Cardwellia sublima
Castanospermum australe
Casuarina cunninghamii
  equisetifolia
  glauca
  inophloia
  torulosa
Ceratopetalum apetalum
  gummiferum
Cryptocarya obovata
  triplinervis
Cupaniopsis anarcardioides
Darlingia darlingiana
  ferruginea
Elaeocarpus bancroftii
  grandis
  reticulatus
Endiandra sieberi
Erythrina indica
  verspertilio
Erythrophleum chlorostachys
Eucalyptus alba
  bigalerita
  bleeseri
  clavigera
  confertiflora
  grandis
  maculata
  miniata
  papuana
  peltata
  ptychocarpa
  tereticornis

  tessellaris
  torelliana
Eugenia eucalyptoides
Ficus benjamina
  destruens
  macrophylla
  microphylla var. hillii
  obliqua
  rubiginosa
  watkinsiana
Geijera salicifolia
Flindersia australis
  bourjotiana
  brayleana
  maculosa
  schottiana
Floydia praelta
Gmelina leichhardtii
Grevillea hilliana
  parallela
  pinnatifida
  robusta
Hakea salicifolia
Harpullia pendula
Hibiscus tiliaceus
Hymenosporum flavum
Lagunaria patersonii
Livistonia australis
  benthamii
  decipiens
  muelleri
Macadamia integrifolia
  ternifolia
Melaleuca argentea
  armillaris
  bracteata

  cajuputii
  dealbata
  leucadendron
  linariifolia
  quinquenervia
  styphelioides
  symphiocarpa
  aff symphiocarpa
  viridiflora
Melia azedarach
Nauclea coadunata
Oreocallis wickhamii
Pandanus pedunculatus
Pittosporum rhombifolium
  undulatum
Planchonella australis
Podocarpus amarus
  elatus
Rhodosphaera rhodanthema
Schefflera actinophylla
  versteegii
Stenocarpus salignus
  sinuatus
Sterculia quadrifida
Syncarpia procera
Syzygium coolminianum
  cormiflorum
  fibrosum
  floribundum
  moorei
  paniculatum
Terminalia catappa
Toona australis
Tristania conferta
  neriifolia
Xanthostemon chrysanthus

Schefflera actinophylla makes a fine specimen plant for tropical and sub-tropical regions.

Plant Lists and Glossary

Graceful small eucalypts are decorative, as well as supplying shade and shelter.
Foreground — *Eucalyptus pulchella;* Background — *Eucalyptus nicholii*

Melaleuca styphelioides makes a handsome tree for parks.

SPECIMEN TREES

Temperate Regions

Acacia acuminata
  aneura
  decurrens
  elata
  excelsa
  melanoxylon
  prominens
  salicina
Acmena hemilampra
  smithii
Acronychia acidula
Agathis microstachya
  robusta
Agonis flexuosa
Angophora costata
  floribunda
  hispida
  melanoxylon
  woodsiana
Araucaria bidwillii
  cunninghamii
Argyrodendron actinophyllum
  peralatum
  polyandrum
  trifoliolatum
Banksia grandis
  integrifolia
  serrata
Brachychiton acerifolium
  discolor
  gregorii
  populneum
  rupestre
Callistemon salignus
  shiressii
  viminalis
Callitris columellaris
  rhomboidea
Capparis mitchellii
Castanospermum australe
Casuarina cristata
  cunninghamiana
  fraserana
  glauca
  huegeliana
  littoralis
  leuhmannii
  obesa
  stricta
  torulosa
Codonocarpus cotiniifolius
Doryphora sassafrass
Eucalyptus alba
  astringens
  bancroftii
  caleyi
  calophylla
  camaldulensis
  chapmaniana
  citriodora

cladocalyx
cloeziana
coccifera
cordata
cornuta
dalrympleana
deanei
elata
eximia
ficifolia
gardneri
globulus
gomphocephala
grandis
gummifera
gunnii
haemastoma
kitsoniana
lane-poolei
leucoxylon
maculata
mannifera
megacornuta
melliodora
morrisbyi
neglecta
nicholii
occidentalis
pauciflora
polyanthemos
pulchella
risdonii
rudis
saligna
scoparia
sideroxylon
stellulata
stricklandii
tenuiramis
tereticornis
urnigera
viminalis
Ficus macrophylla
  obliqua
  rubiginosa
  watkinsiana
Flindersia australis
Geijera parviflora
Gmelina leichhardtii
Grevillea hilliana
  robusta
  striata
Hakea salicifolia
Heterodendron oleifolium
Lagunaria patersonii
Leptospermum laevigatum
  phylicoides
Livistona australis
Melaleuca armillaris
  cuticularis

A good example of parkland that has been built around existing trees.

decora
ericifolia
halmaturorum
lanceolata
leucadendron
linariifolia
minutifolia
preissiana
rhaphiophylla
styphelioides
Melia azedarach
Myoporum platycarpum
Nothofagus cunninghamii

Pittosporum bicolor
    phillyreoides
    undulatum
Planchonella australis
Stenocarpus sinuatus
Syncarpia procera
Syzygium coolminianum
    floribundum
    leuhmannii
    paniculatum
Tristania conferta
    laurina

STREET TREES

Tropical and Subtropical Regions

Acacia bidwillii
    dimidiata
    dunnii
    excelsa
    fimbriata
    gnidium
    mountfordiae

salicina
torulosa
Acmena hemilampra
    smithii
Acronychia oblongifolia
    pubescens
Albizia basaltica

canescens
Aleurites moluccana
Alphitonia excelsa
    petriei
    whitei
Alstonia constricta
    scholaris
Angophora costata
    floribunda
Archontophoenix alexandrae
    cunninghamii
Banksia dentata
    integrifolia
Barringtonia acutangula
    asiatica
    calyptra
    racemosa
Bauerella simplicifolia
Brachychiton acerifolium
    bidwillii
    discolor
    diversifolium
    populneum
Buckinghamia celsissima
Callistemon citrinus
    polandii
    salignus

shiressii
viminalis
Callitris columellaris
    intratropica
Calophyllum inophyllum
Capparis mitchellii
Carpentaria acuminata
Cassia brewsteri
Casuarina cunninghamiana
    equisetifolia
    glauca
    inophloia
    littoralis
    torulosa
Clerodendrum tomentosum
Cryptocarya triplinervis
Cupaniopsis anacardioides
Denhamia obscura
Dillenia alata
Elaeocarpus bancroftii
    grandis
    reticulatus
Elaeodendron australe
Endiandra sieberi
Erythrina indica
    verspertilio
Eucalyptus alba

313

Plant Lists and Glossary

Eucalyptus cloeziana
  crebra
  ferruginea
  miniata
  papuana
  peltata
  phoenicea
  polycarpa
  populifolia
  porrecta
  ptychocarpa
  setosa
  torelliana
  tessellaris
  tereticornis
Eugenia eucalyptoides
Eupomatia laurina
Euodia elleryana
Flindersia bourjotiana
  maculosa
  pubescens
  schottiana
Geijera parviflora
  salicina
Glochidion ferdinandii
Gmelina leichhardtii
Grevillea banksii
  glauca
  hilliana
  parallela
  pinnatifida
  robusta
Gronophyllum ramsayii
Hakea salicifolia
Hibiscus tiliaceus
Jagera pseudorhus
Lagunaria patersonii
Leptospermum brachyandrum
  longifolium
  petersonii
Livistona australis
  benthamii

Lysiphyllum carronii
  cunninghamii
Macaranga tanarius
Melaleuca argentea
  alternifolia
  armillaris
  bracteata
  dealbata
  leucadendron
  linariifolia
  nervosa
  quinquenervia
  nervosa
Melia azederach
Morinda citrifolia
Myristica insipida
Pandanus pedunculatus
Peltophorum pterocarpum
Pithecellobium grandiflorum
  pruinosum
Pittosporum melanospermum
  rhombifolium
Pleiogynium timorense
Pongamia pinnata
Schefflera actinophylla
Stenocarpus sinuatus
Sterculia quadrifida
Syzygium coolminianum
  cormiflorum
  fibrosum
  leuhmannii
  moorei
  suborbiculare
Terminalia arostra
Thespesia populnea
Toechima dasyrrhache
  tena
Tristania conferta
  exiliflora
  laurina
  suaveolens
Xanthostemon chrysanthus

Johnsonia lupulina is an unusual rush-like plant from WA.

STREET TREES

Temperate Regions

Acacia acuminata
  baileyana
  floribunda
  iteaphylla
  longifolia
  podalyriifolia
  pravissima
  pycnantha
  retinodes
  salicina
  spectabilis
Acmena smithii
  juniperina
  parviceps
Angophora costata
  floribunda

  hispida
  intermedia
  melanoxylon
Banksia ericifolia
  integrifolia
  marginata
  spinulosa
Brachychiton acerifolium
  discolor
  populneum
Callistemon brachyandrus
  citrinus
  macropunctatus
  pallidus
  phoeniceus
  salignus

  shiressii
  viminalis
Callitris columellaris
  endlicheri
  huegelii
Casuarina cunninghamiana
  huegeliana
  littoralis
  muellerana
  obesa
  stricta
  torulosa
Eucalyptus annulata
  blakelyi
  bridgesiana
  burdettiana
  caesia
  calophylla
  cinerea
  cornuta
  crenulata
  decipiens
  decurva
  dielsii
  elata
  eremophila
  erythronema
  ficifolia
  gardneri
  globulus
  kitsoniana
  lansdowneana
  lehmannii
  leucoxylon
  loxophleba
  macarthurii
  macrandra
  maculata
  maidenii

  mannifera ssp *maculosa*
  megacornuta
  melliodora
  microcarpa
  micrantha
  nicholii
  occidentalis
  pauciflora
  platypus
  polyanthemos
  pulchella
  rossii
  rubida
  sargentii
  scoparia
  sideroxylon
  smithii
  spathulata
  steedmanii
  stricklandii
  torquata
  viminalis
  woodwardii
Geijera parviflora
Grevillea robusta
Hakea laurina
  oleifolia
  salicifolia
Lagunaria patersonii
Leptospermum laevigatum
  petersonii
Melaleuca armillaris
  bracteata
  cuticularis
  decussata
  ericifolia
  incana
  lanceolata
  lateritia

leucadendron
linariifolia
nesophila
raphiophylla
squarrosa
styphelioides
Melia azedarach

Pittosporum phillyreoides
undulatum
Syzygium coolminianum
paniculatum
Tristania conferta
laurina

TUFTS AND TUSSOCKS

Agrostocrinum scabrum
Amphibromus gracilis
neesii
Anigozanthos bicolor
flavidus
manglesii
pulcherrimus
rufus
viridis
Arthropodium milleflorum
Astelia alpina
Blancoa canescens
Blandfordia grandiflora
punicea
Blechnum cartilagineum

minus
nudum
patersonii
wattsii
Borya nitida
Calectasia cyanea
Carex fascicularis
inversa
Celmisia asteliifolia
longifolia
Cheilanthes tenuifolia
Chloris truncata
Chorizandra enodis
Conostylis aculeata
candicans

Low tussock plants give a natural appearance to a garden.

setigera
setosa
teretifolia
Crinum pedunculatum
Cymbopogon ambiguus
exaltatus
obtectus
refractus
Cyperus digitatus
exaltatus
Dampiera alata
Danthonia caespitosa
pallida
pilosa
Dianella caerulea
revoluta
tasmanica
Dichelachne crinita
Dichopogon fimbriatus
strictus
Diplarrena moraea
Doodia aspera
caudata
media
Doryanthes excelsa
palmeri
Enteropogon acicularis
Festuca dives
Gahnia clarkei
microstachya
sieberana
trifida
Glischrocaryon behrii
Helmholtzia acorifolia
Hyparrhenia hirta
Johnsonia lupulina
Juncus australis
pallidus
polyanthemos
Laxmannia brachyphylla
gracilis
sessiliflora
Lepidosperma concavum
elatius
Leptocarpus tenax
Libertia paniculata

pulchella
Lomandra effusa
filiformis
glauca
leucocephala
longifolia
Loxocarya fasciculata
Macropidia fuliginosa
Orthrosanthos laxus
multiflorus
Panicum decompositum
prolutum
Patersonia fragilis
glabrata
longifolia
occidentalis
sericea
Poa caespitosa
billardieri
Polystichum proliferum
Restio complanatus
tetraphyllus
Scirpus nodosus
Sowerbaea juncea
laxiflora
Stipa elegantissima
nervosa
semibarbata
variabilis
Stylidium bulbiferum
corymbosum
graminifolium
schoenioides
spathulatum
uniflorum
Stypandra caespitosa
glauca
Tetratheca ciliata
Themeda australis
Thysanotus multiflorus
Xanthorrhoea australis
minor
quadrangulata
Xyris juncea
operculata

VARIEGATED FOLIAGE

The following Australian plants have variegated foliage. Some of these have been named as cultivars, and these names are listed where known. Some are based on old records and it is uncertain if the plants are still in cultivation.

Acacia iteaphylla variegated form
melanoxylon variegated form
suaveolens variegated form
Acmena smithii 'Mrs Elizabeth Isaac'
Agonis flexuosa variegated form
Alocasia macrorrhiza variegated form
Banksia integrifolia variegated form

Pleasing visual effect, with shrubs, trees and climbers.
Paul Thompson landscaping and photo

Ceratopetalum gummiferum 'Christmas Snow'
Commelina cyanea variegated form
Commersonia echinata 'Bancroftii'
Corchorus cunninghamii variegated form
Cordyline terminalis 'Baileyi'
Crinum pedunculatum variegated form
Cudrania cochinchinensis 'Bancroftii'
Dracaena angustifolia 'Honoriae'
Eucryphia lucida 'Leatherwood Cream'
Ficus rubiginosa variegated form
Geitonoplesium cymosum variegated form
Grevillea 'Golden Sparkle'
  ilicifolia variegated form
  'Poorinda Firebird' variegated form
  victoriae var. *tenuinervis* variegated form
Hakea salicifolia variegated form
Hibiscus tiliaceus variegated form
Hypocalymma cordifolium 'Golden Veil'
Lagunaria patersonii variegated form
Leptospermum laevigatum 'Flamingo'
Olearia argophylla variegated form
Prostanthera cuneata 'Alpine Gold'
  ovalifolia variegated form
Syzygium paniculatum variegated form
Tristiana conferta 'Perth Gold'
  conferta 'Variegata'

WEEPING GROWTH HABIT

Acacia cognata
  howittii
  iteaphylla (narrow leaf
    form)
  leiophylla
  leprosa
  pendula
  pravissima
  retinodes (forms)
  salicina
  stenophylla
  uncinata
  verniciflua
  vestita
Agonis flexuosa
Baeckea frutescens
  linifolia
Callistemon paludosus
  salignus
  sp. *weeping*
  viminalis
Calytrix fraseri
Cassinia arcuata
Casuarina equisetifolia
  stricta
  torulosa
Eucalyptus caesia 'Silver
  Princess'

  elata
  melliodora (some forms)
  pauciflora (some forms)
  scoparia
  sepulcralis
Eugenia eucalyptoides
Exocarpos cupressiformis
  sparteus
Ficus benjamina
  microcarpa var. *hillii*
Geijera parviflora
Leptospermum phylicoides
Maniltoa schefferi
Melaleuca argentea
  decussata (forms)
  gibbosa (form)
  hypericifolia
  incana
  polygaloides
  raphiophylla
Myoporum floribundum
Pittosporum phillyreoides
Pultenaea cunninghamii
  graveolens
  laxiflora
Syzygium floribundum
Terminalia arostrata
Viminaria juncea

316

Glossary of Technical Terms

aberrant Unusual or atypical, differing from the normal form.

abrupt Changing suddenly rather than gradually.

abscise To shed or throw off.

abscission Shedding of plant parts, e.g. leaves. This may be natural resulting from old age or premature as a result of stress.

accessory buds Lateral buds associated with a main bud such as in a leaf axil. They usually develop only if the main bud is damaged.

acerose Very slender or needle-shaped.

achene A small dry one-seeded fruit which does not split at maturity, e.g. *Clematis, Senecio, Helichrysum.*

acicular Needle-shaped.

actinomorphic Symmetrical and regular, usually applied to flowers, e.g. *Wahlenbergia.*

aculeate Bearing short, sharp prickles.

acuminate Tapering into a long drawn out point.

acute Bearing a short sharp point.

adnate Fused tightly together so that separation without damage is impossible.

adventitious Arising in irregular position, e.g. Adventitious roots, Adventitious buds.

aerial roots Adventitious roots arising on stems and growing in the air.

aff. affinity A botanical reference used to denote an undescribed species closely related to an already described species.

after-ripening The changes that occur in a dormant seed and render it capable of germinating.

aggregate fruit A fruit formed by the coherence of ovules that were distinct while in the flower, e.g. *Rubus.*

alternate Borne at different levels in a straight line or in a spiral.

amino acid An organic compound which is a structural unit of protein.

androecium Collectively the male parts of a flower (i.e. the stamens).

angiosperm A major group of plants which bear seeds within an ovary.

annual A plant completing its life cycle within 12 months.

anomalous An abnormal or freak form.

anther The pollen bearing part of a stamen.

anthesis The process of flowering.

apetalous Without petals.

apical dominance The dominance of the apical growing shoot which produces hormones and prevents lateral buds developing while it is still growing actively.

apiculate With a short pointed tip.

apomixis Seed development without the benefit of sexual fusion.

appendage A small growth attached to an organ.

appressed Pressed flat against something.

aquatic A plant growing wholly or partially submerged in water.

arborescent With a tree-like growth habit.

arboretum A collection of planted trees.

aril A fleshy or papery appendage produced as an outgrowth from the outer coat of a seed.

aristate Bearing a small bristle.

articulate Jointed or having swollen nodes, e.g. the culms of grasses.

asexual reproduction Reproduction by vegetative means without the fusion of sexual cells.

attenuated Drawn out.

auricle An ear-like appendage, e.g. surrounding the bases of the fronds of *Angiopteris.*

auriculate Bearing auricles.

auxin A growth regulating compound controlling many growth processes such as bud-break, root development, seed germination, etc.

awn A bristle-like appendage, e.g. on the seeds of many grasses.

axil Angle formed between adjacent organs in contact; commonly applied to the angle between a leaf and the stem.

axillary Borne within the axil.

axis The main stem of a plant, or part of a plant.

barbed Bearing sharp backward sloping hooks as on *Calamus* or *Rubus.*

bearded   Bearing a tuft of hairs.

berry   A simple, fleshy many seeded fruit with 2 or more compartments which do not split open when ripe.

biennial   A plant completing its life cycle in 2 years, usually growing vegetatively in the first year.

bifid   Deeply notched for more than half its length.

bifoliolate   With 2 leaflets to a leaf.

bifurcate   Forked into 2 parts.

bilobed   Two-lobed.

bipinnate   Twice pinnately divided.

bisexual   Both male and female sexes present.

blade   The expanded part of a leaf.

bole   The trunk of a tree.

bottom heat   A propagation term used to denote the application of artificial heat in the basal region of the cutting.

bract   Leaf-like structure which subtends a flower stem or inflorescence.

bracteole   A small leaf-like structure found on a flower stem.

branchlet   A small slender branch.

bristle   A short stiff hair.

bulb   An enlarged thickened stem containing a bud surrounded by thickened leaf scales.

bulbil   A small bulb produced in a leaf axil; a specialized bud produced at the junction of main veins on the fronds of certain ferns.

bulbous   Bulb-shaped.

burr   A prickly fruit.

bush   A low, thick shrub, usually without a distinct trunk.

caducous   Falling off early.

caespitose   Growing in a tuft or tussock.

calcareous   An excess of lime, as in soil.

callus   Growth of undifferentiated cells; in orchids an organelle developed on the labellum.

calyx   All of the sepals.

cambium   The growing tissue lying just beneath the bark.

campanulate   Bell-shaped.

cane   A reed-like plant stem.

canopy   The cover of foliage of a tree or community.

capitate   Enlarged and head-like.

capitulate   An inflorescence consisting of sessile flowers in a head as in the family Asteraceae.

capsule   A dehiscent dry fruit containing many seeds.

carinate   Bearing a keel.

carpel   Female reproductive organ.

catkin   A pendent spike-like inflorescence composed of unisexual apetalous flowers; often used loosely for any rod-like inflorescence.

caudex   A trunk like axis in monocotyledons and some ferns.

cauliflory   The production of flowers from the trunk and larger branches.

cauline   Attached to the stem.

chlorophyll   The green pigment of leaves and other organs, important as a light absorbing agent in photosynthesis.

ciliate   With a fringe of hairs.

cladode   A stem modified to serve as a leaf.

clavate   Club-shaped.

claw   The narrowed base of a sepal or petal: the staminal bundles of the flowers of the genus *Melaleuca*.

cleistogamous   A term applied to self pollinating flowers which do not open, e.g. *Viola*.

clone   A group of vegetatively propagated plants with a common ancestry.

coccus   A single unit of a multiple fruit which splits at maturity.

column   A fleshy growth in the flowers of orchids formed by the union of the stigmas and stamens.

compound leaf   A leaf with two or more separate leaflets.

compressed   Flattened laterally.

cone   A woody fruit in gymnosperms formed by sporophylls arranged spirally on an axis; other woody fruits such as those of the genera *Banksia* and *Casuarina* are also called cones.

congested   Crowded closely together.

conifer   A cone-bearing tree with needle-shaped or scale-like leaves; a gymnosperm.

connate   Fused or joined together.

contorted   Twisted.

contracted   Narrowed.

contractile root   A specialized root developed by bulbs to maintain the bulb at a suitable level in the soil.

convoluted   Rolled around and overlapping as in the leaves of a young shoot.

coppice shoot   A shoot developing from a dormant bud in the trunk or larger branches of a tree; a very common feature of eucalypts.

cordate   Heart-shaped.

coriaceous   Leathery in texture.

corolla   All of the petals.

corymb   An inflorescence where the branches start at different points but reach about the same height to give a flat topped effect.

cotyledon   The seed leaf of a plant.

crenate   The margin cut regularly into rounded teeth.

crenulate   The margin cut into fine, rounded teeth.

crisped   The margins very wavy or crumpled.

cross Offspring or hybrid.

cross-fertilization Fertilization by pollen from another flower.

cross-pollination Transfer of pollen from flower to flower.

crown That part of a shrub or tree above the first branch on the trunk.

crozier Young coiled fern fronds.

culm Flowering stem of grasses or sedges.

cultivar A horticultural variety of plant or crop.

cuneate Wedge-shaped.

cyme An inflorescence where the branches are opposite and the flowers open sequentially downwards starting from the terminal of each branch.

cymose Divided like a cyme.

damping-off A condition in which young seedlings are attacked and killed by soil borne fungi.

deciduous Falling or shedding of any plant part.

decumbent Reclining on the ground with the tips ascending; as of branches.

decurrent Running downward beyond the point of junction; as of leaves, phyllodes, leaflets, lobes etc.

decussate Opposite leaves in four rows along the stem.

deflexed Abruptly turning downwards.

dehiscent Splitting or opening when mature.

dentate Toothed.

denticulate Finely toothed.

depauperate A weak plant or one imperfectly developed.

depressed Flattened at the end.

determinate With a definite cessation of growth in the main axis.

dichotomous Regularly forking into equal branches.

dicotyledons A section of the Angiosperms bearing two seed leaves in the seedling stage.

diffuse Widely spreading and much branched: of open growth.

digitate Spreading like the fingers of a hand from one point.

dimorphic Existing in two different forms.

dioecious Bearing male and female flowers on separate plants.

diploid Having two sets of chromosomes.

disc floret The tubular flowers in the centre of heads of the family Asteraceae.

dissected Deeply divided into segments.

distichous Alternate leaves arranged along the axis in two opposite rows.

divaricate Widely spreading and straggling.

divided Separated to the base.

dormancy A physical or physiological condition that prevents growth or germination even though external factors are favourable.

dorsal sepal Sepal subtending the column of orchid flowers.

drupaceous Drupe-like.

drupe A fleshy indehiscent fruit with seed(s) enclosed in a stony endocarp.

drupelet One drupe of an aggregate fruit made up of drupes, e.g. *Rubus*.

dune A mound formed from wind blown sand.

ecology Study of the interaction of plants and animals within their natural environment.

effuse Very open and loosely spreading.

elliptic Oval and flat and narrowed to each end which is rounded.

elongate Drawn out in length.

emarginate Having a notch at the apex.

embryo Dormant plant contained within a seed.

endemic Restricted to a particular country, region or area.

endocarp A woody layer surrounding a seed in a fleshy fruit.

endosperm Tissue rich in nutrients surrounding the embryo in seeds.

ensiform Sword-shaped.

entire Whole, not toothed or divided in any way.

enzyme A specialized protein capable of promoting a chemical reaction.

ephemeral A plant completing its life cycle within a very short period, e.g. 3-6 months.

epicarp The outermost layer of fruit.

epidermis The outer layer of cells which protects against drying and injury.

epiphyte A plant growing on or attached to another plant but not parasitic.

erect Upright.

evergreen Remaining green and retaining leaves throughout the year.

exocarp Outermost layer of the fruit wall.

exotic A plant introduced from overseas.

exserted Protruding beyond the surrounding parts.

exstipulate Without stipules.

falcate Sickle-shaped.

family A taxonomic group of related genera.

farinaceous Containing starch, appearing as if covered by flour.

fasciculate Arranged in clusters.

ferruginous Rusty brown colour.

fertilization The act of union of the pollen gametes and egg cells in the ovule.

fibrillose Bearing fine fibres or threads.

fibrose Containing fibres.

filament The stalk of the stamen supporting the anther.

319

filiform   Long and very slender: thread-like.
fimbriate   Fringed with fine hairs.
flabellate   Fan-shaped.
flaccid   Soft, limp, lax.
flexuose   Having a zig-zag form.
floccose   Having tufts of woolly hairs.
flora   The plant population of a given region: also a book detailing the plant species of an area.
floral leaf   A specialized leaf subtending flowers or an inflorescence and differing from normal foliage leaves.
floret   The smallest unit of a compound flower.
floriferous   Bearing numerous flowers.
foetid   Having an offensive odour.
foliaceous   Leaf-like.
foliolate   Bearing leaflets.
follicle   A dry fruit formed from a single carpel and which splits along one line when ripe.
forest   A plant community dominated by trees.
forked   Divided into nearly equal parts.
form   A botanical division below a species.
free   Not joined to any other part.
frond   Leaf of a fern or palm.
fruit   The seed bearing organ developed after fertilization.
fruitlet   Small fruits forming part of an aggregate fruit, e.g. *Rubus*.
fugacious   Falling or withering away very early.
fungicide   A chemical used to control fungus diseases.
fused   Joined or growing together.
fusiform   Spindle-shaped: narrowed to both ends from a swollen middle.

galea   A hood or helmet-shaped structure formed by fusion of petals and sepals, e.g. *Pterostylis*.
gamete   One of the sex cells, either male or female.
gemma   A vegetative bud by which a plant propagates.
gene   A hereditary factor located in linear order on a chromosome.
geniculate   Bent like a knee.
genus   A taxonomic group of closely related species.
germination   The active growth of an embryo resulting in the development of a young plant.
gibbous   Humped.
glabrous   Without hairs, smooth.
gland   A fluid secreting organ.
glandular   Bearing glands.
glaucous   Covered with a bloom, giving a bluish lustre.
globoid   Globe-like, globular, spherical.

glume   The bract subtending the spikelets of grasses and sedges.
glutinous   Covered with a sticky exudation.
granular   Covered with small grains.
growth regulator   A synthetic compound which can control growth and flowering responses in plants and seeds.
gymnosperm   A major group of plants which bear seeds not enclosed within an ovary.
gynoecium   Collectively the female parts of a flower.

habit   The general appearance of a plant.
habitat   The environment in which a plant grows.
halophyte   A plant which grows in saline soils.
haploid   Having a single set of chromosomes.
hastate   Shaped like an arrow head with spreading basal lobes.
head   A composite cluster of flowers — as in the Asteraceae.
herb   A plant which produces a fleshy rather than woody stem.
herbaceous   A perennial plant which dies down each year after flowering.
herbicide   A chemical used to control weeds.
hermaphrodite   Bearing both male and female sex organs in the same flower.
hilum   The scar left on the seed at its point of detachment from the seed stalk.
hirsute   Covered with long, spreading coarse hairs.
hispid   Covered with stiff bristles or hairs.
hispidulous   Minutely hispid.
hoary   Covered with short white hairs giving the surface a greyish appearance.
hormone   A chemical substance produced in one part of a plant and inducing a growth response when transferred to another part.
hybrid   Progeny resulting from the cross-fertilization of parents.
hybrid swarm   Variable population resulting from complex crossing such as between the hybrids themselves or between the hybrids and the parents.
hybrid vigour   The increase in vigour of hybrids over their inbred parents.
hypocotyl   Part of the embryo between the cotyledons and primary root.

imbricate   Overlapping.
incised   Cut sharply and deeply.
incurved   Curved inwards.
indehiscent   Not splitting open at maturity.
indeterminate   Growing on without termination.
indigenous   Native to a country, region or area.
indumentum   The hairy covering on plant parts.

indusium A membrane covering a fern sorus; a cup-shaped structure protecting the stigma in Goodeniaceae.

inferior Below some other part; often used in reference to an ovary when held below other layers of the perianth.

inflorescence The flowering structure of a plant.

inhibitor A chemical substance which prevents a growth process.

insecticide A chemical used to control insect pests.

internode The part of a stem between two nodes.

involucre A whorl of bracts surrounding an inflorescence.

involute Rolled inwards.

jointed Bearing joints or nodes.

juvenile The young stage of growth before the plant is capable of flowering.

keel A ridge like the base of a boat; in pea shaped flowers the basal part formed by the union of two petals.

labellum A lip: in orchids the petal in front of the column.

laciniate Cut into narrow slender segments.

lamina The expanded part of a leaf.

lanceolate Lance-shaped: narrow and tapering at each end especially the apex.

lateral Arising from the main axis; arising at the side of.

lax Open and loose.

leaflet A segment of a compound leaf.

legume A dry fruit formed from one carpel and splitting along two lines.

lemma The lower bract enclosing the flower of grasses.

liana, liane A large woody climber.

lignotuber A woody swelling containing dormant buds, at the base of a trunk, e.g. mallee eucalypts.

ligule A strap-shaped organ: in grasses a growth at the junction of leaf sheath and blade.

ligulate Strap-shaped.

linear Long and narrow with parallel sides.

littoral Growing in communities near the sea.

lobe A segment of an organ as the result of a division.

loculus A compartment within an ovary.

mallee A shrub or tree with many stems arising from at or below ground level.

mangrove A specialized plant growing in salt water and gathering oxygen through specialized roots (pneumatophores).

marginal Attached to or near the edge.

maritime Belonging to or growing near the sea.

marlock A shrub or tree with waxy stems arising from a point on the trunk above ground level.

marsh A swamp.

mealy Covered with flour-like powder.

membranous Thin textured.

meristem A growing point or an area of active cell division.

mesocarp Middle layer of a fruit wall.

midrib The principal vein that runs the full length.

miticide (also *acaracide*) A chemical used to control mites.

moniliform Constricted at regular intervals and appearing bead-like.

monocotyledons A section of the Angiosperms bearing a single seed leaf at the seedling stage.

monoecious Bearing male and female flowers on the same plant.

monopodial A stem with a single main axis which grows forward at the tip.

monotypic A genus with a single species.

morphology The form and structure of a plant.

mucronate With a short, sharp point.

mucronulate With a very small point.

mutation A change in the genetic constitution of a plant or part of a plant.

myccorrhiza A beneficial relationship between the roots of a plant and fungi or bacteria resulting in a nutrient exchange system. Some plants cannot grow without such a relationship.

nectar A sweet fluid secreted from a nectary.

nectary A specialized gland which secretes nectar.

nematicide A chemical used to control nematodes.

nematode A minute worm-like animal, some species of which attack plants.

nerves The fine veins which traverse the leaf blade.

node A point on the stem where leaves or bracts arise.

nodule A small swollen lump on roots; in legumes the nodules contain symbiotic bacteria of the genus *Rhizobium*.

nut A dry indehiscent one-seeded fruit.

nutlet A small nut enclosing a single seed.

obcordate Cordate with the broadest part above the middle.

oblanceolate Lanceolate with the broadest part above the middle.

oblique Slanting: unequal sided.

obovate Ovate with the broadest part above the middle.

obtuse Blunt or rounded at the apex.

offset A growth arising from the base of a plant.

olivaceous Dark olive-green.

operculum A structure formed from the fusion of petals and sepals and protecting the stamens and style when in bud (e.g. *Eucalyptus*.)

opposite Arising on opposite sides but at the same level.

orbicular Nearly circular.

organelle A small plant organ.

order A taxonomic group of related families.

osmosis Diffusion of water through a membrane caused by different concentrations of salts on either side of the membrane.

oval Rounded but longer than wide.

ovary The part of the gynoecium which encloses the ovules.

ovate Egg-shaped in longitudinal section.

ovoid Egg-shaped.

ovule The structure within the ovary which becomes seed after fertilization.

palea The upper bract enclosing the flower of grasses.

paleaceous Clothed with papery scales.

palmate Divided like a hand.

palmatifid Lobed like a hand.

panicle A much branched racemose inflorescence.

paniculate Arranged in a panicle.

pappus A tuft of feathery bristles representing a modified calyx, on the seeds of Asteraceae.

parasite A plant growing or living on or in another plant, e.g. mistletoe.

parthenocarpy Development of fruit without fertilization and seed formation.

pectinate Toothed like a comb.

pedicel The stalk of a flower in a compound inflorescence.

pedicellate Growing on a pedicel.

peduncle The main axis of a compound inflorescence or the stalk of a solitary flower.

pedunculate Growing on a peduncle.

peltate Circular with the stalk attached in the middle on the undersurface.

pendent Hanging downwards.

penninerved The veins branching pinnately.

perennial A plant living for more than two years.

perfoliate United around the stem, as in leaves.

perianth A collective term for all of the petals and sepals of a flower.

pericarp The hardened ovary wall that surrounds a seed.

persistent Remaining attached until mature: not falling prematurely.

pesticide A chemical used to control pests. The word pests in this case refers to a range of plant enemies including fungi, bacteria, nematodes, insects, mites etc.

petal A segment of the inner perianth whorl or corolla.

petaloid Petal-like, resembling a petal.

petiole The stem or stalk of a leaf.

petiolate Bearing a petiole.

phloem Part of the vascular system of plants concerned with the movement and storage of nutrients and hormones.

photosynthesis The conversion of carbon dioxide from the atmosphere to sugars within green parts of the plant, using chlorophyll and energy from the sun's rays.

phylloclade A stem acting in the capacity of a leaf (cladode).

phyllode A modified petiole acting as a leaf.

pilose With scattered long, simple hairs.

pinna A primary segment of a divided leaf.

pinnate Once divided with the divisions extending to the midrib.

pinnatifid Once divided with the divisions not extending to the midrib.

pinnule The segment of a compound leaf divided more than once.

pistil The ovule and seed bearing organ of the gynoecium.

pistillate Female flowers.

plicate Folded longitudinally.

plumose Feather-like from fine feathery hairs.

pneumatophore Specialized roots of mangroves carrying oxygen to the plant.

pod A dry, nonfleshy fruit, that splits when ripe to release its seeds.

pollen Haploid male cells produced by the anthers.

pollination The transference of the pollen from the anther to the stigma of a flower.

pollinium An aggregated mass of pollen grains found in the Orchidaceae and Asclepiadaceae.

polyembryony The condition where a seed produces more than one embryo.

polygamous Having mixed unisexual and bisexual flowers together.

polymorphic Consisting of many forms: a variable species, e.g. *Grevillea glabella*.

prickle A small spine borne irregularly on the bark or epidermis.

procumbent Spreading on the ground without rooting: as of branches.

prostrate Lying flat on the ground.

proliferous Bearing offshoots and other processes of vegetative propagation.

proteoid roots A specialized root development found in species of the family Proteaceae. Numerous short roots develop in a compact mop-like clump.

protuberance A swelling or bump.

pseudobulb Thickened bulb-like stems of orchids bearing nodes.

pubescent Covered with short, soft downy hairs.

punctate Marked with spots or glands.

pungent Very sharply pointed; also smelling strongly.

pyriform Pear-shaped.

raceme A simple unbranched inflorescence with stalked flowers.

racemose In the form of a raceme.

radical Arranged in a basal rosette.

radicle The undeveloped root of the embryo.

ray floret The outermost, flattened florets of the inflorescence in the family Asteraceae.

recurved Curved backwards.

reflexed Bent backwards and downwards.

regular Symmetrical especially of flowers.

reniform Kidney-shaped.

reticulate A network: as of veins.

retuse With a slight notch at the apex.

revolute With the margins rolled backwards.

rhachis The main axis of a compound leaf or an inflorescence.

rhizome An underground stem.

rosette A group of leaves radiating from a centre.

rostrate With a beak.

rotate The lobes of the corolla spreading horizontally like the spokes of a wheel.

rugose Wrinkled.

rugulose Finely wrinkled.

runner A slender trailing shoot forming roots at the nodes.

saccate Pouch or sac-like.

sagittate Shaped like an arrow head, with the basal lobes pointing downwards.

samara An indehiscent winged seed.

saprophyte A plant which derives its food from dead or decaying organic matter.

scabrous Rough to the touch.

scale A dry, flattened, papery body: sometimes also used as a term for rudimentary leaf.

scandent Climbing.

scape Leafless peduncle arising near the ground, it may bear scales or bracts and the foliage leaves are radical.

scarious Thin, dry and membranous.

sclerophyll A plant (or forest) with hard stiff leaves.

scrub Strictly a plant community dominated by shrubs, often used loosely for rainforests.

scurfy Bearing small, flattened, papery scales.

section A taxonomic subgroup of a genus containing closely related species.

secund With all parts directed to one side.

seed A mature ovule consisting of an embryo, endosperm and protective coat.

seedcoat The protective covering of a seed also called testa.

seedling A young plant raised from seed.

segment A subdivision or part of an organ, e.g. sepal is a segment of the calyx.

self pollination Transfer of pollen from stamen to stigma of same flower.

sepal A segment of the calyx or outer whorl of the perianth.

sepaloid Sepal-like.

septate Divided by partitions.

serrate Toothed with sharp, forward pointing teeth.

serrulate Finely serrate.

sessile Without a stalk, pedicel or petiole.

seta A bristle.

setaceous Shaped like a bristle.

setose Bristly.

shrub A woody plant that remains low (less than 6 m) and usually has many stems or trunks.

simple Undivided, of one piece.

sinuate With a wavy margin.

sinus A junction: a specialized term for flowers of the orchid genus *Pterostylis* describing the point of junction of the lateral sepals.

slip A cutting.

sorus A cluster of sporangia on the fronds of ferns.

spadix An inflorescence which is a fleshy spike with flowers more or less sunken in the axis, and usually enclosed by a spathe.

spathe A large sheathing bract which encloses a spadix.

spatulate Spatula-shaped; with a broad top and tapering base.

species A taxonomic group of closely related plants, all possessing a common set of characters which sets them apart from another species.

spicate Arranged like or resembling a spike.

spike A simple unbranched inflorescence with sessile flowers.

spikelet A small spike bearing one or more flowers: in grasses a small unit composed of glumes and florets.

spine A sharp rigid structure.

spinescent Bearing spines or ending in spines.

spinule A weak spine.

spinulose With small spines.

sporangium A case that bears spores.

spore A reproductive unit which does not contain an embryo.

sporeling A young fern plant.

spur A tubular sac-like projection of a flower, often containing nectar.

323

stamen　The male part of a flower producing pollen, consisting of an anther and a filament.

staminate flowers　Male flowers.

staminode　A sterile stamen: often of different form, e.g. petaloid.

standard　The dorsal petal, usually confined to flowers of the family Fabaceae.

stellate　Star-shaped or of star-like form.

stem-clasping　Enfolding a stem.

sterile　Unable to reproduce.

stigma　The usually enlarged area of the style receptive to pollen.

stipe　A stalk or leaf stalk.

stipitate　Stalked.

stipule　Small bract-like appendages borne in pairs at the base of the petiole.

stolon　A basal stem growing just below the ground surface and rooting at intervals.

stoloniferous　Bearing stolons, spreading by stolons.

strain　An improved selection within a variety: also cultivar.

strand plant　A plant growing near the sea.

stratification　The technique of burying seed in coarse sand so as to expose it to periods of cold temperatures or to soften the seed coat.

striate　Marked with narrow lines or ridges.

strobilus　A cone.

strophiole　An appendage arising from the seed-coat near the hilum.

strophiolate　Bearing a strophiole.

style　Part of the gynoecium connecting the stigma with the ovary.

subfamily　A taxonomic group of closely related genera within a family.

sub　Beneath, nearly, approximately.

subcordate　Nearly cordate.

subspecies　A taxonomic subgroup within a species used to differentiate geographically isolated variants.

subulate　Narrow and drawn out to a fine point.

succulent　Fleshy or juicy.

sucker　A shoot arising from the roots or the trunk below ground level.

sulcate　Grooved or furrowed.

superior　Above some other part; often used in reference to an ovary when held above other layers of the perianth.

symbiosis　A beneficial association of different organisms.

taproot　The perpendicular main root of a plant.

taxon　A term used to describe any taxonomic group, e.g. genus, species.

taxonomy　The classification of plants or animals.

tendril　A plant organ modified to support stems used in climbing.

tepal　A term used for the perianth segments when the sepals and petals are alike, e.g. Liliaceae.

ternate　Divided or arranged in threes.

terminal　The apex or end.

teratology　The study of abnormal or aberrant forms.

terete　Slender and cylindrical.

terrestrial　Growing in the ground.

testa　The outer covering of the seed, the seed-coat.

tetragonous　With four angles.

tetrahedral　With four sides.

thorn　A reduced branch ending in a hard, sharp point.

tomentose　Densely covered with short, matted, soft hairs.

tomentum　A covering of matted, soft hairs.

tortuous　Twisted, with irregular bending.

transpiration　The loss of water vapour to the atmosphere through openings in the leaves of plants.

tree　A woody plant that produces a single trunk and a distinct elevated head.

triad　A group of three.

tribe　A taxonomic group of related genera within a family or subfamily.

trifid　Divided into three to about the middle.

trifoliolate　A compound leaf with three leaflets.

trigonous　With three angles.

trilobed; trilobate　With three lobes.

tripinnate　Divided three times.

triquetrous　With three angles or ridges.

truncate　Ending abruptly as if cut off.

trunk　The main stem of a tree.

tuber　The swollen end of an underground stem or stolon.

tubercle　Small tubers produced on aerial stems, eg. *Dioscorea*.

tuberculate　With knobby or warty projections.

tuberoid　The swollen end of an underground root.

tuberous　Swollen and fleshy, resembling a tuber.

tufted　Growing in small, erect clumps.

turgid　Swollen or bloated.

twiner　Climbing plants which ascend by twining of their stems or rhachises.

type form　The form of a variable species from which the species was originally described.

umbel　An inflorescence in which all the stems arise at the same point and the flowers lie at the same level.

umbellate　Like an umbel.

undulate　Wavy.

unequal　Of different sizes.

unilateral   One-sided.

unisexual   Of one sex only — staminate or pistillate.

united   Joined together, wholly or partially.

urceolate   Urn-shaped.

valve   A segment of a woody fruit.

valvate   Opening by valves; with perianth segments overlapping in the bud.

variegated   Where the basic colour of a leaf or petal is broken by areas of another colour, usually white, pale green or yellow.

variety   A taxonomic subgroup within a species used to differentiate variable populations.

vascular bundle   The internal conducting system of plants.

vascular plant   A plant bearing water conducting tissue in its organs.

vegetation   The whole plant communities of an area.

vegetative   Asexual development or propagation.

vein   The conducting tissue of leaves.

veinlet   A small or slender vein.

velamen   A veil: spongy epidermis of epiphytic roots.

venation   The pattern formed by veins.

vernalization   The promotion of flowering.

verrucose   Rough and warty.

verticillate   Arranged in whorls.

viable   Alive and able to germinate: as of seeds.

villous   Covered with long, soft, shaggy hairs.

virgate   Twiggy.

viscid   Coated with a sticky or glutinous substance.

viviparous   Germinating while still attached to the parent plant, e.g. mangroves.

watershoot   A strong rapid growing shoot arising from the trunk or main stem.

whorl   Three or more segments (leaves, flowers etc.) in a circle at a node.

wing   A thin, dry, membranous expansion of an organ: the side petals of flowers of the family Fabaceae.

woolly   Bearing long, soft matted hairs.

xeromorph   A plant with drought resistant features.

xerophyte   A drought resistant plant.

zygomorphic   Asymmetrical and irregular, usually applied to flowers, e.g. *Anigozanthos*.

zygote   A fertilized egg.

Further Reading

Anderson, R. H. (1967) *The Trees of New South Wales*, Government Printer, New South Wales.

Aston, H. I. (1973) *Aquatic Plants of Australia*, Melbourne University Press.

Bailey, F. M. (1909) *A Comprehensive Catalogue of Queensland Plants*, Government Printer, Queensland.

Baker, K. F. (Ed) (1957) *The U.C. System for Producing Healthy Container-Grown Plants*, University of California.

Beadle, N. C. W., Evans, O. D. and Carolin, R. C. (1972) *Flora of the Sydney Region*, A. H. & A. W. Reed, Sydney.

Beadle, N. C. W. (1971-76) *Students Flora of North Eastern New South Wales*, Parts 1-3, University of New England, Armidale.

Beard, J. S. (Ed) (1965) *Descriptive Catalogue of West Australian Plants*, Society for Growing Australian Plants, Sydney.

Bentham, G. and Mueller, F. (1863-78) *Flora Australiensis*, Parts 1-7, Lovell Reeve & Co., London.

Black, J. M. (1943-57) *Flora of South Australia*, Parts 1-4 Government Printer, Adelaide.

Blackall, W. E. (1954) *How to Know Western Australian Wildflowers*, Part 1, University of Western Australia Press, Perth.

Blackall, W. E. & Grieve, B. J. (1956-75) *How to Know Western Australian Wildflowers*, Parts 2-4, University of Western Australia Press, Perth.

Blake, S. T. and Roff, C. (1972) *The Honey Flora of Queensland*, Government Printer, Queensland.

Blombery, A. M. (1967) *A Guide to Native Australian Plants*, Angus & Robertson, Sydney.

Blombery, A. M. (1972) *What Wildflower is That?*, Paul Hamlyn, Sydney.

Boomsma, C. D. (1972) *Native Trees of South Australia*, Woods and Forests Department, South Australia.

Bonney, N. B. (1977) *An Introduction to the Identification of Native Flora in the Lower South East of South Australia*, South East Community College, Mt. Gambier.

Bridgeman, P. H. (1976) *Tree Surgery*, David & Charles Ltd., London.

Brooks, A. E. (1978) *Australian Native Plants for Home Gardens*, 6th Edition, Lothian Publishing Co., Melbourne.

Brown, A. & Hall, N. (1968) *Growing Trees on Australian Farms*, Forestry & Timber Bureau, Canberra.

Burbridge, N. T. (1963) *Dictionary of Australian Plant Genera*, Angus & Robertson, Sydney.

Burbridge, N. T. & Gray, M. (1970) *Flora of the Australian Capital Territory*, Australian National University Press, Canberra.

Canberra Botanic Gardens (1971-) *Growing Native Plants*, (Series), Australian Government Publishing Service, Canberra.

Chippendale, G. M. (Ed) (1968) *Eucalyptus Buds and Fruits*, Forestry & Timber Bureau, Canberra.

Chippendale, G. M. (1973) *Eucalypts of the Western Australian Goldfields*, Australian Government Publishing Service, Canberra.

Cochrane, R. G., Fuhrer, B.A., Rotherham, E. R., & Willis, J. H. (1968) *Flowers and Plants of Victoria*, A. H. & A. W. Reed, Sydney.

Conabere, B. & Garnet, J. Ros (1974) *Wildflowers of South-Eastern Australia*, Volumes 1-2, Thomas Nelson (Australia) Ltd., Melb.

Cribb, A. B. & Cribb, J. W. (1974) *Wild Food in Australia*, Collins, Sydney.

Curtis, W. M. (1956-67) *The Students Flora of Tasmania*, Parts 1-3, Government Printer, Tasmania.

Curtis, W. M. and I. Morris, D. K. (1975) *The Students Flora of Tasmania*, Part 1, Second Edition, Government Printer, Tasmania.

Dockrill, A. W., (1969) *Australian Indigenous Orchids*, Volume 1, Society for Growing Australian Plants, Sydney.

Eichler, H. (1965) *Supplement to J. M. Black's Flora of South Australia*, 2nd Edition, Government Printer, Adelaide.

Elliot, R. (1975) *An Introduction to the Grampians Flora*, Algona Guides, Melbourne.

Erickson, R. (1968) *Plants of Prey in Australia*, Lamb Publications, Osborne Park, Western Australia.

Erickson, R. (1958) *Triggerplants*, Paterson Brokensha Pty. Ltd., Perth.

Erickson, R., George, A. S., Marchant, N. G., Morcombe, M. K. (1973) *Flowers and Plants of Western Australia*, A. H. & A. W. Reed, Sydney.

Everist, S. K. (1974) *Poisonous Plants of Australia*, Angus & Robertson, Sydney.

Fairhall, A. R. (1970) *West Australian Native Plants in Cultivation*, Pergamon Press, Sydney.

Galbraith, J. (1977) *Collins Field Guide to the Wildflowers of South-East Australia*, Collins, Sydney.

Gardner, C. A. (1975) *Wildflowers of Western Australia*, West Australian Newspapers Ltd., Perth.

Goodman, R. D. (1973) *Honey Flora of Victoria*, Department of Agriculture, Victoria.

Guilfoyle, W. R. (about 1927) *Australian Plants Suitable for Gardens, Parks, Timber Reserves etc.*, Whitcombe & Tombs Ltd., Melbourne.

Hadlington, P. W. & Johnston, J. A. (1977) *A Guide to the Care and Cure of Australian Trees*, New South Wales University Press Ltd.

Hall, N., Johnston, R. D., Chippendale, G. M. (1970) *Forest Trees of Australia*, Australian Government Publishing Service, Canberra.

Hall, N. (1972) *The Use of Trees & Shrubs in the Dry Country of Australia*, Forestry and Timber Bureau, Canberra.

Harmer, J. (1975) *North Australian Plants*, Part 1, Society for Growing Australian Plants, Sydney.

Harris, T. Y. (1977) *Gardening with Australian Plants — Shrubs*, Thomas Nelson (Australia) Ltd.

Hartmann, H. T. and Kester, D. E. (1975) *Plant Propagation Principles and Practices*, Third Edition, Prentice Hall, U.S.A.

Hearne, D. A. (1975) *Trees for Darwin & Northern Australia*, Australian Government Publishing Service, Canberra.

Holliday, I., and Watton, G. (1975) *A Field Guide to Banksias*, Rigby Limited, Adelaide.

Jones, D. L., and Clemesha, S. C. (1976) *Australian Ferns and Fern Allies*, A. H. & A. W. Reed, Sydney.

Jones, D. L., and Gray, B. (1977) *Australian Climbing Plants*, A. H. & A. W. Reed, Sydney.

Kelly, S. (1969) *Eucalypts*, Volume 1, Thomas Nelson (Australia) Ltd.

Lazarides, M. (1970) *Grasses of Central Australia*, Australian National University Press, Canberra.

Leeper, G. W., (Ed) (1970) *The Australian Environment*, CSIRO and Melbourne University Press.

Lord, E. E. (1964) *Shrubs and Trees for Australian Gardens*, Lothian Publishing Co., Melbourne.

Maiden, J. H. (1889) *The Useful Native Plants of Australia*, Facsimile Ed. Compendium Pty. Ltd., Melbourne.

Mathias, M. E. (1976) *Colour For the Landscape*, Brooke House Publishers, California, U.S.A.

McCubbin, C. (1971) *Australian Butterflies*, Thomas Nelson (Australia) Ltd.

McLuckie, J. and McKee, H. S. (1962) *Australian & New Zealand Botany*, Horwitz-Graeme, Sydney.

Newbey, K. (1968-72) *West Australian Plants for Horticulture*, Parts 1-2, Society for Growing Australian Plants, Sydney.

Nicholls, W. H. (1964) *Orchids of Australia*, Complete Edition, Ed. D. L. Jones, & T. B. Muir, Thomas Nelson (Australia) Ltd.

Penfold, A. R. & Willis, J. L. (1961) *The Eucalypts*, Leonard Hill, London.

Plumridge, J. (1976) *How to Propagate Plants*, Lothian Publishing Co., Melbourne.

Pryor, L. D. and Johnson, L. A. S. (1971) *Classification of the Eucalypts*, Australian National University, Canberra.

Rogers, F. J. C. (1971) *Growing Australian Native Plants*, Thomas Nelson (Australia) Ltd.

Rogers, F. J. C. (1975) *Growing More Australian Native Plants*, Thomas Nelson (Australia) Ltd.

Rotherham, E. R., Briggs, B. C., Blaxell, D. F. and Carolin, R. C. (1975) *Flowers & Plants of New South Wales and Southern Queensland*, A. H. & A. W. Reed, Sydney.

Salter, B. (1977) *Australian Native Gardens and Birds*, Ure Smith, Sydney.

Simpfendorfer, K. J. (1975) *An Introduction to Trees for South-Eastern Australia*, Inkata Press, Victoria.

Society for Growing Australian Plants, *Australian Plants*, Quarterly, Society for Growing Australian Plants, Sydney.

Society for Growing Australian Plants, Canberra Region (1976) *Australian Plants For Canberra Gardens*, 2nd Edition, Society for Growing Australian Plants, Canberra.

Society for Growing Australian Plants, Maroondah Group Vic. Miscellaneous publications, Society for Growing Australian Plants, Maroondah Group, Ringwood, Victoria.

Sparnon, N. (1967) *The Beauty of Australia's Wildflowers*, Ure Smith, Sydney.

327

Spooner, P. (Ed) (1973) *Practical Guide to Home Landscaping*, Readers Digest, Sydney.

Stones, M. and Curtis, W. (1967-75) *The Endemic Flora of Tasmania*, Parts 1-5, The Ariel Press, London.

Stead Memorial Wildlife Research Foundation, Miscellaneous publications, Stead Memorial Wildlife Research Foundation, Sydney.

Tothill, J. C., and Hacker, J. B. (1973) *The Grasses of Southeast Queensland*, University of Queensland Press.

Wells, J. S. (1955) *Plant Propagation Practices*, Macmillan, New York, USA.

Willis, J. C. (1973) *A Dictionary of the Flowering Plants and Ferns*, 8th Edition, Revised by H. K. Airy-Shaw, Cambridge University Press, London.

Willis, J. H. (1962-72) *A Handbook to Plants in Victoria*, Volumes 1 and 2, Melbourne University Press, Melbourne.

Wilson, G. (1975) *Landscaping with Australian Plants*, Thomas Nelson (Australia) Ltd.

Index

Index

Index

Index